Requirements Modelling and Specification for Service Oriented Architecture

Requirements Modelling and Specification for Service Oriented Architecture

Ian Graham

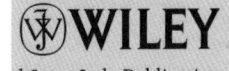

A John Wiley and Sons, Ltd., Publication

Copyright © 2008   John Wiley & Sons Ltd, The Atrium, Southern Gate, Chichester,
West Sussex PO19 8SQ, England

Telephone (+44) 1243 779777

Email (for orders and customer service enquiries): cs-books@wiley.co.uk
Visit our Home Page on www.wileyeurope.com or www.wiley.com

All Rights Reserved. No part of this publication may be reproduced, stored in a retrieval system or transmitted in any form or by any means, electronic, mechanical, photocopying, recording, scanning or otherwise, except under the terms of the Copyright, Designs and Patents Act 1988 or under the terms of a licence issued by the Copyright Licensing Agency Ltd, 90 Tottenham Court Road, London W1T 4LP, UK, without the permission in writing of the Publisher. Requests to the Publisher should be addressed to the Permissions Department, John Wiley & Sons Ltd, The Atrium, Southern Gate, Chichester, West Sussex PO19 8SQ, England, or emailed to permreq@wiley.co.uk, or faxed to (+44) 1243 770620.

Designations used by companies to distinguish their products are often claimed as trademarks. All brand names and product names used in this book are trade names, service marks, trademarks or registered trademarks of their respective owners. The Publisher is not associated with any product or vendor mentioned in this book.

This publication is designed to provide accurate and authoritative information in regard to the subject matter covered. It is sold on the understanding that the Publisher is not engaged in rendering professional services. If professional advice or other expert assistance is required, the services of a competent professional should be sought.

Other Wiley Editorial Offices

John Wiley & Sons Inc., 111 River Street, Hoboken, NJ 07030, USA

Jossey-Bass, 989 Market Street, San Francisco, CA 94103-1741, USA

Wiley-VCH Verlag GmbH, Boschstr. 12, D-69469 Weinheim, Germany

John Wiley & Sons Australia Ltd, 42 McDougall Street, Milton, Queensland 4064, Australia

John Wiley & Sons (Asia) Pte Ltd, 2 Clementi Loop #02-01, Jin Xing Distripark, Singapore 129809

John Wiley & Sons Ltd, 6045 Freemont Blvd, Mississauga, Ontario L5R 4J3, Canada

Wiley also publishes its books in a variety of electronic formats. Some content that appears in print may not be available in electronic books.

Library of Congress Cataloging-in-Publication Data

Graham, Ian, 1948-
  Requirements modelling and specification for service oriented architecture / Ian Graham.
      p. cm.
  Includes bibliographical references and index.
  ISBN 978-0-470-77563-9 (pbk. : alk. paper) 1. Web services. 2. Software architecture.
3. Computer network architectures. 4. Business enterprises – Computer networks.
5. Computer software – Specifications. I. Title.
  TK5105.88813.G73 2008
  006.7'6 – dc22
                                                                 2008031767

British Library Cataloguing in Publication Data

A catalogue record for this book is available from the British Library
ISBN 978-0-4707-7563-9

Typeset in 11/13 Palatino by Laserwords Private Limited, Chennai, India
Printed and bound in Great Britain by Bell & Bain, Glasgow
This book is printed on acid-free paper responsibly manufactured from sustainable forestry in which at least two trees are planted for each one used for paper production.

Contents

Foreword by Mark McGregor ix
Foreword by Professor Neil Maiden xi
Preface xiii

1 Principles of SOA 1
   1.1 Why Projects Fail 1
   1.2 Aligning IT with Business – Speaking a Common Language 3
       1.2.1 Models 6
   1.3 What is Service Oriented Architecture? 8
       1.3.1 The Real User 16
   1.4 Business Drivers for SOA 19
   1.5 Technology Drivers 20
   1.6 Benefits, Pitfalls and Prospects 23
       1.6.1 Pitfalls 24
       1.6.2 Post-SOA Benefits 25
   1.7 Migration Strategies 26
   1.8 Summary 27
   1.9 Bibliographical Notes 30

2 Architecture – Objects, Components, Services 31
   2.1 What is Architecture? 31
       2.1.1 Architecture as High Level Structure 32
       2.1.2 Architecture as Design Rationale or Vision 37
       2.1.3 Architecture and Reuse 41
   2.2 Architecture through the Ages 42
   2.3 Objects and Components 49
       2.3.1 Components for Flexibility 53
       2.3.2 Large-Scale Connectors 54
       2.3.3 How Services Relate to Components 56
   2.4 Architecture and SOA 57
   2.5 Stateless Services 63

	2.6	Practical Principles for Developing, Maintaining and Exploiting SOA	66
	2.7	Summary	68
	2.8	Bibliographical Notes	70

3 Approaches to Requirements Engineering — 71
- 3.1 Conventional Approaches — 71
  - 3.1.1 Approaches Based on Human Factors — 73
- 3.2 Classic Requirements versus Use Cases — 78
  - 3.2.1 UML Basics — 78
  - 3.2.2 Use Case Models — 80
  - 3.2.3 Formulating Requirements — 83
- 3.3 Problem Frames — 85
- 3.4 Requirements and Business Rules — 88
- 3.5 Establishing and Prioritizing the Business Objectives — 89
- 3.6 Soft Techniques for Requirements Elicitation — 93
  - 3.6.1 Using Interviewing Techniques — 93
  - 3.6.2 Repertory Grids — 96
  - 3.6.3 Hierarchical Task Analysis — 97
  - 3.6.4 Object Discovery Techniques — 101
- 3.7 Summary — 106
- 3.8 Bibliographical Notes — 110

4 Business Process Modelling — 111
- 4.1 The Origins of and Need for Business Process Modelling — 111
- 4.2 Business Process Modelling in a Nutshell — 114
- 4.3 UML Activity Diagrams — 116
- 4.4 BPMN — 118
  - 4.4.1 Fundamental Business Process Modelling Patterns — 121
  - 4.4.2 A Practical Example — 124
- 4.5 WS-BPEL — 127
- 4.6 Orchestration and Choreography — 129
- 4.7 Process Algebra and Petri Nets — 130
- 4.8 The Human Side of Business Process Management — 135
- 4.9 Summary — 136
- 4.10 Bibliographical Notes — 136

5 Catalysis Conversation Analysis — 139
- 5.1 What is a Business Process? — 139
- 5.2 Conversations — 141
- 5.3 Conversation Stereotypes and Scripts — 145
  - 5.3.1 Handling Exceptions — 147
- 5.4 Conversations as Components — 149
- 5.5 Contracts and Goals — 151
- 5.6 Conversations, Collaborations and Services — 155
- 5.7 Checking Model Consistency — 160
- 5.8 Summary — 161
- 5.9 Bibliographical Notes — 163

Contents

6 Models of Large Enterprises — 165
- 6.1 Business Process Modelling and SOA in the Large — 165
- 6.2 Business Rules in the Mission Grid — 173
- 6.3 The Mission Grid as a Roadmap for SOA — 176
- 6.4 Other Approaches — 177
- 6.5 Summary — 177
- 6.6 Bibliographical Notes — 178

7 Specification Modelling — 181
- 7.1 From Requirements to Specification — 181
- 7.2 Some Problems with the Conventional Approach to Use Cases — 182
  - 7.2.1 Overemphasis on Functional Decomposition — 183
  - 7.2.2 Lack of Clear Definition — 183
  - 7.2.3 Controller Objects — 184
  - 7.2.4 Use Cases and Scenarios — 184
  - 7.2.5 Essential or Generic Use Cases — 185
  - 7.2.6 Atomicity — 186
  - 7.2.7 Level of Abstraction — 186
  - 7.2.8 Exception Handling — 187
- 7.3 Describing Boundary Conversations or Use Cases — 189
- 7.4 Establishing the Type Model — 192
  - 7.4.1 State Models — 193
- 7.5 Finding Services from State Models — 198
  - 7.5.1 Cartooning Using Agents or Co-ordinators — 199
- 7.6 Finding Business Rules — 201
- 7.7 Ontology, Type Models and Business Rules — 207
  - 7.7.1 Rules and Rule Chaining — 208
- 7.8 Documenting the Specification — 212
- 7.9 Associations, Rules and Encapsulation — 212
  - 7.9.1 Integrity Rules, Rulesets and Encapsulation — 216
- 7.10 Summary — 218
- 7.11 Bibliographical Notes — 220

8 Standards — 221
- 8.1 BPM Standards — 221
- 8.2 Web Services Standards — 224
- 8.3 Other Miscellaneous Standards — 224
- 8.4 Bibliographical Notes — 228

Appendix A Requirements Engineering and Specification Patterns — 229

Appendix B The Fundamental Concepts of Service Oriented Architecture — 271

References and Bibliography — 281

Index — 289

Trademark Notice

Biztalk™, COM™, COM+™, DCOM™, SOAP™, Internet Explorer™, Microsoft Windows™, Access™, PowerPoint™, MSMQ™, MTS™, Excel™, Intellisense™, OLE™, Visual Basic™, Visual Studio™ and Microsoft Office™ are trademarks of Microsoft Inc.; Catalysis™ is a European trademark of TriReme International Ltd. and a US service mark of Computer Associates Inc.; CORBA®, IIOP® and OMG™ are registered trademarks of the Object Management Group™, ORB™, Object Request Broker™, OMG Interface Definition Language™, IDL™, CORBAservices™, CORBAfacilities™, Unified Modeling Language™, UML™, XMI™ and MOF are trademarks of the OMG.; IBM™, CICS™, Component Business Model™, DB2™ and Websphere™ are trademarks of International Business Machines Inc.; Tuxedo™ and Weblogic™, are trademarks of BEA Systems; Java™. EJB™, Enterprise Java Beans™, Java Beans™ are trademarks of Sun Microsystems Inc.; Objectory™, Rational Unified Process, RUP, Rose and Requisite Pro™ are trademarks of Rational Inc.; Oracle® is a trademark of Oracle Inc.; Syntropy™ is a trademark of Syntropy Ltd.; Telescript™ is a trademark of General Magic Inc.; Together™ and TogetherJ™ are trademarks of Together Inc.; Other trademarks are the property of their respective owners.

Foreword by Mark McGregor

*Author of Thrive – How to Succeed in the Age Of the Customer and
In Search of BPM Excellence; former Chief Coach BPMG.org*

When I was asked to write a foreword to this book, I was a little surprised. I have known Ian for many years, and he knows me pretty well. 'Why?', I thought, 'would someone with such a strong technology and methodological background ask me, well-known industry cynic, to do such a thing'.

Then I read the book and all started to become much clearer; this really is the first book of its kind that I have read. Instead of trying to squeeze round pegs into square holes, Ian has taken the time to remind us of which pegs go where and then proceeded to provide us with clear guides on how to make it work.

Few could argue that good IT systems aren't critical to the success of almost any business today. Historically, many of the IT problems we see have been blamed on a disconnect between the business users and IT people. In many ways this disconnect has been propagated through books and articles telling us what and how SOA and Business Process Management (BPM) are, and how we should use them.

As someone who has spent much of the last ten years operating in the BPM and modelling sectors, the problem I see is that too much has been written about how BPM and SOA are about technology and, on the other hand, too much about SOA as a purely business problem. Such confusion inevitably slows down, rather than speeds up, technology adoption.

So at last it has happened. Ian Graham has taken a long look and reminded us that if we are to try and solve the right problems, then first we have to put them in the right boxes. More than that, in this book he clearly puts forward logical arguments and gives great examples of how by doing this we can deliver better business results and systems in a faster and more cohesive manner.

Unlike many who write in this area, Ian has experience behind him; SOA is talking to a core part of development that he has spent many years working in, not just as an author, but as a practitioner – speak to him privately and he will show you the scars. For many, SOA is all shiny and new, but to old hands it is just the next logical evolution of the paradigm that started when software development started down the object oriented route. Object Oriented, Component Based, Web Services and now SOA! Ian has been instrumental in pushing the boundaries and helping people leverage these for success right from the very beginning.

For me, this book really works well in putting SOA into the correct context. It reminds us that sometimes business processes are just the words that IT use to describe systems processes, and when they use the phrase they are very often really talking about system requirements capture or analysis.

With the clear step-by-step methodological approach proposed here, any organization that is considering putting SOA in place will find themselves with a head start compared to those who are still mixing up the terms and ideas needed for IT supported business innovation.

I am certain that all readers of this book will finish it with a greater understanding of what to do and have a whole host of ideas that they can readily apply. Thank you, Ian

Mark McGregor

Foreword
by Professor Neil Maiden

City University, London

Ian Graham's new book is most timely and needed. Recent developments in service-centric computing have been rapid, with worldwide spending on web services-based software projects reaching record levels, and more and more projects exploring web service technologies.

These developments are already having a major impact on how to specify and develop service-based systems. However, most projects still lack effective processes, methods and techniques to develop these systems. Fortunately Ian Graham's book provides some solutions. He builds on his previous experiences in requirements engineering and component-based development to link requirement and design practices with web services for the first time.

This book will teach you about web services and their evolution from software components. It will inform you about web service approaches and standards such as BPEL, business process modelling and business process engineering, and topics increasing important to requirements practitioners and web service developers such as ontologies and business rules.

I strongly recommend this book to anyone wanting to understand how to adapt their software development processes to implement service-based applications.

Professor Neil Maiden

Preface

Service oriented architecture (SOA) is becoming the modern way of conceptualizing software engineering best practice. This book covers the early stages of SOA projects and shows how to specify services based on a sound understanding of existing and projected business processes, which can be achieved by good modelling practices, leading to models of business requirements as well as processes and then to well-constructed specifications.

While many companies have invested significantly in SOA and there have been some success stories, there is evidence that these early adopters may not be getting all the benefits that might have been expected. I feel that the need is to return to the basic wisdoms of software engineering, and the approach taken herein emphasizes this, putting a strong emphasis on best practice and business alignment. As new standards for business process modelling such as BPMN and BPEL emerge and evolve, there is also a need for a practical and critical assessment of them. It is particularly apposite to situate this study in the context of organizations moving towards SOA as a strategic direction.

Thus the book covers techniques and notations for requirements modelling, business process modelling and specification: UML, use cases, activity diagrams, Catalysis Conversation Analysis, Mission Grids, BPMN and BPEL. The focus throughout is on SOA. There is also a discussion of applicable standards and technology. A forthcoming companion volume (Graham, 2009) will cover managing SOA projects with agile development practices, governance, skills needed, migration strategy, and so on.

My objectives in writing it are to do the following.

- Provide a basic language-independent introduction to SOA concepts and technology.
- Explicate the business and technology drivers for SOA.

- Offer some new insights into the nature of business processes, especially those that involve human interaction and collaboration.
- Go beyond mere process area modelling and explain how to construct models at every scale.
- Explain the links between BPM and SOA.
- Explain the links between BPM and business rules.
- Provide a comprehensive coverage of modern approaches and notations for requirements modelling and specification.
- Offer and explain some well-tried but possibly unfamiliar practical requirements engineering techniques.
- Present some useful requirements patterns.
- Situate all this in the context of a migration strategy to SOA that is focused on business agility and which will be the subject of the forthcoming book cited above.

Whether I have succeeded, only the reader can judge.

Acknowledgements

There are some people without whom this book, whatever its current defects, would be a great deal weaker. I must thank Derek Andrews, who was the principal developer of Trireme's e-learning course on SOA (www.trireme.com), for many discussions, communications and valuable insights. The first chapter parallels this material quite closely and, I hope, could act as a back-up text for those taking the course. I am similarly deeply indebted to Hubert Matthews for all that he has taught me during long telephone discussions and exchanges of email. Clive Menhinick not only acted the part of a first class technical redactor but made very many vital suggestions as to content and its correctness.

Thanks also to the editorial and production teams at Wiley, who have been very patient and helpful throughout the project.

Ian Graham

CHAPTER 1

Principles of SOA

The physician can bury his mistakes, but the architect can only advise his client to plant vines.
Frank Lloyd Wright (1953)

Computer systems are critical for modern, increasingly global businesses. These organizations continually strive for shorter time to market and to lower the cost of developing and maintaining computer applications to support their operations. However, according to regular reports from the Standish Group between the mid-1990s and the present day, around two thirds of large US projects fail, either through cancellation, overrunning their budgets massively, delivering a product that is never put into production or requiring major rework as soon as delivered. Outright project failures account for 15% of all projects, a vast improvement over the 31% failure rate reported in the first survey in 1994 but still a grim fact. On top of this, projects that were over time, over budget or lacking critical features and requirements totalled 51% of all projects in the 2004 survey. It is not incredible to extrapolate these scandalous figures to other parts of the world. What is harder to believe is that our industry, and the people in it, can remain insouciant in the face of such a shameful situation. Clearly we should be doing something differently.

1.1 Why Projects Fail

The Standish conclusions are further illuminated by the data represented in Figure 1-1, which shows the fate of US defence projects (Connell and

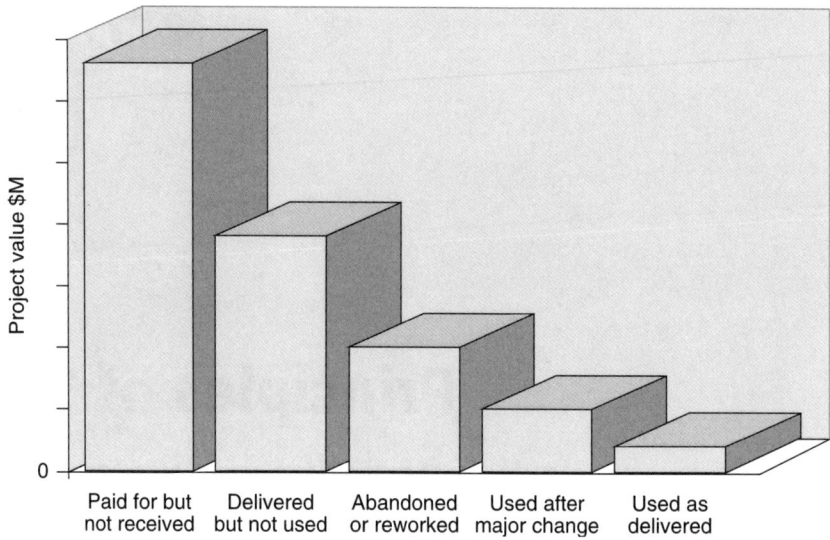

Figure 1-1 The outcome of US defence projects according to US government statistics.

Shafer, 1989). It must be remembered that these systems were mainly mainframe systems written in languages such as PL/1 and COBOL and it may be unfair to make a comparison with systems developed with modern tools. However, the point that something was wrong, even back then, cannot be avoided. Furthermore, the modern evidence seems to suggest that, sadly, not that much has changed.

The Standish surveys also looked into the reasons why people involved in the sample projects thought such projects fail. The reasons given included, *inter alia*:

- lack of user involvement;
- no clearly stated requirements;
- absence of project 'ownership';
- lack of clear vision and objectives.

Why should this be? If the cause really is lack of user involvement (leading to the other three) then we must ask why users are so reluctant. If the system is worth building (and paying for) then, surely, it must be worth spending some time to ensure it does what the user really wants. Is it because they have had bad experiences with IT in the past, perhaps?

Could it be that previous projects involved copious amounts of time spent with that clever C++ programmer (you know, the one with the Ph.D. in Arrogance) poring over huge diagrams that obviously made some sort of sense to him? Could it be that, by the time the system was delivered, the business had moved on so that changes had to be made and these changes took forever and ramped up the cost 'olympically'. Of course I'm too busy!

There are several reasons why our customers are exasperated with us nice IT folk.

- The typical IT person is more concerned with specification than with modelling requirements. The project manager wants to rein in everything to inside the system boundary and the designers think that a sexy system architecture is cool.
- IT folk do not speak the same language as their users. We speak UML and you, Mr User, must learn it if you want us to be able to communicate successfully.
- The architecture of our systems is driven by fashionable technology and short term project goals. This means that the principles of software engineering best practice are usually ignored in the scramble to cut and test the code. This accounts for the discrediting of the various volleys of silver bullets over the past years: structured design, object-oriented methods, component based development, etc. SOA, in some ways is a repackaging of the same (good) ideas – as we will see in the next chapter.
- Furthermore, the level of abstraction at which we work tends to be far too low.

IT departments are often culturally and technically miles away from the concerns and thought processes of the customers they serve. The problem is, thus, far broader than the need for SOA or any other technological solution; the real problem we have to solve is how to align IT practice with business need and begin to speak a common language. If this can be achieved there is a chance the SOA will not suffer the ignominy of its illustrious predecessors.

1.2 Aligning IT with Business – Speaking a Common Language

To believe that adopting the latest technology fad, be it service oriented architecture, business process modelling or even a business rules management system will, on its own, solve this problem is nothing short of naïve. To align IT with business we must consider all these along with innovative approaches to requirements engineering and system modelling.

The problem of requirements engineering is a modelling problem. We must model the business: its processes, its goals, its systems, its people and structure and even its culture. But we also need to model potential solutions: in this context, networks of loosely coupled services (applications) that make sense to the business and contribute to its goals. Ideally, the services (the technology, if you must) will map clearly onto the business needs and processes. This implies that we need a language rich enough to describe both the business and its systems and, more importantly, a language that can be understood by all stakeholders.

If one adopts the common misconception that understanding a client's requirements is the same as specifying a system that will meet those requirements, one can then blithely infer that use case analysis is the only requirements modelling technique needed. Jackson (1998) pours scorn on this idea, arguing that use cases are useful for specifying systems but that they cannot describe requirements fully. Use cases connect actors – which represent *users* adopting rôles – to systems. Requirements, on the other hand, may be those of people and organizations that never get anywhere near the system boundary.

In Figure 1-2 we see a depiction of part of Jackson's argument. A requirements document must be written in a language whose designations concern things in the world in which the system is embedded (including of course that system). Specifications need only describe the interfaces of the system and therefore depend on different designations. A specification *S* describes the interface of phenomena shared between the world and the system; use cases may be used to express these. A requirements model *R* is a description over these and other phenomena in the world. *R* depends on both the specification *and* the world. Jackson also states that 'the customer is usually interested in effects that are felt some distance from the machine'.

Ignoring non-user interactions can lead to us missing important re-engineering opportunities. I once worked on a rule-based order processing and auto-pricing system, whose aim was to take orders from customers electronically and price them automatically using various, often complex, pricing engines. The problem was that some orders were too complex or too large to admit of automatic handling. These had to be looked at by a salesman who would of course have an interface with the 'system'. So

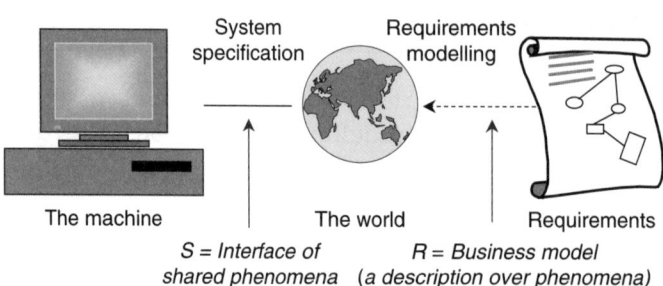

Figure 1-2 Specifications are not requirements models.

far, so good: a rule engine would screen 'illegal' or 'handle manually' orders. The salesman would then apply his various spreadsheets and other routines to such orders. But a further problem existed: some orders were so complicated as to be beyond the skills of the salesman, who did not have expertise in financial mathematics. For these orders, the salesman had to go across the office and talk to a specialist trader. He/she did have the requisite Ph.D. in Financial Engineering. We also modelled this conversation as the 'pseudo-use-case' shown as 'Help!' in Figure 1-3 and, as a result, when our domain expert looked at the simulation we had built, he/she realized immediately that if we gave the trader a screen (for orders re-routed) we could radically improve the workflow, and thereby customer service. Even this relatively minor excursion away from the system boundary thus had a big cash import because the orders for complex products were precisely the most profitable orders – by a long way. In many, more complex cases, the importance of going beyond the boundary will be greater still. Jackson gives an example of patient monitoring wherein sensors are attached to a patient's vital signs, and alarms (i.e. variances from tolerance) are forwarded to a nurse's workstation. The problem is that, should an alarm be triggered, the nurse is not normally the actor who will save the patient's life. She must run down the corridor to fetch a doctor. Thus, the critical use case is not at the system boundary and would be ignored in the conventional approach. Put starkly, concentrate on the use cases at the system boundary and people may die.

My interpretation of Jackson's argument is that we need a specific technique for modelling business processes distinct from, but compatible with, use case models of specifications. The alternative is to fall back on a veritable 'Russian doll' of nested models described in terms of 'business

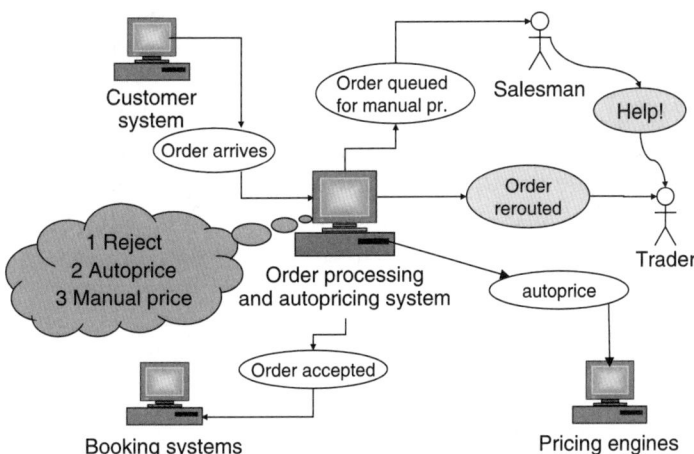

Figure 1-3 A process for order processing.

use cases' (Jacobson *et al.*, 1995): an approach that is not only clumsy but fails to address the above arguments. Thus, we need to know the answers to the following two questions before we can proceed.

- What is a model?
- What is a business process?

We defer dealing with the second question until a later chapter. Later in this book we will explore various notations and approaches to business process modelling. Let us first look at the nature of models.

1.2.1 Models

Modelling is central to software engineering practice and especially within the context of service oriented architecture. A **model** is a representation of some thing or system of things with all or some of the following properties.

- It is always *different* from the thing or system being modelled (the *original*) in scale, implementation or behaviour.
- It has the shape or appearance of the original (an iconic model).
- It can be manipulated or exercised in such a way that its behaviour or properties can be used to predict the behaviour or properties of the original (a simulation model).
- There is always some correspondence between the model and the original.

Examples of models abound throughout daily life: mock-ups of aeroplanes in wind tunnels; architectural scale models; models of network traffic using compressed air in tubes or electrical circuits; scaled models of silting up in river estuaries; software models of gas combustion in car engines. Of course, *all* software is a model of something, just as all mathematical equations are (analytic) models.

Jackson (1995) relates models to descriptions by saying that modelling a domain involves making designations of the primitives of the domain and then using these to build a description of the properties, relationships and behaviour that are true of that domain. For example, if we take the domain of sending birthday cards to one's friends, we might make designations:

```
p is a friend;
d is a date (day and month);
B(p,d) says that p was born on d.
```

Then we can make descriptions like: for every p, there is exactly one B. Jackson suggests that modelling is all about ensuring that the descriptions

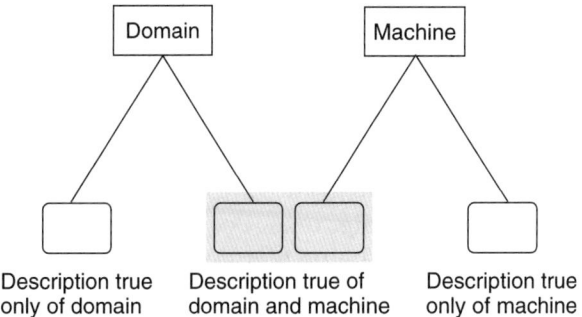

Figure 1-4 M is for model (after Jackson, 1995).

apply equally well to the model and to the original domain. In the context of computer models this might mean that the instances of a class or the records of a database are made to correspond uniquely to domain instances of our friends. Most usefully, Jackson presents this concept as the M configuration shown in Figure 1-4.

The Domain and the Machine are different; in the domain friends do not reside in disk sectors. There are many things in the domain that are not in our model, such as our friends' legs or pimples. There are also things that go on in computers that we are not concerned with in a model, such as load balancing. The model comprises the features shared between the domain and the machine.

This understanding of what a model is can be applied to the problem of service modelling. We must understand clearly that a service is both a model of the domain and a potentially implementable machine model. But we must begin with a model of the domain to understand and validate the requirements.

This understanding leads also to another common difficulty with computer systems: they can get out of synch with the world. The most topical example of this is probably identity theft; the computer model thinks you live somewhere else! It is therefore a key requirement of most systems that there should be a mechanism for re-synching the models should they become out of kilter.

Good models are abstract but 'real'; they ignore unnecessary detail but correspond exactly to the true state of the business. Good models are re-synchable. Good models are understandable to non-technical people.

Applying this understanding to modelling services, a service is derived from a model of the business domain and of the potential implementation domain. Defining the services precisely is the only way we can be sure that they meet current needs. Modelling unifies and clarifies those services and allows us to know what they are. Precise definition also provides a contract for the software developers.

Note that services may have relationships between them and often do: this service can only be accessed after that one; these services can be done in parallel; this service enables or disables that one; etc.

These relationships are about business rules. If we change the relationship, we will change the way we do business or re-engineer the business. Such an approach helps us to integrate different parts of the business and be more agile. It also supports greater reuse because we can know exactly what the service is. Additionally, it helps identify services required from other businesses that, hitherto, we might have been forced to create from scratch, thus duplicating them.

In later chapters we will return to the question of how to construct a sufficiently rich language for business modelling that is equally understandable to the user and to IT staff. We will focus on techniques for modelling requirements, system and business processes specifications on the way to delivering an SOA that can support them properly and allow for flexible and low-cost evolution. But first we must understand the principles and basic concepts of service oriented architecture.

1.3 What is Service Oriented Architecture?

Service oriented architecture (SOA) is an architectural concept in software design that emphasizes the use of combined loosely coupled services to support business requirements directly. In SOA, resources are made available to service consumers in the network as independent artefacts that are accessed in a standardized way. This adherence to standardization is definitional. SOA is precisely about raising the level of abstraction so that requirements and business processes can be discussed in a language understood by business people as well as IT folk.

The main idea behind SOA is the desire to build applications that support a business process by combining a number of smaller 'business services' into a complete business process or workflow. Each of these services is a stand-alone piece of software providing business functionality that is loosely coupled to the other services (other pieces of software) which make up the application. Examples of a business service could be checking details about a customer, validating a customer payment, sending an invoice to a customer, synchronizing or transferring data between systems, or converting a document from one format to another. Many of these services will be particular to a business; however, some will also be standard services that could either be purchased as software or will be readily available on the internet in the form of web services. New services can also be created from existing applications or by writing new ones using your preferred development framework.

Many definitions of SOA identify the use of web services (using SOAP and WSDL) in its implementation; however it is possible to implement SOA using any service-based technology. Though built on similar principles, SOA is *not* the same as web services. SOA is independent of any specific technologies.

A software architecture is a representation of a software system – how all the pieces fit together. It describes the most effective way to design the system within a set of constraints or a defined infrastructure. An architectural style is a family of architectures sharing common themes and a recognizable common vision, in the same way that we can recognize the shared vision of Gothic or Georgian architecture. Service oriented architecture is an architectural style whose goal is to achieve loose coupling among interacting software agents. A software agent is an application, a piece of software, a component, a program, etc; also known in older terminology as a module – a piece of software that does work. A **service** is a unit of work carried out by a **service provider** to achieve some desired result for the **service consumer**. Typically, a unit of work would be some sort of (business) transaction. The service consumer has a goal in mind, and the task of the service provider is to achieve that goal on behalf of the consumer or help the consumer to do so. Both provider and consumer are rôles played by (possibly software) agents.

Although a service is just an interface, it will thus be implemented by a software component, or collection of software components, that implements a reusable business function, such managing customers or managing customer accounts. Services are defined by their interfaces, which describe what the services can do. How the service works is hidden inside the component or components that provide the service.

Service-oriented architecture is an approach for designing and building applications by constructing them from loosely coupled services (existing services where possible) and discovering and writing new services as necessary.

The SOA approach encourages loose coupling between the services that make up an application; contrast this to traditional monolithic architectures, which are characterized by tight interdependence between the parts of an application.

Figure 1-5 illustrates how a user might interact with a product ordering or quotation service. The user asks a question and gets a straightforward and useful answer. To assemble this response the system actually relies on four lower level services, including one which could well be rule-based, since tax regulations vary quite often.

The most important properties of a service are as follows.

- Every service has a **contract**: a description of what the service will do for the user and what it requires of the environment and indeed the

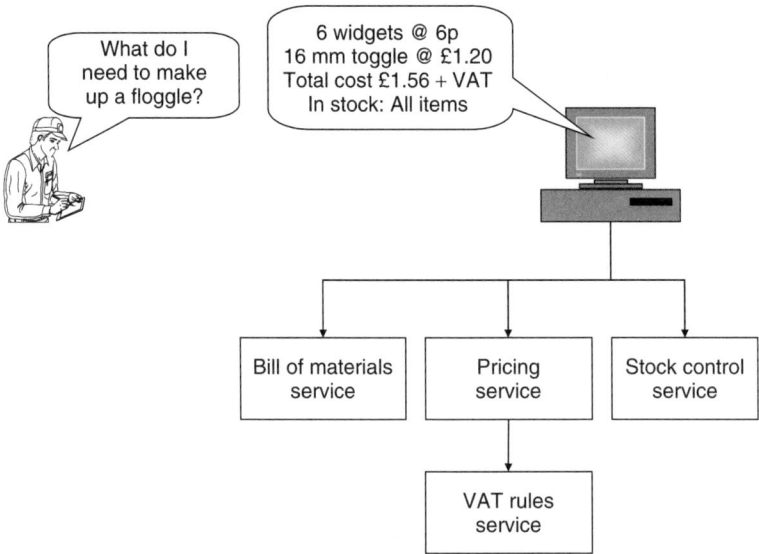

Figure 1-5 Composing loosely coupled services.

user. This is what enables the loose coupling between services and is the basis for 'discovering' [services over a distributed environment]. Clearly defined contracts are essential if we are to achieve composition and reuse of services.

- Services can be **discovered**. They are designed to have a description in a directory, so that they can be found and accessed via a discovery mechanism. This too helps make services more readily reusable. Discovery is a property that can be given to any piece of software – but it doesn't necessarily mean anyone will find that software actually useful.
- Services are **abstract** – the only part of a service that is visible to the outside world is the service description (the contract). This contributes greatly to service reusability or sharing.
- Services are **autonomous**: they have control over the logic they encapsulate; they decide how any arriving messages should be processed or forwarded. This enables service composition and makes reuse easier to achieve.
- Services can be **composed** – they can be combined with other services to satisfy a set of business requirements, to solve new problems.
- Services should be **loosely coupled** to other services. This enables composition and encourages autonomy.
- Services are **stateless with respect to complete transactions**. Services minimize the storage of information specific to an activity (a use of

the service). This too helps with composability. A stateless service is an ideal that should always be strived for, but we can weaken this requirement by passing the state either directly or indirectly with any message exchange.
- Services should be **reusable**. Systems are best divided into services with the conscious intention of promoting reuse.

One needs to focus on precisely these eight properties of a service when developing a new service or identifying and wrapping existing applications as services. Looking closely at these, we can see that reuse depends on all the other properties.

- Abstraction helps with packaging for reuse.
- An autonomous and stateless service is more likely to be reusable.
- Loose coupling means minimizing dependencies on other software and this encourages reuse.
- A service that is discovered can be used, and used again; it can be reused.

Also, adversely:

- Reuse takes place when a service is composed with other services.
- A service that is autonomous and stateless is easier to compose with other services.
- It is precisely loose coupling that allows composition.

Thus both reuse and composition result from the other six properties.

There is an even more important property that we have not listed here. As shown in Figure 1-6, a service must supply a service to the business. This means that the service does something that achieves a business goal. It will be about a sale, identifying a customer, reserving a seat on an aeroplane or some such. The service will not be about supporting functions in a user interface.

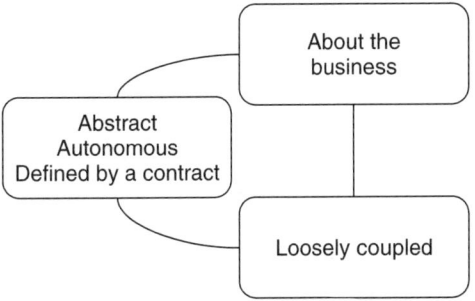

Figure 1-6 The key properties of a service.

The interface of a service, as presented to the user, displays a set of operations that make up that service. These operations are about supporting the user of the service. But who *is* the user of the service? The usual answer is an actor (using UML use case terminology). An actor is a user adopting a rôle or another system that interacts with the service. However, it is necessary to think more carefully about this. Services are about supporting the business, not supporting a computer user or another system. The service should support something or somebody *in the business,* in the real world: the **real user** of the service. The real user, in this sense may be someone who never comes anywhere near a computer or browser; someone who is far away from the system boundary.

The operations of a service should be abstract and at a high level of abstraction and be about the business. Some examples will illustrate this point.

When reserving a hotel room, say, we need to create a record with all the necessary details obtained from the real user, the person making the reservation; rather than

```
get guest details (name, address, contact tel)
get reservation details (room type, arrival date, days)
get reserver details (name, address, contact tel)
```

These are probably operations supporting a user interface or procedure calls in some programming language. Instead of this, a service invocation (message) should contain all the information that is needed for a coherent transaction to be possible. For example:

```
message<guest name, guest address, guest contact
tel, room type, arrival date, days, reserver name,
reserver address, reserver contact tel>
```

SOA emphasizes building systems for the user, not systems for the IT department: systems for the benefits of employees, customers, suppliers, partners; systems for the 'real' user!

In the past, clerks used 'terminals' to access 'batch systems'; now customers use the web ... or do they?

I was once involved in the design of a web radio station. Our approach soon teased out the fact that the most important business objective behind the initiative was neither to do with entertainment, any Reithian concern with edification nor with selling advertising (they would then have only lost the same revenue from the airtime ads). No, the main purpose was to sell CDs. The target audience was teenagers, so the strategy included providing lots of contents concerning current pop stars and bands. Here is one of the scenarios we explored during one requirements workshop.

Denise Green is visiting her friend Tracey Black. They are eating chocolate and discussing music and decide to log on to the station to check out some groovy sounds and get all the latest poop on their favourite boy bands. To their delight, BoyzInCustard have a new album out today. They *must* have it. So far so good. But there is a problem; neither girl is old enough to have a credit card. Never mind, good old Mum's got one. Mrs Black wouldn't go near a computer if her life depended on it. However, she is precisely the real user so far as the financial part of the radio station's business process is concerned.

Figure 1-7 provides another way to visualize this point.

Loose coupling is about having a simple interface with very low dependency – an interface that mandates collaboration with 50 other services in order for it to do its job and for them to do their jobs would be impossible to extract for reuse. To say that services can be loosely coupled implies that the service interface must be independent of the implementation. There can be unintended consequences of coupling (both good and bad ones). Ideally, services are 'stateless'; which means that, when a message arrives at a service interface, the service processes the message and returns an answer or result to the consumer; it remembers nothing about the message afterwards; it does not even need (apart from the reply address) to know anything about the consumer.

A service can receive a message, process it, return a reply and then forget all about it. At any rate, this is all we can see from the outside. Looking inside the service, however, we might see three types of communication ports or 'endpoints'.

- Ports for messages entering the service; the **entry** ports.
- A departure port for sending the reply message; the **exit** port.
- A **rejected message** port for invalid messages.

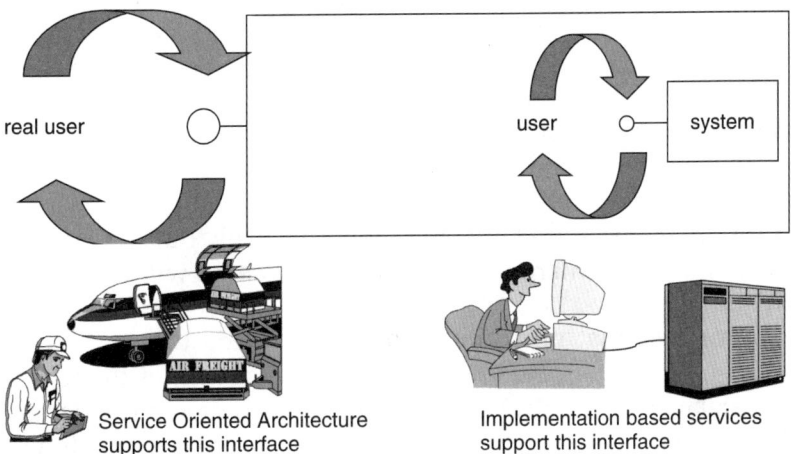

Figure 1-7 Services for customers not clerks.

There could be more ports such as those for queuing application faults or tracking messages, but the above three are the basic ones.

A service will read a message from the entry port, process it and write the reply to the exit port. If the message is invalid (it is not recognized by the service), it is written to the rejected message port. Developing a service in this style is reasonably straightforward. The service knows nothing about the outside environment, it is entirely self-contained and all it needs to do is process a message it recognizes, reject a message it doesn't, send any reply as necessary, and then forget about the message.

Note that this type of service will probably need a complex environment it can exist in. The trick is to make this complex environment easy to configure and use. As we shall see later, enterprise service bus products offer one such configurable environment.

In summary, the perfect service is a black box, loosely coupled to all users. Its overall action is input–process–output, with no memory of the input after producing the output.

It is vitally important that a service can be extended. Businesses change rapidly and so it is important that software changes to reflect this. This will involve changes to service providers, service consumers and the messages. If these changes cannot be made, then everyone is locked into the current version of a service, it will not be possible to extend it to reflect the new business opportunities. What changes can be made to a service without invalidating it for current users?

We can change the implementation providing the interface is still satisfied, we can change the interface by adding function of accepting more types of input and we can add fields to a message. Changes other than these are likely to invalidate or corrupt the service for existing users.

We obtain optimal loose coupling when a service is a perfect black box, in the sense that any user cannot see inside it; and, when once inside the service, you cannot see out; so that the service has no idea of who is using it and what other services are around. Making sure that services really are black boxes really does reduce coupling.

Each SOA service should have a quality of service (QoS) associated with it. Typical QoS elements are security requirements, such as authentication and authorization, reliable messaging, and policies regarding who can invoke services. QoS statements may include SLAs, but in principle they can include more than mere service level agreements. I will give an example of this.

Let us suppose that our quotation service needs to vary the price of widgets dynamically as the open market price of copper fluctuates. This price must be obtained from an on-line information provider such as Reuters or Honest John's Prices Inc. as shown in Figure 1-8. Honest John provides a low cost option but, let's face it, probably isn't anywhere near a reliable as a reputable or well-established firm such as Reuters or

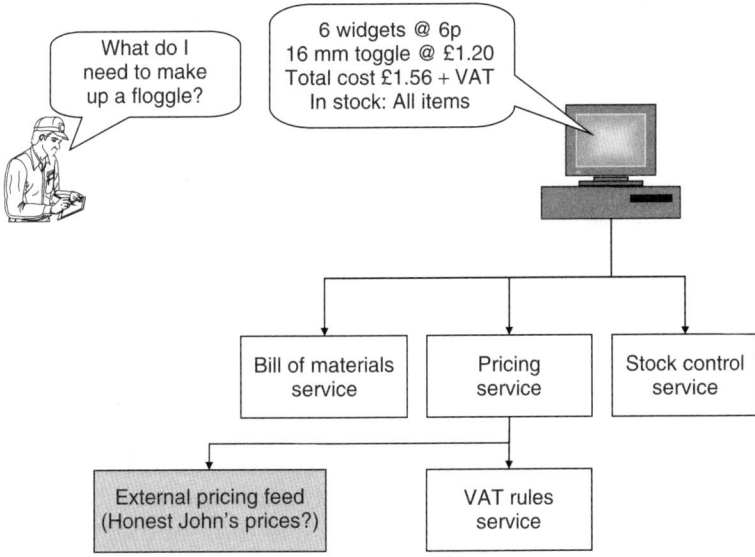

Figure 1-8 External services must be trustworthy.

Thompson (Datastream). We must not know or care about how such a service is implemented but we might well want to specify a level of 'trust' or some surrogate for that quality.

There are other, more mundane, meanings for QoS. The term is most often used to refer to qualities like security or the reliability of message delivery. These are important, of course, but a good service needs to be trusted in every sense of the word.

Application developers or system integrators can build applications by composing one or more services without knowing the services' underlying implementations. For example, a service can be implemented either in .NET or J2EE, and the application consuming the service can be on a different platform or language.

SOA, if done properly, should lead to interfaces that are about the business and not about supporting the user interface; there is end-to-end involvement with both customers and suppliers. Beware especially of just wrapping existing interfaces; this is usually far too low level. Make sure, when modelling, that you understand the business, not just the computer systems. Provide services for *people* to do tasks that deliver them value, whether these people are employees, customers, suppliers, regulators or any other kind of stakeholder. Furthermore, they should be able to understand the system in their own terms rather having to learn the software developers' argot.

SOA should provide services that help people carry out tasks that deliver them value; systems for the user not for the IT department; systems for employees, customers, suppliers, partners and so on. Most importantly, SOA must provide systems for the 'real' user.

1.3.1 The Real User

Traditional, detailed use cases define the interactions among the actors, the direct users who adopt rôles in relation to a system. In several works, Graham (1994, 1996, 1998) reinterpreted use cases to mean goal-oriented conversations or business processes, but the overwhelming number of UML practitioners followed the advice of the creator of the use case (Jacobson, 1992) in restricting use cases to those that involved a human actor or other device interacting with a system at its boundary. But the real user of the system may be far outside the system boundary. The best that could be done in this tradition was to show so-called 'business use cases' at the boundary of a bigger system that incorporated the direct users as components, leading to the kind of Russian doll topology illustrated in Figure 1-9. Is it really credible that all businesses structure themselves in this neat, nested fashioned. I don't think so.

Also, common practice was to create very detailed and over-documented use cases. At the start of the development, if the level of use case captured is too detailed then the analysts are effectively designing the user interface – this is an activity that we can often leave until later. Capturing such detailed use cases leads to vast amounts of documentation with little understanding of the business and its processes. This is exacerbated by anally-retentive project management that insists on a ream of filled-in use cases templates copied from the nearest volume of 'guruware'. As we shall see later, much of the information on the typical template (Cockburn, 2000;

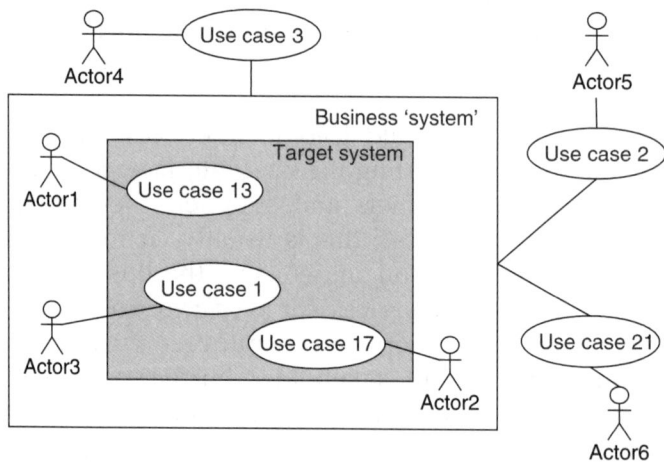

Figure 1-9 Nested use case models.

Fowler, 2003; Jacobson, 1992) is quite redundant from a business analysis viewpoint. There is, however, a need to document the description of the business at a level of detail that provides an understanding of the business. As we will learn, it is 100 % sufficient to do this by writing only the pre- and post-conditions of the use case and noting any possible exceptions, fatal and non-fatal. We return to this in Chapter 5.

In our approach, and in a nutshell, the idea is to start by documenting 'big' use cases: interactions among the real users of the system. These big use cases are business processes. At a later stage in the development cycle these big use cases will have detail added to give traditional use cases which can be used for the development of the HCI as part of the design phase.

The real user will need to be supported with services; the system user is supported by a user interface. Low level stepwise use cases are about defining the system user interfaces. It should be noted that sometimes the real user of the system is a direct user; but it is still better to find his/her goals with respect to the business rather than with respect to the system.

For example, in a lending library the real users of the system are the library members as well as the librarians (who are direct users of the library administration system). A member wants a reservation to be fulfilled when it is their turn in the queue of library members waiting for a particular book. When they return a book at the end of a loan, they want the transaction recorded so they are no longer responsible for it. Our library members are not that interested in the actual loan being recorded – though the library is, of course, very interested in that particular transaction. Thus, the purpose of the system is to make certain that the business of the library is run properly; that the business processes of the library work correctly.

For another example, consider the refuelling of planes at an airport. The technician carrying out the refuelling will be given instructions on how much fuel should be loaded onto the plane. He might contact a clerk to get the latest instructions that may vary the fuel load.

In this example, the business goal is to load the right amount of fuel onto the plane to enable it to get to its destination safely. (Typically it should arrive at its destination with enough fuel to supply a safety margin – at the other extreme, if everything that can go wrong does, the plane should still arrive safely on the ground in one piece with an empty tank!)

The main message here is that you need to get outside of the system boundary to identify services. The writing of use cases at the system boundary tells you the services the interface designer needs, to support the clerk sitting at the computer, not the real user. By concentrating on the user interface rather than what is happening in the real world, we are focusing on the solution rather than on the problem. We need to move our perception out a level (and up a level of abstraction).

There is a change of emphasis. To find business services, we need to understand the needs (goals) of the real user and supply services to satisfy those needs. We could allow the real user, the technician, to access the system directly with little or no change to the service.

A more familiar example of the real user and the actual user being different is a call centre; the real user is the customer on the end of the phone, not the call centre clerk. The software, however, is usually designed for the clerk; this may explain why call centres are not always very helpful! Note that, when we come to services we will differentiate between business services and utility services; utility services are about satisfying the goals of the developer.

Once services have been identified, the users of a service can be changed and their responsibilities moved around, sometimes radically. Returning to the example of refuelling an aircraft, this might be identified as an outsourcible service and moved out to an external service provider. The business service of refuelling an aircraft uses many other services; to calculate the fuel load of the aircraft, we will need to interrogate:

- the flight schedule, to get details of the destination, route, passenger load, and cargo load;
- the runway allocation services of the departure and arrival airports, to find out the length of the runways;
- get weather information for the complete route, especially at the departure airport.

To order the refuelling we will need:

- the arrival time at the airport;
- the gate number;
- the fuel load.

To schedule the refuelling we will need to tell the fuel company:

- the gate number;
- the refueling time;
- the amount of fuel.

If all of this information is available from various services then we can change the way we do business, to become more efficient. It is much easier for the refuelling service to schedule its fuel bowsers if it can find out when customer aeroplanes actually arrive; the fuel load can be calculated in real time and, for example, cargo can be swapped more profitably for passengers during plane reloading, and the fuel load adjusted accordingly.

Any business process can be outsourced if we view it in the right way, though we may not wish to do this. With an SOA based system, there can be end-to-end involvement with employees, customers, suppliers, etc.

For example, in the air-transport industry:

- we can use other companies' services to order limousines to move passengers from home to the airport and back again (similarly, at their destination);
- we can schedule a courier company to pick-up and deliver the luggage – using our airline if possible;
- we can use the airport system to track passengers and their luggage (RFID tags are being used for this currently);
- the fuel loading can be done just before take-off (the fuel company sorts out the fuel load based on current conditions) and we could add passengers to the load if there is room, removing less profitable non-urgent cargo;
- the aircraft maintenance company could call planes in for routine service, and provide early warning of emergency service requests;
- we could book hotels at the destination and order rental cars, theatre-tickets, tours, and provide even more services to enhance 'the passenger experience' – and make money!

The idea is to cut out the middle men and thus improve our business efficiency and/or flexibility.

A typical approach to services (in all meanings of the concept) is for the client to work out what they want and then make a request to the supplier. In our airline example, he/she might say, 'load my plane with 3 tonnes of fuel; it will be at gate 19 at 15:00'. This means that the supplier has just enough information to satisfy the request, but has little or no access to additional information that could make his/her service more efficient.

If the service supplier has access to more information, they might be able to carry out the task more efficiently. In the airline example, the fuel supplier has full access to the airline's and other services and could probably make better decisions on how to supply their service. For example, they could supply less fuel than is ordered because it has more up-to-date information about the actual fuel requirements, or it could schedule its fuel trucks more efficiently.

It can be seen that there are savings to be made, and these are often best shared between the client and the service supplier.

1.4 Business Drivers for SOA

I have already mentioned the high IT project failure rate as a compelling reason for doing *something* differently but there are other key drivers.

The main driver, in my opinion, is the need for greater business agility: the need to innovate new business processes; the need to conform to rapid changes in regulation; the need to exploit new economies of scale and reuse as opportunities arise. Exploiting and integrating the legacy in a flexible way (EAI) can clearly contribute to business agility.

In addition to this there is a need for greater business focus, a focus on the real customers for competitive edge and, finally, the need for greater consistency arising from sharing common services.

The move to B2B over XML from traditional EDI (Electronic Data Interchange) has also been a driver in some sectors but it is now less urgent since low entry-cost EDI products became available.

Some drivers cross the business–technology categories. Rapidly evolving or poorly understood requirements has been a problem for many years, as has the phenomenon of requirements creep. We have already considered the need for a common language. Involving the business in service definition and delivery. The key thing is to make sure that it isn't the lunatics that are running the asylum. High IT system maintenance costs tie up budgets that could be better used for supporting new business initiates; so that, if SOA can reduce these costs through reuse or – more likely – greater flexibility, this is a strong business argument for SOA. Finally, rapidly evolving technology and platforms present as much of a problem to the business as they do to the IT function.

1.5 Technology Drivers

One of the historical drivers that led up to the widespread interest in SOA was the need to get disparate legacy and newer systems to interoperate or be accessed through a single login. This is the so-called Enterprise Application Integration (EAI). Typically, a large organization would, over the years, have accumulated a goulash of departmental systems and systems transferred through mergers and acquisitions. To link these together various point-to-point connexions would have been established, usually based on the interchange of comma-delimited files over batch tape or FTP links. The resulting spaghetti connexions are suggested by Figure 1-10.

Various technologies have been advanced to address this problem including object request brokers (ORBs) based on the CORBA standard (Common Object Request Broker Architecture) and message-oriented middleware (MOM). The main difference between the two is that ORBs deal with messages synchronously and MOM does so asynchronously. In plainer terms, in an ORB environment, an application sends a message to another application and waits for a reply. If the systems crash, everything will have to start all over again. With MOM, such messages are placed on a queue

Principles of SOA

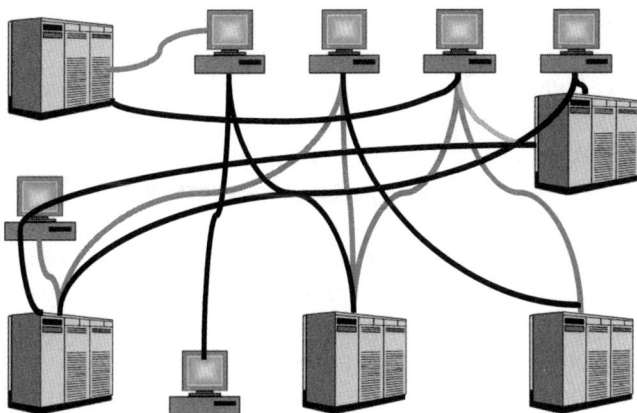

Figure 1-10 Enterprise spaghetti.

for delivery and, if necessary, the sending application can carry on with its business. Usually, eventual delivery of the message is guaranteed by the middleware. Some modern MOM products also include ORB capabilities.

Typical mainstream MOM products include IBM's MQSeries, BEA's Tuxedo, TIBCO, SonicMQ and Microsoft MQ.

Enterprise Service Buses (ESBs) build on MOM to provide a flexible, scalable, standards-based integration technology for building a loosely coupled, highly-distributed SOA. ESBs contain facilities for reliable messaging (*á la* MOM), web services, data and message transformation, content-based 'straight through' routing. Along with web services, ESBs are proving to be the major technical enablers for actual SOA projects.

The architectural simplification provided – at least potentially – by an ESB is illustrated in Figure 1-11. All we need to do is create interfaces or

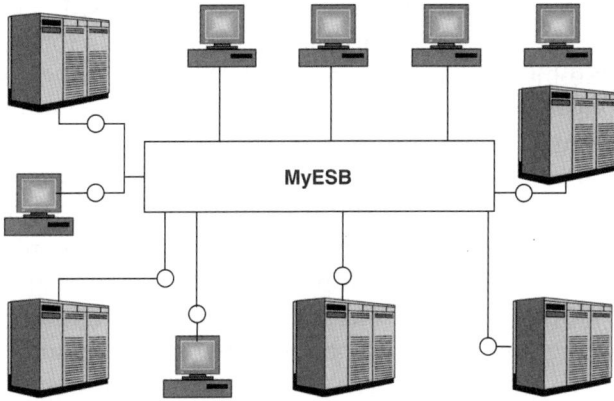

Figure 1-11 The Enterprise Service Bus.

APIs to the systems and the bus takes care of message formats and routing. Well it can if you know what you are doing!

Typical mainstream ESB vendors include BEA, Cape Clear, IBM, SeeBeyond (Sun) and Sonic (Progress).

ESBs are designed to replace conventional 'hub and spoke' EAI brokers and to compliment or replace application servers, such as Websphere and WebLogic.

Another technology that is very pertinent to SOA is that of business rules management systems (BRMSs). This technology allows systems to store business rules separately from raw computer code and in a form that can be maintained directly by business experts with little or no IT skills. Decision processes based on rules can be presented as services within an SOA. I shall have more to say about this in later chapters, when we look into business process modelling, because there is a strong connexion between the two.

Here typical mainstream products include JRules, Blaze Advisor, HaleyRules, PegaRules and Versata.

As I have repeatedly emphasized, the key technology to master when embarking on an SOA project is modelling. Modelling is core to defining good, sharable, reusable, composable, autonomous services. This book will explore how to model requirements, system specifications and business processes. Its companion volume explores modelling within the context of project management – specifically agile software development processes and business rules management.

The final core enabling technology for SOA that I want to mention is standards and, in particular, web services standards.

Web services offer a practical, standardized way of interoperating amongst applications, regardless of the platforms on which they are running. Concrete agents communicate by passing messages that conform to defined standard protocols. The environment is open, so that agents can leave or join without disrupting the whole. Web services standards are myriad but the most important ones have been XML, WSDL, UDDI and SOAP. WS-* refers to a whole family of standards for things such as security, reliable messaging, and so on. The point is that these standards have meant that users and vendors can co-operate to exchange service definitions and realizations and safely pass messages around a corporate or even external network.

TCP/IP is the basic message transport mechanism. XML is a mark-up language that can have tags to define, identify and manipulate structures representing things like customers, products and standard business transactions. WSDL (Web Services Description Language) is machine and programming language independent. SOAP (originally standing for Simple Object Access Protocol) is a communication protocol for exchanging information between applications. It can run over HTTP, JMS or other proprietary middleware. SOAP builds on XML and uses WSDL.

UDDI (Universal Description, Discovery and Integration) is a 'worldwide' business service registry. It too builds on WSDL.

This book is not about the details of these enabling standards but we will look at them in the context of SOA projects in Chapter 8. There are also important emerging standards for business process modelling that we will consider in detail later, primarily BPEL, BPMN and UML. In the context of business rules (mentioned above) the important standards are OWL, SVBR and (again) UML.

Lastly, there is a multitude of extant and emerging vertical industry standards based on XML. These mostly define the semantics of messages within the business contexts that they address. Typical examples are the domain models for the general insurance business (ACORD) and another for Oil and Gas, which was, I think, one of the earliest established. Some business rules management system vendors offer business rules 'knowledge packs' based on these standards.

Web services have self-describing interfaces in platform-independent XML documents. Web Services Description Language (WSDL) is the standard used to describe the services, at least partially (no semantics).

Web services communicate with messages defined in a language (possibly XML). Communication among consumers and providers or services can happen in heterogeneous environments, with little or no knowledge about the provider. Messages between services can be viewed as key business documents processed in an enterprise.

Web services are maintained in a registry that acts as a directory listing. Applications can look up services in the registry and invoke them. Universal Description, Definition, and Integration (UDDI) is the standard used for service registry.

But quality? Trust? Supplier reliability? Unfortunately, UDDI is not currently expressive enough to encase these factors.

1.6 Benefits, Pitfalls and Prospects

The potential benefits of adopting service oriented architecture may be summarized as follows.

- Faster development.
- Faster maintenance.
- More reusable business logic.
- Greater consistency across the enterprise.
- Better alignment and understanding between business and IT.

We shall deal first with the business benefits arising from SOA, then the technical ones.

SOA offers the possibility of being able to plug in new services without disrupting existing operations (business agility). This is especially true if one is using an enterprise service bus. Modularity is based on business concepts rather than technical models, so that business goals should be better supported. Services can be shared across organizational units, companies and maybe even geographical regions, leading to both greater consistency and, potentially, more reuse. Services can be delivered on the web. Finally, there is the opportunity to share your savings with your partners (and vice versa, of course).

The technical benefits include a better separation of concerns, an improvement in the way software is built, leading to lower maintenance costs (as we shall see in the next chapter), greater productivity, greater modularity and more code reuse. Building or assembling services based on small reusable components both supports and depends on the adoption of a culture of good design. Finally, building shared understanding and a common language should lead to less conflict and better business alignment.

Economic benefits include achieving a better understanding of the business. Often, changing business rules or processes (the order in which you do things) can simplify things and thus save costs or add value. SOA supports making such changes without massive delays.

You can add value to your own business by doing things better or by using other companies' services. Also you might add value to other people's business by offering them access to your services. You might also contract out development with better control using SOA.

SOA, as I argue in Chapter 2, ought to decrease the costs associated with both development and maintenance and all within a faster development cycle, as I argue in a companion volume (Graham, 2009).

1.6.1 Pitfalls

However, there are some pitfalls to watch out for too. New challenges for those adopting SOA include security and versioning. Quality may be more of a problem than with earlier systems, though making QoS more explicit could be seen as a benefit. Testing services may need new approaches and new tools are emerging, e.g. Parasoft, SOAPSonar, etc. With services, errors are visible globally – and customers may desert because of even one bad service experience. And, of course, there is a possibility of unforeseen legal problems and the ever-present governance issues such as technical politics and reuse management.

None of these problems is insuperable. The biggest dangers are those I have already warned of:

- Modelling systems and not the business.
- Ignoring the real users.

- Abstractions at too low a level.
- Legacy wrapping as opposing to business service design.

In addition to these there is a danger of vendor (or product line) lock-in preventing unforeseen variation. This is especially true if you are adopting an enterprise service bus (ESB). If you know what such products are capable of and use them well this shouldn't be a problem. But if you go for the quick fix implementation using an ESB, there is every danger that you will end up with hidden spaghetti (in the ESB).

To illustrate this, consider Figure 1-12 and compare it with Figures 1-10 and 1-11.

To avoid this kind of disaster we need considerable skill in modelling, we need to pay attention to architectural layering and to simplifying and rationalizing our technology base technology. Then, maybe, one needs to use a top flight ESB product and understand the full range of its capabilities. Use high-level self-describing messages; embed data format translations; use rule-based routing.

1.6.2 Post-SOA Benefits

Once we have created and bedded down an SOA, what benefits should we be able to see?

We might see that services have enabled us to change who does what or even to have reengineered the business so that we have:

- stopped doing old unprofitable things;
- installed more efficient business processes;
- obtained more business process reuse;

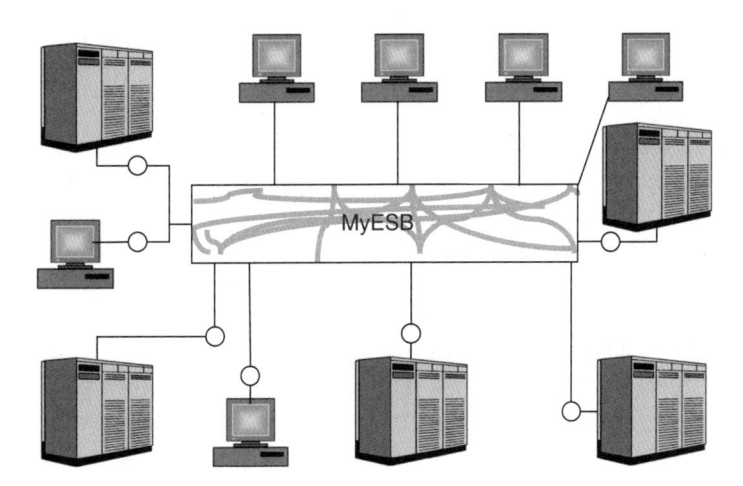

Figure 1-12 Hiding the spaghetti in the ESB.

- obtained the concomitant cost reductions;
- focused more on the business, as opposed to sexy software.

If SOA was done right, it should now be possible to keep on innovating in these dimensions as our business and markets evolve. Business process improvement is now normal practice.

SOA should have helped with granularity by giving better modularity of business processes and the services associated with them.

Building new systems on top of services – system assembly from components – is a routine part of everyday life, rather than a cause for sighs and headshakes in the 'application backlog' department.

It is now possible to share services with customers and suppliers. You are almost certainly contracting out some services now. Maybe you are contracting in some services too; doing new things by using other peoples' services. It may even be possible to use published services from other businesses, sharing pre-competitive expertise with the market, though, it has to be said that most current SOA projects are 'behind the firewall'. We will discuss this further in Chapter 3 when we consider UDDI.

1.7 Migration Strategies

As with any technology transformation programme, one of the problems that is likely to divert or derail the process is change management. Hearts and minds must be won from the IT teams, through the business units and right on to the senior business management.

Looking at change programmes that have succeeded, it seems that the first thing to secure is the understanding and strong support of the most senior operational management. Securing management 'buy in' is not only difficult but crucial. You do not start this by asking them if they 'want an SOA'. The benefits must be discussed entirely in terms of ROI, margins, shareholder wealth, markets and business processes.

Start with manageable but visible projects; no one will notice if you fail with a no-so-visible project – but no one will notice if you succeed either. The early projects should be able to demonstrate a tangible business benefit. Some 'quick wins' will help cement business support and assist the process is change management process greatly.

As I argued at the outset of this chapter, rebuilding trust between IT and the business is a key challenge and may not be easy if the atmosphere has been sullied by past failures. Therefore, be agile: don't resist changes to requirements mid project; learn how to descope rather than run late. Fix the business objectives by all means, but don't fix the specification. Test as you go to avoid unpleasant surprises during user acceptance testing.

Education and training will be important. Teaching the IT guys how to talk plain English is a good start!

On the technical side of change management, define the long-term architecture and define the (local) domain model. Make sure you are *all* clear about the software development method you are following. Publish the models, method and architecture. The companion volume on agile processes provides explicit techniques for these issues.

Finally, manage expectations. Do not let people assume that the existence of a working prototype means that all technical and business issues have been resolved. Warn your sponsors that success with service oriented architecture is a long-term investment yielding long-term benefits – though, of course, one may hope for short-term wins too. An SOA is not just for Christmas!

In my opinion, the critical success factors for SOA are these.

- Senior management support.
- Users who are prepared to get involved.
- A watertight business case for any pilots that are contemplated.
- Good modelling skills on the IT side. These should include UML, business process modelling and domain and service modelling skills.
- You have thought (i.e. done the modelling) before deciding to buy infrastructure products such as an ESB.
- Your team has good (non-IT) communication skills.
- A reuse culture is at least conceivable in the IT department.

    ...and, right down at the bottom of the priority list

- The requisite technical and product skills are in place or obtainable.

If any of these are not present then question whether this is the right time (or the right company) to start an SOA project in.

1.8 Summary

Too many software projects fail. Software engineering practice has not delivered on its promises and needs to change. The chief problem is how best to align IT practice with business need.

Requirements engineering is mainly a modelling problem as is specification. But they are *not* the same problem. The requirements engineer must look beyond the system boundary and understand the business and the real users of services. Discovering business rules is an important part of requirements engineering.

Service oriented architecture is an architectural concept in software design that emphasizes the use of combined loosely coupled services to support business requirements directly. In SOA, resources are made available to service consumers in the network as independent artifacts that are accessed in a standardized way. This adherence to standardization is definitional. SOA is about raising the level of abstraction, so that requirements and business processes can be discussed in a language understood by business as well as IT people. The main idea behind SOA is the desire to build applications that support a business process by combining a number of smaller business services into a complete business process.

Though built on similar principles, SOA is not the same as eb services. SOA is independent of any specific technologies.

A service is a unit of work carried out by a service provider to achieve some desired result for the service consumer. A service is a loosely coupled black box that can be found and (re)used as part of a current or new software application. The more loosely coupleable it is, the more (re)useable it is. Such black boxes can be assembled in different ways to do business in different ways. The IT function can then adapt to changing requirements more easily. It should also supply a service to the business; the operations that make up the service are about supporting the business, not the user interface.

Although a service is just an interface, it will thus be implemented by software components that implement a reusable business function, such managing customers or managing customer accounts. Services are defined by their interfaces, which describe what the services can do. How the service works is hidden inside the components that provide the service.

Services must be autonomous, abstract, composable, discoverable, reusable black boxes defined by contracts.

A service can receive a message, process it, return a reply and then forget all about it. Looking inside the service, however, we might see three types of communication ports or 'endpoints'.

- Ports for messages entering the service; the **entry** ports.
- A departure port for sending the reply message; the **exit** port.
- A **rejected message** port for invalid messages.

Each SOA service should have a quality of service (QoS) associated with it. Typical QoS elements are security requirements, reliable messaging and policies regarding who can invoke services. QoS statements may include SLAs, but in principle they can include more than mere service level agreements.

The main business drivers for SOA are as follows:

- The need for greater business agility: the need to innovate new business processes.
- The need to conform to rapid changes in regulation.

- The need to exploit new economies of scale and reuse as opportunities arise. Exploiting and integrating the legacy in a flexible way through EAI. This can clearly contribute to business agility.
- Rapidly evolving or poorly understood requirements.

The chief technology driver has been getting disparate legacy and newer systems to interoperate or be accessed through a single login: Enterprise Application Integration.

Enterprise Service Buses build on MOM to provide a flexible, scalable, standards-based integration technology for building a loosely coupled, highly distributed SOA. ESBs contain facilities for reliable messaging, web services, data and message transformation, content-based 'straight through' routing. Along with web services, ESBs are proving to be the major technical enablers for actual SOA projects.

The key technology to master when embarking on an SOA project is modelling. Modelling is core to defining good, sharable, reusable, composable, autonomous services. Standards and, in particular, web services standards, provide core enabling technology for SOA.

The potential benefits of adopting service oriented architecture may be summarized as follows:

- Faster development.
- Faster maintenance.
- More reusable business logic.
- Greater consistency across the enterprise.
- Better separation of concerns.
- Better alignment and understanding between business and IT.

There are economic benefits too. These include achieving a better understanding of the business; if everyone knows the rules of the business there are less likely to be conflicts. Often, changing business rules or processes (the order in which you do things) can simplify things and thus save costs or add value. SOA supports making such changes without massive delays.

The potential pitfalls include the following:

- Modelling systems and not the business.
- Ignoring the real users.
- Abstractions at too low a level.
- Legacy wrapping as opposing to business service design.
- The danger of vendor lock-in preventing unforeseen variation.

Education and training will be important in migrating to SOA. Teaching the IT guys how to talk plain English is a good start!

The critical success factors for SOA are these.

- Senior management support.
- Users who are prepared to get involved.
- A watertight business case for any pilots that are contemplated.
- Good modelling skills on the IT side. These should include UML, business process modelling and domain and service modelling skills.
- You have thought (i.e. done the modelling) before deciding to buy infrastructure products such as an ESB.
- Your team has good (non-IT) communication skills.
- A reuse culture is at least conceivable in the IT department.
- The requisite technical and product skills are in place or obtainable.

Businesses strive for shorter time to market and lower development and maintenance costs. Using business process modelling and possibly BRMSs together with better requirements engineering and business modelling within the context of SOA should decrease development costs and dramatically shorten development and maintenance cycles.

1.9 Bibliographical Notes

Erl (2005) is a very good introduction to the technology and broad concepts of SOA but does not emphasize the importance of modelling or provide guidance thereto.

Chappell (2004) is an informed discussion of ESBs by an innovator in that area but, unfortunately, its undoubted technical value is marred by very poor use of the American language, making it rather difficult to read. Chapell builds on the notation developed by Hohpe and Woolf (2004), who describe 65 patterns for developing enterprise integration projects using asynchronous messaging along with lots of useful code examples. Many of the ideas in this book are of considerable significance to those implementing SOA.

Graham (2006) provides a detailed discussion of and tutorial on business rules management systems and references to the literature on that subject. Another forthcoming companion volume to this book is Graham (2009).

CHAPTER 2

Architecture – Objects, Components, Services

Ladies and gentlemen, the story you are about to hear is true. Only the names have been changed to protect the innocent.

Dragnet radio series (1949–1951)

Is SOA the next step in software development? Is it just component based development operating under a new logo? Is it object-orientation under a new badge? Could it even be dataflow (with dynamic links) under a new badge? Is it perhaps all of these?

In this chapter we will examine the whole concept of software architecture and the origins of the notion of service oriented architecture in particular. We point up the similarities and differences with earlier fashionable ideas in computing and try to discover what characterizes an architecture as service-oriented.

2.1 What is Architecture?

Software architecture is a hot topic that has been palpably growing in importance since at least 1992, with a clear separation in schools of thought surrounding its nature appearing only more recently. However, the metaphor has a much longer genealogy than the modern debate is sometimes prepared to admit. The notion of software architecture has a pedigree at least as long as those of 'software engineering' and the 'software crisis'. These latter two terms are commonly accepted to have originated in the historic NATO conference of 1968 (Naur and Randall, 1969). Fred Brooks referred in a number of influential articles to architecture

(Brooks, 1975) but credits Blaauw (1970) with the first use of the term in 1970. According to one attendee at that conference, the idea of 'software architecture' and the rôle of 'software architects' were common currency in its deliberations – the analogy was, however, considered by the proceedings' editors too fanciful a notion to be reflected in the official minutes. It is symbolic indeed that the idea was co-nascent with that of the software crisis and that it was largely discarded in the intervening period, while the discipline of software engineering, as it has been practised, has manifestly failed to cure the malaise it was ushered in to redress.

2.1.1 Architecture as High Level Structure

Most contemporary discussions of architecture reach conclusions such as these.

- Architecture is about the gross structure of a system.
- Architecture guides decisions on how to build a system.
- Architecture is what remains when you cannot take away anything and still understand the system and explain how it works.
- Architecture is about requirements and constraints.

I would add that architecture is about the things that are difficult and expensive to change. Design is then said to be about selecting an architecture, deciding on a design philosophy and asserting that 'this is the way we will do things around here'.

Despite this, there is still no clear and unambiguous definition of what software architecture is. What consensus does exist to date seems to revolve around issues of high level design and the gross structure of systems, including both their static and dynamic properties. Larry Bass and his colleagues (Bass et al., 1998) for example, in a much-quoted definition, say that the software architecture of a program or computer system is the structure or structures of the system, which comprise software components, the externally visible properties of those components and the relationships among them. In the same spirit, Mary Shaw and David Garlan in their influential book on software architecture go so far as to date its origins from the moment software systems were first broken into modules (Shaw and Garlan, 1996). At the same time they recognize that, historically, such architectures have been implicit. In attempting to render architecture more explicit and formal, they introduced the important notions of software 'architectural style' and of software architectural description languages (ADLs).

Shaw and Garlan treat the architecture of a specific system as a collection of computational components together with a description of the interactions, or connectors, linking these components. An architectural style, according to them, defines a family of systems in terms of this structural organization. Clients and servers, pipes and filters, layers and databases are all given as possible examples of components, while example connectors are procedure calls, event broadcasts, database protocols and pipes. Had they been writing now, perhaps they would have included mash-ups, (web) services and self-describing messages in their lexicon.

Shaw and Garlan's position and that of others at Carnegie Mellon University (CMU) and at the so-called Software Engineering Institute (SEI), which is also home to Bass *et al.*, may be characterized as the view that architecture is equivalent to the high level structure of a system. The inclusion of object-orientation in their table itself highlights an issue with an approach that reduces architecture to one of merely components plus connectors. Many of us believe that architecture is more than just boxes and lines; to make sense it must include a notion of architectural *vision*: the unifying concept that we all recognize equally when we see an elegant software system, an *Île de France* Gothic cathedral or a Nash terrace, or, more importantly, when we have to build one.

The other significant contribution made in the Shaw and Garlan book is to introduce ADLs. Their six key requirements for an ADL are reminiscent of the features of an SOA as enumerated in Chapter 1. They are:

1. *Composition*. It should be possible to describe a system as a composition of independent components and connectors.
2. *Abstraction*. It should be possible to describe the components and their interactions within software architecture in a way that clearly and explicitly prescribes their abstract rôles in a system.
3. *Reusability*. It should be possible to reuse components, connectors, and architectural patterns in different architectural descriptions, even if they were developed outside the context of the architectural system.
4. *Configuration*. Architectural descriptions should localize the description of system structure, independently of the elements being structured. They should also support dynamic reconfiguration.
5. *Heterogeneity*. It should be possible to combine multiple, heterogeneous architectural descriptions.
6. *Analysis*. It should be possible to perform rich and varied analyses of architectural descriptions.

Shaw and Garlan point out, correctly in my opinion, that the typical box-and-line diagrams that often pass for 'architectural description' focus on components often to the exclusion of the connectors between them. They are therefore under specified in a number of crucial contexts, notably when dealing with third-party 'packaged' components, multi-language systems, legacy systems and, perhaps most critically of all, large-scale real-time embedded systems. Additionally, the boxes, lines and the adjacency between boxes often lack semantic consistency from diagram to diagram, and sometimes even within the same diagram. Also, the boxes and lines approach ignores the need to structure interface definitions. This points to a minimum of two levels of structure and abstraction that are typically missing: abstractions for connexions, and segmentation of interfaces. As it stands, such diagrams rely heavily on the knowledge and experience of the person in the architect's rôle, and this knowledge is usually held informally. Thus, ADLs can add rigour and formality to the description and analysis of structure.

The broader question arises, however, as to how much increased formality in and of itself will help in addressing the fundamental problems of software development. The roots of the research into architecture at CMU lie in Shaw's pursuit of a definition of the software engineering discipline itself (Shaw, 1990). She opines that the maturity of an engineering discipline is marked by the emergence of a 'sufficient scientific basis' to enable a critical mass of science-trained professionals to apply their theory to both the analysis of problems and the synthesis of solutions. Further progress is observed when science becomes a forcing function. She presents, therefore, a model that contends that the emergence of a sound engineering discipline of software depends on the vigorous pursuit of applicable science and then the reduction of that science to a practice.

This linear model of science preceding practice and reducing engineering to 'mere' problem solving is, of course, the received wisdom of traditional Computer Science. But the problem is what is the 'applicable science'? There is now a growing challenge to the old orthodoxy, which used to see computing as essentially a specialized branch of mathematics. Borenstein (1991), for example, in his marvellously named book *Programming as if People Mattered*, notes that the most interesting part of the process of building software is the human part, its design and its use. Inasmuch as human-oriented software engineering is the study of this process, it could be argued that it is more properly a branch of anthropology than of mathematical sciences. The study of software design may, in fact, be grossly misclassified in the academic world today, leading to an overemphasis on formal models and a lack of basic work in collecting raw material that usually comes in anecdotal, or at least in a non-quantitative form.

Interestingly, Borenstein upholds what Shaw and Garlan and indeed everyone else at CMU and the SEI appear to bemoan, the informality and unquantifiable characteristics of current software design practice. Bruce Blum, a former VP of Wolf Research and an erstwhile research scientist at Johns Hopkins University, has called for the redesign of the disciplines of Computer Science and Software Engineering on similar grounds to those advocated by Borenstein (Blum, 1996, 1998). In his work he has questioned the epistemology of the received orthodoxy on both the grounds of the philosophy of science and of practice. He points to a dialectical contradiction in the making of software that traditional Computer Science is blind to. In a way reminiscent of Michael Jackson's arguments (cf. Section 1.2), he distinguishes between the 'program-in-the-computer' and the 'program-in-the-world'. The program in the computer is subject to the closed abstractions of mathematics and is, theoretically at least, verifiable against some specification. Indeed the core of interest in the 'program-in-the-computer' is the extent of the difficulty of its construction. But what is in the computer must also exist, on completion, as a 'program-in-the-world' where the one and only test is its usefulness. Its value depends upon its ability to transform the pre-existing situation into which it now inserts itself, both impacting upon and being impacted by that situation. As a result the 'program-in-the-computer' exists in a stable, well-known and formally representable environment, but the very same software as 'the program-in-the-world' is dynamic and incompletely understood. A key issue is this: formal approaches work primarily by a process of selection from an existing or theoretical universe of extant, well-defined formal abstractions. Selection is easier than creating from scratch and therefore all such gains are valuable, but a total solution using formal methods is possible only once *all possible* design solutions have been formalized. Hence, no doubt, the SEI's interest in collecting architectural styles. However, Blum's criticism suggests that such a task is not only a Herculean labour but that, because it too rests on a mythology: the received wisdom of Computer Science, it can never be completed.

In fact, as we began to see in Chapter 1, one of the challenges in implementing a service oriented architecture is to ensure that a proper recovery can be made if the program-in-the-computer gets out of kilter with the program-in-the-world.

Fred Brooks, in his article *Aristocracy, Democracy and System Design* (in Brooks, 1975), argued that the single most important consideration in system design is its conceptual integrity. This was for him the defining property of software or system architecture, and the chief charge of the architect. Brooks stated that it is far better to reflect a coherent set of design ideas, and if necessary omit feature or functionality in order to maintain that coherence, than it is to build a system that contains heterogeneous or uncoordinated concepts, however good they each may be independently. This posits the following questions.

- How can conceptual integrity be achieved?
- How can one ensure that the architects do not deliver unimplementable or over-costly implementations?
- Is it possible to maintain conceptual integrity without creating a barrier between a small, 'architectural' elite and a larger group of plebeian implementers for a system?

- How does one ensure that the architecture is adequately reflected in the detailed design?

It was in answering these questions that Brooks made a conscious appeal to the metaphor of architecture in the built environment. He carefully distinguished between architecture and implementation. Echoing Blaauw he gave the simple example of a clock, whose architecture consists of its face, its hands and its winding knob. Having learnt the architecture of a clock, a child can tell the time whether using a wristwatch, a kitchen clock or a clock tower. The mechanism by which the time-telling function is delivered is a detail of implementation and realization, not architecture.

'By the architecture of a system', says Brooks, 'I mean the complete and detailed specification of the user interface. For a computer this is the programming manual. For a compiler it is the language manual. For a control program it is the manuals for the language or languages used to invoke its functions. For the entire system it is the union of all the manuals the user must consult to do his entire job' (p. 45).

While this definition may seem inadequate today, it has at least the virtue of establishing that the architect is the client's agent, not the developers' pawn. It strongly suggests that the conceptual integrity of the system, represented by the architecture, gains its shape from the perceived needs of the client and that the final test of what constitutes a 'good' architecture is its usefulness and, indeed, its safety – as pointed out by Nurse Nightingale![1]. In this important aspect there is a strong thread of continuity between the ideas of Brooks and Blum – although ironically Blum does not use the words 'software architecture' – and a symmetrical discontinuity between Brooks and the SEI despite their claims to the contrary. It is also worth noting that this view of the software architect as the client's agent is also a preoccupation of the World Wide Institute of Software Architects. In this sense, the move to service oriented architecture is precisely a move away from the centralized architectures of COTS packages and, indeed, poorly thought out 'product line' architectures based on them, and towards a fully composable and client-centric approach.

Again following Blaauw, Brooks suggests that the overall creative effort involves three distinct phases: architecture, implementation and realization. For Brooks, architecture appears to end with the complete and final specification of the system: the design 'of module boundaries, table structures, pass or phase breakdowns, algorithms, and all kinds of tools' belongs to implementation. Brooks believed that all three phases could occur to some extent in parallel and that successful design requires an ongoing conversation between architects and implementers. Nevertheless, the boundaries of the architects' input to the dialogue are confined

---

[1] See the quotation at the start of Chapter 3.

to the external specification of the system. There is clearly some tension between this idea of the architect's rôle and Brooks' insistence on the need to maintain the conceptual integrity of the system. In modern service-oriented systems at least, which involve issues of scale and distribution that did not exist in 1975, traceability of a construction back through its structure to its specification and to the needs that inspired it is crucial to maintaining the integrity of the system.

2.1.2 Architecture as Design Rationale or Vision

There appears to be the need for a marriage between the idea of the architect as the client's agent championing the conceptual integrity of the system on the one hand, and ideas about the internal structures of the system on the other. Many modern theorists of software architecture draw inspiration from a seminal paper written by Dewayne Perry and Alexander Wolf (Perry and Wolf, 1992). They defined software architecture in terms of an equation:

```
Software Architecture = Elements + Form + Rationale
```

Barry Boehm is said to have qualified the last of these terms to read 'Rationale/Constraints'. An influential interpretation of this idea, applied specifically to object-oriented development, has been offered by Phillipe Kruchten in his '4+1 View Model' of software architecture (Kruchten, 1995). This view underpins IBM's Rational Unified Process and is responsible, in large part, for the claim that it is 'architecture-centric'. Kruchten concedes that software architecture deals with abstraction, with composition and decomposition, and also with style and aesthetics. To deal with all these aspects, especially in the face of large and challenging systems developments, Kruchten proposes a generic model made up of five different views as follows.

- The **logical** view is an object model of the design.
- The **process** view models the concurrency and synchronization issues of the design.
- The **physical** view gives a model of the mapping of software onto hardware, including distribution issues.
- The **development** view reflects the static organization of the software in its development environment.
- A **scenarios**-based view consists of the usage scenarios from which the architecture is partially derived and against which it is validated.

Kruchten applies the Perry and Wolf equation independently to each view. The set of elements, in terms of components, containers and connectors, is defined for each view, as are the forms and patterns which work in the particular context in which the architecture is to be applied. Similarly, the rationale and constraints for each view are also captured, connecting the architecture to the requirements. Each view is captured in the form of a blueprint in a notation appropriate to the view – in the original paper, which predated the UML, subsets of the Booch notation were used for each view.

Criticizing a rather linear, four-phase (sketching, organizing, specifying and optimizing), twelve-step process for architecture proposed by Witt *et al.* (1994), Kruchten proposes an iterative, scenario-driven approach instead. Based on relative risk and criticality, a small number of scenarios are chosen for an iteration. Then a straw man architecture is put in place. Scenarios are scripted to derive the major abstractions (components, collaborations, processes, subsystems, etc.) and then decomposed into object–operation pairs. The architectural elements that have been discovered are laid out on to the four blueprints: logical, physical, process and development. The architecture is then implemented, tested, measured and analysed, possibly revealing flaws or opportunities for enhancement. Subsequent iterations can now begin. The documentation resulting from this process is in fact two sets of documents: a *Software Architecture Document* and a separate *Software Design Guidelines* which captures the most important design decisions that must be respected to maintain the conceptual integrity of the architecture. The essence of the process is this: the initial architectural prototype evolves to be the final system.

Bosch (2000) addresses the problem of adopting and evolving a product-line approach based on the work of the Research in Software Engineering (RiSE) group at the University of Karlskrona-Ronneby and its industrial collaborators. Product-line approaches, if properly implemented, can be quite close to those of component-based development. The core of Bosch's approach involves first the development of what he calls a 'functionality-based architectural design' from the requirements specification. This activity involves a search for key problem-driven architectural abstractions which he calls 'archetypes'. These archetypes are object types whose roots are in the problem space but which, for product-line development, normally have to be generalized and abstracted further from the concrete phenomena that the analyst or architect first encounters – just as one must often do with service abstraction. Bosch posits further that many archetypes are actually cross-domain in character, once again demonstrating the similarity of his archetypes to modern services. As with product line architectures, vendors can impose a proprietary architecture by insisting, for example, on a particular ESB. One should beware of this otherwise tempting path, especially because of the danger, already alluded to, of basing services on low-level APIs rather than business-centric abstractions.

A small and stable set of archetypes is chosen from a wider candidate list, often merging initial candidates to produce higher level abstractions – at least within a green-field development. The abstract relations between these archetypes are then identified and selected. The structure of the software architecture is then created by recursively decomposing the set of archetypes into well-defined components and establishing the relationship between them. A 'system instantiation' can then be described in order to validate the work done thus far. This requires the further decomposition of components into lower level components and the population of these components with instantiated archetypes. Since product-line architectures have to support a wide variety of systems with different specifications as well as different implementations, variability has to be addressed at this early point. Therefore, multiple such instantiations are produced to validate the match between the architecture and the requirements.

Architectural assessment involves another fairly novel idea: that of a *profile*. A profile is a set of scenarios, but they are not necessarily usage scenarios. That is to say, even if use cases are deployed in order to give traceability to functional requirements they will form only a subset of the overall number of scenarios described. Other scenarios, related to quality attributes (non-functional requirements or NFRs), such as *hazard scenarios* (for safety-critical systems) or *change scenarios* for flexible maintenance, are also specified. The profiles allow for a more precise specification of quality attributes than is typical in most software development. As will be seen in Chapters 3 and 5, our approach insists that all NFRs can be, and many should be, part of the usage scenarios (use cases, conversations). We have already seen in Chapter 1 that services must include quality requirements (e.g. QoS indicators).

Bosch reports that between four and eight categories of scenarios are typical. Scenarios are identified and specified for each category, and each one assigned a weighting. Weightings can be, if necessary, normalized. Scenario-based assessment follows in two main steps: impact analysis and quality attribute prediction. The impact of the running of each scenario in a profile is assessed and then a predictive value for a quality attribute measured. So, for example, the number of changed and new components resulting from a change scenario in a maintenance category estimated in impact analysis could lead to a cost of maintenance effort estimation when brought together with a change frequency figure, based, say, on historical data in the second (predictive) phase. Profiles and scenarios can be used in a variety of ways, including simulated assessments in which both an executable version of the system and implemented profiles can be used to verify the architecture dynamically.

During such assessments, it is normal for one or more quality requirements to fail to be satisfied by the architecture, normally as a result of conflicting forces acting upon the overall design – for example, performance constraints being violated because of the levels of indirection built into the architecture in order to meet changeability requirements.

In these circumstances what Bosch calls 'architectural transformations' are required. Four categories of architectural transformation are identified and used in the following order, each next transformation carrying the expectation of relatively decreasing impact.

- Impose architectural style (*à la* Shaw and Garlan, 1996), which could be SOA.
- Impose an architectural pattern (or mechanism) – by which Bosch means apply a rule locally to specify how the system will deal with one aspect of its overall functionality, e.g. concurrency or persistence.
- Apply a design pattern (maybe *à la* Gamma *et al.*, 1995).
- Convert quality requirements to functionality, e.g. provide context-sensitive help in order that the quality of the users' experience is not damaged by them getting despairingly stuck.

The final step is to distribute quality requirements to identified components or subsystems in the overall architecture.

Bass *et al.* (1998) also offer a technique of architectural assessment and, usefully, apply it to product evaluation and comparison. Their technique is less rounded out than Bosch's but either would work. The basic idea is to specify scenarios or use cases that the proposed product can already support. Then other desirable scenarios are posited by the potential users. The vendor is then asked what the estimated cost would be of enhancing the product to support some or all of the new features. *In extremis* these estimates can be written in the contract. It is a very practical and effective approach when combined with a simple decision model to select for a shortlist of products. For an example, Graham (2006) presents such a technique as applied to selecting business rules management products.

There is actually a fair amount in common among the '4+1' view and the approach to product-line development software architectures used by the RiSE group. Both pay due attention to the full scope of software architecture and deal with conceptual integrity, rationale as well as structure. Both attach non-functional requirements to components or subsystems originally identified by analysing functionality. Both, at a certain point in the process, recommend the application of architectural styles and then design patterns. The key difference is that Kruchten's approach is bottom-up, working from the abstractions discovered in a system requirements specification, while Bosch's approach is decidedly top-down, working from archetypal abstractions and then imposing them upon the development of a particular application or system.

It should be clear that these approaches map readily onto the development of a service oriented architecture, although much current practice seems to contradict this. There is a legacy of systems: the manager has authorized the purchase of an ESB, the CIO says he wants everything done in .NET and the ESB vendor insists 'helping' you to develop the architecture – based, of course, on the standards that there product already supports rather than your business abstractions.

2.1.3 Architecture and Reuse

Making architectural analysis and review an explicit part of the development process helps retain knowledge and facilitates reuse and, of course, developing an architecture is a minimum requirement for establishing any kind of service oriented architecture.

But why choose a particular architecture? For a building, it is the stakeholder requirements that drive the architecture. For one building these might include such criteria as the following:

- We want the building to hold at least 500 people.
- It must give the impression of power to visitors.
- We can use local craftsmen.
- It must have good acoustics.
- It should benefit from natural light.
- It mustn't get too hot.
- It must use energy efficiently.
- We know how to build using stone.
- Diagonal loads need to be spread.

Note the mixture of aesthetic, functional, economic and engineering considerations. It is the architect's task to construct a building that satisfies the stakeholder needs and fits the criteria. As with all design decisions the architect will need to weigh the forces at work and make trade-offs. Patterns can help here. Patterns and patterns languages are discussed in Appendix A.

For software, the concept of architecture is similar. The architecture of a software system must satisfy all stakeholder requirements subject to any imposed constraints. Remember that one group of stakeholders of a system is the developers, and they will have a requirement that the product is easy to maintain. It is the overall design and architecture of the system that will satisfy the non-functional requirements of all the stakeholders; otherwise we could construct any old monolithic system that just satisfies the functional requirements, and ignore ease of use, reliability, good performance and so on.

Well designed services are intended to be shared, so that applications can be built by combining and reusing them in multiple applications. To do this they must not only be correct in themselves but also composable, discoverable, and so on; they must have all the qualities of service oriented architecture *qua* architecture. Requirements analysis and system specification for SOA thus must include paying full attention to both user needs and architecture.

2.2 Architecture through the Ages

Software engineering and software production in general are concerned *inter alia* with the manufacture of high quality systems for a reasonable outlay of effort and thus cost. Attempts to attack the issue of software quality have come from innovations in programming languages and from several structured approaches to system development methods. When there are claims that up to 80% of the cost of a system is accounted for by software costs, and that even good programmers have been generally unable to produce resilient, correct code to budget, then something is seriously amiss. Structured methods, 4GLs, CASE and modelling tools, prototyping techniques, database systems, code generators and MDA, object-orientation and component based development all represented attacks on this problem.

The extent to which structured methods based on modular design succeeded was questioned in reports from the Butler Cox Group in the 1990s that showed that the users of, for example, structured design were actually impairing both their productivity and the quality of the end-product. As we saw in the previous chapter, the impetus to structured methods came largely from the realization that many systems were either not finished, not used or were delivered with major errors.

Following hard on the heels of this discrediting of structured methods, object-orientation (OO) represented a significant architectural shift towards loose coupling and Larry Constantine's complimentary idea of maximizing cohesion (Yourdon and Constantine, 1979). The ideas of OO and its core principles of encapsulation and polymorphism were clear to its proponents and it was widely advanced as the cure to the software ills I have presented. However, when it came to practice, people ignored these principles, probably under pressure to produce short-term fixes but also because of what one might call 'language inertia': the most widely used language in this period was C++, which was an extension of C and, when Java largely supplanted it, the latter presented a thoroughly C-like syntax to the world. One of the principal symptoms of this miasma of misunderstood principles was the proliferation, in code and designs, of classes that were 'too small': classes at totally the wrong level of abstraction.

To the rescue of this abused damsel rode the knights of component based development (CBD). Components were to be bigger than objects and it was an opportunity to reapply those forgotten principles of good software engineering. I wrote at the time that CBD was just OO 'done right'. While much work of lasting value, especially on design, was done in that period (Allen and Frost, 1998; Szyperski, 1998; D'Souza and Wills, 1999; Cheesman and Daniels, 2000), CBD also failed to some extent because of misperceptions and yet more rampant short-termism – in the wake of the Exxon and Viacom scandals and the bursting of the dot com bubble. So now we have services. Curiously, many of the principles of SOA are the same as those of structured design, OO and CBD. Let us look at services from this point of view.

First, why do we need a new approach to architecture at all? Lientz and Swanson (1979) analysed the reasons for maintenance requests in a survey of nearly 500 large projects, as shown in Figure 2-1. Although these data are old, all the indications are that these sources of cost are still present in roughly the same proportions.

The chief significance of this breakdown is that most change requests are, where they are not a result of incorrect specification, unavoidable. The 'changes in user requirements' heading may, of course, be partly a surrogate for inadequate specification, but also reflects the dynamic character of modern businesses. In a changing world, software must be adaptable, and this is precisely the point addressed by the need for systems to be extensible and modular; services must be loosely coupled and development processes must be agile.

Second only to changes arising from evolving requirements come changes in data structures, and here encapsulation offers the greatest promise as a technique for making systems resilient to changes in implementation. (Recall from Chapter 1 that services must be 'black boxes'.) All of the year 2000 date bug problems would have been avoided had all programs called upon date objects or services: the implementation of 4- instead of 2-digit year fields would have been transparent to client programs.

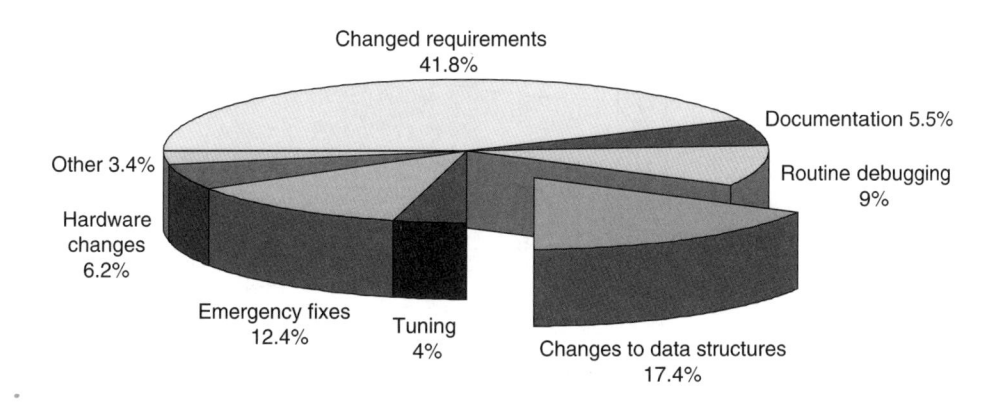

Figure 2-1 Sources of maintenance costs.

Another point to be made about the need for constant change relates to the way *ad hoc* or panic changes are made. Emergency fixes in conventional code often produce unexpected effects.

So, if maintenance accounts for 90% of IT spend, then changes to data structures account for around 16% of all IT spending. Let us try to understand why this is so for conventional computer systems and see how SOA might help to reduce the burden if properly applied.

Being based on the so-called Von Neumann architecture of the underlying hardware, a conventional computer system can be regarded as a set of functions or processes together with a separate collection of data: whether stored in memory or on disk does not matter. This static architectural model is illustrated in Figure 2-2 which also indicates that, when the system runs, the dynamics may be regarded as some function, which without loss of generality we will label f(1), reading some data, A, transforming them and writing them to B. Next some other function, call it f(2), reads some data, perhaps the same data, does whatever it does and writes data to C. Such overlapping data access gives rise to complex concurrency and integrity problems but these can be solved well by using an intervening database management system. The question that I ask you to consider before reading on is: what must be done when part of the data structure has to change?

Considering this from the point of view of the maintenance programmer, the only conclusion that one can come to is that every single function must be checked to see if it may be destabilized by the change. Good, up to date documentation can help with this but is rarely available in practice. Part of the reason for this is that good documentation would itself be a by-product of an object-oriented description of the system and is unlikely to be divorced from a properly conceived object-oriented design, although

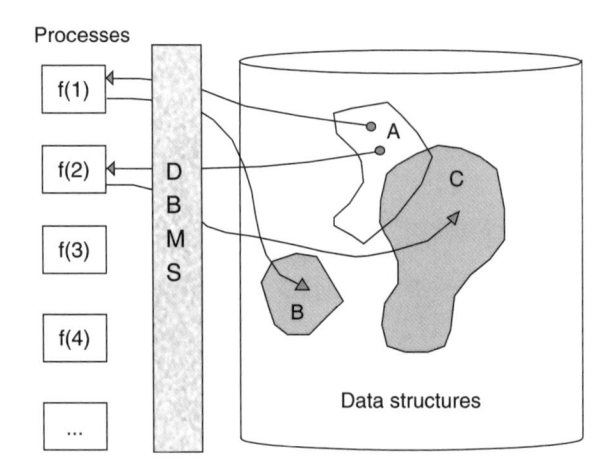

Figure 2-2 The architecture of a conventional computer system.

without this a CRUD matrix, relating processes to data entities, would be a reasonable substitute in many cases.

As well as the need to find and change the functions, every function that has changed to reflect a new data structure may have side effects in other parts of the system, and so the process is horribly iterative.

This problem, I assert, accounts for the extraordinarily high costs of maintenance. If you don't believe me, just think back to the huge costs associated with what must be the tiniest change to a data structure of all time: the change to four-digit dates in AD2000.

Figure 2-3 illustrates a completely different architectural approach to systems. Here, all the data that a function needs to access are encapsulated with it in packages called objects, components or services *a piacere* and in such a way that the functions of no other object, component or service may access these data. Using a simile suggested by Steve Cook, these islands of functionality may be regarded as eggs. The yolk is their data structure, the white consists of the implementation of the functions that access these data and the shell represents the interface to these black-boxed functions: the publicly visible services and their calling format. The shell, or interface, hides the implementation of both the functions and the data structures. Now suppose again that a data structure is changed in the egg 'shelled' for maintenance in Figure 2-3. Now the maintenance programmer need only check the white of this particular egg for the impact of the change. If the implementation changes, no other egg can possibly be affected; maintenance is not eliminated but it *is* localized. This is **encapsulation**: data and processes are combined and hidden behind an interface. It is one of the core architectural ideas behind OO, CBD and SOA.

As I have presented it so far, there is a problem with this model. Suppose that every service interface hides a function that needs the same datum. In that case the potential for data duplication is staggering and the approach would be quite impracticable; pretty soon every egg will need to encapsulate the entire corporate database. The solution is to permit

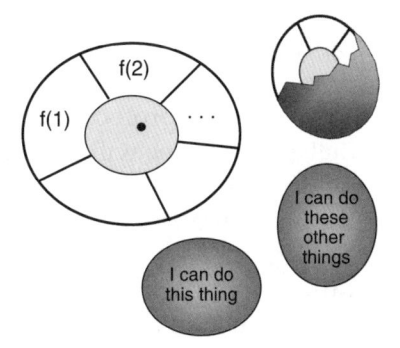

Figure 2-3 The architecture of a service-oriented or component-based system.

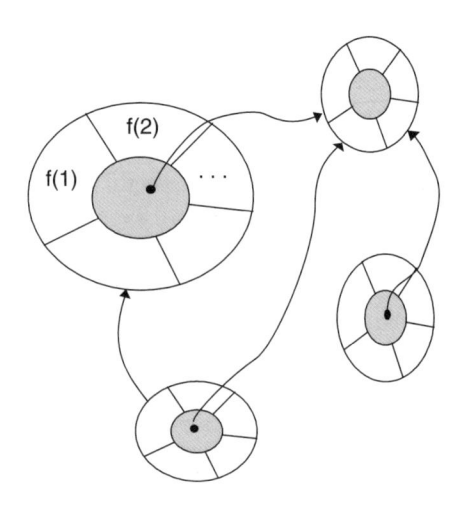

Figure 2-4 Message passing eliminates data duplication.

the eggs to send messages to each other. In this way egg X may need data A but not encapsulate them. Provided that X stores in its yolk the identity of another egg, Y, that does contain the required data, X may send a message requesting the data or even some transformed version of them. This is depicted in Figure 2-4, where the small sperm-like dots represent the identity of a target egg and the arrows show the outward direction of the messages. This, in a nutshell, is 50 % of the idea behind object technology, component technology and SOA. The other 50 % involves the concept known as polymorphism. In OO this is mostly realized by allowing the objects to be classified; inheritance. With SOA, other mechanisms may be used. We shall return to this point shortly. For now, consider the benefits of encapsulation.

The astute reader may detect that the way messaging is handled could be different in OO and SOA. In OO, the sender must know not only the address of the receiver but also the calling format: what parameters are required and in what order. As soon as XML is used as the message transport we have the possibly that a message broker of some sort (possibly an ESB) can intervene to transform the format of messages, making such detailed knowledge of the recipient's protocols unnecessary. Of course, this does not guarantee that the receiver will not reject the message but it does promote looser coupling. Thus, SOA does add value to the object-oriented metaphor, even if it is fundamentally based on the same principle of encapsulation.

So, with this approach, the maintenance problem is localized and thus greatly simplified. When a data structure changes, the maintainer need only check the functions in the albumen that encapsulates it. There can be no effect elsewhere in the system unless the shell is cracked or deformed; that is, if the interface changes. Thus, while we may claim to have reduced the maintenance problem by orders of magnitude, we now have to work very hard to ensure that we produce correct, complete and stable interfaces for our eggs, be they objects, components or services. This implies that sound analysis and design modelling are even more worthwhile and necessary than they were for conventional systems. This extra effort is worthwhile because it leads to some very significant benefits.

Having said this in full sincerity, it must be admitted that getting interfaces right first time is usually not possible for an analyst who is less than prescient. If you change the implementation (of either data structures or functions) no other component object can possibly be affected – thanks to encapsulation. But if the interface changes then *every* other object might be affected – because the messages they send may not be understood. Luckily, polymorphism can be marshalled to save the day.

In programming, the ability to use the same expression to denote different operations is referred to as **polymorphism**. This occurs where + is used to signify real or integer addition and when the message 'add 1' is sent to a bank account and a list of reminder notes: the same message can produce quite different results. This special case is called 'operator overloading'. Formally, polymorphism – having many forms – means the ability of a variable or function to take different forms at run time, or more specifically the ability to refer to instances of various classes. Polymorphism represents the ability of an abstraction to share features. Inheritance, like overloading, is a special kind of polymorphism that characterizes object-oriented systems.

Typically, polymorphism in the form of inheritance is used to allow an interface to be extended with new features while keeping the original interface intact. This approach is not confined to computer systems either, as I will now illustrate with an example from the history of science.

Zoologists, after the time of the great Swedish botanist Carolus Linnaeus, classified the animal kingdom in a hierarchy that is still familiar to most people, despite its being superseded by a DNA-based system in modern times. As suggested by Figure 2-5, creatures are classified as vertebrate or invertebrate. Insects, for example are invertebrates, having no internal skeleton, and thus form a subclass of the latter. Vertebrates can be divided into at least reptiles, birds, fish and mammals. Mammals in turn are classified *inter alia* as dogs, cats, bats, primates and so on. Individuals can be included in the hierarchy too – using the IsA inheritance relationship: Fido is a dog, Guy is a gorilla, Inksy is a spider, Leo is a lion. This system worked very well from the 18th Century until nearly the present day. Well, it did until Australia was opened up. The problem was the humble duck-billed platypus.

Thinking like a programmer for a moment, if you want to find out about Fido you might send him a message such as: 'do you have forward pointing eyes, bodily hair and give birth to live young?'. Fido doesn't know, so he

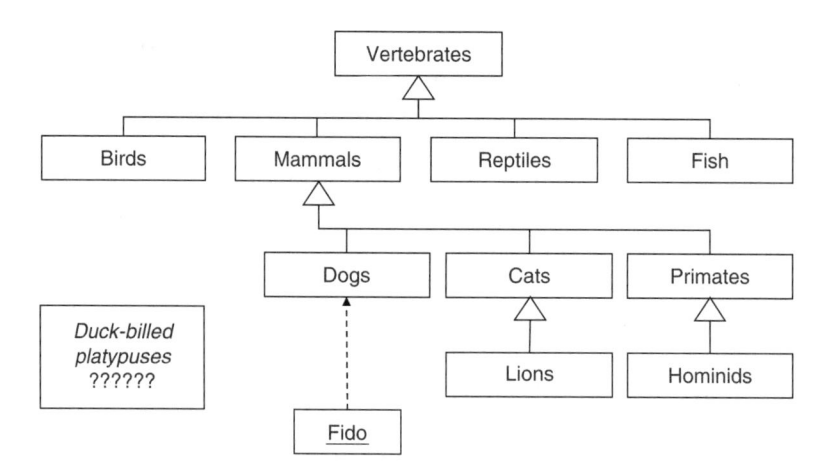

Figure 2-5 Part of the Linnaean order.

asks the Dog class to which he belongs. Dog doesn't know either, so it asks Mammal. 'That's, easy', thinks Mammal, 'that's how my interface defines me'. The message 'yes' is relayed, via Fido, back to his client.

But now we have the pesky duck-bill. It looks like a mammal except that it lays eggs. We got the interface wrong; we screwed up! We'll have to change the interface and everything in Zoology might go pear-shaped.

Wrong! We can keep the definition of mammal and still deal with the new suborder. Historically, this was Monotremata, which are regarded as special mammals, but I will present a better solution from the programmer's viewpoint. You keep Mammal with its interface unchanged – so that all messages sent to it by legacy clients can be processed – and create two subclasses: Lower Mammals and Higher Mammals, as shown in Figure 2-6.

The interface of Higher Mammals is exactly the same as that of Mammals. Lower Mammals overrides all the stuff about bearing live young and having mammary glands. New clients can send messages to these classes with confidence and old clients will still get serviced nicely by Mammals. You *can* have your cake and eat it.

Some authorities have claimed that polymorphism is *the* central idea in object-oriented systems, but there are non-object-oriented metaphors that take this point further, as exemplified in programming languages such as ML or Miranda. Polymorphism is the second core principle of object-orientation after encapsulation. Does it apply to service oriented architecture?

Clearly, a service too can be classified within a network of more generalized or more specialized services. For example, a bubble-sorting service might specialize a very general service offering all kinds of sorting algorithms. For a real world – rather than computing – example, consider shoe cleaning and hairdressing as specializations of personal services.

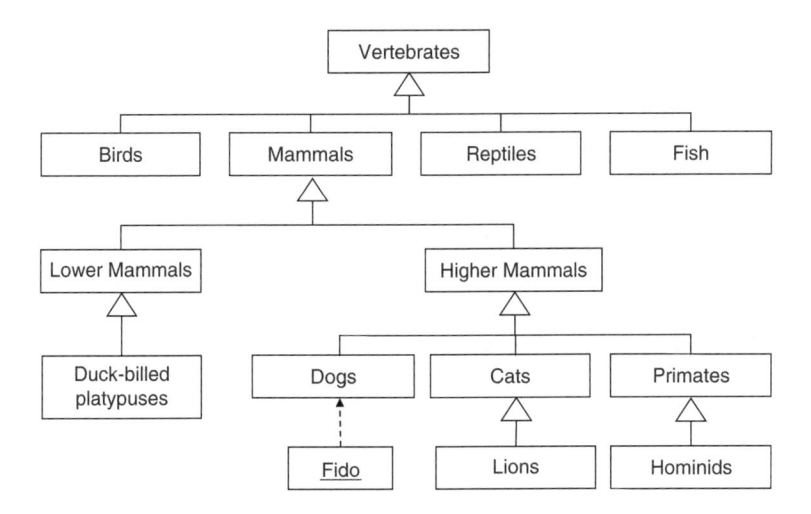

Figure 2-6 Part of the Linnaean order.

So it can be seen that service oriented architecture incorporates at least the features of object-oriented and component-based architecture. However, SOA adds more because of its richer notions concerning messaging, which can now be asynchronous as well as synchronous and messages become first class citizens, along with services and the components that implement them. Messages can be self-describing and contain routing data. Self-description and internal structure make it possible to transform the format of a message according to which service it is being sent.

As I argue in Appendix B, The fundamental static concepts of SOA are encapsulation (abstraction/identity) and polymorphism (inheritance/classification/discoverability/visibility/composability). The fundamental dynamic concepts are message passing and rule embedding, which lead to rule-based routing and contract-based transformation as subsidiary (but no less important) fundamental concepts.

If the services of an SOA must be implemented, we must have an implementation architecture. In practice, this is nearly always a component-based architecture. Therefore, we must now look at the topic of component based development and its history in relation to object-orientation, before returning to service oriented architecture *per se*.

2.3 Objects and Components

Writing in *Byte*, John Udell once announced that 'Objects are dead!' and said that they would soon be replaced by components. He wrote this in May 1994, whereas objects didn't really hit the mainstream of information technology until around 1996. In fact, most CBD offerings that were popular in 1994, such as OpenDoc, OpenStep and Hyperdesk, didn't survive for very long after that. Probably the only significant survivor was the humble VBX. There are, even now, several understandings of what the term 'component' means. Some commentators just use it to mean any module. Others mean a deliverable object or framework: a unit of deployment. Still others mean a binary that can create instances (of multiple classes). Serious writers on object-orientation tended to mean a set of interfaces with *offers* and *requires* constraints. The *requires* constraints are often called **outbound interfaces**. Daniels (2000) questioned this and showed that while these aspects of a component must be defined, they do not form part of the component's contract. Szyperski (1998) defined a component as 'a binary unit of independent production, acquisition and deployment' and later as 'a unit of composition with contractually specified interfaces and explicit context dependencies only'. We prefer 'a unit of executable deployment that plays a part in a composition'.

In many ways, VB was the paradigm for component-based development, though now largely overtaken by C# or Java for much development work or by web-specific languages. Components were needed initially because object-oriented programming languages were restricted to one address space. Objects compiled by different compilers (even in the same language) could not communicate with each other. Thus arose synchronous distribution technologies such as RPCs, DCOM, CORBA and so on. In every case, interfaces were defined separately from implementation, making object-oriented programming only one option for the actual coding of the objects.

In the late 1990s, ERP vendors that surfed on the crest of the year 2000 and Euro conversion issues did well because their customers needed quick, all-embracing solutions. When that period ended their market was threatened by a return to more flexible systems that were better tailored to companies' requirements. One vendor was even quoted as saying that a large customer should change its processes to fit the package because the way they worked was not 'industry standard'. This arrogance would no longer be tolerable after 2000 and the vendors were seen to rush headlong to 'componentize' their offerings, i.e. introduce greater customizability into them.

A lot of the talk about components being different from (better than) objects was based on a flawed idea of what a business object was in the first place. Many developers assumed that the concept of an object was co-extensive with the semantics of a C++ class or instance. Others based their understanding on the semantics of Smalltalk objects or Eiffel classes or instances. Even those who used UML classes or instances failed to supply enough semantic richness to the concept: typically ignoring the presence of rules and invariants and not thinking of packages as wrappers.

Furthermore, an object will only work if all its required servers are present. This was the standpoint of methods such as SOMA (Graham, 1995), which always allowed message–server pairs as part of class specifications. These were the equivalent of what Microsoft then called outbound interfaces.

From one point of view, outbound interfaces violate encapsulation, because the component depends on collaborators that may change and so affect it. For example, the client of an order management service should not have to know that this component depends on a product management one; an alternative implementation might bundle everything up into one object. For this reason Daniels (2000) argued that collaborations do not form part of an object's contract in the normal sense. He distinguished usage contracts from implementation contracts. The latter do include dependencies, as they must to be of use to the application assembler. It was his suggestion that QoS constraints were needed to capture the **effects** of collaborations.

From a vendor's point of view, components are usually larger than classes and may be implemented in multiple languages. They can include their own metadata and often be assembled without too much programming. They need to specify what they require to run. Such component systems are not invulnerable to criticism. The size of a component is often inversely proportional to its match to any given requirement. Also, components may have to be tested late; an extreme case being things that cannot be tested until the user downloads them (although applets are not really components in the sense we mean here). There is a tension between architectural standards and requirements, which can limit the options for business process change. Finally there is the problem of shared understanding between developers and users. Szyperski (1998) discusses at length the different decision criteria used by each of infrastructure vendors and component vendors. He says nothing about the consequences for users. Can we deduce that users don't care about how components are developed? As with services, they certainly care about how they are assembled into applications.

CBD, like object modelling, is about not separating processes from data. It is about encapsulation: separating interfaces from implementation. It is about polymorphism: inheritance and pluggability. It is about design by contract: constraints and rules. The basic principles must be consistently applied to programming, analysis, business process modelling, distributed design and components. However, there is a difference between conceptual models and programming models. In conceptual modelling both components and classes have identity. Therefore components are objects. Inheritance is as fundamental as encapsulation for the conceptual modeller. In programming models on the other hand components and classes do not have identity (class methods are handled by instances of factory classes). Thus components are not objects, class inheritance (or delegation) is dangerous and pluggability is the thing. So is there a rôle for inheritance? CBD plays down 'implementation inheritance' but not interface inheritance, but at the conceptual level this distinction makes no sense anyway.

When it comes to linking requirements models to analysis models, we can either 'dumb down' to a model that looks like the programming model (as most UML-based methods tend to do) or introduce a translation process between the models in the style of MDA, which we shall discuss in Section 2.4. The trade-off concerns the degree to which users and developers can share a common understanding.

It is worth revisiting another aspect of the philosophy behind object-oriented development and *a fortiori* CBD. A key feature of the idea is that software is based (at least approximately) on the real world. So that for every object in the real world that the program deals with, there is a corresponding chunk of code in the software.

The two chief benefits of this close correspondence are that (a) programmers can (at least potentially) talk in the same language as users, which makes it more likely that the program will do what its users want and (b) changes are easier to make, because when users describe required changes (in their language) we can more easily see which parts of the program need changing. And of course, changes constitute the most expensive part of the software lifecycle. As we have seen (Figure 2-1), changes in business requirements, coming after first delivery, account for upwards of 60%, often more like 90%. So the big win of object-orientation (and its successors: component based development and service oriented architecture) is that they all make software easier to change and thus help reduce the most significant element of the IT budget.

If we want to base our software on the real world, the first thing we have to do is understand that world: only by understanding the real world can we identify the *right* services. In the real world we will find entities, things that are, that are of interest to us. We will also be interested in relationships between entities and so both entities and relationships will appear in our model. But none of these help much with discovering services, because services are about doing things – as opposed to the thing that they are done with or to. Services do things that help satisfy user goals. So we also need to consider what happens in the business: simple actions and complex business processes – and the goals of these business processes. Services are there to help run the business processes and to help the users achieve their goals. Thus, we must model business processes and identify the goals of those business processes. Once done, this model will help us identify the services and components that are needed to support the business processes. How to do this is the subject of Chapters 3 to 6.

The strategy we will adopt is to build very abstract models of the business processes and entities they refer to, with the aim of understanding the business and identifying and specifying services. It will also help with integrating different parts of the business if all services are specified using a common semantics or 'ontology'. Again subsequent chapters discuss how best to do this. Building such abstract models of the business will also aid in the best way to integrate and reuse legacy systems. Having identified possible services, we can consider the best technology to support the services and develop an enterprise systems architecture, in this case a service-oriented one. In this way, we need to complement our top down, business focused approach with a technology focused, bottom up one, when we can identify reusable components, services, devices, etc.

Getting to a solid SOA means identifying the *right* services, and this means understanding the business, not just new or old computer systems. As we will now see, SOA goes hand in hand with CBD. Thus any technology that supports CBD can be beneficially used.

2.3.1 Components for Flexibility

Component-based development is concerned with building extensible families of software services or software products from new or existing kits of components. The latter may range in scale from individual classes to entire (wrapped) legacy systems or commercial packages. Doing this proved hitherto an elusive goal for software developers. The trick is to realize that we need to define the interface protocols of objects in such a way that they can be plugged together in different ways. The number of interfaces needs to be small compared to the number of components. To improve flexibility these interfaces should permit negotiation in the same way as with facsimile machines or the clipboard interfaces in Microsoft's products and the like.

An example may suffice to explain the point. Consider an hotel support system that is originally written for a small chain of Scottish hotels. The original is a great success and pays for itself quickly. But the price of success is rapid expansion and the company now acquires several more hotels in England, Wales, France and Germany. In Scotland rooms are always allocated to new arrivals on the basis of the empty room nearest the reception desk – to save visitors wearing out their shoes walking long distances. But the spendthrift and gloomy English want peace and quiet more than these savings; so that rooms are allocated alternately, to leave empty rooms separating occupied ones when the hotel is not full. The Germans allocate rooms with French widows first. The different states involved also have different rules about wage payments. The system is amended piecemeal and soon there are several versions to maintain: one with nearest desk allocation and French payment rules, another with least-recently-used room allocation and UK staff payment laws and an *ad hoc* patch for management Christmas bonuses in Ireland and the Netherlands, and so on. A maintenance disaster of some proportion!

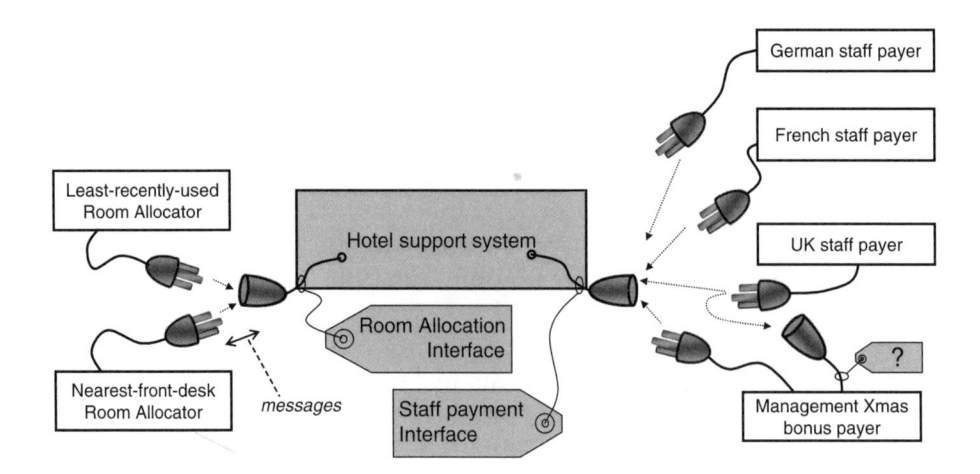

Figure 2-7 Plug-points (well-designed service interfaces) add flexibility.

A considerable improvement on arbitrary modification is shown in Figure 2-7. There is a basic framework, which does everything that is common between the requirements of all the hotels. Each separate variable requirement has been moved into a plug-in component: for example, there are different room allocators and different staff payment components. This arrangement makes it much easier to maintain and manage variants of the system. We separate the rôles of the framework-designer and the designers of the plug-in components – who are not allowed to change the framework.

This makes it very clear that the most suitable basis for choosing components and services is that they should correspond to variable requirements. This is a key rule which people sometimes forget, while still claiming to be doing component-based development.

One problem is that it is not always easy to foresee what requirements will be variable in the future. The best advice we can give here is as follows:

- Follow the principle of separation of concerns within the main framework, so that it is reasonably easy to refactor.
- Don't cater for generalizations that you don't know you are going to need: the work will likely be wasted. Observe the eXtreme Programming (XP) maxim: 'You ain't gonna need it!'.
- Where you do need to refactor the framework to introduce new plug-points, make one change at a time, and re-test after each change.

2.3.2 Large-Scale Connectors

The big advantage of connectors over point-to-point interfaces is that we try to design a small number of protocols common to the whole network of components, so that they can easily be rearranged. We can pull components out of a bag and make many end products; for large systems, it means that you can rearrange the components more easily as the business evolves. This is a common problem faced by many companies large and small.

For example, our hotel system might have a web server in Amsterdam, a central reservations system in Edinburgh, a credit card gateway in New Zealand and local room allocation systems in each hotel world-wide. We would like to define a common connector, a common 'language' in which they all talk to one another, so that future reconfigurations need not involve writing many new adapters. Typical events in our hotels connector protocol will be customers arriving and leaving, paying bills; properties will include availability of rooms. The component kit architecture for such a network will have to specify:

- the low level technology it will use;
- a basic model of the business – what types of object are communicated between the components, customers, reservations, bills, etc.;
- the syntax of the language in which the model will be transmitted – XML is often the solution;
- a description of the logic of business transactions – e.g. how a reservation is agreed between the reservations system and a local hotel;
- business rules, e.g. is a customer allowed to have rooms in different hotels at the same time?

This point about business rules is sometimes forgotten at the modelling stage. But it is very important: if one component of the system thinks a customer can have two rooms whereas another thinks each customer just has one, there will be confusion when they try to interoperate. And it is not just a question of static invariants; the sequences in which things should happen matters too. For example, imagine a company that comprises two divisions as a result of a merger. One is a modern internet site on which the business demands payment before delivery is made, while in the other, a traditional mail-order catalogue operation, payment is demanded after delivery is made. The different business régimes can be illustrated by the two state transition models in Figure 2-8.

Problems will arise if these systems pass orders to each other to fulfil, because when an on-line customer orders a widget from the catalogue, they pass the request to the on-line system in the `ordered` state. That system assumes payment has been made and delivers – so that the lucky punter never pays a penny. Conversely, the poor loyal catalogue 'agent' who orders on the internet is asked to pay twice.

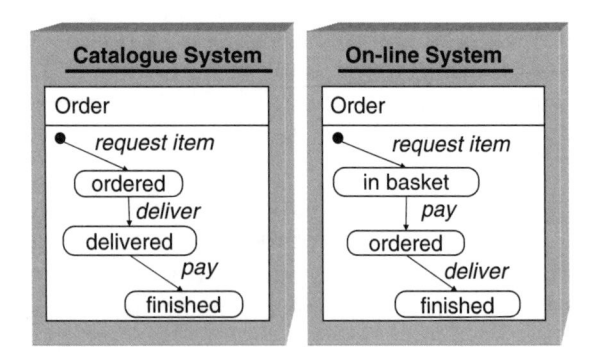

Figure 2-8 Incompatible business processes.

2.3.3 How Services Relate to Components

Components can be used to implement services and, indeed, are an ideal tool for so doing. Figure 2-9 illustrates the relationship between services and the components they rely on in such a case, as part of a metamodel for SOA. Services, which are possibly composites of smaller services, have at least three and possibly more endpoints or ports: the entry ports, departure or exit ports and a rejected message port. Each service is defined by its one or more operations – also called interfaces. However, the metamodel reserves the term 'interfaces' for those of components, although the idea is fundamentally the same. A component interface can implement one or more service operations.

Components, as we know, are defined by their interfaces and the rest of their specification: the rules and constraints they obey. These specifications must match the corresponding services' contracts exactly if the implementation is going to perform as expected. Rules can also relate the

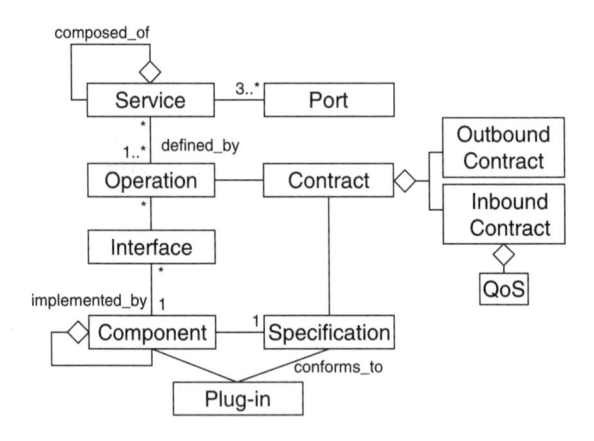

Figure 2-9 Part of a metamodel for SOA.

operations of a service and so the service as a whole can have a contract as well as its individual operations having one.

The idea is that, given any service, we decompose it into its non-composite or **atomic** services. For each operation of these atomic services we find or build a component whose interfaces include an identical specification – implying that we must check at this point that the rules of the contract and the specification match. Note, *en passant*, that this matching check is itself a business rule: we are using the pattern ASSOCIATION LOOPS CONCEAL RULES, because there is a cycle in the diagram of Figure 2-9 (see Appendix A or Chapter 7).

Service oriented architecture and component based development are complimentary technologies – one can be done without the other, but they are best done together. Typically, a service will be realized by one or more components. (One could argue that a component that does not satisfy the properties of a good service is not a good component.) Developing services for an SOA must lead to interfaces that support the business: it is not about supporting the user interface (or other existing software). Prior to SOA, the typical approach was to develop interfaces to the application that support the interactions of a direct user of the system (use cases) – these interfaces are at too low a level. Analysis must be done to identify high level services that are *about the business* and it is these that should be implemented.

2.4 Architecture and SOA

Let us look at two, quite similar, definitions of software architecture. As we saw earlier, the SEI say that the software architecture of a program or a computer system is the structure or structures of the system, which comprise software elements, the externally visible properties of those elements, and the connexions among them. The first version of Catalysis (D'Souza and Wills, 1999) regarded the architecture of a system as consisting of the structure or structures of its parts, the nature and relevant externally visible properties of those parts, and the relationships and constraints between them.

Apart from noting the woeful absence of architectural vision from these definitions[2], we should note that both of them are about building systems from components: black boxes that have externally visible properties. Services satisfy these criteria perfectly. So, as we have seen, SOA is about building systems from loosely coupled services, which in turn are built from black boxes (components) that implement service operations,

---

[2] Actually it was present in Catalysis but hidden away in the Catalysis notion of a 'kit of components'.

possibly (but invisibly) by delegation. Adding to this the requirement that services should be reusable leads to the conclusion that, for ease of construction and maintenance, the components too should be loosely coupled.

As a corollary of this, a good approach to SOA is to separate service design from system design.

We should build systems from service components, with the service interfaces being the link between services and their use. To do this, it is necessary first to identify the right services. As services are about the business, to find them we need to understand the business. This can be done by building a domain model (a model of the business objects) and a business process model (a model of what the business does) and the services needed to support the business within the processes. Chapters 3 to 6 address how to go about this in some detail.

This business or **domain model** must be transformed into a **specification model**, which describes the functions that the system is to supply and identifies relevant systems and their place within the business processes. The business process model helps identify the needed functions directly but sometimes only makes sense in the presence of a system specification model. This model also shows the services and their interactions. As we know from the domain and specification models what each service does, we can use this information to work out how the services can be woven together to supply the necessary functions that support the business now and as it evolves. Thus, if attention is not paid to business and specification modelling then any SOA will soon degenerate into a hard-to-maintain mess, or worse be built from the start as a hard-to-maintain mess.

Migration without modelling has usually been a failure or a mess. Successful integration and migration need sound models of the business (processes, objectives, etc.) and models of the systems (specifications, architecture, etc.).

The final model we need is the **implementation model**, which describes how the services will be programmed to supply the necessary operations identified in the system model. From the requirements for a given application, we can identify those services that are of use and work out how they must be orchestrated or choreographed (how they collaborate) to satisfy those requirements. The design problem is how that collaboration should be implemented.

A useful way to look at the necessary transformations between models is provided by the OMG's Model Driven Architecture (MDA) standard, which also gives us some useful terminology. MDA has two principal aspects:

1. The prospect of generating code from models.
2. A central role for modelling in the development lifecycle.

The former aspect is catered for by a number of emerging tools, while the latter is only poorly or partially served by current technology, although one may expect this situation to improve.

MDA mandates that there are three model types which, in order, are a **computer[3] independent model** (CIM) that is the equivalent of our domain and specification models and eschews mention of any platform. A CIM based on services collaborating with business processes is quite permissible. The CIM must then be transformed into a **platform independent model** (PIM) which permits mention of design decisions that do involve the choice of particular products or technology. Thus, the PIM might assume the use of a relational database or an ESB but would not say which one. In our approach, we would split this into two models: the former corresponding to the specification model and the latter adding such architectural and design decisions. Finally, when the technology has been selected – .NET or J2EE, Oracle or SQL/Server, Websphere or Weblogic – the **platform specific model** (PSM) is created.

Well, not quite finally! We still need a model in the form of code. The assumption behind MDA is that this will be generated automatically from the PSM using a code generator. MDA also assumes that the transformation between the PIM and the PSM is rule-based and will be automated too. Several commercial tools exist that can perform this task. All of them assume that the PIM contains specifications for classes (the components) and their methods; the latter must be described in a particular language, usually OCL (Object Constraint Language) or ASL (Action Semantics Language), which subsumes part of OCL. Sadly, both languages are very low level and a suitable 4GL for method specification is yet to emerge. With this approach, when platforms evolve or are superseded, systems can be regenerated entirely automatically from the PIMs; the only proviso being that the transformation rules must be rewritten to suit the new platform.

While acknowledging the power and benefits of the approach, there are some problems with it currently. Most companies exist with a goulash of legacy systems with a range of different hardware, all sorts of languages and all sorts of interconnexions. The problem is using MDA in the context of both new and existing (legacy) systems. First, current MDA tools concentrate on. NET and/or J2EE (and relational databases). So MDA tools are fine if you are just dealing with new systems and wrappers for legacy APIs. But what if you want to extend the legacy? As suggested in Figure 2-10, transformation tools for the legacy or for other platform technologies are still thin on the ground.

The second problem is also pointed up in the figure. How do you transform the CIM into a PIM? Some authorities claim that CIM to PIM

---

[3] Actually, the word in the standard is 'computational' but this gives a phrase so meaningless in English that I am forced to translate to retain the intended meaning.

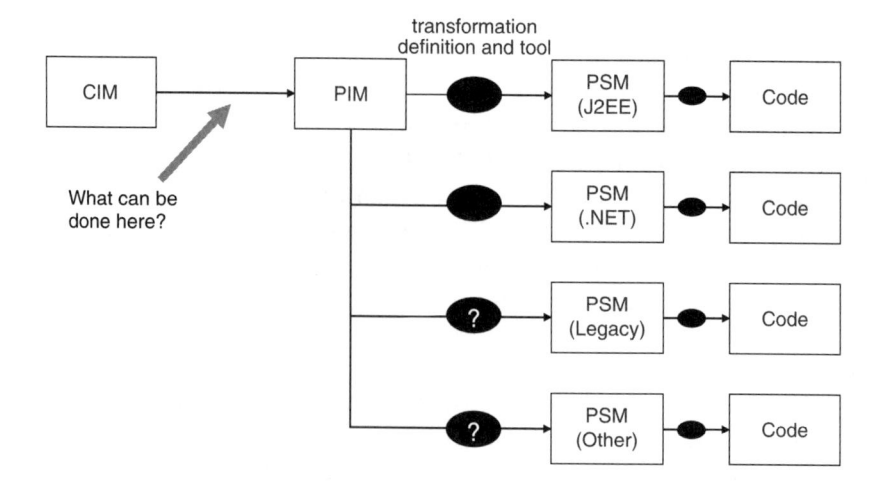

Figure 2-10 MDA model transformations.

transformation tools are impossible because every transformation is a human judgment (e.g. Kleppe *et al.*, 2003). I question that; part (though perhaps not all) of the process *can* be automated, as I will demonstrate in subsequent chapters.

Each of the models is influenced by an architecture, and should conform to an architectural style and vision. The design problem is about how the services – and thus the components – that make up the system should be structured. What architecture should we best use? There are at least three levels that we must considered as shown in Figure 2-11:

- the business architecture;
- the service architecture;
- the technical or IT architecture.

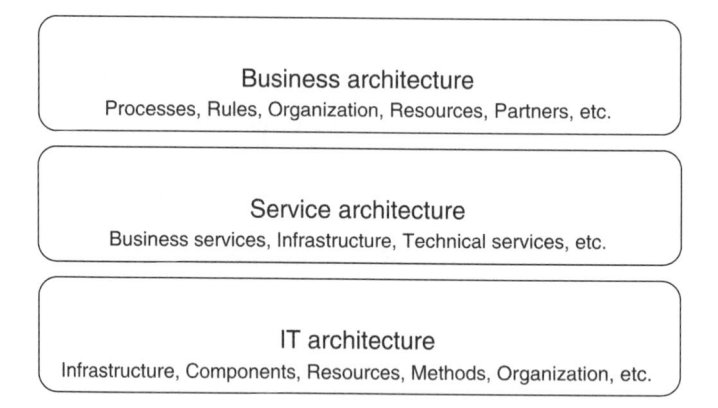

Figure 2-11 Architecture layers.

One possible IT architecture that supports SOA is to choose to use web services and SOAP (and their related technologies) as a RPC mechanism across a network, but there are others options. In that case we design and implement a component that will coordinate the use of the chosen services and do any other additional work that is needed. This component uses the services by calling them via SOAP. We could also base our SOA on an ESB and MOM technology, perhaps adopting the architecture recommended by a vendor.

This architectural style that dictated using SOAP over an HTTP network (this could be either the internet or an intranet) is a technical architecture. It will heavily influence the way we assemble applications. In such a case, a coordinating component will orchestrate the services to supply the required function. We discuss orchestration in Chapter 4.

The service architecture model would dictate that we document the specification of each service, the collaborations among the services, as orchestrated by the coordinator component, and specify the messages. The implementation, i.e. the IT architecture, would then be RPC across a HTTP enabled network.

Another approach is to route all the necessary information in messages between the services, and allow the routing to manage the collaborations. It may be necessary to carry out message transformations so that messages are in the right format for the services they are sent to. Here, the technical architecture is messaging across a message bus – with the bus supplying basic messaging functionality (e.g. JMS) or a full-blown set of functions (an ESB). The application architecture would then involve the specification of each of the services, specifying the message formats and any transformations, enrichments and routing that was required. Any orchestration that was required would also need to be specified. The technical architecture would specify that each of the services be plugged into a message bus.

In many companies, services are developed by separate teams who either don't speak to each other at all or, if they do, may not agree on common semantics, preferring instead their own interpretation or local jargon. In this situation, all communications between services require transformations. This is trivial in pilot projects because the number of transformations required is similar to the number of services. However, as services are added, the number of transformations required does not grow linearly but explodes in proportion to the square of the number of services. Thus, unless semantics are agreed and standardized in the corporate ontology model, you have entered a *cul-de-sac*. Model or die!

Within product lines, such as SAP or Seibel, there are, of course, agreed semantics with each product, but as soon as we, in order to increase business flexibility, break open business process in this short-sighted way, without the benefits of shared semantics, multiple translations are needed and there ensues the predictable maintenance nightmare.

This is not to say that a team of analysts should take five years to model the entire enterprise; we learnt how disastrous that could be way back in the days of so-called corporate data models. No, our models must be built piece by piece and remain at a level of abstraction and detail appropriate to the job in hand. Of course, do the 'big stuff' first, i.e. make sure that the key business concepts are covered, but don't attempt a detailed model of everything. And whatever you do, cut down to a minimum the bureaucracy associated with model change control. Actually it's a lot easier to build a good ontology than you might think. If you follow the methods outlined in this book, a good model should emerge almost automatically as a side effect of business process modelling; a good analysis will produce models 'like a silk worm produces silk'.

In a nutshell, what you do is this.

1. Model the key business processes. This should not be a massively costly project for most organizations.
2. Write pre- and post-conditions for the processes or use cases.
3. Examine these pre- and post-conditions for the vocabulary they use.
4. Include the concepts used in the first-cut ontology.

And, Bob's your uncle: you have a common semantics and a much reduced need to code transformations. Of course, you will refine the model as you implement more and more services, possibly using finite state models to uncover missing detail. We will look at this process in detail in subsequent chapters.

Designing and coding components to implement and use services involves more work than conventional monolithic designs; there are more design decisions that need to be made in any one piece of software.

- We must discover services across the whole problem domain from an examination of the business process model (see Chapter 7 for how to do this).
- The resultant software will be slower as there are more calls between components and services.

Payback is made over the longer term: the system is more flexible, maintainable and reusable. The web-style approach pays dividends here because you can exploit technologies such as load balancing, fail-over, low-cost scalability, backups, etc. However, the investment is only returned if you distribute with care the tasks across the various components and services that make up the system. At the very least, the system must be well decoupled.

There is another, though related, area in which we need models of interoperability that are separate from any particular implementation choices. This is when assembling applications using our carefully crafted services. The skills required of the people making software products from existing services are quite different from those needed by the service developer.

Application development with SOA is like using Lego® bricks or logic chips or modern car design. We have, or plan, a kit of services that can plug together in a variety of ways to make many systems. Among other things, this kit embodies our architectural vision, or at least should do. The danger that your architectural vision is blind to all semantics.

SOA implies a separation of programming rôles. In building a future end product, your aim will be to understand the needs of the users and satisfy them by wiring services together very rapidly. There are languages or tools to help, such as those supplied with some ESBs, but it still requires careful service modelling and design.

Service design is more thoughtful. The aim is to satisfy a longer-range demand for services and components that can be used reliably in many different situations. You don't know what other systems yours will be used with, so you have to be careful to adhere to interface specifications. This is different from designing in a traditional modular environment, where you know who your neighbours are.

Much more care is needed with SOA, mainly in the definition of the transactions that can go on between the services. This is not just a matter of defining messages; you must pay attention to defining protocols, conceptual models, rules and operations too.

2.5 Stateless Services

As we saw in Chapter 1, services are usually regarded as 'stateless'. An object, service, system or protocol is said to be **stateless** if it does not keep a persistent state between transactions. Services that do have this property are called **stative**[4]. It is a axiom of the architectural vision or rationale of SOA that all services should be stateless.

A stateless service treats each message as an independent transaction that is unrelated to any previous request. For example, a web server is stateless because processes requests to display pages require neither any context nor any memory of previous requests. Contrast this with an FTP server conducting an interactive session with a user; a request to the server for a file might assume that this user has been authenticated and that the current directory and file transfer mode have been set, requiring a remembrance of things past.

---

[4] I refuse to use the utterly barbarous 'stateful' since there is already a perfectly good word in existence and which anyway means something quite different – according to the OED: full of state or dignity, stately.

Statelessness helps ensure loose coupling and reusability. Statelessness also simplifies service design; services do not need to allocate memory dynamically to deal with conversations in progress or worry about freeing it if a client crashes mid-transaction.

The main disadvantage of statelessness is that it may be necessary to include more information in messages. This extra information will need to be interpreted each time, thus impacting performance.

However, objects and components have responsibilities and may 'remember' things, so they cannot be completely stateless; *a fortiori* nor can services built upon them. Services are best implemented by components. Services and the underlying components are black boxes. For this very reason, it is impossible to know if a service has state.

For example, consider a spell-checking service that relies on some dictionary of reference; for English this would be the OED, for French, Larousse, for American, Webster, and so on. Although these dictionaries are constantly updated (their state changes) they are unlikely to be superseded. Thus, the service should store the location of the relevant dictionaries. This is transparent to service consumers but does represent persistent data.

So services can and should store state. However, we do not want services to become tightly coupled. To avoid this we therefore forbid services to store the state of *transactions*. Services, therefore, are not necessarily completely stateless and are more properly described as **transactionally stateless**.

The notion of state is critical in business process modelling; without it, we would have systems with no history or audit trail. Indeed, most computer systems hitherto have either been responsible for storing state (databases) or acting upon that state (applications). Transactions can be rolled back if need be. In other words, without persistent state we can't process transactions properly. So, do we have a contradiction?

As we shall see in Chapter 4, one important reason for composing services is to implement business processes, and processes must be stative, since, after all, one instance of a process may be in a different state to another. How best to maintain process states in an environment of stateless services is a critical issue for architects planning and implementing SOA. Implement process state improperly, and the loose coupling benefits of stateless services, and hence the SOA itself, are soon lost.

Two of the features that characterize SOA are loose coupling and encapsulation. Resultant from this there are fewer unnecessary restrictions on the behaviour of service consumers. So, perhaps the service state can be maintained internally after all and merely not exposed to service consumers, lest changes of state require changes to those consumers. But we still need to store the state of long-running processes that span organizational or company boundaries visibly plus there must be some representation of state for most security, governance and quality processes that maintain a context across multiple services.

Even with the web it was soon found that one had to maintain session data across individual queries, each of which maintain no state on their own. Two approaches emerged: storing cookies that maintain state across multiple interactions, or tracking state somehow on the server side, using protocol exchanges for maintenance of a session. Cookies only work because they are a feature of HTTP, the underlying transport protocol of the web, and every browser therefore supports HTTP. But with SOA we must allow for arbitrary system-to-system communication, with no expectation that the service consumers are all browsers, or support any particular protocol. That leaves the message itself as the only place we can maintain state.

This message-based approach to maintaining state begs the question as to how to manage the processes that the service compositions represent. Traditional business process management tools utilize a runtime composition engine that maintains state on behalf of all running processes. The advantage of this approach is that it makes running processes visible and maintains state across relevant services.

However, this approach has some problems: a central process execution environment can only maintain state for services and compositions that are visible to the server. Once a service request passes outside the boundaries of the system, the process tool can no longer control the process. Secondly, the robustness of the processes depends upon the robustness of the process tool; if the tool crashes and loses state information, then there is no way to recover the process instances that were in progress. And of course, any centralized process execution environment reduces loose coupling, because all service providers and consumers must defer control over the processes to the centralized tool.

So, how can we implement stative systems with stateless services? Can we maintain process state in a service-oriented manner, offering state management via contracted services whose purpose is to maintain state for process instances? The answer is to use messages as events that the state maintenance services can audit, log and analyse to determine state. This approach regards state as a side effect of a running system rather than something that some runtime process environment must know about. This event-driven, service-oriented approach tracks all relevant events, and a separate set of services can then analyse the event stream and perform specific actions based on process requirements, policies and service contracts.

Now when a process management service goes down no process information is lost, because the messages that the service providers and consumers are exchanging contain the persistent tokens that represent the process state. Instead of being lost, messages to the process management service merely queue up, waiting for it to come back online. Once it does recover, it can continue executing the process logic where it left off; the queued messages will tell it everything it needs to know about the current process state.

Good architects and designers know that good design always involves trade-offs and compromise. While statelessness is desirable for independent services to achieve agility through loose-coupling, stative services may be needed for business processes to achieve their goals. The architect must therefore meet both of these needs in a service-oriented manner.

The architect must think about state in a service-oriented way. Services should not maintain transactional state unless they are specifically contracted to do so – state management services. They manage the state of running processes that are external to the state management service itself. In no case should the architect allow a service to manage its own transactional state, because a service consumer would then have to know the internal state of the service in order to determine whether to send a message to that service. That situation would violate the loose coupling and encapsulation principles of SOA.

2.6 Practical Principles for Developing, Maintaining and Exploiting SOA

To convert existing systems to SOA involves identifying the services that are needed by the business (the real users) and then providing new interfaces that supply those services. This means that a wrapper or adapter will need to be developed that exposes the business service at the outside interface and maps the operations of that service into low level calls to the legacy API. It may well mean that a service call with the associated request message will involve taking the message apart and making multiple calls to the API. Thus, great care must be taken when wrapping existing legacy systems.

When wrapping an existing application, to use it as a service, just wrapping the existing API will *not* provide business services; it will just give existing systems a very minor face-lift. They may look sexier, but there is no new substance. All that is usually done is to turn the system's parameters into XML messages and the RPC-style calls to calls done using SOAP. If the original interface supported the direct user, then just exposing it as a set of operations that are part of a service will not lead to the right level of granularity for the real user.

To develop services successfully, you must understand the business, not just the computer systems. The idea is to provide services for people to do tasks that deliver value to them. These could be employees, customers, regulators, partners, suppliers, in fact any stakeholders. These people need to be able to understand the system in their own terms, not the terms convenient to the software developers, and the services should support the goals of these people, not the fancies of technicians. One good test is this. If we document the interface of a service, then the business people should be able to understand the documentation just as easily as the developers can.

The following points state some of the principles.

- Reuse, granularity, modularity, composability, componentization and interoperability.
- Compliance with standards (both common and industry-specific).
- Externalizing business rules.
- Monitoring, tracking and process improvement.
- Service identification and categorization, provisioning and delivery.

In addition, the following factors should also be taken into account when defining an SOA implementation.

- Governance.
- Life cycle management.
- Efficient use of system resources.
- Service maturity and performance.

Introducing SOA is often seen as presenting a set of purely technical difficulties. People think as follows:

- We need to understand SOAP, XML, WSDL, UDDI, BPEL and several relevant WS-* standards.
- We need to wrap our applications or expose their APIs to use these standards.
- We must learn to use new products such as an ESB and messaging middleware.
- We need to use SOAP for all remote procedure calls.

This usually leads to a SOA migration plan that involves the following steps:

- Adopt XML, SOAP, etc.
- Institute training and recruitment programmes for the new technologies.
- Evaluate products from vendors and select a platform and technical architecture based on the product(s) selected.
- Start to wrap existing legacy applications to use SOAP rather than (remote) procedure calls.
- Identify anything that looks remotely like a service, extract it from an existing application if necessary, wrap or rewrite and then publish it.
- Write new applications using the new toys.

Here be dragons! Adopting SOA is *not* just about these things, important though some of them are. XML, though it is necessary to have a standard for interchanging information rather than just data, is only part of the solution – and, anyway, there is no guarantee that XML will not be replaced by more efficient future languages. SOAP, though it is nice to have a standard way of calling a remote service that is language independent, is only part of the solution too. Wrapping legacy systems, perhaps using some sort of tool – though good tools are useful once you know what you are doing – is only part of the solution. Worse still is the prevalent practice of exposing hundreds of tiny APIs and thinking that this automatically gives you a service-oriented architecture. Introducing MOM or an enterprise service bus, though this could be a useful approach, is only part of the solution. These are important issues, but they do not encompass the essence of what SOA is really all about.

These issues concern how to *implement* services; they are about technical architecture. The service architecture must emerge from a consideration of both the technical architecture and the business architecture. The service architecture shows how the two relate; how the IT architecture can support the business architecture using services as the delivery mechanism. Doing this well starts with good modelling.

Finally, insisting on modelling as a necessary condition for the success of an SOA is as much part of governance as are people, processes and measurement.

2.7 Summary

Despite the huge number of people employed as practising software architects, there is still a lack of clarity about the definition of architecture in the theoretical architecture. Most people can agree that architecture is about the gross structure of a system and that architecture guides decisions on how to build systems, so that architecture is about requirements and constraints. Architecture is what remains when you cannot take away anything and still understand the system and explain how it works. A good architecture should promote reuse. I would add that architecture is about conceptual integrity and that there must be a coherent unifying rationale: an **architectural vision**. Thus we assert that: Software Architecture = Elements + Form + Rationale.

Architecture is also about the things that are difficult and expensive to change. Design is then about selecting an architecture, deciding on a design philosophy and asserting that 'this is the way we will do things around here'.

Service-oriented architecture mandates that systems are assembled from services. Well designed services are intended to be shared, so that applications can be built by combining and reusing them in multiple applications. To do this they must not only be correct in themselves but also autonomous, abstract, composable, discoverable, transactionally stateless, reusable black boxes defined by their contracts. Ideally, service oriented architecture is based on standards.

To help reduce the massive burden of maintenance, software architecture has evolved away from the original von Neumann architecture, that separated data from processes, to architectures that unify them: object-oriented, component-based and, now, service-oriented. All emphasize encapsulation and polymorphism in support of pluggability and composability. The emphasis on messaging has grown steadily throughout this evolution.

Services are best implemented as components but these can only be successfully designed based on an understanding of the business processes involved and a model of the ontology of the domain. To move to a service-oriented architecture we must work at three levels and understand:

- the business architecture;
- the service architecture;
- the technical or IT architecture.

A good approach to SOA is to separate service design from system design.

As we will see in later chapters, use cases are one way to model business processes. If the level of the use cases is such that they provide too much detail, then we are probably designing the user interface. This is an activity that we can and should leave until later. Frequently, this approach leads to too much documentation of the use cases, and little understanding of the business, its processes and rules. There is a need to set the description at a level that provides both understanding and provides a basis for detailed development of the HCI later.

In an SOA, the number of interfaces needs to be small compared to the number of components.

Use messages as events that state maintenance services can audit, log, and analyse to determine state. This regards state as a side effect of a running system rather than something that some runtime process environment must know about. This event-driven, service-oriented approach tracks all relevant events, and a separate set of services can then analyse the event stream and perform specific actions based on process requirements, policies, and service contracts

In this chapter we saw that there are some principles that can guide a successful move to SOA. In addition we must consider governance, life cycle management, efficient use of system resources and service maturity and performance. There are great dangers in much current practice. Sound architecture and good modelling skills are the main guarantors of successful migration to SOA.

2.8 Bibliographical Notes

In this chapter, I restricted myself to the discussion of software architecture as given by Bosch (2000). There is a substantial second part dealing with the actual development of product lines. The interested reader is recommended to consult this book.

A complementary discussion of architecture in a service-oriented context is provided by Erl (2005).

Dikel *et al.* (2001) provide an interesting slant on the topic of software architecture, in that they equate it much more with architectural vision than do most approaches. These authors view architecture mainly as the unifying vision that makes it possible to put together systems across departmental and organizational boundaries, in contrast with the islands of automation that Americans call 'stovepipes'. Sounds like SOA? The book is definitely pre-SOA but does have some useful insights. They focus almost entirely on 'product line' development, which was the fashion for a while – presumably because someone at the Sloan School of Management said once that there was money to be made, based on the common but absurd Empiricist premise that 'what was true yesterday will be true tomorrow'. SOA removes the need for a lot (though by no means all) of what is recommended: it *is* an architectural vision. Nevertheless, the book is worth a look at, especially because it presents much of its wisdom in the form of patterns and includes useful links to other relevant published patterns.

Graham (2009) discusses architectural assessment in the context of managing SOA projects.

CHAPTER 3

Approaches to Requirements Engineering

It may seem a strange principle to enunciate as the very first requirement in a Hospital that it should do the sick no harm.
Florence Nightingale *(Notes on Hospitals, 1863)*

In this chapter, I survey some of the many different approaches to requirements engineering that have been taken to help software developers uncover, structure and document requirements and understand them better. I also introduce some of the Unified Modelling Language (UML) notation that we will need in subsequent chapters.

The chapter then begins to lay out a practical approach to requirements engineering that is suitable for SOA projects.

3.1 Conventional Approaches

Classic requirements engineering proceeded with the ultimate aim of producing a functional specification, which was often embodied in a number of giant-sized ring binders. The intention was that the customer would read, understand and correct the document, thus ensuring that the correct system was built. Such documents typically contained report layouts, screen mock-ups, Entity-Relationship (ER) and other technical diagrams and numbered lists of statements describing what the customer expected the system to do: the requirements. These were often written using a rather absurd vocabulary laid down originally by the US military, which insisted on the words that could be used as follows.

The word 'shall' (which in English implies duty) must be used for all statements of requirement. The word 'will' (in English this implies intention) must only be used to connote statements of fact. Goals can use the word 'should'. Michael Jackson (1995) pours scorn on this, challenging the reader to speak aloud and interpret the following two sentences. 'I shall drown, no one will save me. I will drown, no one shall save me'.

Whatever you think about this convention, enshrined as it is in an IEEE standard (Dorfman and Thayer, 1990), there are a number of points that the conventional approach sensibly insists upon. Most importantly, requirements should be numbered and cross-referenced to features and implementation status, and requirements should be concise descriptions of features that are necessary, attainable and verifiable.

Classic problem analysis techniques used within requirements analysis were of three basic kinds: data-centred, function-centred and behaviour-oriented. Data-centred techniques included Jackson System Development (JSD) (Jackson, 1983) and Entity Relationship (ER) modelling (Chen, 1976). Function-centred techniques included *inter alia* data flow diagrams (DFDs) with data dictionaries, Yourdon, SADT and SSADM. Finally, behaviour-oriented techniques included statecharts, Petri nets, decision trees and tables and prototyping. Many behaviour-oriented techniques persist within modern approaches (as indeed does ER modelling).

The technical nature of the descriptions of features contained in most requirements specifications meant that users often lacked the patience and time, if not the skills, to interpret them properly; so they were signed off even when incorrect or inadequate, leading to the imbroglio of failed project that we are familiar with. It just so happens that many users are *not* able to interpret ER diagrams or state charts. They do *not* understand pseudocode. More critically they can't tell the difference between a feature being missing or present because it's not needed and one that is missing or present because of the limitations of (current) computer technology. Further to this, add in the limitations of the imagination of IT staff. I recently worked on a business rules project where it soon became clear that the IT guys and their business analysts (tamed ex-users) had no conception of what such systems could do: their ambitions were trammelled by what a programmer could do in COBOL, PL/1 or Java.

A parallel approach to requirements engineering, often used for safety-critical systems or systems with high intended levels of reuse, such as operating systems, is the use of various formal methods. Formal specifications are written in a mathematical notation such as Larch (Guttag *et al.*, 1985), Object-Z (Carrington *et al.*, 1990) or VDM (Jones, 1986). These are all based on logic (usually first order predicate calculus or similar) and require some mathematical acumen but have the advantage that certain things can be proved about a specification written in such a way.

While I have no need to nor intention of deprecating formal methods, it must be said that they do not address the problems of requirements engineering; they only deal with *the specification of systems* and cannot possibly help understand the nature of the need for such systems or the ways in which they can be used. Formal methods become beneficial under two provisos:

- The additional cost in terms on time and specialized staff is justified on the grounds of safety or mass reuse.
- The requirements are properly understood *before* the formal specifications are written.

Latterly, since the use of object-oriented methods became widespread in the 1990s, it has become common to identify requirements work with use case analysis (Jacobson *et al.*, 1992). We will concentrate on use-case-centred modelling later in this chapter and it will be seen that our approach (Chapters 4 to 7) is greatly influenced by use cases. For now I should only note that Jacobson's use cases, like formal methods, fail to address the whole problem of requirements; they too are tools for system specification – at least if interpreted in the ways suggested by Jacobson and his epigones. We will see later how formal methods can be incorporated into use case analysis.

One significant response to the failure of use cases to address requirements was the technique of Jackson Problem Frames (Jackson, 2001) which I discuss below.

Of course in many IT shops, mixed approaches dominate. Typically, IEEE-style requirements statements are written and cross-referenced to features that include copious use cases. Indeed, several tools exist to help with this: DOORS, Requisite Pro, etc. It is almost equally common to find an IT organization using a requirements engineering method known as Just Do It (JFDI); in other words, the approach is hidden inside the heads of the developers.

In reality, the best approach to take will depend on the culture of customer and type of problem under consideration.

3.1.1 Approaches Based on Human Factors

Pohl (1993) defined requirements engineering to be the systematic process of developing requirements through an iterative co-operative process of analysing the problem, documenting the resultant observations in a variety of representations and checking the accuracy of the understanding gained. This definition, while it leaves some questions unanswered, is a good starting point because it suggests that there is more to requirements engineering than just writing a functional specification. By contrast, the IEEE standard defines a requirement as one of the following.

1. A condition or capacity needed by a user to solve a problem or achieve an objective.
2. A condition or capability that must be met or possessed by a system or system component to satisfy a contract, standard, specification or other formally imposed documents.
3. A documented representation of a condition or capability as in (1) or (2).

This leaves out the issue of context completely and emphasizes the presence of a requirements document but is notable for the inclusion of the idea of a contract.

Macaulay (1996) suggests that the Pohl definition raises a number of important questions, including whether one can be systematic in the face of vaguely understood requirements, how one can know whether the requirements are complete in the context of iteration, how to define co-operation among agents, what representation formalisms can be used and, finally, how can a genuine shared understanding be reached. The approach laid out in this book offers answers to all of these questions in the context of SOA.

We can distinguish two aspects of requirements elicitation and analysis. Requirements elicitation is the process whereby a development agency discovers what is needed and why. It is a branch of the discipline of knowledge elicitation and will use many techniques developed within that discipline. Requirements analysis, on the other hand, is the process of understanding and modelling the requirements that have been or are being elicited. This is where the requirements engineer will ask questions about the completeness and consistency of the knowledge discovered. This distinction is represented by the division of most work on requirements engineering into two fairly distinct camps. One group focuses on knowledge elicitation techniques and is represented by work that uses *inter alia* ethnomethodology, human factors theories, soft systems methods and ergonomics. A second group emphasizes formal methods of systems analysis. Examples range from traditional systems analysis approaches such as JSD (Jackson, 1983) to overtly mathematical formal methods such as VDM and Z.

One of the problems with formal specification is that it can actually ignore the true requirement just as easily as an informal document-oriented approach. An example will suffice to illustrate this. An infamous case occurred in the case of aircraft design. A requirement was stated that an aeroplane's reverse thrusters should not cut in until the aircraft was in contact with the runway. The designers reasoned that one could only be sure that the plane had touched down when its wheels began to spin forwards, which would be the case when in contact with a runway or similar. Therefore they arranged the system such that the thrusters would fire automatically when the wheels so span. This worked very well ... until the first time the plane had to land on a runway covered with water and aquaplaned! The plane overshot the runway. So, even if the system can be proved to meet its specification – and there is no principled reason why this could not have been done in our aircraft example – then there is still no guarantee that the specification meets the true requirement. This is especially the case when there are conflicting requirements. In the example just given the conflict was between the need to eliminate human error and the need to land safely in all conditions.

Formal methods emphasize proving the correctness of the code against the specification. This is achieved by writing the specification in a language based on some variant of formal logic. Mathematical proofs of correctness may then be constructed. There are two major problems with this. First, the proofs require great mathematical skill and for large systems can be quite intractable. On the other hand the effort may be worthwhile for safety-critical systems or systems upon which mission-critical systems depend. One of the largest projects of this kind involved the specification of the CICS transaction monitor at IBM's Hursley laboratory. The second defect is, in my opinion, far more damning. The problem is that using logic as a specification language is tantamount to programming in logic. All the formal proofs can do is to show the equivalence of the two programs; they say nothing at all about whether the specification meets the users' requirements.

In contrast to formal and semi-formal techniques, approaches such as ETHICS (Mumford, 1986) stress participation and the harmonization of the social and the technical aspects of systems. ETHICS (Effective Technical and Human Implementation of Computer-based Systems) advocates twelve main steps:

1. Specify the work mission.
2. Describe current activities and needs.
3. Consider and measure job satisfaction.
4. Decide on changes needed.
5. Set objectives for job satisfaction, efficiency and effectiveness.
6. Consider the organizational options.
7. Reorganize.
8. Select computer solutions.
9. Train the staff.
10. Redesign jobs.
11. Implement.
12. Evaluate.

ETHICS thus is strongly echoed by more recent work on business process re-engineering and workflow analysis, though it is less associated with rigid and bureaucratic workflow systems of the sort commonly implemented in Lotus Notes and the like. I feel that all the above twelve issues must be addressed during requirements engineering and systems analysis, though not necessarily in that order. Implicitly ETHICS encourages the empowerment of teams and the use of formal inspections to facilitate self-correction of defects. The major problem with ETHICS is that it provides no guidance on how to go about modelling itself, which is the critical success factor for step (8). Nor does it integrate ideas from business process re-engineering, rapid application development or object technology into its approach. Thus, while not ignoring the advances of ETHICS, we must go well beyond it.

Ethnography and ethnomethodological techniques, deriving from Anthropology, have been applied to requirements engineering in order to recognize that task analysis based on studies of individuals is flawed if it fails to recognize that all business activity takes place in a social context. The behaviour of groups is studied over some time and conclusions about requirements drawn. Suchman (1987) provides an excellent case study: applying the method to the design of photocopying machinery. We adopt an approach that focuses on networks of social commitments but does not require extensive observational studies, though these are by no means ruled out.

Participatory design is a general label for approaches that emphasize user involvement throughout the specification and design process. Leading proponents include Ehn (Ehn *et al.*, 1990; Ehn and Kyng, 1991). Requirements are not fixed at some arbitrary point as in conventional structured approaches. This view is consistent with the evolutionary process model described in Chapter 9. Also important to the advocates of participatory design is that systems should not be used to downgrade and de-skill users' work. Webster (1996) provides some pretty horrifying counter-examples in the context of the degradation of work when looked at from a gender-specific viewpoint – and that includes the degradation (or elimination) of the work of both sexes. I believe that all relevant social factors should be taken into account when designing systems (including perhaps, age, culture, gender and physical ability) and that designers have a social responsibility at least to *predict* the effects of their technology.

Research into human computer interaction (HCI) has led to approaches based on user-centred and task-centred design. These can utilize direct user involvement, observational studies or even questionnaires and surveys. Eason (1989) is a leading exponent of user-centred design whose approach has much in common with ETHICS although he gives more emphasis to socio-technical design and cost-benefit analysis. The task-centred approach descends from the educational technology movement of the 1950s and 1960s. User task analysis is a key influence on the approach presented in this chapter, but we combine these ideas with those of use cases, semiotics (part of ethnomethodology) and script theory from artificial intelligence. I advocate the use of a number of other techniques derived from knowledge engineering, discussed later.

Contextual enquiry (Beyer and Holtzblatt, 1997) is a set of tools and techniques whose basic tenet is that business processes are best apprehended in the context of the workplace. Modelling techniques include flow models, task scenarios, artefacts used, culture and the physical environment. It does not emphasize user interface design and is most suitable for automating existing manual processes.

Usage-centred design (Constantine and Lockwood, 1999) builds on many of the above ideas and emphasizes user interface design, task analysis, user rôles and the use of 'essential' use cases. It has much in common with the approach presented herein.

Quality function deployment or the so-called 'house of quality' has been put forward as a way of discovering users' requirements based on correlating them pairwise with product features. I believe that the techniques described in this book make this kind of approach superfluous.

The CREWS approach to requirements engineering (Maiden *et al.*, 1998) emphasizes techniques based on scenarios for checking that specifications are consistent and – more especially – complete.

An approach to the analysis of workflow systems developed by Winograd and Flores (1986) has much to recommend it and is integrated into our approach. It emphasizes the network of commitments that exists between the agents in a business and their sequenced conversations. However, the approach has been criticized for leading to over-rigid work practices in the implementations that it arrives at. I believe that delving deeper than the workflow aspects of the conversations and analysing the stakeholders' tasks as well can overcome this.

ORCA (Object-Oriented Requirements Capture and Analysis) (MacLean *et al.*, 1994) represents one of the few attempts to make requirements engineering for object-oriented development in any way rigorous. It advocates the use of soft systems style 'rich pictures' as a starting point and then makes a clear distinction between models of the world and models of systems.

Soft systems research (Checkland, 1981; Checkland and Scholes, 1991) is concerned with apprehending an entire, situated problem in the context of an organization and the purposes of the whole problem solving activity. Emphasis is on elicitation of behaviour and problem dynamics from multiple perspectives. The foundation of soft systems work was in general systems theory and Cybernetics. The same traditions are at the root of approaches to business process re-engineering such as that of Senge (1990). The approach usually begins by drawing a rich picture of the problem situation.

Checkland's famous mnemonic, CATWOE – standing for: Customers, Actors, Transformation processes, Weltanschauung, Owners and Environment – is used within SSM as a guide to what the components of a system model should cover. The key concepts in the Soft Systems method are as follows:

- A transformation process (T) that converts input to output – a system.
- Customers: the victims or beneficiaries of T. The modern term would be stakeholders, although some are singled out as actors or owners.
- Actors: those who would do T.
- Owners: those who could stop T, including sponsors.
- Weltanschauung: the worldview that gives meaning to T in context. This includes what we would call goals, objectives, measures, assumptions, exclusions, etc.
- Environmental constraints: the elements outside the system over which we have no influence.

SSM also recommends an approach that consists of the following steps:

1. Find out about problem situation, i.e. establish the objectives and possibly build a business process model.
2. Express the situation (the rich picture).
3. Select viewpoint and produce root definitions.
4. Build conceptual models of what the system must do for each root definition. This could be a use case model.
5. Compare the conceptual model with the world.
6. Identify feasible and desirable changes.

We will build on this in the approach taken in this book.

3.2 Classic Requirements versus Use Cases

The use case approach was developed by Ivar Jacobson at Ericsson in the context of his Objectory method, which emerged in an object-oriented form in the 1990s. Subsequently it was absorbed into the Unified Modelling Language (UML), which was then adopted as an OMG standard.

3.2.1 UML Basics

UML is a language for describing models of software artifacts and their designs. A **model** is a representation of something that differs from the thing itself and is (usually) simpler than the original. There are many kinds of model: iconic models (e.g. in architecture, wind tunnels, fine art, etc.); graphical models (e.g. in UML); simulation models (digital and analogue models of traffic flow, say); textual models (e.g. classic requirements models); prototypes; mathematical models (e.g. designing a car engine, getting to the moon, etc.); axiomatic (realization) models. Some models fall into more than one of these categories.

Specifically, the models of UML are meant to be based on the object metaphor. Object modelling has its roots in simulation modelling (cf. Graham, 2001) and is the foundation for use-cased-based specifications. UML models should be easy to understand for both analysts and users, but only if done well. UML is certainly useful in allowing developers to communicate among themselves, either using documents or at the whiteboard. Its models record what objects there are and how they are related, what tasks they can perform and how they collaborate. These models are meant to be abstract in that they avoid detail of code but are detailed enough to generate at least some of it. Using UML helps developers and analysts clarify important issues earlier on in projects by exposing models using a precise and relatively rigorous formalism. Precise may not be quite the right word here, since natural language is capable of infinite precision – often at the expense of great verbosity. UML walks between these extremes. Such analysis helps expose gaps and inconsistencies early on although UML contains no explicit guidance on how to achieve this, e.g. it does not specify how its various model are related nor impose cross-model consistency checks.

So, UML is a language and is thus about communication ... but communication with whom? Current practice restricts its usefulness, making it only an effective tool for inter-developer communication. This clearly will not do for the requirements engineer, who must communicate with all the stakeholders.

Also, UML is not a method; it has strong syntax but weak semantics and there are no links between diagram types. Neither is it a complete solution to all modelling problems, as we will see in this book; other notations or languages are often essential. Nor is it a substitute for common sense and hard work.

Figure 3-1 illustrates some of the origins and influences on UML.

Among the benefits of adopting UML we can identify these:

- It is a widely accepted standard, so that new recruits are likely to have had exposure to it at college or in employment.
- It provides a very effective common language for developers.
- There is good tool support.
- It encourages modelling.

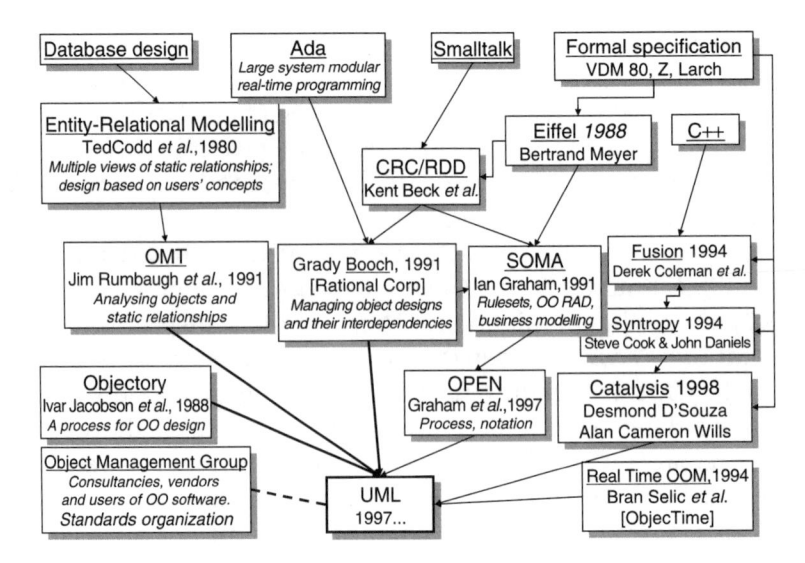

Figure 3-1 UML's origins and influences.

However, there are some risks too. There is a great deal of bad practice out there in industry and academia alike – some of it encouraged by interpretations built into tools. Because it has no defined semantics, there are many variations of interpretation. Lastly, UML is still subject to revision, although upward compatibility has been mostly maintained so far.

UML has many diagram types but only a few are in widespread, mainstream use in commerce. The basic diagram types are as follows:

- Use case diagrams.
- Class diagrams (often used for and confused with type diagrams).
- Sequence diagrams.
- Collaboration diagrams (actually just another notation for sequence diagrams).
- State transition diagrams.
- Activity diagrams.

The various other notations, such as deployment and module diagrams are described succinctly in an appendix to Graham (2001) and in full on the OMG web site.

UML also contains its own formal specification language, OCL (Object Constraint Language).

3.2.2 Use Case Models

According to Jacobson, a use case is 'a behaviourally related sequence of transactions in a dialogue with the system' (Jacobson *et al.*, 1992) and 'a sequence of transactions in a system whose task is to yield a result of measurable value' (Jacobson *et al.*, 1995). Elsewhere, he says implicitly that a use case is a class of scenarios but defines a scenario as 'an instance of a use case', which of course is rather circular. Also the mathematics of such statements is rather suspect (Graham, 1998). The vagueness of these and other definitions is suggestive of a number of problems with the theory, not least the introduction of the procedural idea of a 'sequence of transactions'. In systems analysis, one should usually be concerned not with the sequencing of events but with their outcomes. On this basis, it might be better to say that use cases describe required or permissible business or system interactions and their desired outcomes.

There is a further ambiguity in the interpretation of what it means for one use case to 'extend' another, but this need not detain us here.

The other key concept in use case modelling is that of an actor. Jacobson's original definition was 'a user adopting a rôle'. Later, this is softened to admit non-human actors like sensors, clocks and computing or control devices, but the sense is very strongly that use cases mediate between a system and the people or things that touch it: direct rather than real user, in our terminology. This makes the use case a useful tool for system specification rather than for requirements engineering or business analysis.

To get over the latter problem, Jacobson *et al.* (1995) point out that a business is a system, though not a computer system. As such it may have users who interact with a business unit and only use its computer systems indirectly; these indeed can be our real users. However, this leads to the view that organizations are hierarchically nested entities – in the manner of a Russian doll: systems within systems within systems. All my practical experience suggests that this is a most unrealistic view of the nature of businesses. Nevertheless, the idea has resulted in the notion of business (as opposed to system) use cases, which is useful.

In practice, use cases are rarely used this way and are most often used in software specification to record which activities the software should support. Sometimes it is also useful to note those that it doesn't support. The kind of diagram usually drawn is shown in Figure 3-2. Such a picture is often called a context diagram; it shows a system boundary (the context) and the interactions that take place across it (the system use cases).

This diagram also shows how the business use case 'arrival' is often represented in practice. The scenario depicted is this:

1. Someone arrives and asks the receptionist to check him/her in. He/she asks for a credit card or cash. There is no computer interaction.
2. The receptionist interacts with the computer to check the guest in. This involves subsidiary use cases that the 'check in' use case

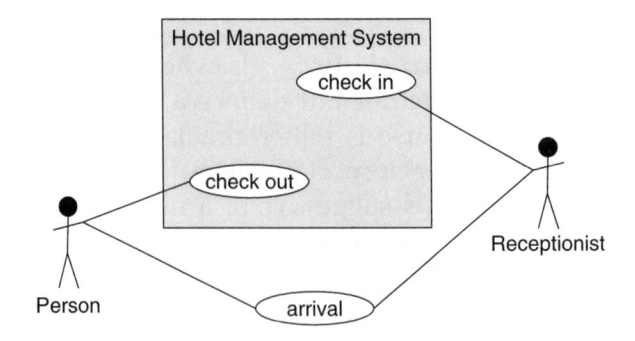

Figure 3-2 A use case model with a system boundary.

'includes'. These, in no particular order, might be 'swipe card details', 'allocate room', 'book alarm call' and so on.

3. This hotel management system allows guests to 'check out' themselves using a touch screen.

There is nothing wrong with doing things this way at design time, but it is totally wrong as a technique for understanding requirements or specifying systems initially. It focuses attention on the system and its boundary rather than on business need or, indeed, business processes. Don't do it!

For such higher level purposes it is often better to draw what I call, following Checkland (1981), a 'rich picture'. The same UML notation may be used, as shown in Figure 3-3.

What I have done here is to utilize the UML idea of a stereotype. Instead of using a context box, I represent the hotel management system as an actor but, instead of stereotyping it as a pin-man (which what most case tools do) I make it look like what it is: a system. This makes it far easier to

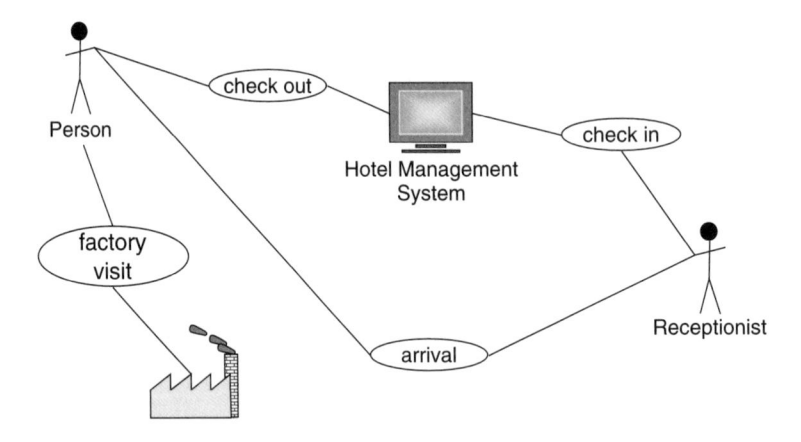

Figure 3-3 A rich picture.

discuss the diagram with non-technical people and emphasizes the fact that the system is part of a business process. I show this further by recording that the guest has checked in only in order to visit his firm's factory the next day. This may assist the hotel in its marketing strategy. The north-lit, smoke-belching factory is another actor, stereotyped to look like what (to anyone of my generation at least) looks like a factory.

Such a rich picture enables one to discuss the basic business processes and business rules with users. In subsequent chapters we will see how to take this analysis further.

3.2.3 Formulating Requirements

All requirements statements, whether expressed as use cases or not, should be:

- correct;
- complete;
- unambiguous (although fuzzy statements are permissible under certain circumstances);
- verifiable;
- modifiable;
- implementation independent;
- clear;
- concise;
- consistent;
- understandable (by customers too);
- well organized;
- traceable.

But if they are all these things there is a contradiction. In practice they get too big to be usable. Which is one reason why use cases are so popular.

It is convenient to classify requirements into categories. This can act as an *aide memoire* to completeness, i.e. help you to avoid missing key requirements. The most obvious category concerns what are called functional requirements in the conventional approach and are the ones most usually expressed as use case. These concern the following kinds of issue.

- Product features.
- System capabilities.
- Performance issues such as speed and efficiency, availability, accuracy, throughput, portability, response and recovery time and resource usage. (Note that conventional requirements engineers

would put this in the non-functional category, but I disagree; doing X fast enough is just as much a matter of functionality as doing X at all; if it's too slow it ain't working properly!)
- Security.
- Reliability issues such as the frequency and severity of failure, mean time to failure, accuracy (e.g. of calculations), recoverability and predictability.

The non-functional aspects are of two kinds.

- Usability issues. These include aesthetics, ergonomics, consistency in the user interface, online and context-sensitive help, documentation and training materials and learnability and, indeed, forgetability.
- Maintainability issues. These include testability, extensibility, adaptability, localizability (internationally), compatibility, configurability, serviceability and installability.

Finally, there are the constraints on possible implementations. These are of two kinds: constraints that are constraints of functions or use cases and others. The use case constraints split further into two categories.

- Implementation constraints: standards, existing systems, resource limits, database integrity policy, implementation languages, operating environment, etc.
- Interface constraints: external interactions and their formats, timings, etc.

The other constraints will obviously vary but they often include physical constraints such as:

- material;
- size, shape, weight, etc.;
- physical network configuration;
- hardware manufacturer.

All requirements can, in principle, be expressed as use cases and vice versa, but it is not always sensible to do so. Specifically, some of the 'other' constraints may have arisen from an earlier use case; for example, suppose we discover that our client requires that the systems run on hardware supplied by a preferred manufacturer, such as IBM. This doesn't look much like a use case but it could be the post-condition arising from an earlier conversation between the manufacturer and the procurement department. We can represent this by the business use case shown in Figure 3-4. Of course, this may be quite a clumsy representation in practice, so one must use common sense to decide which is the clearest representation: use case of textual statement.

[Figure 3-4 diagram: IBM —— arrange discount —— Procurement]

Figure 3-4 A latent use case.

The key to successful requirements engineering is being able to model: to model the business, the system and its users, both direct and real. This will be a constant theme in later chapters. For now, we look at a slightly different approach that was inspired by the same belief.

3.3 Problem Frames

A more profound approach is due to Jackson (1995, 2001). He defines a problem frame as a structure consisting of principal parts and a solution task. The principal parts correspond to what we have met as actors, use cases and business objects, along with other actions and goal-oriented conversations. The solution task is the work one has to do to meet some requirement concerning these parts or objects. He then abstracts from the objects to problem domains and the phenomena that are shared between them: in the sense of the elements that can be described in the languages of both domains.

In Figure 3-5, the rectangles represent problem domains and the connecting lines shared phenomena: shared events, states and values. These are sometimes labelled and expanded, so that the connector labelled 's' lets the machine read off *inter alia* the safe ranges for the sensors attached to a patient's body. The annotation PMS indicates that it is the machine

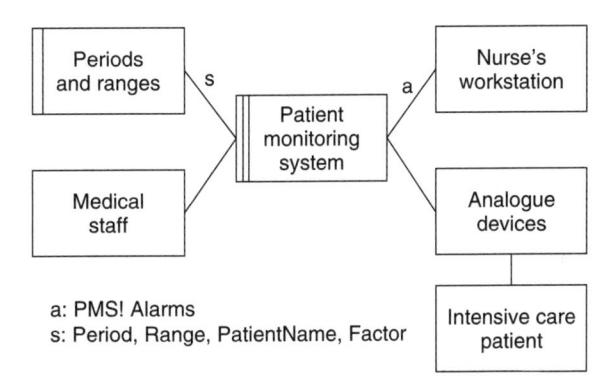

[Figure 3-5 diagram: Patient monitoring system connected to Periods and ranges (s), Nurse's workstation (a), Medical staff, Analogue devices, Intensive care patient.
a: PMS! Alarms
s: Period, Range, PatientName, Factor]

Figure 3-5 A problem context diagram.

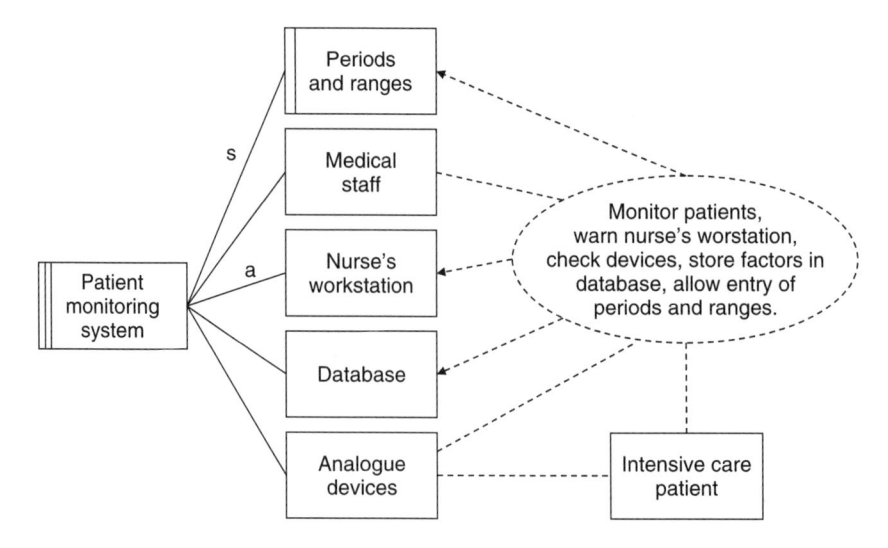

Figure 3-6 A problem diagram (after Jackson, 2001).

that initiates any alarms. Rectangles with a double vertical line represent machine domains – one per frame and those with a single represent domain that must be designed – as opposed to being part of the uncontrollable world.

Each frame may have a set of rules that connect pairs of domains. Problem context diagrams become problem diagrams with the addition of **requirements**, represented by dashed ellipses; the dashed connectors are **requirements references**. The latter may be directed to indicate that the reference is a constraint on the solution. Figure 3-6 shows a problem diagram for the same patient monitoring system.

Problem frames abstract from commonly occurring problem or subproblem diagrams that have the same basic structure or topology. Each frame may have a set of rules that connect pairs of domains.

I think that problem frames provide not only a requirements engineering technique but potentially also an architectural technique because they describe not a solution but a suitable approach to finding a solution. They also suggest the patterns that we deal with in the next section. The idea is focused more on the problems of the requirements analyst trying to understand a problem and select an approach than the software designer who has already selected the architectural style and implementation technology.

Jackson emphasizes the use of problem frames in requirements understanding and analysis. His approach is fundamentally that of an analyst but he pays far more attention to the human issues than is traditional in requirements analysis. He stresses formality but without using the kind of alienating symbolism found in the formal methods tradition. Most importantly of all, Jackson points out that the generality of a method is in inverse proportion to its applicability. To this end he proposes the building of a library of problem frames to cover commonly encountered problem types and appropriate methods to go with them. This, of course, suggests that problem frames are architectural patterns.

Typical problem frames include the following:

- CONNEXION: introduces a separate problem domain between the application and solution domains. Examples: a post office; CORBA; ESBs.
- TRANSFORMATION (JSP): helps to describe a program in terms of its input and output streams. Example: a typical accounting or stock control system.
- COMMANDED BEHAVIOUR: describes the situation where known control rules are applied to a controllable phenomenon. Examples: embedded real-time controllers; vending machines.
- SIMPLE INFORMATION SYSTEMS: the real-world analogue of the JSP frame. The problem concerns users requesting and updating information about some domain. Example: database systems.
- INFORMATION DISPLAY: a machine collects information from the world and presents it in a specified form.
- SIMPLE WORKPIECES: describes the way operators' commands are linked to the manipulation of objects. Example: text editors.

Figure 3-7 shows the commanded behaviour frame and suggests the highly abstract nature of frames. There is no need here to explain the details of the notation.

Jackson's problem frames, taken together, represent a pattern language since realistic problems usually involve several frames. He argues that identifying the frame is a precursor to selecting an appropriate method. He characterizes, by way of example, the use case approach as such a method and points to some of its limitations – as we shall in Chapter 5 – with the aim of showing that its use is restricted to problem frames where user I/O dominates. This is quite correct for the conventional interpretation of what a use case is.

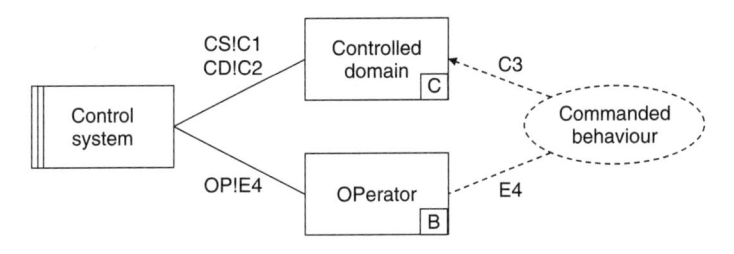

Figure 3-7 The COMMANDED BEHAVIOUR problem frame (after Jackson, 2001).

Jackson's method goes on to introduce frame concern diagrams wherein the problem domain properties are modelled. This phase of the analysis makes heavy use of state-transition diagrams but this is not the place to consider these. We will do so in Chapter 7.

3.4 Requirements and Business Rules

It is a common error to confuse business rules with requirements but they are not the same thing at all.

A business rule is a compact, atomic, well-formed, declarative statement about an aspect of a business that can be expressed in terms that can be directly related to the business and its collaborators, using simple unambiguous language that is accessible to all interested parties: business owner, business analyst, technical architect, customer and so on. This simple language may include domain-specific jargon.

The term 'well-formed' comes from Logic and needs explanation. The rules must be executable on a machine if they are to be of much use in a business rules management system. This implies that they must be convertible into statements in some formal logic: statements that are well-formed with respect to that logic.

One corollary of the declarative principle is that business rules do not describe business processes; they do, however, constrain what processes are permissible.

Business rules are statements expressed in a language, preferably a subset of a natural language such as English. I see two clear kinds of statements that must be distinguished: assertions and rules. Assertions or facts have the form: 'A is X' or 'P is true'. These are equivalent forms, e.g. I can convert the former into '"A is X" is true'. Simplifying slightly, until later in this book, rules have the equivalent forms: 'If A then X'; 'X if A'; 'When A then X'; and so on. Here X can be a fact or an action. Statements are always statements *about* something. Ross refers to these somethings as **terms**. Other authors refer to the **vocabulary** of the domain or even the **domain ontology**.

Strictly, Ontology is the philosophical science concerned with what exists: the science of Being. Here, though, it is used to mean the model of the domain that we work with including the things we can discuss, their properties and how they relate to each other. I will take the view in this book that the domain ontology is precisely an object model, usually expressed by a UML type diagram; but more on that later. Some readers might like to think of the ontology as the database schema – at least for the time being. The ontology tells us what we are allowed to discuss when we write rules. Without a sound ontology the rules are meaningless and any attempt at writing them in natural language is certainly doomed. This means that we must modify our definition slightly. We can do so by adding just one sentence. **Business rules are always interpreted against a defined domain ontology.**

Having defined what business rules are, there is still much more to say about them, such as how they may be linked together to derive new facts (inference), how they are best written (rule structure) or how they are to be discovered (knowledge elicitation). Graham (2006) discusses these issues in detail and in the context of service oriented architecture.

It should be clear now that, while business rules constitute statements about the business that are true, they are not quite the same thing as statements of what is required. They may represent constraints or show how business processes must proceed (action rules); they might even show how latent information can be uncovered or inferred. But they do not state what is required of a new or modified system.

The relationship between requirements and business rules could be as follows.

- There can be a requirement stating that certain rules must be enforced by the system.
- Rules can arise from requirements as use case or problem frame constraints.
- Rules can form part of the description of a business process.
- Rules can arise from requirements as a result of analysing domain models and type diagrams (e.g. ASSOCIATION LOOPS CONCEAL RULES).

Problem analysis should pay careful attention to the discovery of business rules provided that the analyst is clear about their rôle and provenance.

3.5 Establishing and Prioritizing the Business Objectives

We intend to use UML as our primary modelling notation for requirements analysis and specification. However, there are some things that just cannot be modelled with UML, so we need other representations. This is most true at the outset of a requirements engineering exercise.

Let us suppose that we are looking to improve a particular business area. It is enormously beneficial to be able to state what the business area does. This can be captured in a mission statement – sometimes called a project charter. If we think of the business area as providing a service then the mission statement should capture, as succinctly as possible, what this service is.

A manufacturing process might state, for example, that it should 'make a high quality product at a reasonable price, while maintaining an adequate profit margin'. If we are developing a word processing service, our mission could be to create the easiest to use and most comprehensive word processor available. Clearly, UML has no diagram type that can represent these ambitions; natural language seems to fit the bill perfectly though.

Mission statements, such as the above, can be quite vague. To pin down the requirements we must ask for much more precise objectives within each service or process area. These objectives may refer to several services that the business area provides to its customers or internally.

For any given process-oriented business area, once we have defined its mission, we are in a position to define the specific objectives of the process or service. Once again, natural language is the best modelling tool. Ideally, a joint requirements workshop will be the forum for this activity.

In a workshop, the facilitator will ask other participants to call out and discuss objectives. These are written on a flip chart or other visible medium (e.g. text can be projected from the computer with which the requirements analyst or scribe records the session). Experience has taught that there are usually about 13 objectives, either due to the fact that people run out of ideas after that much discussion, that 13 objectives comfortably fills two flip chart pages or, as a more remote possibility, reflecting some obscure law of nature yet to be articulated by rational Man.

No activity should be allowed to produce a deliverable without it being tested. This principle must be applied to the objectives by seeking a measure for each objective. For example, if our business is running a hotel and an objective is to provide a high quality service then the measure might be a star rating system as provided by many tourist boards or motoring organizations. Of course, there are cases where a precise measure is elusive. Discussing the measures is an important tool for clarifying, elucidating and completing the objectives shared and understood by the group. The discussion of measures helps a group think more clearly about the objectives and often leads to the discovery of additional ones or the modification of those already captured. Setting aside plenty of time for the discussion of the measures is seldom a waste of time. An objective that cannot be measured and/or prioritized must be rejected or, at least, consigned to a slightly modified mission statement.

The minimum requirement, from a project manager's point of view, is that it must be possible to prioritize all the objectives. A formal preference grid can be elicited by asking that each pair of objectives be ranked against each other. In workshops, this is far too time consuming and a quicker, more subjective technique is needed. One way to come quickly to the priorities is to allow participants to place votes against each objective. We usually permit each person a number of votes corresponding to about 66% of the number of objectives, e.g. 9 votes for 13 objectives. A good way to perform the voting is to give each eligible participant a number of small, sticky, coloured paper discs, of the sort that are sold in strips by most stationers. Then the rules of voting are explained: 'You may place all your stickers on one objective or distribute them across several, evenly or unevenly according to the importance you place on the objectives. You need not use all your votes; but you are not allowed to give – or sell – unused votes to other participants'. Then everyone must come up to the flip charts all at once. No hanging back to see what others do is permitted. This helps inject a dynamic atmosphere into the proceedings and stops people waiting to see what the boss does before voting.

Usually, two rounds of voting should be done, under different interpretations of what a vote signifies. The results are added together to reach a final priority score for each objective. Of course, two colours are then needed for the sticky discs. An example of two possible interpretations that can be combined is:

1. Vote from your point of view as an individual user.
2. Vote from a corporate viewpoint.

I sometimes try to help the voters remember which is which by using red and blue stickers and explaining that blue is the 'selfish' right wing or 'Thatcherite' vote and red is the lefty 'socially aware' vote. Another pair might be:

1. Vote from the supplier's viewpoint.
2. Vote from the customer's viewpoint.

Figure 3-8 illustrates the sort of things that might appear on a flip chart during this process. Every objective has a measure and I have used black and white stickers for the two rounds of voting. Note that the white vote straddling the line under the third objective constitutes a spoilt ballot paper and indicates the importance of drawing these lines. Note also that objective 5 has no votes, even though at least one voter must have suggested it. This does happen. Usually, it is because the objectives overlap; in this case if we achieve the second and third objectives then the fifth will already be gained. As a result we delete the fifth objective from our list. Adding the scores gives the result shown in Table 3-1.

Of course, the ranking would be different if there were more objectives.

For those readers familiar with DSDM, you might wonder how this approach stands up against the MoSCoW approach. Put simply, this is a *much* better way to go about things. If you just ask stakeholders which objectives are 'Must-have's then, often, everyone will say that their pet objective is an M leading to an impasse. The voting and numerical ranking is less susceptible to this. MoSCoW rankings can be added after a consensus has emerged from the full discussion that follows voting.

92 Chapter 3

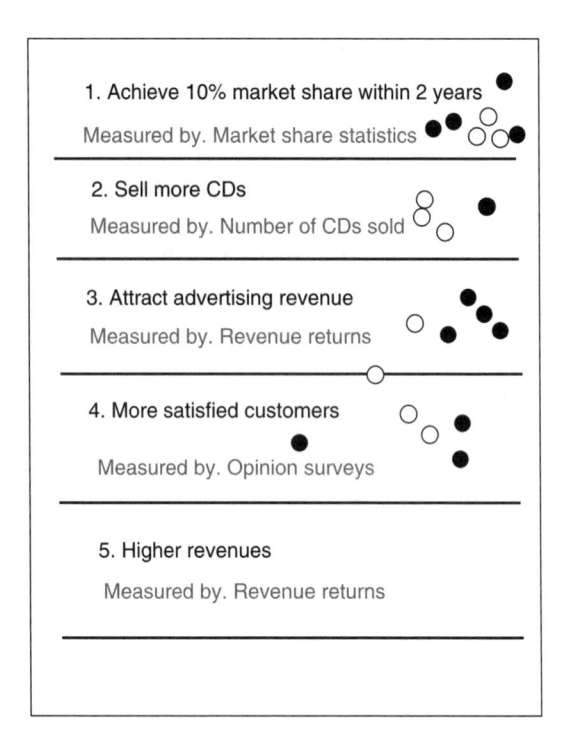

```
1. Achieve 10% market share within 2 years  ●
   Measured by. Market share statistics  ●● ○○○●
───────────────────────────────────────────
2. Sell more CDs                    ○
   Measured by. Number of CDs sold  ○○  ●
                                      ○
───────────────────────────────────────────
3. Attract advertising revenue            ●●
   Measured by. Revenue returns    ○   ● ●
───────────────────────────────────○───────
4. More satisfied customers    ○      ●
                               ●   ○○
   Measured by. Opinion surveys         ●
───────────────────────────────────────────
5. Higher revenues
   Measured by. Revenue returns
```

Figure 3-8 A flip-chart page with some objectives, measures and votes.

Table 3-1 Priorities for the objectives.

Objective number	White votes	Black votes	Total	Priority	MoSCoW rating
1	3	4	7	1st	M
2	3	4	7	1st	M
3	1	1	2	3rd	C
4	2	3	5	2nd	W

The results often generate further useful discussion and one should allow for re-prioritization at this point, if surprising results have emerged. This is often due to overlap between objectives that is highlighted by the priorities given or a subtle misunderstanding of the wording. Allow time for this and strive for a final ranking that everyone can agree upon.

Often a discussion around these issues elicits new objectives, clarifies existing ones or leads to their recombination or even placement in the overall mission statement. Issues that cannot be resolved are recorded with the names of the people responsible for resolving them. Specific assumptions and exclusions should also be recorded.

The priorities are a key tool for project management since they determine from the point of view of the business sponsor what must be implemented first. Technical dependencies must also be allowed for, of course. They also allow the project manager to negotiate on descoping projects that are in danger of overrunning a time box deadline. For this reason, the objectives must be regarded as fixed for the duration of the project even though the requirements may evolve and change quite substantially. Graham (2009) discusses this further.

We now have a mission statement, linked to several measurable and prioritized business objectives. We can now begin to construct a model of the business area and its processes using the techniques described in Chapters 4 and 5. Before doing that, let us look at a few general techniques that can help us elicit requirements in workshop or interview situations.

3.6 Soft Techniques for Requirements Elicitation

Requirements engineering is about discovering knowledge, some of which is latent; people don't know what they know. The principal things that the requirements engineer must discover are business objectives (as discussed in Section 3.5), business processes, business tasks, business rules, business services and the ontology of the business: the things and concepts that the processes manipulate and the rules and services can talk about. This section discusses an assortment of techniques that I have found useful for such knowledge discovery. We start with some insights from interview theory and knowledge engineering which may also be useful in a workshop context, with a facilitator leading discussion.

3.6.1 Using Interviewing Techniques

Many techniques that can be used in normal interviews can be readily extended for use in workshops once they are well understood. This subsection discusses just a few of the techniques that I have found particularly useful.

It is usual to divide interviews into structured and focused interviews. Typically, structured interviews are at a high level of generality and take place earlier in the discovery process. A structured interview aims to grasp an overview of the topic which is broad but shallow. It will result in elicitation of the key services, objects and concepts of the domain but not go into detail. In a workshop this corresponds to running a scoping session, where the same techniques can be used.

Focused interviews or detailed workshops go into the detail of one area and are typically narrow and deep. During the elicitation process it is essential to search for reusable elements – the grey rectangles in Figure 3-9. Applying the Pareto principle, analysts should select the area that gives

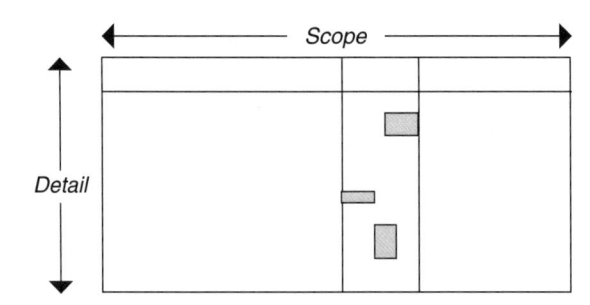

Figure 3-9 Narrow and deep versus broad and shallow approaches to interviews.

either 80% of the benefit or 80% of the predicted complexity or reuse potential as the first area to explore – preferably both. This corresponds, ideally, to about 20% of the scope of the system. This broad and shallow followed by narrow and deep scenario corresponds closely to the approach that should be followed during application prototyping.

Structured interviews follow a plan that should be prepared in advance and state the objectives of the interview or workshop session. At the start of the session, participants should agree an agenda. Then, for each agenda topic, interviewers or workshop facilitators ask questions, put out 'probes', review the results at each stage and move to the next topic. Finally, one must review the overall results and compare them with the plan, asking whether the objectives have been achieved. If not, the exercise can be repeated. It is essential that questions are open rather than closed. Open questions do not permit an answer such as 'Yes' or 'No' that closes further discussion or elaboration. **Probes** are merely particularly useful types of open question. Table 3-2 sets out some probe types with examples. Probes can use all of the six question words alluded to by Rudyard Kipling as follows.

> *I keep six honest serving men*
>   *(They taught me all I knew);*
>   *Their names are* What *and* Why *and* When
>   *And* How *and* Where *and* Who.

You might think that it is pointless to classify and label questions in this way; after all, we all learn how to ask this kind of question in infancy. The justification is that one can fall back on it in those moments in which one is lost for the right question to ask next, just as a salesman falls back on standard techniques for handling objections, such as the so-called *assumptive* close: 'Would you like some washing powder for your new washing machine?' If you can't think what to say, why not try a mode change probe?

Table 3-2 Types of probe.

Probe type	Example
Definitional	What is a …?
Additive	Go on …
Reflective	What you're saying is …
Mode change	How would your colleagues view that?
	Can you give a more concrete example?
Directive	Why is that?
	How?
	Could you be more specific?

Focused interviews are less easy to describe in the abstract than are structured ones. Their form depends more on the domain. However, techniques such as teachback, repertory grids and task analysis are commonly the ones used.

Teachback involves interviewers presenting their understanding to the users formally, maybe using slides, and receiving corrections thereby. It is a more formal version of the reflective probe. The analyst presents his/her understanding to the experts and users and hopes for criticism that will uncover gaps and errors in the understanding achieved so far. A teachback session that results in the experts agreeing that you have everything right is completely unproductive.

Basden (1990a,b) suggested another useful questioning technique, again in the context of knowledge acquisition for expert systems. He offers the example of a knowledge engineer seeking for high level rules of thumb based on experience (heuristics). Suppose, in the domain of 'gardening', that we have discovered that regular mowing produces good lawns. The knowledge engineer should not be satisfied with this because it does not show the boundaries of the intended system's competence – we do not want a system that gives confident advice in areas where it is incompetent. We need to go deeper into the understanding. One question next asked of the expert might be of the form: 'why?' The answer might be: 'because regular mowing reduces coarse grasses and encourages springy turf'. What we have obtained here are two attributes of the object 'good turf' – whose parent in a hierarchy is 'turf', of course. Why does regular mowing lead to springy turf? Well, it helps to promote leaf branching. Now we are beginning to elicit methods as we approach causal knowledge. To help define the boundaries, Basden suggests asking 'what else' and 'what about …' questions. In the example we have given the knowledge engineer should ask: 'what about drought conditions?' or 'what else gives good lawns?'

A good interviewer or facilitator plans and prepares sessions and sets clear objectives. However, adaptability is the key skill and one must be prepared to adapt or even abandon a plan that is not working. Some domain knowledge is prerequisite to facilitate open discussion, as is a good understanding of the technology to be used.

3.6.2 Repertory Grids

One of the most useful knowledge engineering techniques for eliciting objects and their structure is that of Kelly, or repertory (repertoire), grids. These grids were introduced originally in the context of clinical psychiatry by Kelly (1955). They are devices for helping analysts elicit 'personal constructs': concepts which people use in dealing with and constructing or construing their world.

Constructs are pairs of opposites, such as slow/fast, and usually correspond to attributes or associations in the business ontology. The second dimension of a grid is its **elements**, which correspond to objects of the same ontology. Elements are rated on a scale from 1 to 5, say, according to which pole of the construct they correspond to most closely. These values can then be used to 'focus' the grid: a mathematical procedure which clarifies relationships among elements and constructs. In particular, focusing ranks the elements in order of the clarity with which they are perceived and the constructs in order of their importance as classifiers of elements.

To illustrate the usefulness of Kelly grids, suppose we need to interview a user. The technique involves first identifying some elements in the application. These might be real things or concepts but should be organized into coherent sets. For example, the set {Porsche, Jaguar, Rolls Royce, Mini, Driver} has an obvious odd man out: Driver.

The use of the Kelly grid technique in its full form is not recommended. However, questioning techniques based on Kelly grids are immensely powerful in eliciting new objects and extending and refining classification structures. There are three principal techniques:

- Asking for the opposites of all elements and concepts.
- Laddering to extract generalizations.
- Elicitation by triads to extract specializations.

In Figure 3-10, we may have discovered that the concept of cars being Sporty was key. Asking for the opposite produced not 'Unsporty' but 'Family' cars; not the logical opposite but a totally new one. Thus, asking for the opposite of a class can reveal new objects or attributes. Applying this to services one might ask: 'what is the opposite of a regulatory service?'

In the technique of **laddering**, users are asked to give names for higher level concepts. 'Can you think of a word that describes all the concepts {speed, luxury, economy}?' that might produce a concept of 'value

	ELEMENTS					
Concept	Rolls Royce	Porsche	Jaguar	Mini	Trabant	Opposite
Economical	5	4	4	2	2	Costly
Comfortable	1	4	2	4	5	Basic
Sporty	5	1	3	5	5	Family
Cheap	5	4	4	2	1	Expensive
Fast	3	1	2	4	5	Slow

Figure 3-10 A Kelly grid. Scores are between 1 and 5. The left-hand pole of the concept corresponds to a low score for the element and the right (its opposite) to a high one. The grid is not focused.

for money'. This technique elicits both aggregation and classification structures. It usually produces more general concepts. For example, asking for a term that sums up both Fast and Sporty we might discover the class of 'ego massaging' cars.

Elicitation by triads is not a reference to Chinese torture but to a technique whereby, given a coherent set of elements, the user is asked to take any three and specify a concept that applies to two of them but not to the third. For example, with {Porsche, Jaguar, Mini}, top speed might emerge as an important concept. Similarly, the triad {Mini, Jaguar, Trabant} might reveal the attribute CountryOfManufacture, or the classes BritishCars and GermanCars. As a variant of this technique, users may be asked to write all the concepts or elements on index cards and divide them into two or more groups on a table. They must then name the groups to reveal the appropriate generalization or specialization. This is known as **card sorting**.

All these techniques are first-rate ways of getting at the conceptual structure of the problem space, if used with care and sensitivity. Exhaustive listing of all triads, for example, can be extremely tedious and can easily alienate users.

3.6.3 Hierarchical Task Analysis

Several of the other methods developed by knowledge engineers can be used to discover concepts. These concepts often map onto the domain ontology.

Broadly, task analysis is a functional approach to knowledge elicitation that involves breaking down a problem into a hierarchy of tasks that must be performed by a user. The approach is very similar to that of use case analysis, but it has a longer history and contains several useful insights that are not always found in expositions on use cases. Like a use case, a task is a procedure that achieves a goal. There can be many tasks that achieve the same goal.

Early versions of task analysis were developed independently, and somewhat differently, in the USA and Britain during the 1950s. In both cases, the motivation and background was mainly training needs analysis to help overcome a chronic post-war labour and skills shortage. The British concentrated on the hierarchical decomposition of tasks and on taxonomies of human skills while the Americans focused on issues such as psychometric testing. Substantive tasks were decomposed into their requisite psychological abilities; viewed as perceptual, motor and problem-solving skills. The model of human cognition was fairly primitive at this time and not able to analyse complex tasks such as programming.

A **task** is an activity or set of actions undertaken by an agent assuming a rôle to change a system's state to some goal state. Goals may have subgoals and be achieved by executing procedures (sets of actions). It is a matter of some skill to set goals at the appropriate level; neither too abstract nor too specific. Tasks involve objects, actions and taxonomies (classification structures). Sometimes the goals are clear. In other cases the goal is not known at the start or may change during the task, as new factors emerge. UI designers should consider people, rôles, organizations and technology in their approach. A goal is a desired state and a task is the means of reaching it. For example, my goal might be to stop feelings of hunger. The corresponding task is to eat. This may involve setting subgoals (or implied tasks) such as finding food, chewing, etc.

There are two kinds of task: **internal tasks** are the tasks that the user must carry out to use the system (having knowledge, depressing certain keys in sequence, etc.); **external tasks** are those tasks that the user must perform using the system to support them (interpreting reports, writing documents, etc.). Internal tasks enable external tasks.

Just as there are two kinds of task there are two approaches to design. We can attempt to merely support each of the external tasks. This approach does not challenge the underlying business processes or attempt to change them and Barfield (1993) suggests that it amounts to building 'intelligent notebooks'. The alternative is to attempt to build a model underneath the task level including some understanding of what is being done and why. If the existing task can be modelled then the model can be criticized and optimized. This may lead to suggestions as to how to improve the business processes. Building internal task models is tantamount to building a knowledge model in cases where the task is not merely a sequence of simple external tasks. The skills of the knowledge engineer are then useful. When the task normally involves group interaction, as with CASE or group work, then some internal task knowledge may become externalized. Typically these kinds of system are the hardest to model and Barfield points out forcibly, and correctly in my view, how this is evinced by most CASE tools that usually enforce too many trivial tasks and sometimes miss out the important ones.

To be useful for system builders, task knowledge should be central, typical and representative. **Centrality** means that the task is critical to achieving the goal. If most users mention it, it is likely to be central. **Representativeness** holds when the mental model corresponds closely to the domain model that experts would hold. **Typicality** occurs when the task knowledge is typical of most users.

There is a link between task analysis and AI planning theory in that an actor searches for subgoals in order to execute a task, just as in constructing a plan in a domain such as job-shop scheduling.

There are three fundamental activities (which may be regarded loosely as steps) involved in task analysis. These activities are: to define the objectives of the system, perform task knowledge elicitation and finally carry out a knowledge analysis – looking for the knowledge and skills involved in task performance. Again there is a strong link here to the domain of expert systems and the skills of the knowledge engineer. Typically, knowledge engineers carry a tool bag of more or less formal knowledge elicitation techniques which includes such approaches as task analysis itself, topic analysis, Kelly grids and card sorts, rating scales and frequency counts, skill profiles and taxonomies of human performance. These techniques will be described further in Chapter 7 when we deal with the object identification techniques within SOMA. Other techniques include reading about the domain, introspection, examining sample output, observation (both direct and indirect), structured and focused interviews, protocol analysis (both concurrent and retrospective), brainstorming, questionnaires and having the analyst perform the task after instruction from the user or expert (also called teachback). Direct observation involves the physical presence of the observer whereas indirect observation could utilize video recordings. Both are time consuming and may be intrusive. Concurrent protocols require the expert to give a running commentary on the task being performed while retrospective ones are reports on task performance given afterwards.

Tasks are usually expressed in a simple task–action grammar whereby each task has the form:

```
Subject-Verb-Direct object-[Preposition-Indirect object]
```

Typically, the verb will be a transitive verb. The subject corresponds to either an actor or to some active component of a system. For example, a deal capture task could be expressed as 'Dealer enters bargain details', where there is no indirect object, or a deal confirmation task as 'System sends confirmation to counterparty', where there is. It is important that tasks are only decomposed to **atomic** level; that is, to the lowest level that introduces no terms extraneous to the domain. We would thus exclude tasks such as: 'Dealer enters bargain details with keyboard'. The term 'keyboard' is not within the trading domain.

The objectives of task analysis in general can be outlined as the definition of:

- the objectives of the task;
- the procedures used;
- any actions and objects involved;
- time taken to accomplish the task;
- frequency of operations;
- occurrence of errors;
- involvement of subordinate and superordinate tasks.

The result is a task description, which may be formalized in some way, using flowcharts, logic trees or a formal grammar, as above. The process does not, however, describe knowledge directly. That is, it does not attempt to capture the underlying knowledge structure but tries to represent how the task is performed and what is needed to achieve its aim. Any conceptual or procedural knowledge and any objects that are discovered are only elicited incidentally.

In task analysis, the objective constraints on problem solving are exploited, usually prior to a later protocol (i.e. textual) analysis stage. The method consists in arriving at a classification of the factors involved in problem solving and the identification of the atomic 'tasks' involved. The categories that apply to an individual task might include:

- time taken;
- how often performed;
- procedures used;
- actions used;
- objects used;
- error rate;
- position in task hierarchy.

This implies that it is also necessary to identify the actions and types in a taxonomic manner. For example, if we were to embark on a study of poker playing we might start with the following crude structure.

```
Types: Card, Deck, Suit, Hand, Player, Table, Coin
Actions: Deal, Turn, See, Collect
```

One form of task analysis assumes that concepts are derivable from pairing actions with types, e.g. 'See player', 'Deal card'. Once the concepts can be identified it is necessary to identify plans or objectives (win game, make money) and strategies (bluff at random) and use this analysis to identify the knowledge required and used by matching object–action pairs to task descriptions occurring in task sequences. This is important since objects and services are always best identified in relation to purposes.

Another approach to cognitive task analysis (Braune and Foshay, 1983) is based on human information processing theory. It is less function-oriented compared to the basic approach to task analysis as outlined above and concentrates on the analysis of concepts. The second stage of a three-step strategy is to define the relations between concepts by analysing examples, then to build on the resulting schema by analysing larger problem sets. The schema that results from the analysis is a model of the knowledge structure of an expert, similar to that achieved by card sorting methods, describing the 'chunking' of knowledge by that expert. This chunking is controlled by the idea of 'expectancy' according to the theory of human information processing; i.e. the selection of the correct stimuli for solving the problem, and the knowledge of how to deal with these stimuli.

In some ways it could be held that the use of a formal technique such as task analysis in the above example can add nothing that common sense could not have derived. However, its use in structuring the information derived from interviews is invaluable for the following reasons. First, the decomposition of complex tasks into more primitive or unitary actions enables one to arrive at a better understanding of the interface between the tasks and the available implementation technology, as will be seen in the above analysis. This leads to a far better understanding of the possibilities for empirical measurement of the quality of the interface. The second factor is that the very process of constructing and critiquing the task hierarchy diagrams helps to uncover gaps in the analysis, and thus remove any contradictions.

Task analysis is primarily useful in service identification rather than for finding objects, although objects are elicited incidentally.

3.6.4 Object Discovery Techniques

When building systems within a service oriented architecture, we need to construct models. These models include models of our business objectives, business processes, business services and business rules, all of which will probably not be rendered in UML. All these only make sense if the model includes references to business objects: entities and concepts. Thus our models are meaningless unless we can relate them to a **business ontology**: a model of the objects of the domain that probably *will* be expressed in UML. We will go into the details of this in Chapter 7 but, for now, I will explore a few techniques with which analysts can use to make a first cut at identifying the domain objects.

To understand these object identification approaches it is useful to digress briefly and consider some of the insights that philosophers have had on the topic. The dominant philosophical view in Western scientific thinking has been, for a very long time, Empiricism. I believe that this clouds our view of what objects are in various subtle ways and must be overcome by the analyst. For example, Empiricism holds that objects are merely bundles of properties. An Empiricist would maintain that objects are out there just waiting to be perceived and an extreme version holds that this is easy to do. A phenomenologist view, on the contrary, recognizes that perception is an active, iterative, creative process and that objects come both from our intentions and from the objectively existing world in an ever-repeating dialectical process. When we see a tree we bring our ideas about trees to bear before we make the perception. As the biologist J. Z. Young (1986) puts it, when we look: 'The whole process [of vision] is the search for information that may answer a question asked, so that to a large extent *we know already what we are going to see*' (emphasis in original, p. 145).

An even richer view suggests that real-world abstractions are a reflection of social relations and processes, as well as having an objective basis – as we will explore in Chapter 5. Objects may be apprehended by an analyst familiar with a domain in many different ways; choosing the 'best' representation is a fundamental contribution that human intelligence always makes to computer systems. Some objects correspond directly to real-world objects such as people or chairs, but others, such as stacks or quarks, correspond to invented abstractions. Abstractions, whether they represent objects or services, sum up the relevant divisions of the domain. What is relevant may depend on the application, but this will compromise the reusability of the abstraction and so the designer should try to think of abstractions with as wide an applicability as possible. On the other hand, care should be taken not to compromise efficiency with over-general abstractions. The more high level our systems become, the more they are to be regarded as tools for enhancing communication between humans. The more the human aspect is emphasized, the more the subjective factor in object identification comes to the fore.

Analysts and designers can learn much from two key branches of Philosophy: Epistemology and Ontology. Epistemology is the theory of knowledge; what knowledge is, how it is possible and what can be known. Ontology is the science of Being: what is and how it comes about. These two sciences are intimately related because we are interested in true knowledge: knowledge of what really is. Both disciplines are concerned with the nature of objects and are therefore directly relevant to the identification of objects in analysis and design. This view is taken by Wand (1989) who proposed a formal model of objects based on Bunge's mathematical ontology. Unfortunately, this ontology is atomistic: it conceives things as reducible to irreducible components. Nevertheless, the principle of an ontologically based model, albeit not a formal model, is a sound one.

The simplest approach to object identification, first suggested by Abbott (1983), is **textual analysis**. One extracts the objects and methods from a

Table 3-3 Textual analysis.

Part of speech	Model component	Example
Proper noun	Instance	J. Smith
Improper noun	Class/type/rôle	Toy
Doing verb	Operation/service	Buy
Being verb	Classification	'Is an'
Having verb	Association/aggregation	'Has an'
Stative verb[a]	Pre- or post-condition	'Are owned'
Modal verb	Business rule, pre-condition, post-condition or guarantee	'Must be'
Adjective	Attribute value or class	Unsuitable
Adjectival phrase	Association	The customer with children
	Operation	The customer who bought the laptop
Transitive verb	Operation	Enter
Intransitive verb	Exception or event	Depend

[a] Stative verbs are verbs that indicate that a state of affairs holds and which are always compound constructions in English that use 'to be' as an auxiliary. 'To be happy' is a stative verb whereas 'to increase' is not.

textual description of the problem such as a specification or a use case goal. Objects then correspond to nouns and services to verbs. Verbs and nouns can be further subclassified. For example, there are proper and improper nouns, and verbs to do with doing, being and having. Doing verbs usually give rise to methods or services, being verbs to classification structures and having verbs to associations or aggregation. Transitive verbs generally correspond to methods, but intransitive ones may refer to exceptions or time-dependent events; in a phrase such as 'the shop closes', for example. Table 3-3 gives some examples. This process is a helpful guide but it must be understood that this is **not** a formal technique in any sense of the word. Intuition is still required to get hold of the best model.

As we will see in later chapters, just spotting the nouns and verbs in the post-conditions of use cases is a very useful technique for establishing the vocabulary of the domain and thereby the static type model.

A complementary approach is to use some simple patterns. Coad *et al.* (1999) say that there are exactly five kinds of archetypal components and give standard features for each one. Each archetype is associated with a colour – based on the colours of commercially available pads of paper stickers. Their archetypes are components representing:

- descriptions (blue);
- parties (e.g. people, organizations), places or things (green);
- rôles (yellow);
- moments in or intervals of time (pink), better called episodes, I think;
- interfaces and plug-points (white).

Each of these comes equipped with default attributes and operations that can be adapted to specific problems or domains, although we have found limited use for this.

It is difficult to be completely convinced at first that the world is really so simple but the idea is a very useful one during specification and I have yet to find anything missing.

In addition to object identification, there are few checks that we can do on the internal consistency of the ontology; again we take philosophical enquiry as a guide.

Brooks (1986) notes the difference between essence and accidents in software engineering. The distinction is, in fact, a very old one going back to Aristotle and the mediaeval Scholastics. The idea of essence was attacked by modern philosophers from Descartes onwards, who saw objects as mere bundles of properties with no essence. This gave rise to severe difficulties because it fails to explain how we can recognize a chair with no properties in common with all the previous chairs we have experienced. A school of thought known as Phenomenology, represented by philosophers such as Hegel, Brentano, Husserl and Heidegger, arose *inter alia* from attempts to solve this kind of problem. Another classical problem, important for object-oriented analysis, is the problem of categories. Aristotle laid down a set of fixed pairs of categories through the application of which thought could proceed. These were concepts such as Universal/Individual, Necessary/Contingent and so on. Kant gave a revised list but, as Hegel once remarked, didn't put himself to much trouble in the doing. The idealist Hegel showed that the categories were related and grew out of each other in thought. Finally, the materialist Marx showed that the categories of thought arose out of human social and historical practice:

> *My dialectic method is not only different from the Hegelian, but is its direct opposite. To Hegel, the life-process of the human brain, i.e. the process of thinking, which, under the name of 'the Idea', he even transforms into an independent subject, is the demiurgos of the real world, and the real world is only the external, phenomenal form of 'the Idea'. With me, on the contrary, the ideal is nothing else than the material world reflected by the human mind, and translated into forms of thought (Marx, 1961).*

So, we inherit categories from our forebears, but also learn new ones from our practice in the world.

All phenomenologists and dialecticians, whether idealist or materialist, acknowledge that the perception or apprehension of objects is an active process. Objects are defined by the purpose of the thinking subject, although for a materialist they correspond to previously existing patterns of energy in the world – including of course patterns in the brain. A chair is a coherent object for the purposes of sitting (or perhaps for bar-room brawling) but not for the purposes of sub-atomic physics. You may be wondering by now what all this has got to do with object-oriented analysis. What does this analysis tell us about the identification of objects?

The answer is that it directs attention to the user and his/her tasks. It means that we must ask about purpose when we partition the world into objects. It also tells us that common purpose is required for reusability, because services designed for one set of users may not correspond to anything in the world of another set. In fact, reuse is only possible because society and production determine a common basis for perception. A clear understanding of Ontology helps to avoid the introduction of accidental, as opposed to essential, objects. Thus, Fred Brooks, in my opinion, either learned some Ontology or had it by instinct alone.

Some more useful tips for identifying important, rather than arbitrary, objects can be gleaned from a study of philosophy, especially Hegelian philosophy and modern Phenomenology. Stern (1990) analyses Hegel's concept of the object in great detail. The main difference between this notion of objects and other notions is that objects are neither arbitrary 'bundles' of properties (the Empiricist or Kantian view), nor are they based on a mysterious essence, but are conceptual structures representing universal abstractions. The practical import of this view is that it allows us to distinguish between genuine high level abstractions such as Man and completely contingent ones such as Red Objects. Objects may be judged according to various, historically determined, categories. For example 'this rose is red' is a judgment in the category of quality. The important judgments for object-oriented analysis and their relevant uses are those shown in Table 3-4.

The categorical judgment is the one that reveals genuine high level abstractions. We call such abstractions **essential**. Qualitative judgments only reveal contingent and accidental properties unlikely to be reusable, but nevertheless of semantic importance within the application. Beware, for example, of abstractions such as 'red roses' or 'dangerous toys'; they are qualitative and probably not reusable without internal restructuring. Objects revealed by qualitative judgments are called **accidental**. Accidental objects are mere bundles of arbitrary properties, such as 'expensive, prickly, red roses wrapped in foil'. Essential objects are universal, in the sense that

Table 3-4 Analysis of judgments.

Judgment	Example	Feature
Quality	This ball is red	Attribute
Reflection	This herb is medicinal	Relationship
Categorical	Fred is a man	Generalization
Value	Fred should be kind	Rules

they are (or belong to) classes which correspond to objects that already have been identified by human practice and are stable in time and space. What they are depends on human purposes; prior to trade money was not an object. Reflective judgments are useful for establishing usage relationships and methods; being medicinal connects herbs to the sicknesses that they cure. Value judgments may be outside the scope of a computer system, but can reveal semantic rules. For example, we could have, at a very high business analysis level, 'employees should be rewarded for loyalty' which at a lower level would translate to the rule: 'if five years' service then an extra three days' annual leave'.

For business and user-centred design, the ontological view dictates that objects should have a purpose. Service operations too should have a goal. This is usually accomplished by specifying post-conditions.

A useful rule of thumb for distinguishing essential objects is that one should ask if more can be said about the object than can be obtained by listing its attributes and methods. It is cheating in the use of this rule merely to keep on adding more properties. Examples abound of this type of object. In a payroll system, an employee may have red hair or be able to fly a plane. Nothing special can be said about the class of employees who can fly, unless, of course, we are dealing with the payroll for an airline. What is essential is context sensitive.

It is not only the purposes of the immediate users that concern us, but the purposes of the user community at large and, indeed, of software engineers who will reuse your services. Therefore, analysts should keep reuse in mind throughout the requirements elicitation process. Designing or analysing is not copying user and expert knowledge. As with perception, it is a creative act. A designer, analyst or knowledge engineer takes the purposes and perceptions of users and transforms them. He/she is not a *tabula rasa* – a blank sheet upon which knowledge is writ but a creative participant.

3.7 Summary

Many different approaches to requirements engineering have been taken. These include the following major styles.

- Classic requirements engineering, usually involving the production of large, complex, written functional specifications.
- Formal methods based on logic; though these really only deal with the *specification* of systems and not requirements *per se*.
- Use cases. When used in the usual style these too fail to address the whole problem of requirements; they too are tools for system specification.

- Various approaches based on human factors.
- The Soft Systems Method.
- Jackson Problem Frames.
- Mixed approaches.
- Just Do It (JFDI) – which is to say that some approach exists but is unarticulated, so that it is hard to repeat or share with other teams.

The approach that is most appropriate depends heavily on the cultures of development organization and the customer and upon the type of problem: real-time, safety critical, embedded, mass-market, etc.

Requirements elicitation is the process whereby a development agency discovers what is needed and why. **Requirements analysis** is the process of understanding and modelling the requirements that have been or are being elicited.

UML is a notation and not a method. It has its origins in several earlier notations and methods originated in database design, programming languages, formal methods and the object-oriented analysis and design methods of the 1990s. It is a widely accepted standard and provides a common language for developers. There is good tool support and, used with MDA, encourages modelling.

There are many diagram types but the most used are these.

- Use case diagrams.
- Class diagrams (often used for and confused with type diagrams).
- Sequence diagrams.
- Collaboration diagrams (actually just another notation for sequence diagrams).
- State transition diagrams.
- Activity diagrams.

UML also contains OCL: its own formal specification language.

Use cases are a useful representation for specification and some of the requirements. But there have been problems with the theory, not least the introduction of the procedural idea of a 'sequence of transactions'. Also, generally, attention is focused on some system boundary, violating Jackson's caveats and warnings. A better way to do things is to utilize the use case notation along with UML stereotypes to create rich pictures á la Soft Systems Method. A rich picture enables one to discuss the basic business processes and business rules more easily with users. In this way, use cases can be used to represent much more of the requirements space.

All requirements can, in principle, be expressed as use cases and vice versa, but it is not always sensible to do so.

All requirements statements, whether expressed as use cases or not, should be:

- correct;
- complete;
- unambiguous (although fuzzy statements are permissible under certain circumstances);
- verifiable;
- modifiable;
- implementation independent;
- clear;
- concise;
- consistent;
- understandable (by customers too);
- well organized;
- traceable.

It is convenient to classify requirements into categories as follows.

- Product features.
- System capabilities.
- Performance issues.
- Security.
- Reliability issues such as the frequency and severity of failure, mean time to failure, accuracy (e.g. of calculations), recoverability and predictability.

Non-functional issues are of two kinds.

- Usability issues. These include aesthetics, ergonomics, consistency in the user interface, online and context-sensitive help, documentation and training materials and learnability and, indeed, forgetability.
- Maintainability issues. These include testability, extensibility, adaptability, localizability (internationally), compatibility, configurability, serviceability and installability.

Finally, there are the constraints on possible implementations. These are of two kinds: constraints that are constraints of functions or use cases and others. The use case constraints split further into two categories.

- Implementation constraints: standards, existing systems, resource limits, database integrity policy, implementation languages, operating environment, etc.

- Interface constraints: external interactions and their formats, timings, etc.

The other constraints will vary but may include physical constraints such as material, size, shape, weight, etc., physical network configuration and hardware manufacturer.

A **problem frame** is a structure consisting of principal parts and a solution task. The principal parts correspond to actors, use cases and business objects, along with other actions and goal-oriented conversations. The solution task is the work one has to do to meet some requirement concerning these parts or objects. Each frame may have a set of rules that connect pairs of domains. Problem context diagrams become problem diagrams with the addition of **requirements**, represented by dashed ellipses; the dashed connectors are **requirements references**. The latter may be directed to indicate that the reference is a constraint on the solution. Problem frames provide not only a requirements engineering technique but potentially also an architectural technique because they describe not a solution but a suitable approach to finding a solution. Problem frames form a pattern language, since realistic problems usually involve several frames. The main problem is that the technique is quite hard to grasp the idea of, maybe because of its roots in formality.

A business rule is a compact, atomic, well-formed, declarative statement about an aspect of a business that can be expressed in terms that can be directly related to the business and its collaborators, using simple unambiguous language that is accessible to all interested parties: business owner, business analyst, technical architect, customer and so on. This simple language may include domain-specific jargon. One corollary of the declarative principle is that business rules do not describe business processes; they do, however, constrain what processes are permissible. It is a common error to confuse business rules with requirements but they are not the same thing at all.

The relationship between requirements and business rules could be as follows.

- There can be a requirement stating that certain rules must be enforced by the system.
- Rules can arise from requirements as use case or problem frame constraints.
- Rules can form part of the description of a business process.
- Rules can arise from requirements as a result of analysing domain models and type diagrams (e.g. ASSOCIATION LOOPS CONCEAL RULES).

The vocabulary in which we can discuss the rules – their subject matter – is called the domain ontology and can be represented by a UML type model. Business rules are always interpreted against a defined domain ontology.

Our approach to requirements engineering starts by establishing the project mission and a set of measurable (i.e. testable) business objects. Setting aside time for the discussion of the measures is seldom a waste of time. Next we must prioritize all the objectives with numerical ranking. This is best done using a simple voting scheme. The priorities are a key tool for project management.

There are several soft requirements elicitation techniques that the analysts should know about. These include planning and conducting structured and focused interviews, probes, teachback, task analysis, repertory grids, card sorting and textual analysis. Also the following questioning techniques are handy.

- Asking for the opposites of all elements and concepts.
- Laddering to extract generalizations.
- Elicitation by triads to extract specializations.

Finally, we looked at several useful object and service discovery techniques, including task analysis, textual (protocol) analysis and the analysis of judgments.

3.8 Bibliographical Notes

Several standard texts describe conventional approaches to requirements engineering. These include those by Davis (1993), Gause and Weinberg (1989) and Macaulay (1996). Wieringa (1996) is a popular text that provides extensive guidance on how to analyse requirements using functional decomposition, entity–relationship models and JSD, and emphasizes the production of written requirements specifications but says little about knowledge elicitation. The approach is basically an extension of Information Engineering or SSADM and, as such, would not suit either a service-oriented or agile approach to development.

This chapter only gave a tiny glimpse of Jackson's (2001) problem frame method. The reader is strongly encouraged to study the original text – though warned that it is not exactly bedtime reading. His 1995 book on requirements engineering is a modern classic.

The topic of how to use business objective priorities in project management is discussed further by Graham (2009).

CHAPTER 4

Business Process Modelling

*I have no precious time at all to spend,
Nor services to do, till you require.*
William Shakespeare (Sonnet LVII)

Once the mission of a business area and its measurable business objectives have been established and the latter prioritized, the next step in requirements engineering for service oriented architecture is to understand the key business processes that the area is responsible for. We do this by modelling them as we continue to probe the knowledge of our users and domain experts. Having modelled existing processes we can move on to designing alternative and, it is to be hoped, better processes.

After some preliminary justifications and a little history, this chapter introduces some popular and powerful notations for business process modelling (BPM). We restrict the discussion in this chapter to what I call *network* process models, which are the conventional ones used by the business process management movement. In Chapter 5, I present a more innovative but very practical approach to BPM that can be used with or instead of the methods of this chapter but is particularly useful when one wishes to explore the collaborative, human aspects of business processes.

4.1 The Origins of and Need for Business Process Modelling

Although people have been modelling businesses since Adam Smith and drawing network model diagrams (such as procedure flow charts) at least since the 1940s, the modern business process management movement grew out of an earlier focus on what was called business process re-engineering (BPR). BPR became a fashionable topic during the first half of the 1990s and received much attention. It was locally, but not universally, successful, but it did help a few businesses to reorganize their operations and change their relationship to information technology radically and irreversibly. Typically this has been also associated with a move to evolutionary and agile development and sometimes with the adoption of new computer technology and e-commerce.

Business process re-engineering is the radical rethinking and redesign of an entire business, its processes, organizational structure, management, jobs and value system. Its aim is dramatic performance improvement. It is accomplished by first identifying the key processes needed to do business and then breaking through organizational and functional divisions that could impede these processes. Processes are viewed from new angles and new organizational structures invented to support them. Increasing global competition still makes many businesses feel compelled to consider BPR and business process management as enablers of greater business agility.

BPR and business process management projects must be driven by business requirements and backed fully by senior management, with regular and open feedback to staff. IT is usually an enabler of business process management, because the legacy must be removed or wrapped before changes become feasible. Also, IT staff often have a cross-functional perspective that eludes many line managers.

The idea of BPR was to redefine jobs by making corporate information accessible to all and giving those in direct contact with the task the power to make decisions. Unfortunately, it is largely an art rather than a science because the analyst has to leap intuitively to what is sometimes called 'the great idea'. The examples quoted in the literature all have such a great idea, e.g. (Hammer, 1990; Davenport and Short, 1990). Ford was able to reduce the size of its Accounts Payable headcount from 500 to 125 by paying for goods upon receipt rather than matching invoices and orders. This was enabled by a computer system but the great idea was generated from the observation that Mazda had an equivalent department with only five people in it. Mutual Benefit Life similarly reduced its underwriting turnaround from 24 to 4 hours by making a 'case manager', equipped with expert systems technology, responsible for the whole process. Here it seems the great idea arose directly from the technological potential of expert systems combined with the propensity to think outside current organizational constraints. One might also note that, in these case studies, the benefits are highly similar to those now claimed for SOA projects.

These days, increasingly zealous regulatory environments make employee empowerment less of a priority than the need to enforce and audit procedures. Business process management is thus used to understand and enforce existing processes as well as to change them. SOA plays an increasing important rôle in providing (and orchestrating) support for process workers.

The total quality and BPR movements both emphasized process over functional specialization. More recently the term BPR is seldom used; instead people talk about business process innovation or (continuous) process improvement and current commentators on business process management, such as those contributing to (Towers and McGregor, 2005), echo the sentiments of the BPR movement under these banners. Of course, the idea is basically the same. Business process management is the umbrella term used and is also often abbreviated BPM, but we reserve the abbreviation for business process *modelling* in this chapter.

Another formative influence on business process management is variously known as computer supported co-operative work (CSCW), workflow automation, groupware and collaborative work support. It involved various technologies from document image management, scanners, multimedia display, broadband networks, full-content database retrieval and specialized technologies based on insights from linguistics, AI, biology, anthropology and other social sciences. Workflow software, used largely for document information management systems, was designed to automate existing, repetitive, multi-actor processes while groupware tries to support *ad hoc* forms of co-operation and co-ordination. Group work emphasizes the social aspects of work and thought and CSCW emphasized this further. The split reflects a dichotomy within the business process management community, which either emphasizes the automation and streamlining of existing processes and the enforcement of 'best practice' or the entire obliteration of unnecessary work. Successful introduction of groupware correlates with flat organizational structures where the norm is people working in teams to solve problems rather than individuals reporting upwards in order to have their decisions authorized.

Although business process management has strong roots in workflow, there are two significant differences. Firstly, workflow focused on processes where people carried out the tasks (as with document information management) rather than including some automated processes. Secondly, workflow systems tended not to cross organizational boundaries.

An orientation towards process, it is said, helps to produce:

- increases in efficiency and effectiveness;
- cost reductions;
- greater process flexibility and therefore adaptability;
- greater job satisfaction;
- higher quality products.

It has become commonplace to appoint a 'process engineer' to oversee the delivery of these benefits.

Business process management projects fail for many reasons, including the following.

- Refusal to dispose of legacy IT assets, existing management structures and business practices.
- Over-reliance on package software (such as ERP systems) to solve all problems at a stroke.
- Failure to master modelling, so that incompatible systems interact to produce incorrect processes.
- Failure to master modelling, so that every time a new connexion is made a new semantic transformation is required.
- Lack of clear strategy and resistance from 'robber barons' in management positions.
- Failure to flatten management structures radically.
- Resistance to multi-skilling and multi-tasking among staff and management.
- Excessive focus on cost cutting.
- Lack of patience – the budget is cut before tangible results emerge.
- Lack of understanding of customers.

IT practices up to now have tended to lock organizations into their existing methods of working. This is partly a failure of modelling but partly because changes to computer systems take too long. The move to agile development is thus very important for IT within a business that is adopting business process management.

Business process innovation cannot be accomplished without business process modelling. Also, evolutionary agile development is nearly always an opportunity to re-engineer some aspect of the business.

4.2 Business Process Modelling in a Nutshell

Business process management cannot succeed, except in the simplest of cases, without good business process models. It is therefore time to look at this topic. In this chapter we will cover the two most popular network modelling languages and the leading process execution language: WS-BPEL.

As we will see, network business process models look like algorithms: steps with conditional branches, loops and even parallelism. Because of this they can be implemented on a computer, which can accept a process description as input, initiate it and manage or control its execution. Thus, one of the key advantages of using the network modelling notations is that there can be an automatable mapping to an execution language.

The diagrams we draw are process definitions. The computer runs instances of these definitions. In other words, the diagrams are process models. When specific data are provided, it is possible to create and run a process instance. Processes are comprised of tasks and these can be automated (done by machines) or manual (done by people).

A task can be executed when triggered by data or it can be placed on a queue for action by users or external services, e.g. a credit check. Normally, tasks are locked once an agent – machine or human – accepts them for processing. Once completed control is returned with data to the supervening process and the task is removed from the queue.

Network business process modelling lets analysts design the high level logic of an application using a flowchart-style notation.

Despite its power and many benefits, there are some limitations on network BPM. It is only suitable when there is an important set of states that characterize the process. As Havey (2005) points out, such applications should be long running, have persistent state, be event driven or involved in the orchestration of human interactions. He also says that BPM diagrams are a poor fit for other applications such as the design of vending machines and the like, where the sense of state is quite fleeting and inessential. Pawson and Matthews (2002) give a lovely example of an inappropriately enforced process model. Richard Pawson was visiting America and phoned a car-hire company. He was asked to provide the number of his driving licence and a raft of other personal details: a process that took several minutes. Only then was he asked to specify the kind of car he wanted. The response came back quickly: 'We sure don't have any of that kinda automobile, Sir'.

A non process-based model whereby Richard could have given the information in the order that suited *him* would have been a million times more appropriate.

To do BPM we need a design notation or language that is rigorous, business-oriented and computer-oriented: seemingly contradictory requirements. We need the business people to understand the initial representation but also want to convert it into an executable language: one that will run in some unexotic runtime environment such as an application server, which will handle things such as security and scalability. Running process must be monitored if the business is to retain control and prosper. Therefore, not only do we need a mapping between the notation and the executable forms of the model, we need a mapping back to some form understandable by users. Often, in current systems, this form is a management console.

There have been many notations and methods for network business process modelling, including the dreadful but popular IDEF0, but there are two that have emerged as industry standards: UML's activity diagrams and the increasing popular BPMN, both now under the enfolding wing of the OMG. We will only consider these two, starting with activity diagrams.

As an interesting aside, anecdotal evidence from various consultants indicates that developers tend to take readily to activity diagrams whereas business people seem to be more comfortable with BPMN, or at least to a useful subset of it – for it can be fearsomely complex, as we shall see.

4.3 UML Activity Diagrams

UML provides only one notation explicitly for business process modelling: the activity diagram. Activity diagrams are said to be a special case of state charts, which implies that they must describe the state of some thing – or object. However, the way they are used, as Martin and Odell (1998) point out, makes them look dangerously like data flow diagrams, albeit with some characteristics of flow charts added. Their origins were in the Ptech method and Martin/Odell event schemata. The states are usually 'process states'. Figure 4-1 shows an activity diagram in the domain of order processing. You will see that it is entirely unclear which object(s) the process states are states of – unless order processing is itself an object of some sort. We can improve the situation somewhat by adding swimlanes, as we have done in this figure.

In the figure, process states are rounded rectangles and arrows represent, possibly conditional, threads of control flow. The diamonds are decision branches, as in a flowchart. The thick horizontal bars represent forks and joins of control. It is distinctly better to annotate these with pre- and post-conditions (guards), as we have done with the 'order prepared' fork. I have shown two swimlanes with grey outlines and names.

The problem is that, without swimlanes, the processes are entirely 'disembodied' and the notation is not object-oriented at all. By 'disembodied' I mean that the processes are not encapsulated within any business object and that it is unclear who or what initiates or carries out the processes. The advantage of this is that no assumptions about the allocation of responsibilities have been made, so that attention is not focused on any particular implementation of the business process. However, this is only apparently so; in early versions of UML these diagrams were said to be state charts, so the states must be states of something – we just haven't said what explicitly. Using swimlanes makes the assumption more clear. But even here there are problems. Remarkably, Rumbaugh *et al.* (1999) state that, as an organizational unit for activity diagrams, the swimlane 'has no inherent

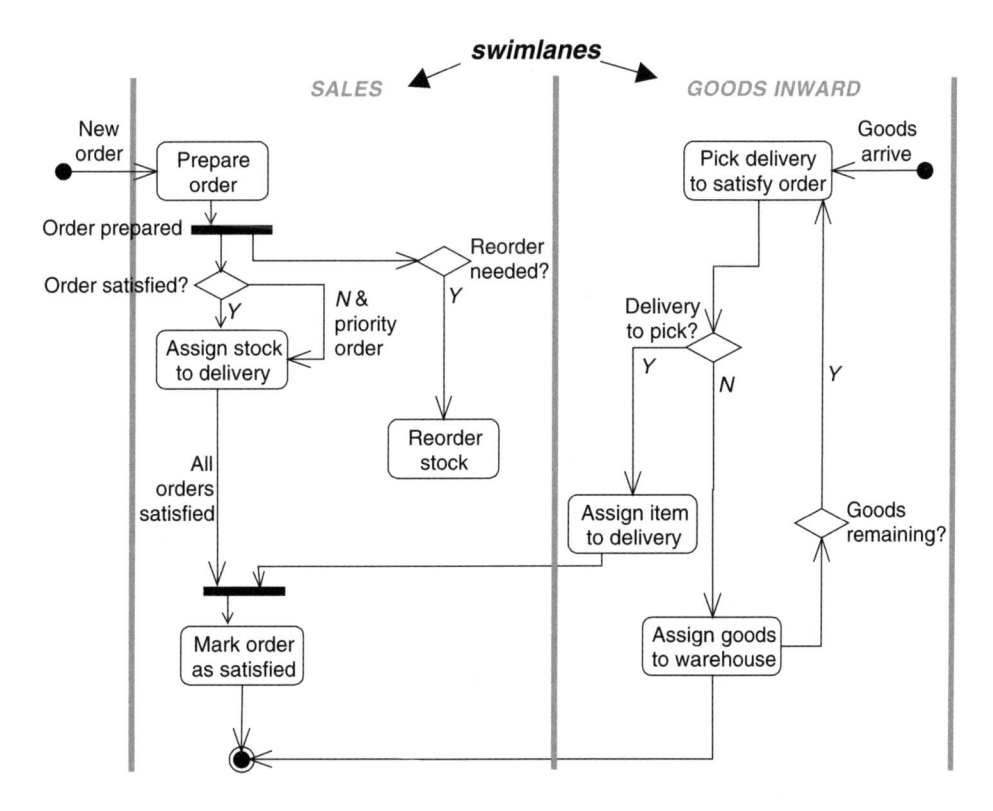

Figure 4-1 An activity diagram for order processing.

semantics': it can mean whatever you like! Most people seem to use them to represent functional units within the organization; so we are straight back to a set of assumptions about business process implementation.

Were we to draw the same process as a state-transition diagram, we would have to make the states (which correspond to the branch points in Figure 4-1) of an order object: states such as Prepared, Satisfied, Arrived, etc. This at least has the advantage of being declarative – as against the procedural style of the corresponding activity diagram – but it loses the feel of the order being an artifact merely subsidiary to some process (one aimed at making money). The other point worth making is that activity diagrams grow more rapidly than statecharts as problem complexity increases and can become unusably large for even averagely complex processes.

Martin and Odell (1998) give the following criteria for deciding whether or not to use this kind of state-based representation. Consider using activity diagrams if:

- an object has complex, significant state (use state charts);
- there is complex interaction between a few objects which trigger state changes in each other – as often found in real-time control systems;

- object behaviour is event driven and single threaded and objects have only one state variable (note that business processes are notoriously multi-threaded);
- the user culture supports their use – as in the telecomms sector.

Avoid them if:

- there are several threads (as in a typical business process);
- there is complex interaction between large numbers of objects;
- objects have several significant state variables.

Activity diagrams are reminiscent of what O&M experts in the 1950s used to call procedure flow charts. One useful application of them is to document system (or system simulation) executions, as we discuss later in this chapter. Sequence diagrams can be used for the same purpose, but activity charts may be better if we want to show control or decision branching, or both. It is very much a pragmatic decision as to which notation is best in each case one meets.

In their essence, activity diagrams are simultaneously flow charts and a special case of the state chart of UML (cf. Chapter 7) although. Simons (2000) argues that activity diagrams are not bona fide state machines because they put the transition logic into the state rather than into events. In Version 2.0 of UML, they are given the semantics of Petri nets (cf. Section 4.7.1; Petri, 1962).

4.4 BPMN

Our second network notation for BPM is BPMN: Business Process Modelling Notation. Similar in general nature to activity diagrams, it is far more expressive and supports a mapping to the most popular process execution language: WS-BPEL. The downside of this is that it is ferociously complex – it has to be to support all the constructs of the BPEL programming language – but can be reasonably tamed for high level business process modelling. WS-BPEL is described briefly in Section 4.5.

The main constructs of BPMN are events, activities, flows and gateways. Flows, as one might expect, are shown as arrows which admit two decorations as shown in Figure 4-2. Undecorated arrows represent normal, unguarded flows between activities, events and gateways.

Default flows are used when flow splits into multiple paths dependent on the evaluation of some condition. Guarded flows are used when the flow is blocked unless the associated condition (guard) evaluates to TRUE. At once we can see that BPMN is slightly more complex than the activity diagram.

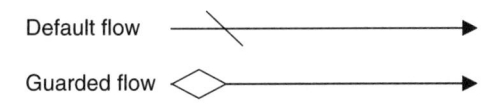

Figure 4-2 Special flows.

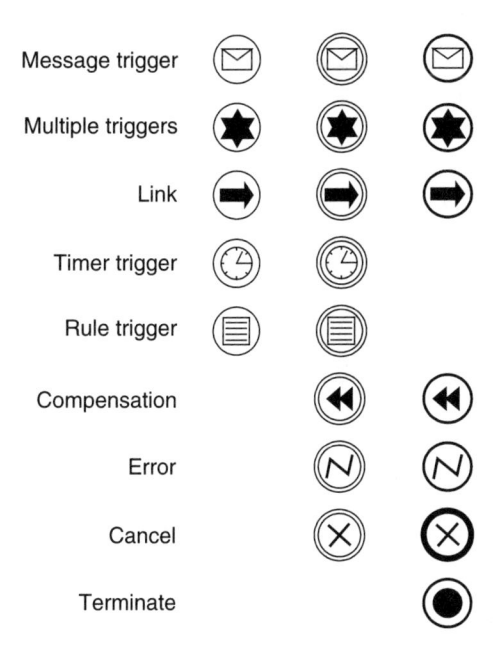

Figure 4-3 BPMN event types.

To give a further feel for the complexity and expressiveness of the notation, Figure 4-3 enumerates all the event types available in the specification. Event types are classified as start, intermediate or end events. When there is no decoration the event is called a basic event, which can act as a placeholder. Start events are represented by a small circle which may, optionally, enclose any of the icons shown in the left-hand column of the figure. For terminal or end events this circle is thick (the right-hand column shows the available icons) and intermediate events use a double line for the circle (centre column). For anyone with even slightly imperfect eyesight, this represents something of a diagram-reading challenge in my opinion; not a show stopping defect but irritating nevertheless.

Some of the names in the figure are self-explanatory. End events, except terminate, end the current process but lead off to some other process, often for exception handling of some sort. Intermediate message events indicate that the process will wait for a message. Intermediate rule events are only used for exception handling within the process. End and start links connect to sibling processes and intermediate ones to other activities. The most complicated type is compensation. It reverses the effect of a previously completed activity, either by rolling back a transaction or using some custom approach where this is not feasible.

Activities are rounded rectangles. Like events they admit various decorations to show activity types such as compensation and looping activities and those with multiple instances. We will not need them in this book. A plus sign in a box indicates that an activity is not an atomic task, i.e. it can be further decomposed into subactivities.

BPMN provides an incredibly rich set of logic gateways, as illustrated in Figure 4-4. These all represent some kind of branching or synchronization. For example, the AND gateways have the same meaning as the thick bars in a UML activity diagram (or, indeed, a statechart).

As with activity diagrams, BPMN supports swimlanes, which are shown as labelled parallel rectangles.

All BPMN elements can be annotated, which is to say they may have attributes in the underlying data model. This is especially necessary if one is to generate executable BPEL processes from the diagrams. Thus we can see that BPMN can serve as a high level process modelling language that can be enhanced and refined to the level of programming – thus its huge complexity. In fact, BPMN currently has constructs with no equivalent in BPEL, so that care is required if requirements information is not to be lost.

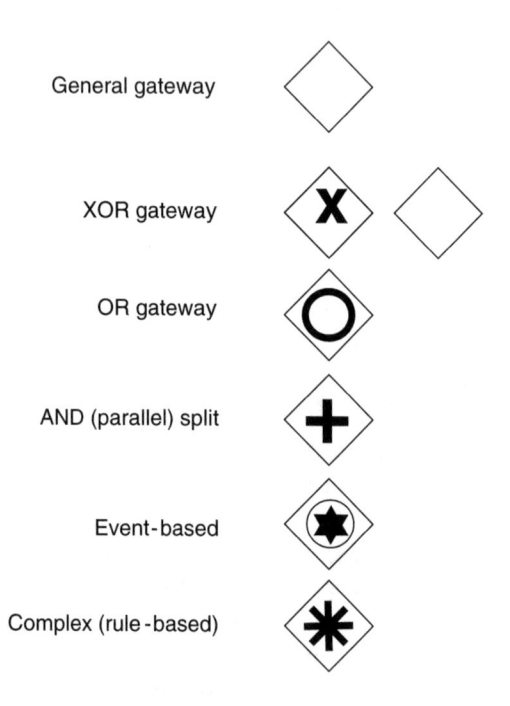

Figure 4-4 Logic gateways in BPMN.

4.4.1 Fundamental Business Process Modelling Patterns

BPMN, with its rich set of gateways is capable of supporting most of the primitive split-and-join process patterns identified by Aalst *et al.* (2003). These patterns include the following.

- SEQUENCE. One damned thing after another!
- PARALLEL SPLIT (AND split). The process splits into processes that run independently and concurrently.
- SYNCHRONIZATION (AND join). All the parallel processes run to completion before merging.
- MULTI-CHOICE (OR split). Run one or more processes in parallel according to a conditional statement evaluating to TRUE or not. This is an example of a pattern that BPEL can only implement indirectly, if at all.
- SYNCHRONIZING MERGE (OR join). Merge when all the active paths from a split are completed.
- EXCLUSIVE CHOICE (XOR split). Only one of the branch activities is performed. The gateway must contain the appropriate rule as an attribute.
- SIMPLE MERGE (XOR join). Continue when the first activity completes.
- MULTI-MERGE. This allows all parallel processes to continue independently though they share the same ending. BPMN and BPEL do not support this multi-threading pattern directly.
- COMPLEX JOIN. The merge happens after a subset (e.g. two out of three) of the parallel activities complete. Obviously, this must be rule-based.

Figure 4-5 illustrates a complex join. Here, the three parallel processes return success if a score exceeds a specified threshold. The Issue permit process can proceed if two out of three successes occur. Clearly, the gateway must contain the logic for this rule somehow.

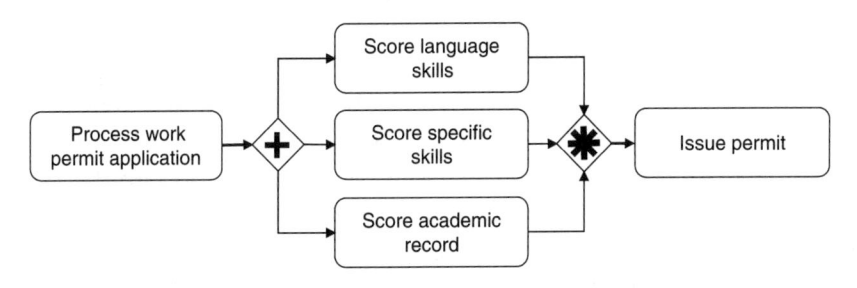

Figure 4-5 Complex join pattern.

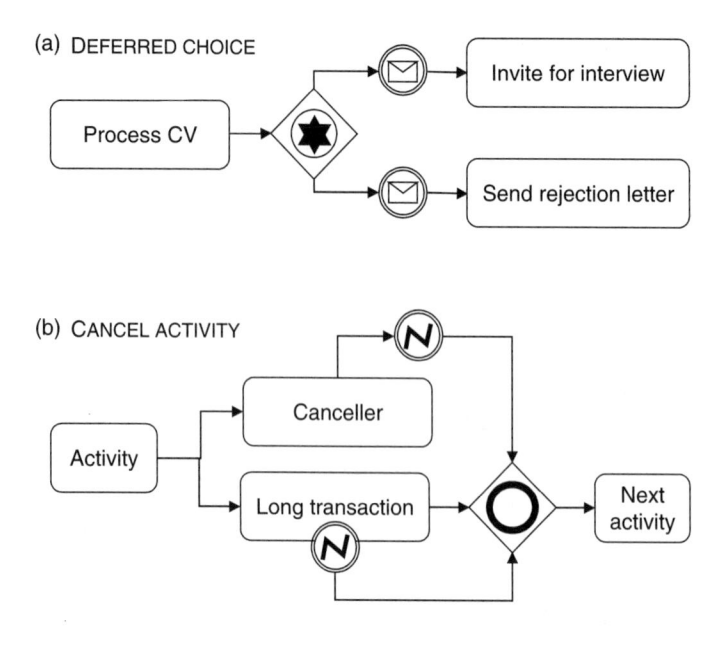

Figure 4-6 DEFERRED CHOICE and CANCEL ACTIVITY as BPMN diagrams.

PARALLEL SPLIT and SYNCHRONIZATION are often used together as in Figure 4-1 and in the example that will follow shortly (Figure 4-7).

Along with the split and join patterns, the paper by Aalst *et al.* also includes the following process patterns, all of which are expressed as simple diagrams of the sort shown in Figure 4-6.

- WITH DESIGN-TIME KNOWLEDGE. This is the same as PARALLEL SPLIT and SYNCHRONIZATION except that the parallel activities are just different instances of the same process. BPMN uses the loop construct and BPEL its flow activities.
- WITH RUN-TIME KNOWLEDGE. The same as WITH DESIGN-TIME KNOWLEDGE but the number of instances is unknown at design time.
- WITHOUT RUN-TIME KNOWLEDGE. The same as WITH RUN-TIME KNOWLEDGE but the number of instances is unknown up until a point during the processing of the instances.
- WITHOUT SYNCHRONIZATION. Run multiple concurrent instances of an activity without synchronization – basically PARALLEL SPLIT in a loop.
- ARBITRARY CYCLES. Perform several processes in a loop until a condition is met using EXCLUSIVE CHOICE to exit the loop.
- IMPLICIT TERMINATION. The process does not have a single termination event. It terminates when all its branches complete.

- DEFERRED CHOICE. The same as exclusive choice but the decision as to which process to run waits for an event.
- INTERLEAVED PARALLEL ROUTING. Several activities are to be performed in strict sequence but the order in which they run does not matter. BPMN and BPEL support this via their *ad hoc* process and serialized scope constructs.
- MILESTONE. An activity cannot start until a certain milestone is reached and cannot proceed after the milestone expires.
- CANCEL ACTIVITY. Branch to a cancellation activity on a trigger. The activity process is killed.
- CANCEL CASE. Branch to a cancellation activity on a trigger. The entire process is killed.

BPM notations and languages can be evaluated according to how many of these patterns they can support. BPMN and BPEL do relatively well against this criterion though neither are perfect as yet. Activity diagrams fare slightly worse. Of course, many of the patterns may never be required in a given practical modelling exercise, but it nice to know they are available.

Havey (2005) suggests a further nine patterns concerned with inter-process communication and workflow, whose names are mostly self-explanatory, as follows.

Communication patterns.
- RECEIVE REQUEST. A process is triggered by a service request.
- CALL PARTNER SERVICE.
- WAIT FOR RESPONSE.
- UNSOLICITED EVENT. A process handles an unforeseen event with an event handler.
- CORRELATE REQUEST AND RESPONSE. A process filters an inbound service request to match conversational identifiers.
- DYNAMIC PARTNER. A process determines the endpoint of a partner process at runtime.

The above six patterns can all be implemented easily in BPEL.

Workflow patterns.
- PRIORITIZATION. Assign a priority at the start of a manual process.
- ESCALATION. Reassign work on time-out.
- RÔLES COMPETE FOR TASKS. Assign a task to many rôles. The task completes when the first rôle does so. Use COMPLEX JOIN.

4.4.2 A Practical Example

I will now present a simple but practical and rather testing example that we will meet again in subsequent chapters. In fact, it represents a pattern, in the sense that it can apply to several business scenarios wherein orders are taken.

Consider first a company that sells stationery and office paraphernalia. We assume that there is some sort of telephone ordering service or call centre. Customers may call in for quotes and with orders. Salesmen may also call known customers to solicit business (but forget this for the time being). Imagine that a customer, Dr Shelley, calls a salesman, Emma.

'Good morning. J. Austen Supplies. Emma here.'

'Hullo, it's Dr Shelley from the Ozymandias Clinic for the Despairing. I need some pads of prescription forms and a box of drawing pins.'

'Hold on, Dr Shelley, I'll just check that we've got them in stock. How many pads do you need?'

'Fifty.'

'Right. Hold the line while I check.'

Emma, in fact, first checks the Ozymandias Clinic's records for any outstanding debt. In this case it is below the company risk threshold and there is no debt older than two months; so that's OK. Now she checks the stock and finds just one box of fifty prescription pads. That's OK too because the stock control system will have reordered them automatically by now.

What Emma has been doing has been automated and she is entering the details of the customer and the order into a computer system that has access to stock records and so on. However, in principle, it could be done by consulting paper stock ledgers and price lists. Essentially, she must first gather the data that are needed and then check various things to see if the sale is possible and permissible.

'Yes, we can get those things to you by tomorrow. The pads are £ 15.80 and the pins £ 0.20. Small order postage and packing brings that to £ 18.75.'

Thank the gods for our new service oriented architecture, she muses.

'That's fine, m'dear. Do you need an order number?'

'No, not for a small amount. Is there anything else?'

'Not unless you've got any vast trunkless legs of stone.'

'Very droll, sir. Bye now.'

'Bye.'

Now the deal is committed to and the price agreed, Emma (or the system) must ensure that the stock levels are adjusted and the necessary paper work sent out: a dispatch instruction to the warehouse and an invoice to Dr Shelley. As far as the call centre is concerned that is the end of the process.

Figure 4-7 shows this process using BPMN. The plus signs in the Check Limits and Send Confirmations boxes indicates that there are subprocesses that need to be expanded, as shown in Figure 4-8.

Exactly the same process could apply in a totally different kind of company. To see this, consider now the dealing room of an investment bank trading foreign exchange on the money markets. The rules are a little more complicated and the jargon is different, but the process is essentially the same.

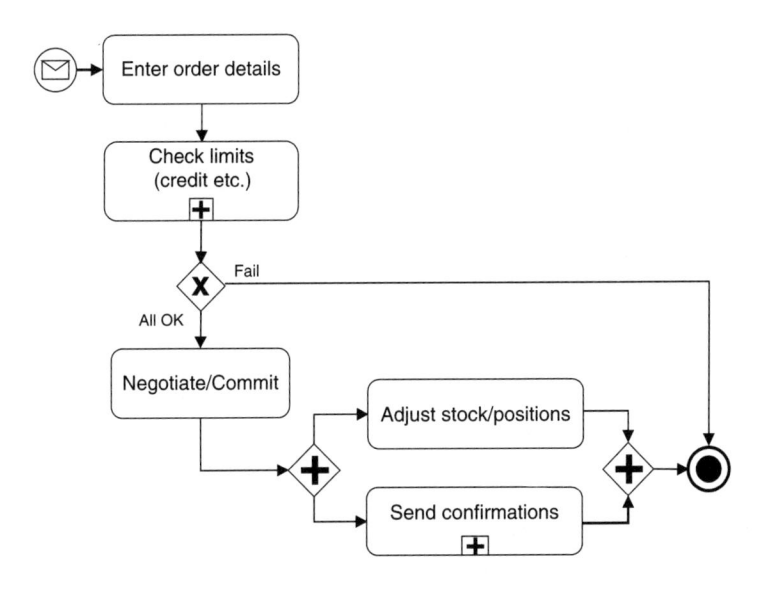

Figure 4-7 A process for entering and validating an order.

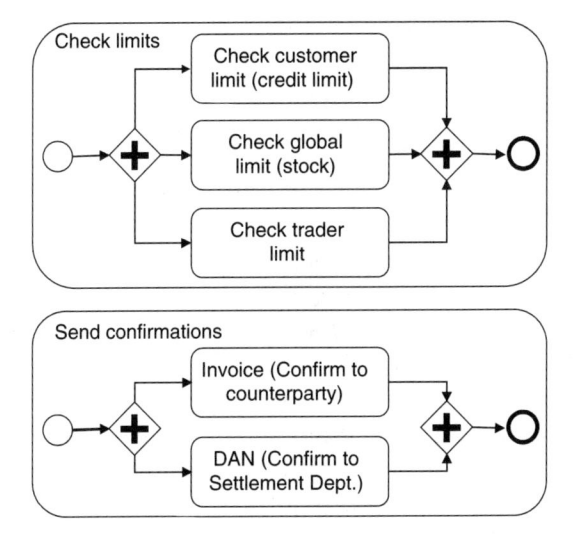

Figure 4-8 Expanded subprocesses for entering and validating an order.

Here, the dealer has various screens in front of her, such as Reuters terminals showing the most recently traded prices for her portfolio of currencies. To keep it simple, let's says she is a cable trader, i.e. she only deals with GBP/USD trades. She also keeps a book, which shows how many pounds and dollars she holds personally on behalf of the bank. Ideally she will be able to find out what the bank's total stock in these currencies is. These figures are called **positions**. The dealer has positions as does the bank. The bank's regulatory régime says that these positions should not exceed certain set limits, e.g. the dealer may not hold more than $100M, in case the price of the dollar should falls dramatically. There may be lower limits too, such as not allowing dealers to 'go short', i.e. sell currency that they do not have. Furthermore, the bank imposes limits on its customers, to mitigate the risk of non-payment between a deal being done and settlement taking place; this is sometimes called an **exposure** limit. All in all, these limits are analogous to the stock and credit checks that Emma made for J. Austen Supplies. The only difference is the distinction between the dealer limit and the bank limit; all J. Austen's stock was available for Emma to trade.

The telephone scenario is a little more complicated too. Alongside the screens is a dealer board: a set of buttons linking the dealer to traders in other banks by telephone. If a button on the dealer board flashes then the dealer, let's call her Monica, knows who is calling. Obversely, if Monica presses a button she will be connected to a known trader, referred to as the **counterparty**. Counterparties not represented on the dealer board will have to dial in – or be dialled.

Imagine Monica at her desk. The phone rings. Since the dealer board doesn't light up, she doesn't know who it is.

'Hi Monica. This is Suresh at The Bank of Baroda. Remember me?'

'Of course,' she lies, and hurriedly checks to see if they have an open account and what its status (position) is.

'What can I do you for, Suresh?'

'I want a price on the cable.'

'How much?'

'Twenty million dollars.'

Monica needs this information because big deals sometimes get a preferential rate – as indeed do preferred customers.

Now, Monica must not know if Suresh is buying or selling; if she did it would affect the price. What she does is to look at the latest trades in the money market and sets her price a little higher or a little lower than the last few trades, according to whether she is trying to unload a large (long) position or not. Actually, she quotes two prices (the 'spread') but let's not complicate matters for the purpose of this example.

'I'll give you 1.97, Suresh.'

'OK. I sell 20 mill.'

And that's it; it's irrevocable. The motto in the City is: 'my word is my bond'. Verbally agreed bargains are binding – and it's all tape recorded!

Suresh can now ring off – after a suitably intimate conversation about the cricket scores, of course – and Monica must update the system by committing all the details she has been entering as the conversation progressed.

Finally, the system must take responsibility for sending out the appropriate confirmations and for updating the positions. It might also calculate Monica's updated P&L – which is one reason why updating the positions in real time is beneficial, so we are back full circle to a business objective.

Notice that the BPMN diagrams abstract away a lot of the subtlety of the process. In Chapter 5, we will return to this example and present a method for capturing it a little more directly in the form of a Catalysis Conversation Analysis.

4.5 WS-BPEL

WS-BPEL, usually abbreviated to just BPEL (pron. Beepell or Beeple), is a programming language that is designed to represent business processes as XML. It is an extension to web services standards that introduces stative constructs to interactions between services that are otherwise transactionally stateless. A BPEL program contains two kinds of file: WSDL files that describe service interfaces and BPEL files that encode the definition and orchestration of processes. In fact, BPEL's messaging facilities depend entirely on the use of the WSDL to describe outgoing and incoming messages. Thus, partner process activities do not address each other using identities but pass messages that encapsulate key data that can be correlated over the duration of the exchange.

The details of process execution languages should not concern the average business analyst and is outside the scope of a text on requirements engineering and specification, such as this one. In fact, since BPEL is limited to web service implementations, which we have already seen are not the only way to implement service oriented architecture, the analyst might want to steer well clear of such implementation decisions. However, since very many current installations use BPEL, this section provides a high level overview of it and how it fits in architecturally – especially with respect to BPMN.

Historically, IBM and Microsoft had both developed process execution languages: WSFL and XLANG. As the business process management movement evolved they, with the help of BEA and several other vendors, decided to combine these languages to create BPEL4WS and submit it to OASIS for standardization. It was renamed in WS-BPEL in 2004, when version 2.0 was adopted. In 2007, Active Endpoints, Adobe, BEA, IBM, Oracle and SAP published the BPEL4People and WS-HumanTask specifications, which describe how human interaction with BPEL processes could be implemented.

BPEL is said to support *programming in the large*. This means it only considers the high-level state transition interactions of an *abstract* process. A BPEL abstract process represents publicly observable behaviour in a standardized fashion. It will include information such as when to send messages, when to wait for them, when to compensate for failed transactions, and so on. Programming 'in the small', on the other hand, deals with short-lived behaviour, single transactions involving access to local logic and resources such as databases. Doing this kind of thing 'in the large' would not only be tricky from a 'clean syntax' point of view but would often incur a quite unacceptable performance penalty. BPEL philosophy is that programming in the large and programming in the small require different types of languages.

BPEL is a web service orchestration language, not a choreography language (cf. Section 4.6).

There is no standardized graphical notation for WS-BPEL. Some vendors – including, for example, IBM and Oracle – invented their own notations. These notations generally follow the block-structured constructs in BPEL, such as sequence, while, pick, scope, etc. This gives a direct visual representation of BPEL process descriptions. However, most of the same vendors have moved to using BPMN for graphical specification, using BPMN as a graphical front-end to capture BPEL process descriptions. The BPMN specification includes a mapping from BPMN to BPEL 2.0. A BPMN-BPEL mapping has been implemented in several vendor tools and at least one open-source tool: BPMN2BPEL.

However, the feasible of a complete and reversible mapping has been questioned (Havey, 2005). It seems that there are fundamental differences between BPMN and BPEL, which make it very difficult, and arguably in some cases impossible, to generate BPEL code from BPMN models. The problem of BPMN-BPEL round-trip engineering is even more tricky. Generally, BPEL is evolving as implementation developers extend the language by adding new tags to the XML as needed. The better ideas will gradually creep into the standard, I suspect.

BPEL also has limitations as an executable process specification language. It omits certain process constructs and so that it is not possible to express all conceivable business processes in BPEL. Therefore, BPEL is often used in conjunction with programming languages, for example Java, or extended by the scripting languages to be found in proprietary workflow or integration broker engines.

BPELJ (BPEL for Java) is an extension to BPEL based on the earlier PD4J. It allows for lower level (or finer-grained) programming constructs, compared to BPEL's definition of processes in terms of high level steps, by permitting the inclusion of in-stream Java code and calls to Java objects and enterprise beans and the like. This not only supports the finer-grained details of process implementations but is attractive to those organizations that wish to use J2EE-based web-servers and ESBs. Efforts are underway to produce the C# equivalent of BPELJ.

The battle between BPEL and BPML is largely over. BPEL syntax triumphed that of BPML but BPML semantics remains victorious. BPEL, as it is continually extended, is evolving slowly but inexorably in the direction of the more formally complete BPML.

Unlike BPEL, whose roots were in workflow theory, BPML was inspired by Milner's pi-calculus. This gave BPML a ready-made complete formal semantics. We will take a brief look at the pi-calculus in Section 4.7.

4.6 Orchestration and Choreography

As noted above, BPEL is a web service orchestration language. This means that a BPEL implementation of a business process will include the control logic that links all the services together from the point of view of a single rôle or process participant. Of course, this rôle will need to interact with other rôles at various points in the process, but these are secondary. If you are a sales clerk taking an order you have an interface to the customer, the credit system and the stock control system, but your focus is on the process by which the order is validated and executed.

Now, in real life, there needs to be what Catalysis called **collaboration** between systems and the processes that they represent. This, in principle, cannot be orchestrated by a central controller – because the systems may be distributed and may well be owned independently (as might be the case if the credit checks are operated by a specialist company). What is needed therefore is not a controller but a **protocol** that enables collaborating processes to talk to each other on demand. The internal logic of the processes in irrelevant, what matters is the language they use to talk to each other: the protocol. Such a protocol requires that there be an underlying common semantics; so yet again we come back to the need for modelling. In business process management circles defining such a protocol is referred to as **choreography**.

The primary difference between orchestration and choreography is that between executability and control. Orchestration specifies an executable process that involves message exchanges with other systems, such that the message exchange sequences are controlled by the orchestration designer. Choreography specifies a protocol for peer-to-peer interactions, defining, for example, the permissible sequences of messages exchanged, with the aim of guaranteeing interoperability. A choreography protocol is not directly executable, as it admits many different compliant realizations. Choreography can be realized by writing an orchestration (perhaps as a BPEL process) for each peer involved. Orchestration exhibits central control of the behaviour of a distributed system – as provided by a 'conductor'. Choreography allows the components of a distributed system without centralized control to 'dance' to the music of the business process.

The choreography also specifies which services each process needs to listen to and to call. This is sufficient information to specify a BPEL stub using the receive and invoke tags.

In practice, choreography is defined using web service standards. The dominant one is WS-CDL (Web Services Choreography Description Language).

WS-CDL is an XML-based process contract description language. The technical contracts so defined capture the common observable behaviour of otherwise autonomous participants that communicate via web service interfaces defined in WSDL. The participants are often distributed and owned by separate organizations. To participate each process must conform to the agreed WS-CDL choreography model.

Adopting a choreography base such as WS-CDL enables collaborative scaleable e-commerce. A process language targeted at business-to-business collaboration such as BPSS (cf. Chapter 8) can be used to add business semantics to WS-CDL.

The major competing choreography standard is WSCI (Web Services Choreography Interface) with a syntax and semantics similar to BPML (which the reader will recall competed directly with BPEL). The industry consensus seems, for the most part, to prefer WS-CDL.

There is a potentially interesting analogy between versus choreography and conversations versus collaborations (defined in Chapter 5). Orchestration looks at a conversation (within a process) from the viewpoint of one rôle whereas choreography defines how several rôles may collaborate to achieve a shared goal.

Activity diagrams and BPMN are given semantics based on Petri nets. WS-CDL, like BPML, is influenced by the semantics of process algebra.

4.7 Process Algebra and Petri Nets

It is claimed that BPML formal semantics are based on, or at least inspired by process algebra, while a BPMN or activity diagram is given its semantics using Petri nets.

Process algebras are mathematical systems that describe concurrent processes. There are various forms of process algebra, going back to

Tony Hoare's Communicating Sequential Processes (CSP) (Hoare, 1985) and Rob Milner's Calculus of Communicating Systems (CCS) (Milner, 1989). Several variants of these have appeared, one of the most relevant to our subject matter being Performance Enhanced Process Algebra (PEPA) (Hillstone, 1993). However, the variant most commonly quoted by the BPM community is Milner's pi-calculus.

PEPA is concerned with the performance of a process and the identification of its bottlenecks, using Markov models such as stochastic or timed Petri nets. However, such models are often intractable computationally, leading to interest in compositional models such as CCS. A compositional approach breaks down a system into subsystems that are more easily modelled; the results can be aggregated to give the desired data. To my knowledge, no one has yet applied PEPA to BPM, despite its obvious relevance.

CCS models a system as a network of **agents** that can perform discrete **actions**. Actions can be internal – so that the agents proceed concurrently – or might involve inter-agent **communications**. Communications take place through channels via named ports (so one begins to see the resonance with web services). Two communicating agents or processes have complimentary actions designated by ports with the same label but with one distinguished by an overbar, e.g. enterorder and $\overline{\text{enterorder}}$.

Similarly, the (Milner, 1993) approach has processes made of actions that can be connected sequentially, in parallel or recursively and communicate via channels.

Returning to our running example, consider the following fragment of a source code representation of some pi-calculus.

```
Cust(enterorder,cust)=enterorder <cust>.cust<result>
```

`Cust` is a process whilst `enterorder` and `cust` are channels. The notation $\overline{\text{enterorder}}$ `<cust>` signifies 'send `cust` on channel $\overline{\text{enterorder}}$'. The dot, which is called the sequence operation, can be read 'then'. So the left hand side of the equation declares the channels available to the Cust process, while the right hand side can be read as saying: that this process first sends a value (cust) on the channel `enterorder` and expects a reply on its dual $\overline{\text{enterorder}}$; then it listens on channel `cust` for a result message.

Of course, there are several operators often than sequence, such as the choice operator S, but business process modellers do not need to understand the details of pi-calculus to do modelling, so I will not elaborate. The interested reader may consult Milner's original (1993) work or Havey's (2005) excellent layman's overview.

Petri nets (Peterson, 1981) are another useful modelling notation for representing concurrent distributed systems. They can also be used to provide semantic models (i.e. concrete interpretations) of business process models. A Petri net consists of **places, transitions**, and **flow relations**: directed arcs linking them. No flow relations may connect two places or two transitions. Places from which an arc runs to a transition are called the input places of the transition and places to which arcs run from a transition are called its output places. As with process algebra, there are several variants of the theory: coloured, stacked, timed Petri nets and so on.

Each place in a Petri net may contain a number of **tokens**. A distribution of tokens over the places of a net is called a marking of the net. If there are tokens in every input place then a transition can **fire**. When a transition fires, it consumes the tokens from its input places, performs some processing task and places a specified number of tokens into each of its output places. Firing is considered to be instantaneous, in a manner similar to a transition in a state–transition diagram (STD) (see Chapter 7 for a description of STDs). Graphically, places are circles, transitions (tasks) are rectangles and tokens are small dots. As we saw with BPMN, the rectangles may need to be annotated in case there are rules or conditions to be evaluated during transition.

Figure 4-9 shows a Petri net simulation of the PARALLEL SPLIT and SYNCHRONIZATION pattern (AND split-join). The grey arrows represent ticks of the simulation clock. Look at the progress of the little black dots that represent tokens from left to right as time ticks along. The order of the fourth and fifth firings is, of course, arbitrary. Note especially the synchronization, which illustrates nicely how all inbound places must be filled before firing can occur.

One can see from this example that to do this analysis for even slightly complex processes would be very time consuming, even with the help of software packages that automates the simulations – the analyst still need to work though them to check for errors. Thus, as with process algebra, it is reassuring to know that such semantic models exist but not very practical in most commercial contexts.

Havey (2005) goes into slightly greater depth, working through some Aalst patterns – including the above example. He also gives a particularly intriguing example of a simple process and its Petri net equivalent. Figure 4-10 shows a similar process (part of that of buying a house for people other than first time buyers) in BPMN. Processes don't get much simpler than this, but the Petri net is pretty complicated. Figure 4-11 is based on the diagram given by Havey.

The place circles and transition rectangles are annotated with the truth table values that enable legal transitions. It takes about a paragraph to explain this to someone to whom it is not obvious that this Petri net

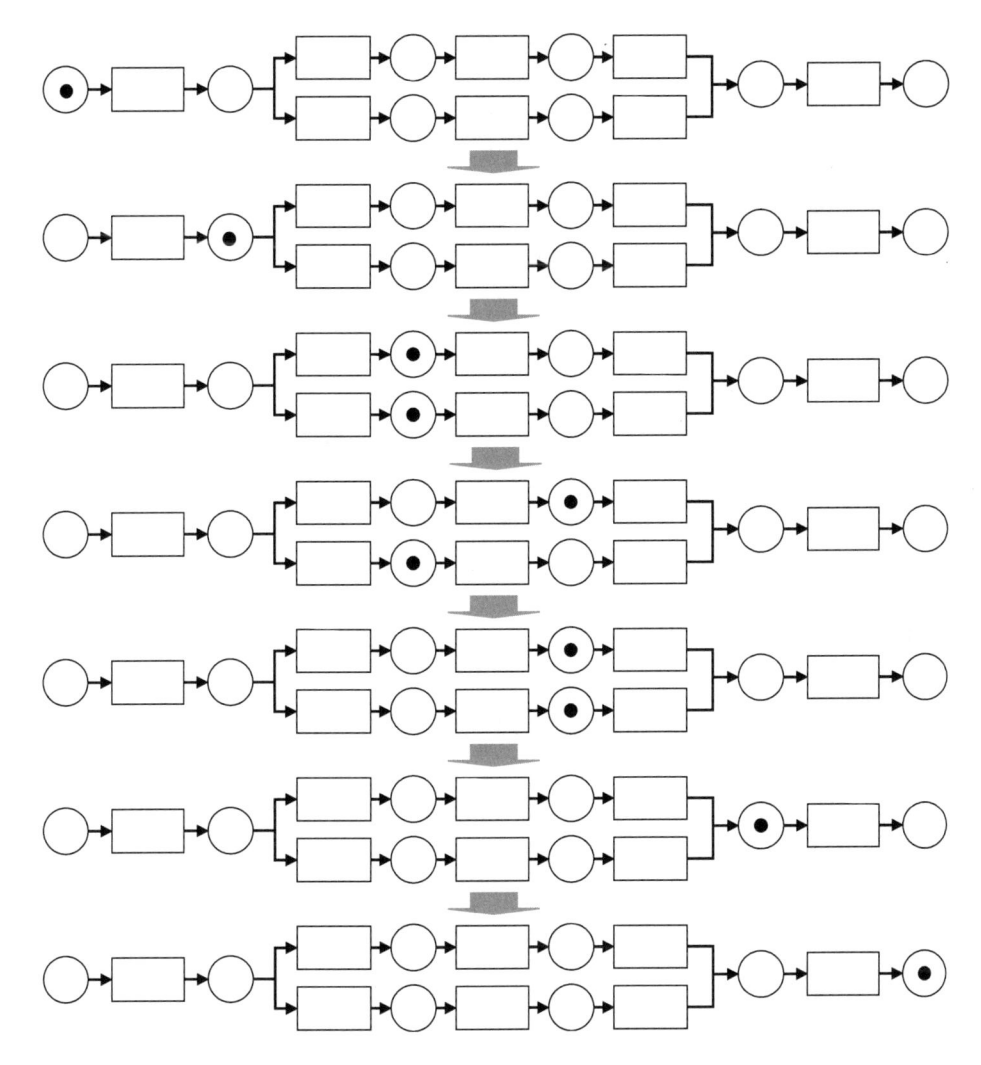

Figure 4-9 Petri net simulation of the AND split-join.

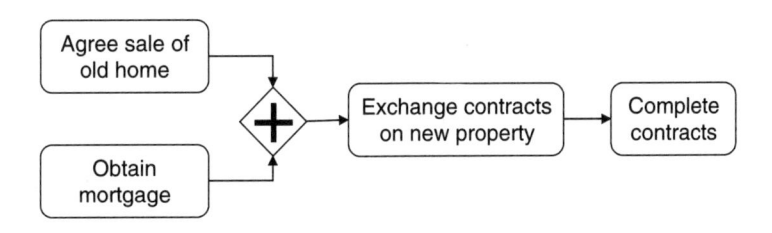

Figure 4-10 Moving home process model.

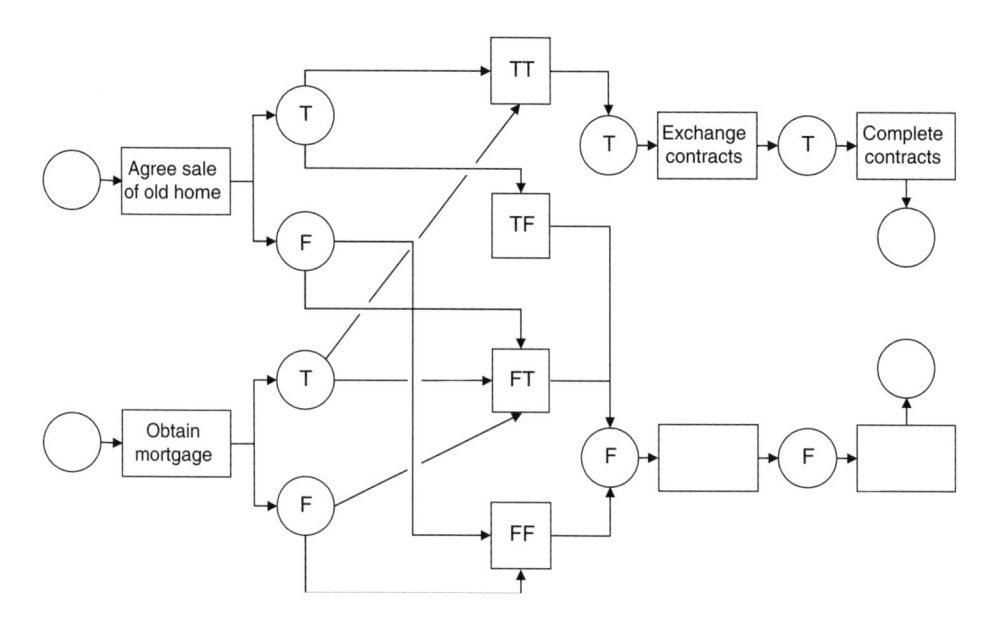

Figure 4-11 A Petri net for moving home (after Havey, 2005).

represents a simple truth table. As is known, all truth tables can be represented as rules. Consider the following ruleset.

```
Complete contracts if contracts have been exchanged.
Exchange contracts if all of the following conditions are
true:
    Sale of old home has been agreed;
    A mortgage has been obtained.
```

Isn't that simple? In fact, in many ways it is simpler than the BPMN diagram – especially for users who didn't get to go on the BPMN training course!

Petri nets and process algebra were developed because set theoretic semantics sometimes give rise to problems where concurrency is involved. However, this arises in an *extremely* small number of practical situations in, for example, operating system design. The same applies to business processes. It is also the case that it has been proven that first order predicate calculus (whose default semantics is set theory) can express any other kind of logic (Hayes, 1979) – though, admittedly, doing so may be the *opposite* of concise. Therefore, on balance, I prefer set theoretic semantics (i.e. business rules) except for the rare case where the Petri net comes into its own. Process algebra remains, to this day, an academic discipline inaccessible to most IT workers, so the same conclusion is reached: such complicated semantic models are usually otiose. Give meaning to your models with business rules.

4.8 The Human Side of Business Process Management

Network business process models tend to emphasize the procedural side of processes, usually focusing on software applications, but in reality there is another side that they often obscure. This is great if you are concerned with enterprise integration or the reuse of the legacy. However, many crucial business processes are essentially based on human ingenuity. Consider such processes: product design, mergers and acquisitions, writing a novel, developing a marketing strategy, pacifying a dissatisfied customer or deciding what proportion of the national product should be allocated to the arts – and to *which* arts?

BPEL and its like were languages designed for programmers to help them build automated process engines and thus orchestrating (often existing) existing computing resources. Such languages were never intended to provide a tool for business analysts to develop high-level process models. Also, BPEL and all the network BPM techniques emphasize transactional activities; but many business processes are not transactional, rather they are what Harrison-Broninski (2005) calls *collaborative*. Consider the examples listed in the previous paragraph: all of them are totally collaborative – except maybe writing a novel, although getting it published is entirely another matter. Ould (2005) insists further that collaboration is at the heart of real-world processes and therefore 'must be at the heart of our process methods' as part of his passionate argument for the development of process-oriented languages.

Harrison-Broninski singles out current CRM systems, noting that no salesman is going to want to return from a day on the road only to spend two hours entering data about his calls into a computer. Such staff are given incentives as individuals and thus are reluctant to put their information into the corporate pool of knowledge.

When considering automated processes it is useful to concentrate on *what* happens and *when*. For collaborative processes it is equally and crucially important to focus on *why* and *how* people do things. Harrison-Broninski points out that, for knowledge workers, the sequencing of process activities is merely a corollary of the why and how, and therefore may vary for occasion to occasion. Such behaviour is not readily captured in a conventional computer program.

However, it is a great deal easier to record such insights in the form of business rules – and, with a good rule engine, even executable business rules. The analyst should think about actions as being the result of business rules firing rather than as a result of previous events or some rigid 'control flow'. The principle is that knowledge workers do things 'if and when they need doing'. Not only are actions rule dependent, so are the rôles that workers take on from time to time, and this must be understood too.

Once again we see that a business rules approach may be crucially useful for many business process modelling projects. There are further remarks on this topic in the bibliographical notes below.

In the next chapter we will examine business processes from a more people-centred point of view and present a technique that both complements network process models and emphasizes the human side much more.

4.9 Summary

Business process modelling is central to requirements analysis and especially relevant in an SOA environment. It has its origins in workflow technology and the BPR movement of the 1990s. Modern business process management has embraced important standards such as UML activity diagrams, BPMN, WS-BPEL and WS-CDL. This chapter described these in outline and introduced the key ideas of network business process modelling techniques.

We described and considered the business process modelling patterns of Aalst *et al.* and showed how some of them might be represented in BPMN before introducing an order processing example that will be used throughout this book.

Next, we looked at WS-BPEL and the notions of orchestration and choreography.

It is claimed that BPML formal semantics are based on, or at least inspired by process algebra, while a BPMN or activity diagram is given its semantics using Petri nets. We examined both these topics briefly and saw that rule-based semantics (i.e. set theory) were a viable and simpler alternative in the majority of cases.

Finally, I noted that business processes may be collaborative rather than procedural; so that business process management has a human side that will be emphasized in subsequent chapters. The importance of business rules came to the fore in this context too.

4.10 Bibliographical Notes

If you are involved in design or architecture as well as specification, you will now benefit immensely from reading Michael Havey's (2005) superb introduction to the more technical aspects of BPM. It goes into much more detail on the syntax of BPEL and WS-CDL and contains an excellent layman's introduction to pi-calculus and Petri nets. I cannot recommend it enough – although the version numbers have moved on a little since it was published. Perhaps there will be a second edition by the time this text hits the streets. I hope so.

Ross (2005) provides an interesting classification of business rules in relation to business process management, saying that there are three important categories: rules at decision points, rules at rejection points and process coördination rules. Decision points typically involve an organization's particular expertise and might include such things as medical diagnosis, paying an insurance claim or detecting a fraud. Businesses cannot be modelled without considering such rules. Rules at rejection points are merely constraints on possible decisions, e.g. you can't marry someone under sixteen. Process co-ordination rules are there to ensure that processes run properly. In an SOA these are especially important because that may determine message routing and filtering. Ross also makes a very good case for combining business process management and business rules management. Graham (2006) provides an introduction to the latter.

Gaur and Zirn (2006) offer tutorial material on BPEL based around the Oracle BPEL notation and toolkit. It contains an especially interesting article on how to integrate a process with a business rules engine exposed as a web service.

CHAPTER 5

Catalysis Conversation Analysis

'What is the use of a book', thought Alice, 'without pictures or conversations?'
Lewis Carroll (Alice in Wonderland)

In the previous chapter we met some popular approaches to and notations for modelling business processes. This chapter introduces another, based on a different set of ideas and using the UML use case notation to model things that are, rather than actions at some system interface, conversations between the agencies involved in the process. It emphasizes the human aspects of business processes more than do the approaches of Chapter 4.

Once again, we assume that the mission is established and that the objectives are clearly stated with defined measures and priorities. We must now create a model of the business area that we are dealing with and its processes.

5.1 What is a Business Process?

To build a business process model we must understand what a business process actually is. Most vendors of business process modelling tools and techniques find it very difficult to answer the question: 'What is a business process?'. Of course, the more unscrupulous may say: 'A business process is anything that you can model with our wonderful software'. Typically, the more erudite might answer that a business is a set of processes connected by data flows, with timings for each process and (possibly) allocations of process responsibility to functional units. In other words, data flow diagrams enhanced with timings or perhaps UML activity diagrams are all that is needed. As we have seen the most sophisticated variant of this kind of approach is BPMN.

Ask the same question of a management consultant or business school and there will likely be a range of different answers. Some answers will emphasize value chains and so on, though not all businesses are value chains. The analysis will rarely drill down lower than the description of workflow into the ontology modelling that is a prerequisite for service oriented architecture.

What all these approaches have in common is that they lack an adequate *theory* of what a business process is above and beyond a basis in process algebra or Petri nets that is focused on the language semantics rather than an enquiry into the nature of business itself. It would be nice to be able to use a more scientific approach. As it turns out the only such work has been done principally by workers in the fields of Sociology, History, Anthropology and even Literary Criticism. Such workers recognize, as an axiom, that organizations are primarily social entities. The science of Semiotics is a key tool for understanding how agents in organizations communicate.

Catalysis Conversation Analysis offers a very definite, theoretically based, perspective on the question of what a business process is, which I now present. The theory is rooted in Semiotics, and especially in the work of Winograd and Flores (1986) on workflow systems.

According to Flores (1997) **a business** is 'a network of commitments' among agents that participate in these commitments. – I would say: 'a network of *goal-oriented* commitments'. Each of these commitments is expressed as a contract between these agents – either explicitly stated or implicitly understood. For example, an employment contract may state that the employee must perform certain tasks or achieve certain results, such as ensuring that desks are cleared at the end of the working day, but it is unlikely that there will be a clause mandating that: 'employees shall wear clothing while in the office'.

To satisfy a goal-oriented commitment or contract, some work must always be done – unless the goal is already achieved in the start state! The contract defines the state of the world that must be achieved on completion of the work task.

How can this be modelled?

Consider some business or enterprise. It could be an entire small company, a division or department of a larger one or even a sole trader. A business process (or business area) is a network of communicating agents. An **agent** is any entity in the world that can communicate; so it could represent a customer, regulator, employee, organizational unit, computer system or even a mechanical device of a certain type, such as a clock, camera or controller. Agents are autonomous and flexible. They respond to appropriate stimuli and they can be proactive and exhibit a social aspect, i.e. communicate. Typically agents exhibit some level of intelligence; human agents certainly so but mechanical agents insofar as they can initiate and respond to communication. This now begs the question of what it means for two agents to communicate.

Agents can be **internal** to the business we are examining or **external** to it. This has nothing to do with whether they are system users, i.e. actors. Agents – like actors in the use case theory – are to be thought of as adopting a rôle.

This 'business' must communicate with the outside world to exist at all and, if it does so, it must use some convention of signs and signals thereto. We could call these signals between agents **semiotic acts**. They are *carried* by some material substratum. They involve a number of semiotic levels from data flows up to implicit social relationships[1]. For example, the substrate may consist of filled-in forms in a paper-based office environment and the social context might be that one assumes that no practical jokes are to be played and no nudity is to be tolerated. If the substratum is verbal (or written) natural language then we can speak instead of **speech acts** or **conversations**. These are the speech acts of Austin (1962) and Searle (1969). Flores (1997) argues that business conversations have a constant recurrent structure based on only five primitive speech acts: assert, assess, declare, offer/promise and request.

Semiotic acts (or conversations as I shall call them from hereon) can be represented by messages, which are directed from the initiator (source) of the communication to its recipient (target). Informally, we could identify semiotic acts, or conversations, with their representation as messages although strictly they are different; the same semiotic act may be represented by many different messages[2]. This defines equivalence classes of messages and we can think of our actual message as a generic representative of its class; many contracts may express the same relationship so we choose one to represent its equivalence class.

5.2 Conversations

A business process is thus a network of commitments represented by conversations and contracts.

---

[1]Semiotics is the comparative study of sign systems and has been important in such diverse fields as mathematical logic, natural language processing, anthropology and literary criticism. It holds that signs can be analysed at at least three levels: those of syntax, semantics and pragmatics. There can be as many as five levels, up to and including the level defined by the social relations of production.
[2]For a trivial example consider that the same conversation may be represented by a message in English, Chinese, German or Urdu.

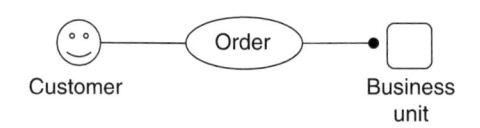

Figure 5-1 A conversation.

A typical conversation is represented as (part of) a rich picture in Figure 5-1 where a typical external customer agent places an order with some business. This message includes the definition of the reply: {order accepted|out of stock|etc.}. We have, quite legitimately I think, used the UML use case symbol to represent the conversation, but stereotyped the UML classifier symbols to represent customer and business unit agents.

A message implies that data flow, so that this approach generalizes the more dataflow-based modelling techniques of Chapter 4. However, it also enriches them considerably. For one thing, data flow in both directions along message links (via the request and hand-over stages discussed below). This is why we have chosen to terminate message links at the recipient end with a filled circle rather than an arrowhead. The line segment is directed from the initiator (when known) of the communication, not from the origin of the data.

We now begin to see that agents can be modelled as objects that pass messages to each other. Clearly agents can also be classified into different types as well. UML actors are a specialization of our agents.

A semiotic or speech act is characterized at the semantic and pragmatic levels by a (possibly implicit) contract that both parties understand. The pragmatics of this contract represent a social relation, just as a message represents a semiotic act.

So we think of a business process as a network of related goal-oriented conversations between agents, represented by messages. It is inconceivable in most businesses that the message initiator does not wish to change the state of the world in some way as a result of the communication. This desired state of the world is the **goal** of the conversation and every conversation (or message) has a goal or post-condition, even if it is often unstated: the contract representing the conditions of satisfaction of the conversation.

A goal is achieved by the performance of a **task**. The innovation here is twofold. Firstly, there is the realization that the tasks we perform can often be reduced to a few stereotypes: typical tasks that act as pattern matching templates against which real tasks can be evaluated and from which real tasks can be generated. This overcomes a possible objection that there could be an explosion in the number of tasks. For example, in a simple foreign exchange deal capture model there are only eleven tasks of which eight are atomic (defined below and illustrated in Figure 5-11). These tasks can be modelled as objects and, of course, are the building blocks of business processes, which in turn take on a stereotypical character.

Clearly, conversations also have the character of transactions. As such they will correspond closely to the business services that we must discover are we to succeed with SOA.

In business, only serious, goal-oriented conversations are relevant and therefore we can argue that each conversation has a sixfold structure as follows:

1. A **triggering event**: a world event that triggers the interaction.
2. A **goal**: a world state desired by the initiator of the conversation.
3. A proposal, which is either an **offer** or a **request**, together with the data necessary for the recipient to evaluate the offer or request.
4. A **negotiation**, whereby the recipient determines whether the goals are shared and the conditions of acceptance, leading to either a **contract** being agreed or the proposal rejected. The contract formalizes the goal and provides formal conditions for knowing when the goal has been achieved satisfactorily.
5. A **task** that must be performed by the recipient of a request to achieve the goal and satisfy the contract.
6. A **handover** of the product of the task and any associated data, which checks that the conditions of satisfaction of the goals have been met.

Note that there are four tasks (the rectangles in Figure 5-2) but that only the performance task is of an entirely unpredictable or variable nature; it will be quite different for each separate conversation.

This structure accords generally with that of a conversation for action in the terminology of Winograd and Flores (Flores, 1997; Winograd and Flores, 1986), although I have added the notion of a triggering event. Figure 5-3 illustrates the structure.

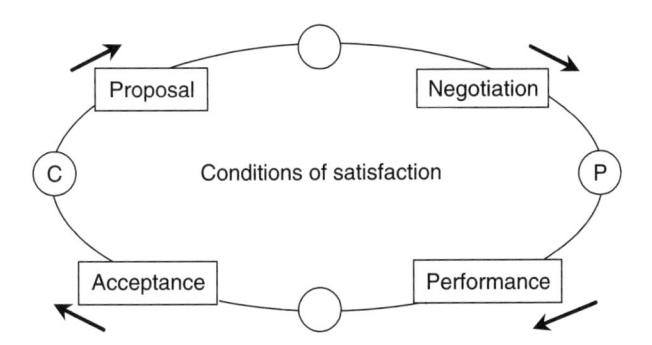

Figure 5-2 A Flores conversation for action with initiator C (customer) and recipient P (performer).

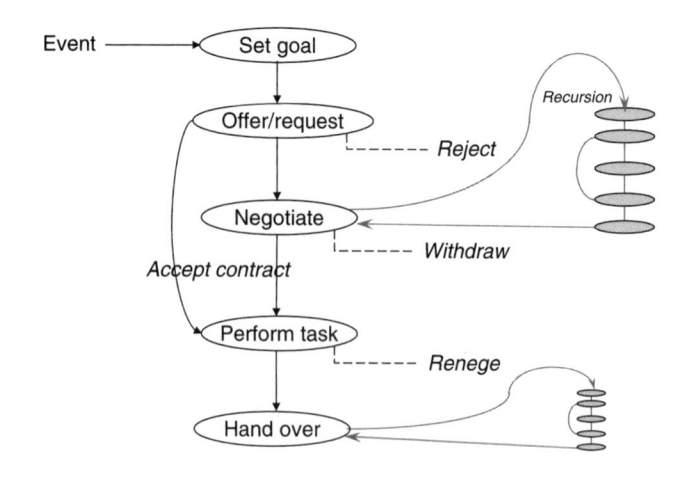

Figure 5-3 The structure of a conversation in SOMA.

Note also that there is symmetry of offers and requests, so that we can replace every offer with an equivalent request by swapping the initiator with the recipient. This gives rise to a notion of **request canonical form** for conversations. Flores presents the theory in terms of a customer (our initiator) and a performer (our recipient) who executes the primitive speech acts – shown in italics in the next paragraph.

The customer *assesses* his/her concerns and *asserts* a request to the performer (dually the performer makes an offer). A process of negotiation then ensues, aimed at defining a contract that can be *promised* by the performer and *accepted* by the customer. This, and other stages in the conversation, may involve recursion whereby subsidiary conversations are engaged in. At the end of negotiation the contract defines the conditions of customer satisfaction, and then some task must be executed to fulfil their promise. Finally, the results of this work are *declared* complete and handed over to the customer who should *declare* satisfaction or decide whether the contract is void.

Figure 5-3 shows that recursion can occur in the negotiation and handover segments of the conversation and that either party may withdraw at each stage.

Consider the concrete example of buying a house. An initiator might say 'would you like to buy my house?' and the recipient would need to know, and would negotiate on, the price. This negotiation could well involve (recursively) subsidiary conversations between the recipient and a mortgage provider and a building surveyor. If everything is agreed then a contract will be agreed and signed (literally in this case). Now there is work to do: in England it is called conveyancing. The work involves searching local government records and land registry documents along with many other, all fairly straightforward, tasks. So this is the place where we might rely on a standard script for the task to be performed, as exemplified for example by the words (or flowcharts) in a book on conveyancing. Finally, when this task completes satisfactorily we can hand over the keys and the contract is said to be *completed*.

Now, such a complex breakdown of conversations is only sometimes necessary or even helpful when analysing a business process. We would normally focus directly on the task segment, taking the other segment for granted unless they have particular significance. In house buying, for example, the discussions with the surveyors and lenders may need to be made explicit, depending on the context in which we are analysing the process. Normally, a simpler representation, such as that of Figure 5-1 will suffice. We really don't need to say that the order conversation involves a request (customer enquiry), since it is obvious in this case. We will however decompose the conversation during later analysis, capturing the negotiation process in so doing. We will also capture the handover segment with the contract. Before going into this, I must explain why and how conversations are regarded as stereotypical.

5.3 Conversation Stereotypes and Scripts

Conversations can be described in several ways but it is most useful to describe a task using a **conversation script**. A script represents a *stereotypical* chunk of behaviour. It is an abstract textual description of such a conversation. As we will see, this provides a notion of generalized exception handling that does not seem to be available to users of the use case approach, where an exception (extends) path is often specific to the use case.

One word of warning is appropriate. This use of the term stereotype has absolutely *nothing* to do with the same word as used in UML; unfortunately there is no other sensible term for the idea that I want to capture here.

As an example, consider a script that describes the process of going to a restaurant. The idea is that one *always* does the same thing when visiting a restaurant. One *always*:

1. Enters the restaurant.
2. Attracts the attention of a waiter.
3. Takes one's seat.
4. Reads the menu.
5. Chooses a meal.
6. Eats it.
7. Pays.
8. Leaves.

This is certainly a good stereotype of the situations normally met with.

Note how the script *defines* the notion of a restaurant. Suppose I were to tell you that, yesterday, I did the following.

1. Entered a building.
2. Attracted someone's attention.
3. Followed that person to a table.
4. Read the items on a list given to me.
5. Choose items from the list.
6. Consumed those items.
7. Paid money;
8. Left the building.

Firstly, I think you would be able to tell me what I was doing very easily indeed.

Secondly, notice that deviations from the script give rise to a feeling of cognitive dissonance between the word and the description. Many readers will have come across advertising for the 'MacDonald's restaurant' chain. This is utterly dissonant because one does not expect to have to clear one's own table when visiting a restaurant. I refrain from any comments about the food at this point and would only point out that most people would have a 'fast food joint' script to cover such eventualities.

The idea of conversation scripts has its roots in the AI script theory of Schank and Abelson (1977) and, to an extent, in hierarchical task analysis. One of the original applications of script theory was interpreting press agency news stories concerning the Vietnam War. It was common for several of the stories to cover the same events and editors needed to know how to filter out the repetition. What the researchers did was to construct objects whose structures represented typical stories. A program then tried to 'fill' all the slots in the script objects with information from the actual wired stories. If all the slots could be filled, the story was deemed to be 'understood'. Editors could then skim stories for new content. There were other applications, including writing children's fiction – within a limited scope – and answering questions about stories and plans. The most significant commercial application was to filtering and correcting natural language elements of SWIFT funds transfer messages. The original was developed for a group of banks and a version is still sold to this day as part of a commercial package.

Our purpose is more limited. We want to write scripts that capture the essence of commonly occurring business conversations. Returning to the order entry and verification example used in Chapter 4, we might write the following script to capture its essence from the viewpoint of the order clerk.

1. Get the details of the customer.
2. Get the details of the required product.
3. Verify that no customer limits have been exceeded, e.g. the customer's account exists and is not blocked.
4. Verify that no product limits have been exceeded, e.g. check the stock.
5. Check the price.
6. Agree and record the sale.
7. Adjust the stock.
8. Send out the paperwork.

Note the complete generality of this stereotypical procedure – all ordering should work this way – but also note that the script is a little overdetermined by the ordering of its steps. We will be able to relax this later and add detail too.

The attentive reader may be wondering how I can claim generality for a process that is clearly going to have exceptions. For instance, what happen when the product is out of stock? What if the customer says: 'No deal', because the price is not right?

Clearly, we need a method for handling exceptions.

5.3.1 Handling Exceptions

There can be two kinds of exception to a business process or the conversations that compose it.

- Something may happen that means that a different set of tasks must be carried out in order to achieve the conversation's goal. This kind of exception is **non-fatal**.
- Something may happen that means that the script cannot achieve its goal at all. We call these exceptions **fatal**, without wishing to imply that they are always life-threatening.

In some cases, the only way to deal with fatal exceptions is to annotate the script to say what happens. I will deal with fatal exceptions later. First, let us look at the non-fatal case, which is more interesting.

Back to the restaurant! No real visit to any restaurant follows the restaurant script exactly. One may, for example:

1. Enter the restaurant.
2. Attract the attention of a waiter.
3. Go to take one's seat.
4. Slip on a banana skin . . .

The script is broken and must be repaired before our culinary cravings can be assuaged. This is accomplished by permitting what we will call side-scripts, which deal with exceptions to the stereotypical course of the conversation. **Side-scripts** are scripts for well-known situations that may be invoked when an exception occurs in another script: we have the mental model of a script 'sending a message' to a side-script to ask for its help in achieving its goal. In this particular case the side-script might proceed as follows:

1. Get up.
2. Utter imprecations and profanities.
3. Brush oneself down.
4. Look around to see who is laughing.
5. Abuse them verbally or punch them.
6. Return to the interrupted task.

The point to note here is that the banana skin script does not just work in the context of the restaurant script. It will work anywhere: in the street, on the factory floor or in the office (if there are no carpets). The graphical notation for this kind of message is illustrated in Figure 5-4.

In practice, scripts can become complicated and have to allow for many exceptions, e.g. what happens when the bill arrives and you find you have lost your wallet or purse? However, the script describes a well-known and stereotypical situation: one that has been encountered many times before. To process such exceptions, conversations are able to send messages to each other.

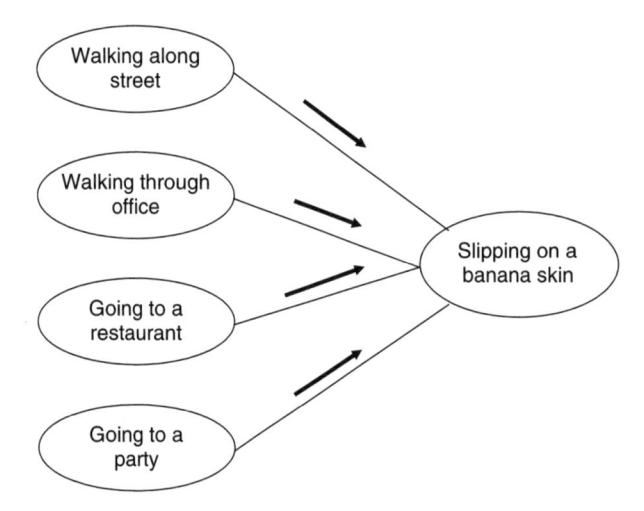

Figure 5-4 Handling exceptions with a side-script.

Parenthetically, we should note that a side-script has exactly the same semantics as what Schank and Abelson called a 'subscript'. The renaming is necessary to avoid confusion with notions of specialization where the prefix 'sub' is commonly used.

5.4 Conversations as Components

If business processes are networks of conversations then it follows that the components of a process are precisely components; in other words conversations can be regarded as reusable, pluggable objects. As such they define services, just as components implement the latter.

We have just seen the utility of permitting OO-style message passing in our models of conversations. It turns out that conversations can also be classified and (de)composed. For example, the scripts for paying one's electricity, gas and water bills can be generalized into a 'pay bill' task script. In other words, they can be regarded as objects within an object model of the business process world. It also happens that we can find uses for the idea of associations between objects. To represent these concepts we use well-known UML notations, as shown in Figure 5-5.

Figure 5-5(a) shows a conversation script with three specializations, while Figure 5-5(b) shows a script with three components. Note that the semantics of this figure is exactly the same as the «uses» relationship between use cases (or «include» as it was originally called), with the arrows pointing down to the components.

Figure 5-5(c) shows an association between scripts. There is no restriction on what kind of association there can be, but we can pick out four canonical ones that are particularly useful for business process modelling:

- Enables. The first conversation must conclude successfully before the second can start.
- Disables. If first conversation concludes successfully then the second may not start.
- Follows (dually Precedes) implies a sequencing between conversations. Note that aggregation does not; the three subscripts in Figure 5-5(a) can happen in *any* order.
- Parallels. The two conversations go on in parallel and may interact.

In Figure 5-5(d) we are using the notation that is normally only found on UML collaboration diagrams to indicate the message passing that occurs when a use case passes control to an exception handling use case or side-script. We shall see in Chapter 7 that this is a far better approach than relying on the flawed «extends» stereotype.

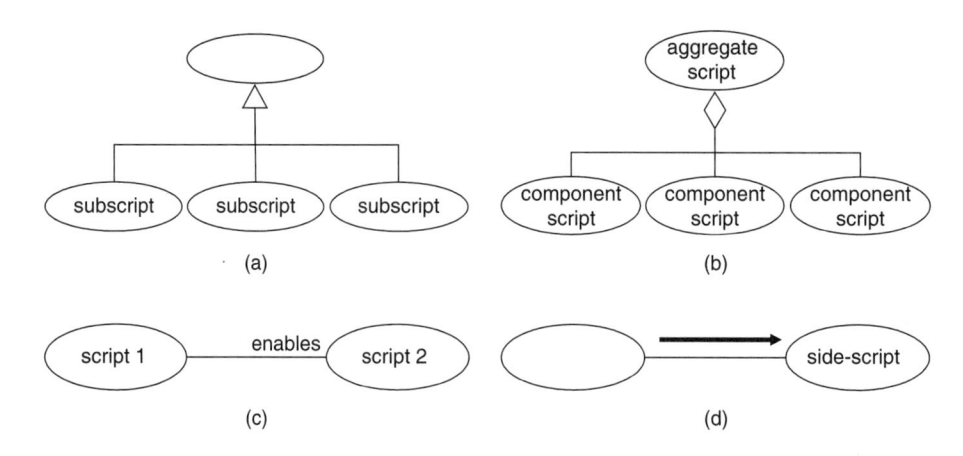

Figure 5-5 Relationships among conversation scripts.

So, conversations can be modelled as *bona fide* objects, where the attributes are the script, its used resources and various performance-related items; the operations are exceptions to the script to be handled by other conversations. Scripts describe stereotypes of business tasks. Recall that the most common approach to analyzing a task is to decompose it into its component tasks, as in Figure 5-5. We can keep doing this until the tasks are atomic. The scripts can then be written, if desired, using a task action grammar in what I call SVDPI form – because all sentences can be arranged into the form: Subject–Verb–Direct object(s)–Preposition–Indirect object(s). Doing things this way enables simple metrics to be collected, such as the number of indirect objects as a surrogate for the data complexity of the task.

Of course, it is always possible to keep on decomposing tasks *ad infinitum*, merely by adding more detail or descending to a lower level of Physics. We stop when words that are not in the vocabulary of the normal user (the domain ontology) would be introduced at the next stage of the decomposition. For example, in order to capture the script 'the clerk moves the mouse to the Quantity field and enters … ' is not atomic because the word mouse is not part of the ontology of ordering. We should have stopped at 'the clerk enters the quantity … '. In other words an **atomic** script is arrived at by decomposing task objects until:

1. The script is a single sentence – ideally in SVDPI format.
2. Further decomposition would introduce terms that are not in the domain ontology.

The outstanding question, then, is how are we to discover the domain ontology? Luckily, a study of the conversations' contracts makes this relatively straightforward.

5.5 Contracts and Goals

Consider now a conversation that is fundamental to all commercial activity: the conversation that leads to a sale or, dually, a purchase. Figure 5-6 shows that a sale always involves a purchaser and a vendor. Since there is a great deal of variation in the way that sales are handled, there is some difficult in writing a completely generic script for this conversation. So, deferring this for the time being, what can be said in general?

We know that every conversation is partly defined by its conditions of satisfaction: its contract or goal. What is the goal of a sale? In other words, how does the world change when a sale takes place? The answer is very simple indeed: after a sale the purchaser has the goods and the vendor has the money. More formally, some thing is owned by the purchaser and the vendor no longer owns that thing, and the vendor has an extra amount of money equal to the price of the thing and the purchaser has less money by the same amount. Logicians and computer scientists would call this statement a **post-condition**.

It is equally easy to see that all sales must satisfy a pre-condition: the vendor must own the thing and the purchaser must have the money.

The pre- and post-conditions of a conversation define that conversation completely. To convince yourself of this, try to vary one of them. Suppose the post-condition becomes: the thing is owned by the purchaser and that thing is no longer owned by the vendor, leaving out the assertions about money. This is no longer a sale! So, what is it?

It could be a theft, but it could equally well be a gift. When a goal is indeterminate between concepts we must refine the post-condition. In this case we might ask, in the post-condition if the vendor is happy to distinguish between the two concepts.

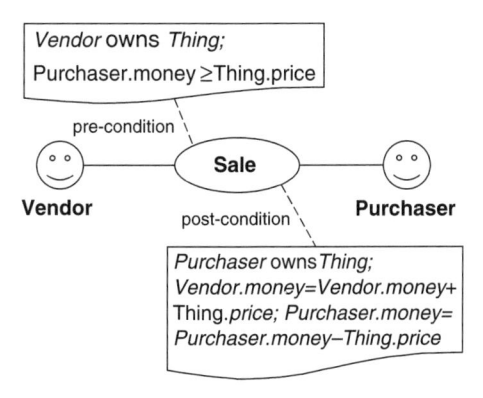

Figure 5-6 The sale conversation.

Summarizing, every conversation has a pre- and post-condition and these conditions characterize it completely. These conditions provide a completely *non-procedural* description of the conversation, whereas the scripts may be procedural, giving the sense of a fixed sequence of steps that may not reflect the business reality accurately. Both viewpoints can be useful but the non-procedural description is essential. Both are stereotypical.

Once we have written pre- and post-conditions for each conversation we can use some of the object identification techniques outlined in Chapter 3 to begin to establish the business ontology. Once again we will use the UML class diagram notation to provide any graphical representations that may be needed.

Textual analysis of the pre- and post-conditions helps to establish any objects, associations and concepts needed for the conditions to make sense. In the sale example, it is immediately obvious that our ontology must provide representations for Purchaser, Vendor and Thing and that these are object types. We will also need to represent Purchaser.money, Vendor.money and Thing.price somehow. More subtly, there must be a way of saying that someone owns a thing. Drawing a UML diagram of the types will help the thought process, but there is a useful Catalysis trick to make this easier: we draw a 'snapshot' of typical instances of the types involved when the pre-condition is true and the sale conversation is yet to take place. Figure 5-7(a) shows one. Jane has £20 in her purse and is currently the proud owner of four things. The vendor has four (different) things in stock and the till holds £200.

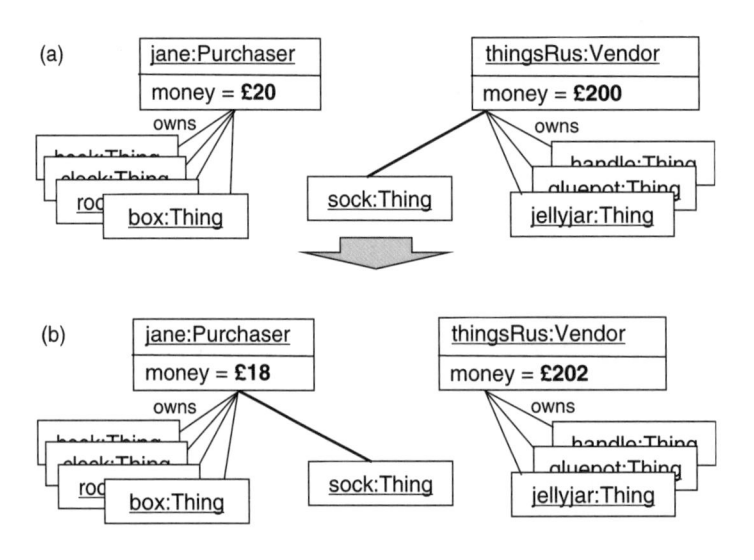

Figure 5-7 Before and after snapshots.

Now let the sale of a sock occur and some things change. Figure 5-7(b) shows the 'after' situation. First, the association between thingsRus and the sock is destroyed and a new one created linking Jane to the sock. Similarly, the amounts of money held by each participant are amended by the price of a sock, £2.

The most convenient way to execute this 'back of envelope' technique is to use two different colour pens. Draw the before diagram in blue and use the red to cross out the associations and values shown in bold in Figure 5-7(a). Then write the new data in red on the same diagram.

Figure 5-8 shows a type diagram consistent with this model. Observing the duplication of the 'owns' attribute in both Vendor and Purchaser makes an abstraction possible: an Owner type. It is just worth pausing to note that, in programming, this would be an interface rather than a class.

Having established the conversation model and its corresponding ontology – which provides a vocabulary to describe the pre- and post-conditions and, indeed, any other business rules that apply – we can go on to identify the business services that our model suggests.

There are two things that need to be done to discover business services from the conversation model. We must decompose the conversations or processes in the model to reveal detail and we can classify the types in our ontology. During decomposition we ask: 'What must the agents have or know to achieve the desired outcome?'. During classification we are asking: 'What collaborations do the components need to carry out amongst themselves?'. It is not a completely mechanical process and requires experience and some skill to do it successfully.

The sale process is very simple and little decomposition is possible unless we impose a particular business model, such as insisting that the money must be handed over before the goods are delivered. But, even at the high level, we can see easily that both the agents must know how much money they have before and after the sale and the vendor at least must be able to check the stock. So there must be two services: a current balance service and a stock service. It's not rocket science.

Implicit in this thought process is that we have, perhaps subconsciously, classified the type model. Vendor and Purchaser are agents and Owner is merely an abstraction of these: Thing is a core component that perhaps

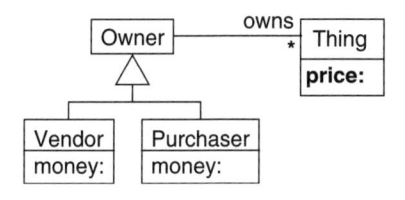

Figure 5-8 Some types in the domain ontology.

should present the stock and balance services to the agents or other service consumers.

My colleagues and I have found it very efficacious to apply Coad's 'colour' classification patterns; introduced in Chapter 3. Recall that this approach distinguishes five domain independent component types as follows.

- Descriptions (blue), which are like catalogue entries. The services associated with these types are almost exclusively CRUD (Create, Read, Update, Delete) services based on the data fields in the catalogue.
- Party/Place/Thing (green) components are the core components of the domain and are usually its most stable and enduring concepts. Every green object has a blue description.
- Rôles (yellow) provide decoupling between green objects and pink ones (which may otherwise have a many-to-many relationship). Our agents are rôles.
- Moment/Interval (pink) components provide a record of some business process that must be recorded. I think Episodes would be a more descriptive and evocative name.
- Interfaces and plug-points (white) become more significant as we move through specification towards design.

Since this book is set in monochrome, it will not present the colour coding, but I will refer to the colours as a convenient shorthand.

It is possible also to discover various heuristic rules associated with these types. For example, if there is an association between two greens this implies that there is a missing pink.

Recalling the discussion in earlier chapters of Jackson's analysis of models, it is important to remember that there is a difference between an event in the world and a (pink) event in the system. In the case of a sale event taking place in the world, we create an instance of the pink type – also called a sale. The sale event must refer to the thing sold (green) through the (yellow) rôles of vendor and purchaser. So there are two trivial services: a buy service accessible by the purchaser and a sell service accessible by the vendor. In general, such services arise as a combination of a pink and a yellow. Such services may have to obey specific business rules. Of course, we must now add the services that we have already discovered: a current balance service and a stock service. These are essentially CRUD services on the blue descriptions of thing, vendor and purchaser. Unfortunately, this kind of analysis does not always reveal the detail that we need for more complex processes. To get to such detail we need to move from simple conversations to more complex collaborations.

In law, a contract is always between exactly two parties. It might be objected that a partnership constitutes a contract between all the partners, but this is not the case. A partnership is said to be 'jointly and severally liable' for its contracts with the outside world. What this means is that, should the partnership be found in breach of contract, it would have to compensate as a whole the aggrieved counterparty. If the fault were attributable to a particular partner then the partnership as a whole would have to sue that individual for damages. For this reason *a conversation may only connect exactly two agents*; if there need to be more we must decompose the conversation somehow.

But if two conversations happen in parallel they may interact and, furthermore, the interaction may be between more than two agents when taken together. To deal with this complexity, we need the notions of a collaboration and a collaboration script.

5.6 Conversations, Collaborations and Services

A conversation involves exactly two agents. A collaboration arises from multiple conversations and therefore may involve two or more agents. Like a conversation a collaboration has a stereotypical script and a goal. The goal is the intersection of all the conversations' post-conditions, i.e. they are combined with the AND operation. The situation with pre-conditions is slightly more complicated. The pre-conditions of each conversation must all be satisfied but one conversation within a collaboration may be the enabler of another. This is because, in the real world, collaborations take time; they are not instantaneous.

In the original version of Catalysis, collaborations were called actions. They were modelled as being instantaneous and simply had a pre- and post-condition.

Let us consider a simple example, returning again to our order processing process. Figure 5-9 illustrates the two conversations that take place when a customer rings in with an order. Note that there is a 'parallels' association between them. Here are the two scripts.

PlaceOrder

1. The customer asks the clerk for a quotation (in general this can be for purchase or sale, but think of a purchase request for now).

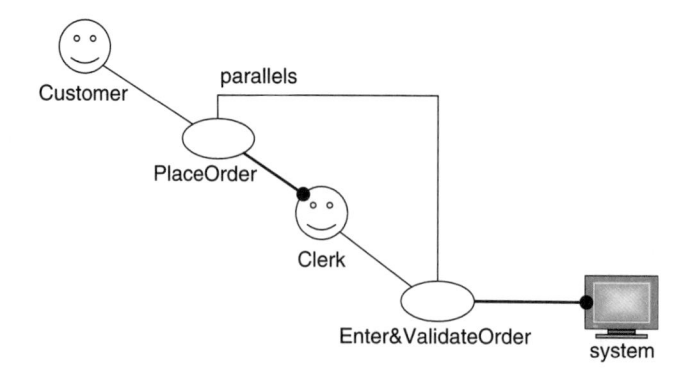

Figure 5-9 The order processing conversations.

2. The clerk gives price and availability.
3. The customer decides whether to accept the quote and places the order.

Pre: None.

Post: The customer has a confirmation that the order has been placed.

Enter&ValidateOrder

1. The clerk checks with the system that the customer is valid and has credit.
2. The clerk retrieves the applicable prices and checks stock levels.
3. The clerk checks with the system that the deal will not violate any limits or regulations.
4. The clerk commits the deal in the system.

Pre: Valid customer and no limit breaches. Product in stock.

Post: The customer has a confirmation that the order has been placed. The stock level is adjusted.

These scripts fail to capture the interaction between the two conversations dismally but the resultant collaboration, shown in Figure 5-10, does so nicely. Here is the script.

PlaceValidOrder

1. The customer asks the clerk for a quotation (in general this can be for purchase or sale, but think of a purchase request for now).
2. The clerk checks with the system that the customer is valid and has credit.
3. The clerk retrieves the applicable prices and checks stock levels.

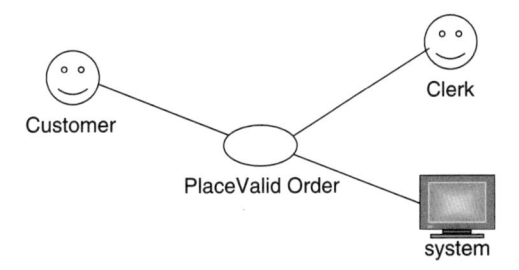

Figure 5-10 The order processing collaboration.

4. The clerk checks with the system that the deal will not violate any limits or regulations.
5. The clerk gives price and availability.
6. The customer decides whether to accept the quote and places the order.
7. The clerk commits the deal in the system.

Pre: Valid customer and no limit breaches. Product in stock.

Post: The customer has a confirmation that the order has been placed. The stock level is adjusted.

This collaboration describes exactly the same business process that we expressed in BPMN in Chapter 4: order processing for foreign exchange dealing. Figure 5-11 shows this process using the conversation object notation developed in this chapter. Note the partial sequencing. Also notice the relative simplicity of the diagram, comparing it with the three BPMN diagrams that we needed to draw in Chapter 4 to express the same process. We can't decide whether to commit to the deal until after we have

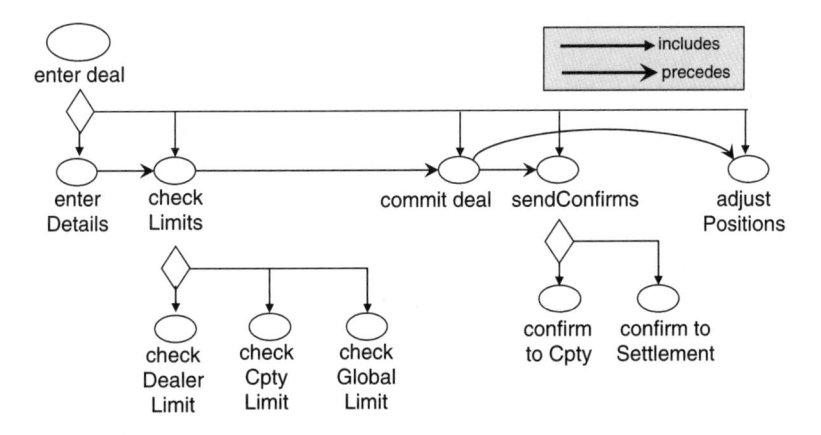

Figure 5-11 Decomposing the order processing collaboration.

checked all the limits, but the order in which we adjust the positions and send out the confirmations does not matter in the slightest. The aggregation (includes) notation does *not* imply left-to-right sequencing, so we have to introduce the precedes associations to express sequencing.

Essentially this process description focuses on the clerk-system conversation though it makes reference to the conversation with the customer. In that sense it is what I call a **boundary conversation**. Some people may wish to think of boundary conversations as similar to use cases, although this might be misleading, given the state of current practice with use cases.

Each of the atomic conversations has a script, and it is at this stage that the SVDPI form becomes appropriate. Here it is.

EnterDetails

1. The dealer enters the counterparty, instrument, amount, rate, buy or sell, and any special settlement conditions.

As a result of their duration, collaborations and, indeed conversations and business processes, may be subject to rely and guarantee conditions. A **rely** clause states a pre-condition that must remain true throughout the execution of the conversation, collaboration or service it refers to. Should it be violated, it is not known what is to be expected as a result. A service implementing a rely clause is not responsible for maintaining the condition. A **guarantee** is a statement that a service must maintain as true throughout its execution.

We must return now to the topic of finding services from conversation analysis. Again we will make use of the Coad colour patterns.

Our intention is to create a service, and thus a component, for order processing. The agents are customer, clerk and system, but the system is merely a surrogate for the service(s) we are trying to define: the boundary conversations. The customer, while still involved in the process, does not partake of any boundary conversations. Thus, we identify the product as a thing; it has a description. Taking an order should result in the creation of a pink episode which breaks down into several component pinks: take details, do checks, commit, send confirmations and adjust stock.

Each of the pink components has a state model that describes the valid process. From this we can extract the candidate services directly. For example, to go from the unvalidated state to the validated state of an order, we need a stock monitoring service and a credit checking service. The presence of these services is a guard on the transition. It is easy to see, in a similar way, that there must be services for pricing and for printing and dispatching.

There is a danger, when carrying out this kind of analysis that one will focus only on the immediate problem and not ask whether there are there services whose use is common to other departments or processes. Often

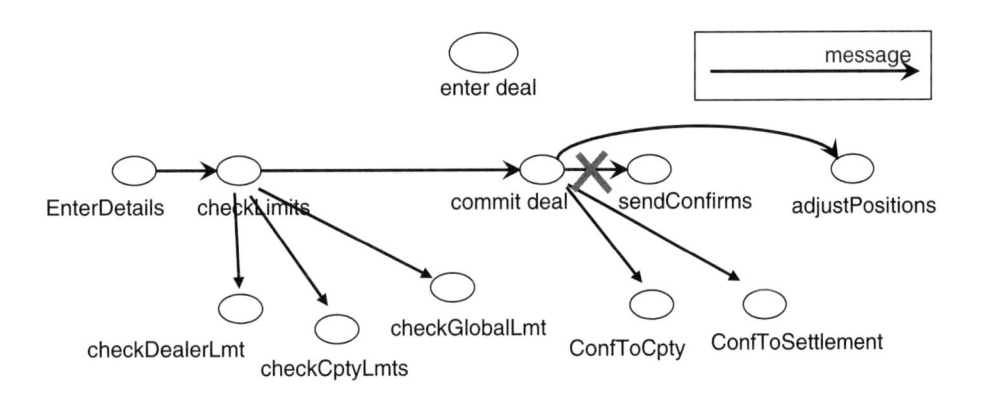

Figure 5-12 Service implementation of the order processing process.

there is little effort needed to spot this kind of common need and the potential payback is large.

Having completed this analysis, we can now think about implementation of the order processing process in a service oriented architecture. This can follow the same structure quite closely as shown in Figure 5-12. The main difference is that we are able to eliminate the sendConfirms process and bundle it up in the commit decision process.

To round off this section, let us look at a simple business process re-engineering (BPR) example. BPR is less fashionable than it was in the early 1990s though still providing an important part of the motivation for many BPM exercises. It provides a good illustration of the value of conversation approach.

Of course, in business process re-engineering, we are eager to capture not just the boundary conversations, such as order placement, but to model the communications among our customers, suppliers, competitors, etc. This provides the opportunity to offer new services to these players, perhaps taking over their internal operations – for a fee of course.

The rich pictures of Figures 5-13 and 5-14 show how this might be applied in the simple case of delivering medical supplies, based on what happened at Baxter Healthcare (Short and Venkatramen, 1992). Originally, Baxter took an order from the hospital's procurement department and delivered to its loading bay. Then the hospital was responsible for storing the goods and delivering them to the appropriate operating theatre, as shown in Figure 5-13. After re-engineering, goods such as surgical gloves are delivered directly by the supplier to the operating theatre where they are required (Figure 5-14). Of course, the conversation labelled `OrderGloves` has been modified. This gives an advantage over other suppliers in terms of service, reduces the hospital's inventory and logistics costs and means that the supplier while remaining competitive can charge a higher price. It also makes the hospital more dependent on the supplier.

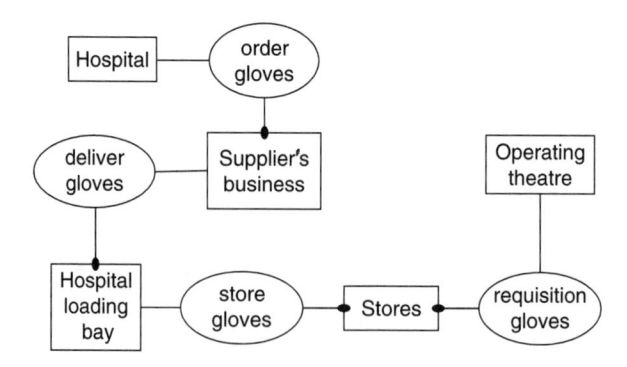

Figure 5-13   Delivery logistics – before.

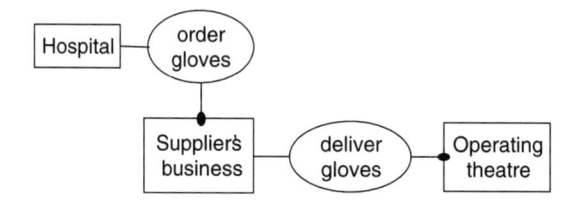

Figure 5-14   Delivery logistics – after.

Of course, we could represent the same before and after processes equally well using BPMN, but I think these rich pictures have a directness of impact that appeals to many non-technical stakeholders, making it easier to discuss the benefits and consequences of the revised service architecture.

5.7   Checking Model Consistency

Having analysed the business process in terms of conversations and collaborations, there is one more critical task for the requirements engineer. Recall from Chapter 3 how we went to a good deal of trouble to establish a set of measurable, prioritized business objectives for each process. Now there is a model of a network of conversations. What is the relationship between the two models? We must now answer two critically important questions:

- Does every conversation support the achievement of *at least one* objective?
- Is *every* objective supported by at least one message?

If the answer to either question is 'no', then the models must be amended. Either we have missed some conversations or we are modelling conversations that do not contribute to the achievement of any stated business objective. Of course, it is possible that we have missed an important objective and, in that case, the users should be consulted to see if the statement of objectives needs to be modified. If not, we have a clear re-engineering opportunity: just stop doing the work that supports no objective.

The simplest way to record the results of the analysis is to construct a simple spreadsheet with the rows representing conversations and the columns objectives. A 'Y' entered in the grid then signifies that 'this conversation has a goal that will contribute to the achievement of this objective'. It takes just a few minutes to create a macro that will highlight any conversations that contribute to no objectives by, say, changing their colour to red. The same macro can also highlight any objectives that are unsupported by any business process, i.e. conversation. Using a different colour for this is a good idea.

The spreadsheet is a tool for discussion with users and further analysis by requirements engineers. It is also a good place to record the measures and priorities. Keeping such a record contributes to the goal of model traceability, in that we can see how our processes and their outcomes (goals) are linked to the business objectives. For fuller traceability, a similar matrix can be built relating the conversations to the components in the ontology: the types mentioned in their pre- and post-conditions. As we will see later, the same components can also encapsulate business rules that apply to processes, giving another layer of traceability.

5.8 Summary

Catalysis Conversation Analysis offers a very definite, graphically simple, theoretically based perspective on the question of what a business process is. The theory is rooted in Semiotics, and especially in the work of Winograd and Flores (1986). A business is thus a network of goal-oriented commitments among agents that participate in these commitments. Each of these commitments is expressed as a contract between these agents – either explicitly stated or implicitly understood.

To satisfy a goal-oriented commitment or contract, some work must always be done – unless the goal is already achieved in the start state! The contract defines the state of the world that must be achieved on completion of the work task.

An agent is any entity in the world that can communicate. Agents are autonomous, flexible and social in nature and, to some extent, intelligent. Agents can be internal or external to the business. Agents – like actors in the use case theory – are to be thought of as adopting a rôle.

A business process is a network of commitments between agents represented by conversations and contracts. Conversations have a fixed, six-phase structure: recognize trigger, set goal, propose, negotiate, perform task, check and handover result. The symbol for a conversation is an ellipse, as for a use case, which is a special case of a conversation or collaboration.

Conversations are described by scripts which are stereotypes of behaviour.

There can be two kinds of exception to a business process or the conversations that compose it. Something may happen that means that a different set of tasks must be carried out in order to achieve the conversation's goal. This kind of exception is **non-fatal**. Something may happen that means that the script cannot achieve its goal at all. We call these exceptions **fatal**. In some cases, the only way to deal with fatal exceptions is to annotate the script to say what happens. Non-fatal exceptions are best dealt with by delegating control to an exception handling process script: a side-script. This considerably reduced the number of scripts that must be documented.

Conversations can have component conversations. Conversations can specialize other conversations. Conversations can be associated with each other. The most useful associations are enables, disables, follows/precedes and parallels.

An **atomic** conversation script is arrived at by decomposing task objects until the script is a single sentence – ideally in SVDPI format – and such that further decomposition would introduce terms that are not in the domain ontology.

Conversations are defined completely by their goals. Snapshots provide a handy technique for exploring what happens when a conversation occurs with respect to the type model.

There are two things that need to be done to discover business services from the conversation model: decompose the conversations or processes in the model to reveal detail and classify the types in our ontology. During decomposition we ask: 'What must the agents have or know to achieve the desired outcome?'. During classification we are asking: 'What collaborations do the components need to carry out among themselves?'. This is not a completely mechanical process and needs some skill. Try to classify the types according to Coad's colour patterns.

A conversation involves exactly two agents. A collaboration arises from multiple conversations and therefore may involve two or more agents. Like a conversation a collaboration has a stereotypical script and a goal. The goal is the intersection of all the conversations' post-conditions. The situation with pre-conditions is slightly more complicated. The pre-conditions of each conversation must all be satisfied but one conversation within a collaboration may be the enabler of another. This is because, in the real world, collaborations are not instantaneous. Collaborations enable us to discuss business processes as a whole and move towards what must happen in conversations at the system boundary.

To move to identifying services, we must focus on the pink episodes in the type model, which will have a state model that describing the valid process.

Check model consistency by asking if every conversation supports the achievement of at least one objective and every objective is supported by at least one message.

5.9 Bibliographical Notes

The Catalysis method was originally developed and popularized by Desmond D'Souza and Alan Cameron Wills (D'Souza and Wills, 1999). Subsequently, it was developed and extended by Derek Andrews as Catalysis II, with input from Alan and others. As a result it now takes account of modern, distributed, layered component architectures such as J2EE and .NET and of SOA. A book on Catalysis II is in preparation.

Conversation theory was developed by Ian Graham between 1991 and 2008 in a number of publications and integrated into Catalysis II with the help of Derek Andrews. Derek's forthcoming book on Catalysis II goes into much more detail on the use of Coad's colour patterns to specify services (Andrews, 2009).

CHAPTER 6

Models of Large Enterprises

I am big. It's the pictures that got small.
Brackett, Wilder and Marshman (*Sunset Boulevard*, 1950)

Business process modelling techniques based on activity diagrams, BPMN or Catalysis Conversation Analysis are all very well for modelling individual process areas within the enterprise. They facilitate the analysis of workflow within a business area and the sort of detailed models that can form that basis of system models and provide a basis for SOA implementation. However, attempts to apply these same techniques or notations to large organizations are doomed to drown in a sea of detail and be caught between the monster of procrastination and the whirlpool of slow progress. They are doomed to, in a word, failure.

In this short chapter we will learn a simple and pragmatic technique for modelling businesses in the large and see how such a corporate model or models can be used to home in upon and organize our more detailed business process models. The model can also provide the basis for a description of the high level structure of a service oriented architecture: SOA in the large.

6.1 Business Process Modelling and SOA in the Large

The aim is to construct an object model of a business. For a small business this is straightforward but, unfortunately, building an object model of a corporation as large as AT&T, British Petroleum, IBM, Toyota or UBS is likely to produce a model of such complexity as to be virtually meaningless. Like earlier attempts to produce corporate data models, the exercise is likely to take so long that it would be out of date years before it was complete. Even approaches based on the Soft Systems Method's rich pictures will not help a great deal with problems of this sort of scale. What then can be done to de-scope such a large problem to a scale where more conventional business process modelling notations are apposite and effective? To answer this question, I propose a technique which I designate mission grid analysis.

A **mission grid** is a two-dimensional matrix of high level business process areas, organized into columns representing logical rôles and rows representing value propositions (goals). The grid may be annotated with various data, metadata and comments including, but not restricted to, business rules, process interactions, service interfaces, existing systems and APIs, process categories and strategy.

In analysing any commercial enterprise, the first question we must ask is: 'who are the customers and other stakeholders in this business?'. Typical stakeholders might include – in addition to the ever-present customers – suppliers, regulatory bodies, trade associations, information providers and competitors. Once these are identified, we can define external goals that are shared with the customers and others. These are variously called shared goals or customer value propositions (CVPs) in the literature. An **external goal** is a goal that the organization shares with its customers. These statements sum up a state of affairs that both the customer and the enterprise would like to achieve on a regular basis. As an example, one external goal might be *to deliver a high quality product at a reasonable price while remaining profitable*. Let us take each of the three subsidiary goals in this proposition in turn.

- *High quality products.* This obviously suits the customers' aims – unless they are very eccentric customers. It suits the business because if the products are of poor quality, competitors may enter the market with a better product. This happened to the British motorcycle industry after the 1960s.
- *Reasonable prices.* This too obviously suits the customer. Again the company's motivation is the danger of low cost competition seducing its customers. The supermarket business is a constant reminder of this, although it is clear that low cost supermarkets have yet to pass the quality benchmark, at least for fresh foods. The one exception I know of solves the equation by subjecting its staff to appalling working conditions. Obviously, I can't name them here.
- *Profitability.* Here it is the company that most obviously benefits. The customer would gain because he wants to buy a product from a reliable supplier who is going to stay in business and continue to

improve the product. Any motorcycle enthusiast who owns a vintage British bike knows this well. Many even make their own spares.

These external goals are insufficient to characterize the goals of a business; we must also define internal goals. **Internal goals** are those that the organization holds to for it own, private reasons and could be to do with cultural or ethical principles. They may also arise from the exigencies of government or industry regulation. Even the law of the land may play a rôle in, for example, such mundane matters as keeping the managing director out of gaol. The latter consideration leads, for example, to the need to file proper accounts and tax returns. These, of course, are services provided by the Accounting business process.

The mission grid technique mandates that we write these goals along one axis of a grid or spreadsheet. Practical considerations have led me to conclude that it is better to let the rows of a spreadsheet represent the goals. This is mainly because they can be quite a number of goals. We will see what the columns represent shortly.

To clarify the separation between internal and external goals, it is a good idea to write internal goals as a separate group of columns from the external goals. Alternatively, one might highlight the two different goal types in different colours. To show what is possible, in terms of presentation of the results of a mission grid analysis, Figure 6-1 presents the goal types at the opposite edge of the page; internal goals on the right hand side.

The next step in completing the grid is creative and challenging; it involves establishing what processes must be carried out in order to contribute to or accomplish the goals, internal and external. Having established the goals we must now identify the high level business processes that are

	Butcher	Master butcher	Cleaner	Accountant	
Make/offer product	Prepare product	Visit markets			
	Cutting	Define cuts	Clean workspace		
	Offer advice	Train butchers			
Inform public of products		Advertise & promote			
				VAT Analysis	**Produce VAT return**
	Take cash		Keep hands clean	Accounting	**Produce accounts**

Figure 6-1 A fragment of a mission grid for a butcher's shop.

needed to achieve these goals. Returning to our example, making and delivering a high quality product at a reasonable price while remaining profitable would seem to imply a need for the following processes.

- Production (unless this is a service industry).
- Logistics (we used the word 'deliver').
- Sales (unless we sell through marketing alone).
- Marketing (including competitive analysis and price monitoring).
- Quality monitoring and control.
- Recruitment.
- Training.
- R&D.

Possibly there will be others, depending on the specifics of your firm.

In some cases it may be tempting to drill down a little further into some processes before going on with the construction of the mission grid. For example, to expedite the production process we might need a factory and this implies some sort of estate or premises management process, including such eminently outsourceable services as site security and providing power for the lathes. Resist this temptation unless you can relate the processes to goals. In this case it is easy to see that power provision is related to economies arising from the employment of capital in the production process and that site security is needed to guarantee the continuous availability of the product to customers. So iterate! Did you miss these goals on the first pass? Do they imply that new processes need to be identified?

The next step in mission grid analysis can be challenging too. It involves assigning each process to a logical rôle. This usually involves a substantial rearrangement of the processes in the grid. A **logical rôle** is a sort of abstract job description that unifies a coherent set of processes that could be accomplished using one basic set of skills, such as those likely to be within the capabilities of a single human agent or department. Assigning the processes to the rôles is quite a difficult thing to do well and the process is bound to be iterative and to involve a lot of interaction with domain experts and users within the business. In Figure 6-1 the rôles are the columns.

During the search for logical rôles one should be trying to see if processes fall into natural groupings. In Figure 6-1, for example, should we see VAT analysis as just a subprocess of Accounting? From the SOA angle, VAT analysis is clearly a potential service that could be useful within Accounting but might also be of value for Order Processing, as we saw in Chapter 1. Therefore if we do bundle it up into Accounting in the mission grid we must record this information in some way. Therefore process documentation must include a list of any services that the process relies upon. In this case we would add VAT Analysis to the documentation of both the Accounting process area and that of Order Processing. Alternatively, we can retain VAT Analysis as an independent process area but should create rules to represent the process dependencies between it and the other two process areas.

The mission grid technique mandates that, except in the unlikely circumstance that this is an entirely new company, before and after grids are constructed. The before grid models the existing situation. Finding the logical rôles is easy for the before grid; they are existing departments and functions. The only really new information is likely to be the assignment of current processes to shared or internal goals. The reason for building a before grid is to facilitate discussion and negotiation about how to improve and re-engineer the business.

The after grid represents a vision of a streamlined, re-engineered more agile business. Ideally, the after grid is developed without reference to the before grid and there is a big danger that people will slavishly copy existing practices, especially existing logical rôles. One may also prepare separate grids for different geographical divisions of the organization.

The mission grid has been found to be an excellent tool for communicating with business leaders about the nature of the business and its strategy in the large. These experts should always be asked to justify the goals and challenge every process: Is it necessary? Do we really want to be in that business? Will that goal be sustainable in forecast market conditions? Could a partner do it for us more efficiently than we could do it?

Taking up the last point as an example, certain rows or columns of the grid, or particular groups of cells (processes), may be candidates for outsourcing. The key desiderata in this respect are:

- Is the process a customer facing process?
- Is the process differentiating?

The phrase **customer facing** signifies that the process involves direct contact with the customer. It is usually unwise to outsource such processes to third parties. The many companies that outsourced their help desks in recent years are beginning to realize their error in relation to this principle. **Differentiating** activities are those that your company does that actually characterize it in the eyes of its customers. For example, if you saw a hoarding advertising an organization that 'guarantees to take a percentage of your income every year while providing no direct service in return', then you could be pretty sure that the ad. referred to the Revenue. This statement differentiates that organization from all others. It is a capital error to outsource customer facing, differentiating processes. Differentiating and customer-facing are examples of **process categories**.

Processes that are neither customer facing nor differentiating are usually the most appropriate for outsourcing. Thus, the mission grid is a

	Not customer facing	Customer facing
Differentiating	R&D, training in industry specifics or non-commodity skills, proprietary production processes, etc.	Unique processes, people, skills or products, customer services process, complaints process, marketing, etc.
Not differentiating	Electricity supply, water supply, recruitment, office cleaning, etc.	Help desk, network infrastructure, billing, call centre operations, advertising, etc.

Figure 6-2 The C-F/D grid.

powerful tool for discussing business process re-engineering with the business. It is also the starting point for the implementation of the systems that must underpin such an enterprise and for object-oriented business modelling.

Figure 6-2 shows a selection of business processes from the mission grid arranged into another kind of grid in which they are classified as to whether or not they are Customer Facing (C-F) and Differentiating (D). We will call this the C-F/D grid for reference. A glance at this C-F/D grid shows that we would be foolish to outsource our complaints process and should think twice about outsourcing, for example, the help desk. On the other hand it reminds us how sensible it is that we buy our water and electricity from a utility company. Of course there are going to be quandaries, those processes for which it is hard to decide exactly where they belong in the C-F/D grid. An example might be customer relationship management (CRM). An IBM survey (Carter, 2007) concluded that 64 % of CEOs believed that their companies could only grow 'by introducing new products ... and differentiating [all] their products through their service'. Therefore, CRM becomes both customer facing and differentiating. On the other hand, much of the CRM process is identical from company to company, as evinced by the proliferation of CRM software packages on the market. The lesson here is to apply the principles that I am advancing intelligently, thoughtfully and with due attention to your concrete circumstances. The devil is in the detail.

The processes in each cell of the grid can be thought of as mission statements for each process-oriented 'business area'. Each of these is likely to be (a) small enough to make the construction of an object model of the business area feasible and (in many cases) (b) suitable for enhancement with a fairly well-focused computer support system. Sometimes the business area corresponds to a small group of closely related cells.

Other process categories are theoretically possible and may be useful in making strategic decisions of a similar type to those we have been discussing. This will be entirely dependent on concrete circumstances. However, I recommend sticking to the C-F/D grid in normal circumstances.

Each process in the grid needs a mission statement that captures its essence and provides a context for any future work that might need to be done on or for it. The mission statement can be quite woolly and will need to be refined into concrete, measurable, prioritized business objectives before requirements analysis of the process area can proceed. Of course, it is this that gives the mission grid technique its name.

Here is a made-up, slightly tongue-in-cheek, mission statement for an order processing process.

Our order processing process will guarantee that only valid orders are recorded and that this will be done in a convivial and familiar atmosphere, enhancing the customer experience and minimizing the human labour required of our clerical staff. Customers will be able to track their orders in real time and contact a representative at any hour of the day.

The process must also have a description of any pre- and post-conditions that apply, in the manner of a Catalysis conversation or collaboration. In other words we must enumerate the condition under which the process, once started, can succeed. These pre-conditions may include process dependencies and external factor. As an example, a Dig-Copper-Mine process might require a certain average copper price to have been attained over an historic period equivalent to its projected lifetime and for the historic trend in price to be upward. (Copper mines usually have a life expectancy of over 25 years.)

The pre-conditions for order processing might include such statements as 'Accounts have a record of customer account,' 'Item is in stock', and so on. Post-conditions describe how the process changes the world; 'Valid order stored. Stock records up to date. Payment processed'; that sort of thing.

Finally, we must assign various priorities to the process areas: priorities for redevelopment, priorities for integration, priorities for outsourcing, priorities for scrapping, priorities for re-engineering, and so on. To this end we ask questions of the following sort for each process area.

- Is the process failing the business in some way?
- Is the process adding value or contributing to profits?
- What are the costs associated with the process?
- What revenues arise directly or indirectly from this process?
- Do our customers report a good experience?
- Is the technology base obstructing business flexibility?

- Are there any forthcoming regulatory requirements that will impose changes?

The list of such questions is possibly endless and will certainly depend on circumstances, industry and culture. Whatever they are, and whatever the answers, the focus must be first on the customer facing, differentiating processes; because it is these that will make or break the company.

Having allocated priorities, the next step is to model the high priority process areas to:

- agree a strategic plan;
- record any existing systems, service interfaces and APIs;
- establish the required services and plan new services;
- elicit any business rules that apply.

I will expand on this process in the subsequent sections of this chapter but, for now, this concludes our high level overview of the mission grid analysis technique.

The normal steps in mission grid analysis are as follows.

- Establish the external goals.
- Establish the internal goals.
- Identify required processes for each goal (before and after).
- Drill down and iterate (before and after).
- Organize the processes according to the logical rôles responsible for them (before and after).
- Agree process categories.
- Find business rules and process interactions.
- Agree strategic plans for each process.
- Record existing systems, service interfaces and APIs. Plan new services.
- Assign process improvement priorities as part of the company strategic plan.

The various annotations that must be made to the process mission statements and descriptions could be viewed as a 7-dimensional hypercube rather than a simple grid. Of course, it may be easier in practice to just store a pointer to 'process documentation' in the cells of a simple spreadsheet but, conceptually, the dimensions of the mission grid hypercube are these.

- Goals.
- Logical roles.
- Process categories.
- Cost and revenue data.

- Business rules.
- Process interactions.
- Service interfaces needed, existing systems/services and APIs.
- Strategy.

The alternative process documentation consists of a document with at least these headings together with a crisp statement of the process's mission, priority and a brief description of its execution that should include any pre-conditions and outcomes. In light of this, the astute reader will have noticed that a process in the mission grid is like a very high level use case or Catalysis collaboration or conversation.

The next step is to refine the analysis of each high priority process using your preferred business modelling technique from the previous chapters and, crucially, perform an SOA-oriented requirements analysis exercise.

6.2 Business Rules in the Mission Grid

The mission grid may be thought of as a matrix of data about the service oriented enterprise or as a, possibly multi-dimensional, spreadsheet. However, there is another useful simile. The mission grid may be thought of as a circuit board. On the edges of the board are gold connectors, linked together by the business process chips mounted on the board. These chips transform input from the logical rôles on one edge to output customer and internal value propositions on the other edge connectors. Clearly, the process chips may collaborate to achieve this and, furthermore, have constraints imposed on their processing. In other words, there are rules.

We have already seen how business rules are endemic in business process descriptions and it is no different at this level of granularity. Processes can be grouped and there can be interactions among processes. Processes obey – or ought to obey – rules.

There will be rules governing individual processes and rules that cross process area boundaries. As an example of an intra-process rule, we might discover that, within the sales process, all contacts should be recorded and all meetings with prospects minuted, and the minutes kept. Of course, we would also have to say what constitutes a contact and a prospect and, indeed, suggest how long such records should be kept or under what circumstances they might (must?) be deleted. Such rules, if discovered should be recorded in the mission grid documentation. If you have a business rules management system, you might even structure its repository to hold the rules.

Inter-process rules are just as common. An obvious example is to say that any financial transaction that completes within the logistics process area must result in a corresponding journal entry in the Accounting process. Now we have to define clearly what constitutes a *financial* transaction, which may not always be entirely trivial. For example, does free accommodation at a supplier's hotel constitute a financial benefit; the tax man might think so. As this example suggests, there could be an entire ruleset capturing the decision criteria based upon, say, taxation law, jurisdictions, dates, and so on. Explicating such detailed rulesets is beyond the remit of mission grid analysis, but their existence should be noted.

As we have seen in earlier chapters, all processes and the services that support them can be characterized and described by pre- and post-conditions: contracts. Such contracts are business rules. Each cell in the grid contains explicit statements of contracts and these are ideally expressed in the company standard rule language, if one has been defined. See Graham (2006), Morgan (2002) or Ross (2003) for detailed suggestions on how to structure rule syntax for this purpose.

An alternative way to capture the business rules inherent in the processes is to use state machine models.

Recall that services at all levels are implemented by components, possibly human components but components nevertheless. At the top level we can define components that manage entire business processes; these might contain objects that record events. An example of such an event might be a book loan from a public library or a reservation for a title. Business components will play particular rôles in a business process event and thus appear in the record of that event. For example, in our library a person plays the rôle of a borrower in a book loan and a reserver in a reservation and a library member in the library. The rôles link to, and represent, business objects. Business rules about the processes can be held in a corresponding process component. The component that manages the loan service would know about the length of a loan, and the maximum number of books that can be borrowed at one time. A process component is less reusable than a core business object since it contains business rules that govern the process. These components are less stable; they tend to change quite frequently as the organization thinks of better and different ways of conducting its business. Even these can be made easier to write and maintain if they can be split into two parts – a generic description of a particular business process together with a part that tailors the description to a particular business process by providing the business rules that restrict the general approach. Returning to the library example, the loan service is about lending books to library members but, with care, it can be refactored to be used in any organization that does loans (books become lendables

```
●──▶[ order ]──▶[ invoice ]──▶[ pay ]──▶[ deliver ]──▶◉
```

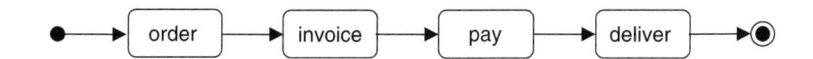

Figure 6-3 Stalinist sales process.

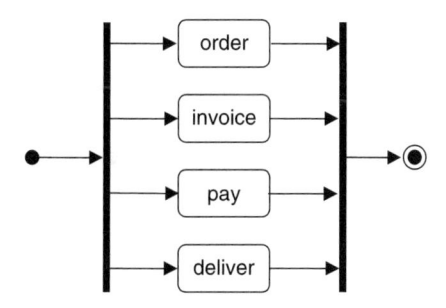

```
       ┃──▶[ order ]──┃
       ┃              ┃
       ┃──▶[ invoice ]──┃
●─────▶┃              ┃──▶◉
       ┃──▶[ pay ]────┃
       ┃              ┃
       ┃──▶[ deliver ]──┃
```

Figure 6-4 A less bureaucratic sales process.

and library members borrowers). The business rules about the business process can be turned into component plug-ins and can then be changed as needed.

This ordering could be weakened to that illustrated in Figure 6-4.

Looking at any business process, one part is about the order in which we do things, and the other is about under which conditions we do things: you can only reserve a horror movie if you are over 18, you cannot buy life assurance if you are over 100, you cannot have a loan if you are an undischarged bankrupt. These later business rules can be encapsulated in a separate part of any component. To introduce generality into the first part we can allow more general order in which we do things and impose business rule to restrict this. Consider the business process of making a sale; our business rules may demand a prescribed order for the activities that make up a sale as shown in Figure 6-3.

The latter allows the activities that make up the business process to be done in any order, or even in parallel. Consider a Christmas club, where we pay for goods before we finally obtain them, and a try-before-you-buy, where they are delivered before being ordered. Business rules are used to enforce the previous order for new or unreliable customers; reliable and well-known customers could benefit from more liberal régimes.

Processes can be grouped, processes may interact and processes obey rules. Process interactions can be of at least three basic types.

- A process can enable or disable a downstream process.
- Two or more processes may typically need to run in parallel.
- A process can need to follow or precede another process.

- A process might affect the way a downstream process is conducted. For example, earlier security vetting may affect the way someone is processed when entering a building.

More complex rules, of course, are possible. Don't forget that process contracts and goals can always be expressed as rules. Doing so may help uncover further rules.

6.3 The Mission Grid as a Roadmap for SOA

In the context of contemporary IT systems, the mission grid is about SOA in the large. Each cell in the grid contains descriptions of the services that a business needs in order to operate: sales, logistics, production, etc. The technique has forced us to decide which processes are differentiating or customer facing. We have been encouraged to assign priories based on this analysis and other factors, such as competitive opportunity or technical innovations. Moving to SOA is now best achieved by organizing it around building SOAs for the high priority process areas.

One of the killer mistakes that people make in implementing SOA is ignoring the need for a common language with shared semantics. Without such a language enterprise integration is doomed to fail. Process relationships and business rules in the mission grid can provide the basis for semantic translations, e.g. prospects from the Sales process become customers when an order is created in Order Processing.

The mission grid construction process starts with shared goals. If services are constructed to support these goals they will be more generic, more reusable and more focused on business agility. The mission grid rules show how process areas will be integrated as, area by area, SOA is introduced.

In summary, the mission grid technique:

- gives a top level view of all the processes that are candidates for migration to enterprise SOA;
- helps us prioritize and order the process of transition to SOA;
- focuses attention on shared semantic concepts that cut across the enterprise as well as those that exist within individual process areas;
- helps uncover business rules;
- helps keep the focus on shared goals throughout migration, supporting greater reusability;
- shows how piecemeal SOA projects will integrate in the long run.

The mission grid is, therefore, an ideal precursor to and roadmap for SOA.

6.4 Other Approaches

IBM has developed a grid-based technique with some similarities to the mission grid; they designate their grid a business component model (BCM). One axis of the grid is the accountability level: Direct, Control or Execute. The reader should note that such old-fashioned hierarchical thinking is discouraged in mission grid analysis. The other axis tends to have labels that are dependent on the specific industry but are always similar to these: Manage, Design, Buy, Make, Sell. The cells within the grid hold individual business process names. Like mission grid analysis, the BCM technique emphasizes customer related goals but these are not made explicit in the structure of the grid.

IBM has developed specific BCMs for some vertical industries. These are very detailed and might well be useful as checklists to ensure that no process area has been inadvertently ignored in a mission grid.

8 Omega is an approach that suggests the tasks that need to be carried out during enterprise business process management exercises. The tasks are classified within a grid the axes of which are as follows.

- Dimensions: Strategy; People; Processes; Systems.
- Task types: Discover; Analyse; Design; Validate; Integrate; Implement; Control.

There are from one to four recommended tasks per cell of the grid. As an example, in the Discover/People cell we find the following three tasks: audit current skills; determine process rôles; map functional activities to customer outcomes (i.e. goals). In the Design/Process cell, one of the tasks is to create a process model and another is to align process priorities with customer goals; directing us, thus, to the use of some specific technique for doing this such as BCM or the mission grid.

The remit of 8 Omega is therefore more general than business process modelling and the mission grid technique could well be used within the context of some parts of an 8 Omega project.

6.5 Summary

Current business process modelling notations are suitable for detailed analysis of business processes and services but are too complex to scale up to model entire enterprises. SOA must be based on business goals.

A mission grid is a matrix of business processes organized by shared business goals and logical rôles. Each process in the grid may be annotated with business rules, process interactions, service interfaces, existing systems and APIs, process categories and strategic plans.

The normal steps in mission grid analysis are as follows.

- Establish external goals.
- Establish internal goals.
- Identify processes (before and after).
- Drill down and iterate (before and after).
- Organize the processes into logical rôles (before and after).
- Agree process categories.
- Find business rules and process interactions.
- Agree strategic plans for each process.
- Record existing systems, service interfaces and APIs. Plan new services.
- Assign process improvement priorities as part of company strategic plan.

Process documentation should include at least the following headings or items.

- Mission statement.
- Process description, including any pre-conditions and any post-conditions not listed as goals.
- Goals.
- Logical roles.
- Process categories.
- Business rules.
- Process interactions.
- Service interfaces needed, existing systems/services and APIs.
- Strategy.

Mission Grid Analysis provides a practical method of analysing and improving business processes in the large. It can be used in concert with other approaches such as BCMs and 8 Omega.

Mission Grid Analysis provides the basis for planning and analysing individual SOA projects in a coherent way that will facilitate consistent SOA implementations across the enterprise.

6.6 Bibliographical Notes

Mission grid analysis is loosely based on ideas developed initially within International Computers Limited during a business process re-engineering project in the 1980s and subsequently used successfully within several other large companies including Swiss Bank Corporation while the present author worked there. The first version of mission grid analysis was described by Graham (1998).

Graham (2006) provides a tutorial on business rules and relates them to service oriented architecture.

Carter (2007) gives a very clear account of IBM's Business Component Model approach. The best source of information on 8 Omega is at `bpmg.org`.

CHAPTER 7

Specification Modelling

Let these describe the undescribable.
Lord Byron (*Childe Harold*)

After modelling the business and its existing and required services, the next step is to home in on the specification of those services and the components that will implement them. We assume also that the architecture has been defined, at least in outline.

This chapter defines an approach to system specification based on Catalysis (D'Souza and Wills, 1999) and various extensions and improvements made to it over the years by my colleagues and I at Trireme International Limited, and especially by Derek Andrews: Catalysis II.

7.1 From Requirements to Specification

As argued already, understanding and modelling requirements requires a richer language than that needed to specify a computer system that will satisfy all or some part of the requirement. In requirements engineering we model a world of which this system may be only a small part. So the style of requirements engineering that says that requirements statement are all of the form: 'The system shall...' misses the point; such statements do not and cannot describe the entire business problem that we are trying to solve or the process that we are trying to support. For example, a system with services that show current cash balances and display stock levels does not, in and of itself, get the goods into the hands of the purchaser, which is the key goal of the process.

Having understood this, once a clear understanding of the business requirements is achieved, it is quite proper to focus on the detailed specification of a system; that is the definition of a set of services that the system will offer. How do we do this?

The requirements model should contain all of the following items.

- Prioritized measurable business objectives.
- Before and after versions of business process descriptions. These may include network models (e.g. models written in BPMN), mission grids or rich pictures based on conversations – or both. They may also include collaborations that show how conversations interact.
- Cross reference tables linking the objectives to the processes and conversations.
- Descriptions of the boundary conversations that apply to existing or projected systems.

It is these boundary conversations that are the starting point for specification. Note that there is no concept of a boundary collaboration. The system will engage in conversations with its users and with any attached devices; these interactions are strictly pairwise. In the conventional wisdom they are use cases.

However, the concept of the use case has been widely applied and inconsistently interpreted. Therefore, we prefer to think of them as boundary conversations, to avoid falling thoughtlessly into bad habits. In what follows I shall use the terms fairly interchangeably, as the need for clarity dictates.

Although there are no collaborations at the system boundary, there may well be collaborations that are internal to the system which it is helpful to include in the specification. For example, three or four components may need to collaborate to provide a service, whether the latter is entirely internal or apparent at the boundary. Of course, specifying these collaborations overlaps with system design – which is not within the scope of this book – but, as established by the original developers of Catalysis, understanding such collaborations is key to specifying the communications protocols that are the difference between a bunch of objects and a genuine kit of components. We will return to this topic later.

7.2 Some Problems with the Conventional Approach to Use Cases

Use cases were first introduced as a technique for specifying telephone switching systems at Ericsson and were later recognized as a brilliant and useful idea by the object-oriented methods community. Most methodologists of that generation integrated use cases into their methods and they are a key feature of UML. Use cases offered possibly the first technique within object-oriented development that did not assume that a written system specification existed at the start of object-oriented analysis.

In this section I consider a number of features of the conventional use case approach that militate against its successful use. In the next we will see how these may be overcome. The problems are, in brief, as follows.

- Overemphasis on functional decomposition.
- Lack of a clear definition and agreed interpretation.
- The inappropriate use of controller objects.
- Confusion over the relationship of use cases with scenarios.
- Lack of a notion of genericity.
- Lack of a notion of atomicity.
- Too much detail and too many use cases as a result of poor abstraction.
- Poor exception handling.

7.2.1 Overemphasis on Functional Decomposition

At first sight, the use case approach appears to have a more functional flavour than an object-oriented practitioner would be comfortable with. Blaha and Premerlani (1998), leading thinkers behind OMT, go so far as to include a treatment of use cases within the dataflow-based Functional Model of that method. This has led critics to claim that use cases are not really object-oriented at all. However, when use cases emerged it was clear that object-oriented analysis and design methods lacked an approach to system specification. Furthermore, most of these methods were entirely data-driven and this led to difficulties in communicating with users who were more comfortable with functionally oriented descriptions of their businesses than with data-centred ones. So, while use cases and the Objectory method within which they were originally situated were indeed rather 'functional' there was at least a small step forward beyond the methods that assumed the pre-existence of the specification. The challenge was to integrate this advance and its functional viewpoint within a genuinely object-oriented, responsibility-driven approach, rather than cobbling it together with a data-driven one.

7.2.2 Lack of Clear Definition

Unfortunately, and despite the standardization within UML, the lack of a precise, semantically complete and universally accepted definition has led to a horrid proliferation of approaches all calling themselves 'use case' based. It seems that every company has their own version of the theory. At a goldfish bowl session at Object Technology 96, held in Oxford, England, participants were asked if they used use cases. Of the 14 who said they did, each was asked to give a definition of a use case. The result was 14 different definitions, even though three of the respondents worked for the same company (in different divisions). Cockburn (1997) obtained similar results in the USA. Subsequent consulting engagements of mine and of my colleagues have done little to persuade me that the situation has improved much.

7.2.3 Controller Objects

The Rational Unified Process (RUP) recommends that its use cases should be linked to three kinds of implementation object: entity objects [*sic*], interface objects and controller objects. The introduction of controller objects in the analysis process can seriously violate the principle of encapsulation, leading to severe maintenance problems downstream. This is because controllers often act as main routines (especially when a data-driven approach is adopted) and have to know a great deal about the other objects that they control. Thus, when one of these objects changes, the controller may have to be modified. This style of implementation, where the controller objects access several entity objects (i.e. datastores), was shown to be inferior to a responsibility-driven design in a study by Sharble and Cohen (1994). A far better approach is the use of rule-based agents.

7.2.4 Use Cases and Scenarios

There has been some confusion over the exact meaning of the term SCENARIO of UML and its predecessors. The problems referred to above are mostly compounded by confusion over whether a use case is the same as a scenario. At OOPSLA 1994 a panel was posed the question of the relationship between scenarios and use cases. Jacobson and Booch agreed that a scenario was 'an instance of a use case' but the point was not elaborated further. The distinction is far better understood as that between abstract and concrete notions than between classes and instances. Use cases and scenarios are *both* instance level concepts. One difference is that scenarios may also include sequencing information.

The use case approach asks developers to begin by discovering behaviourally related sequences of transactions in a dialogue with a system whose task is to yield a result of measurable value to actors who use the system. These descriptions are then mined for concepts and actions that will be implemented as classes and methods in a future system. Several other approaches recommend the study of scenarios of system use. In most cases a scenario is more detailed and specific than a use case and may mention individuals by name. Thus, 'The user enters the number' is a use case whereas 'John enters his wife's number' is a scenario – at least that is the understanding that will suffice for the purposes of this book.

7.2.5 Essential or Generic Use Cases

Another reason for the tendency to find too many use cases is the lack of any notion of essentiality or genericity.

There appears to be an overlap between our notion of collaboration scripts and Constantine's (1995) *essential* use cases. Essential use cases abstract away from the detail of a use case. As an example, the use case that deals with extracting cash from an ATM (Automatic Teller Machine) refers to inserting a card, entering a PIN and so on. The corresponding essential use case merely refers to withdrawing cash. This corresponds to what I refer to below as the *atomicity* of tasks. The atomic level depends on the purpose of the description and excludes terms foreign to the domain at that level of purpose. Constantine defines an essential use case as an abstract use case describing the common structure of use cases representing a single intent or purpose of users in some rôle. An essential use case is expressed in user application domain terms and assumes idealized technology or is technology independent.

In other words, an essential use case is a structured narrative, expressed in a language that users can understand. It is a simplified, abstract, technology-free and implementation-independent description of a user's task, embodying the goal underlying an interaction. These definitions combine what I have called 'generification' and 'atomicity'. I think it is better to separate these concerns. As I show in the next section, a collaboration script represents a generic use case. Thus, I would suggest that a conversation or collaboration that is atomic – or contains (has parts) nothing more specific than atomic conversations – should be called an essential conversation or collaboration. Then an essential collaboration is the same as what Constantine calls an essential use case. Eliciting essential use cases is a key part of Constantine's Usage-Centred Design method (Constantine and Lockwood, 1999): a method that has much to recommend it.

Now we are in a position to define the differences and relationships between the concepts of use cases and scenarios. To overcome the lack of essentiality referred to above, what is required is a generification[1] of the idea of use cases that prevents this explosion in their number. Collaborations

---

[1] The OED describes this word as more precise than GENERALIZATION: 'the abstraction which carries up species into genera'. It is used here in the sense of 'making a generic representative'.

are just such a generic concept that, additionally, allows developers to model the internals of a business process and its implementation.

As remarked, a scenario is often seen as an instance of a use case: it describes an actual occurrence of the use case. Intuitively, too, a use case could be thought of as an instance of a linked set of tasks: it describes a typical path through the business model. Unfortunately, this terminology does not bear closer scrutiny because a scenario is an instance of the class of scenarios and the class of *all* scenarios will not correspond to a sensible use case. The idea, however, is sound and can be rephrased by saying that task actions *generify* use cases in the sense that a set of tasks is a generic use case or an equivalence class of use cases. They do not generalize use cases; they make them generic. A collaboration is a *generic* scenario.

We may now view a use case as an equivalence class of scenarios. A use case is equivalent to the set of scenarios that can implement it. The equivalence relations are easily defined informally and may sometimes be fuzzy relations in the sense of Zadeh (1971). For example, the relation could equate all scenarios where some individual enters the phone number of some other individual, or all 'eating out' use cases.

The advantage of moving to the essential level of abstraction is principally that we abstract away from specific exceptions that tend to increase the total number of use cases to an unacceptable extent.

7.2.6 Atomicity

Another problem is the lack of a notion of atomicity for use cases. Project managers might like to believe that the number of use cases in a requirements document gives some indication of the business benefit of the final system or even of the amount of effort involved in building it. This would help with product pricing and project estimation. However, conventional use cases are notoriously hard to measure, since a use case can be any length.

The lack of a notion of atomicity means that no metrics can be reasonably defined for use case models – unless we change their definition as many companies have indeed done: numbering the sentences of a use case, for example. Our approach includes a notion of atomicity for conversations and collaborations that permits developers to measure task complexity by simply counting the number of single-sentence atomic conversation scripts. Recall from Chapter 5 that a conversation is atomic if further decomposition would introduce terms that are not in the domain ontology.

7.2.7 Level of Abstraction

My experience with use cases dates back to about 1991, when I attempted to use them to capture the requirements for part of a banking application.

I quickly discovered that this relatively simple application was generating hundreds of use cases: far too many to be manageable. Using a precursor of the approach described in this book there were only eleven: an order of magnitude improvement! This defect is potentially very serious, though in some domains (designing equipment such as vending machines or switch gear for example) it may not happen. I have often found that my clients have written hundreds of use cases precisely because they are working at an inappropriate level of abstraction. In such cases there are often many exceptional paths through a business process. The exceptions are not 'errors' as they would be in a computer program; they are important – often business-critical – variants on the use case. Nor are they concrete scenarios, because they themselves are implemented in a multiplicity of concrete executable scenarios corresponding to actual use.

In another case, the analysts had created separate use cases for create record, update it, etc. Surely, I reasoned, most developers would be able to fill in the details of the ubiquitous CRUD use case that combines all the maintenance possibilities; that's a 'divide by four' reduction with hardly *any* strain on the intellect!

7.2.8 Exception Handling

Other related problems are the granularity of the typical use case, the fact that a use case can span several linked but independent tasks and the poor exception handling semantics in the theory.

Severe problems arise if we try to treat use cases as objects: a treatment that Jacobson hints at in several places. One structural link between use cases, the «extends» arrow, points in the wrong direction from the point of view of encapsulation. Therefore, we are not able to treat use cases as *bona fide* objects. In which case they are not going to be really reusable. If we agree that use cases are pure objects, we do not need to invent «includes» and «extends» links but can use existing and properly defined concepts such as composition and message passing to cover the same semantics and, additionally, we get the notions of inheritance and use case associations for free.

UML has two built in stereotypes for use case diagrams. One use case 'uses' or 'includes' another if the latter is 'part of its own description' (Jacobson *et al.*, 1995). Thus, the «uses» relationship (now called «includes» in UML) certainly corresponds to task decomposition: the composition relationship in UML. The difference here is at most one of interpretation.

A use case 'extends' another if it may be 'inserted into' the latter (Jacobson *et al.*, 1992). Thus, «extends» would correspond to our 'is a side-script of', though the arrows are drawn in the opposite sense with the latter, to preserve encapsulation; an extension of a conversation object should not know that it is part of something bigger if we want to reuse conversation-based services.

Jacobson *et al.* (1992) give the example of the design of a vending machine, which accepts used containers for recycling. `Returning item` is the use case that describes a customer inserting a used container into the machine. The `Item is stuck` use case extends `Returning item` and describes what happens when the container jams in the chute. However, it does so in a foreseeable course of events, whereas the restaurant script only uses the `BananaSkin` script (discussed in Chapter 5) in the most exceptional circumstances, which may not be foreseen in the context of any particular use case. One of the consequences of this in terms of implementation is that `EnterRestaurant` may have to perform a search for an appropriate script such as `BananaSkin` rather than store a reference to it statically. Once again, for reasons of encapsulation and the promotion of reuse, it is important that side-scripts do not know which scripts they 'extend', which is why it is important to model this relationship as a message-send to the side-script, possibly involving a search. For example, recall the five conversations illustrated in Figure 5-4, wherein the banana skin exception works for the other four. Using «extends» would lead to the situation shown in Figure 7-1, where every exception potentially *doubles* the number of use cases.

Armed with this critique, we can proceed to understand what the analyst *should* do.

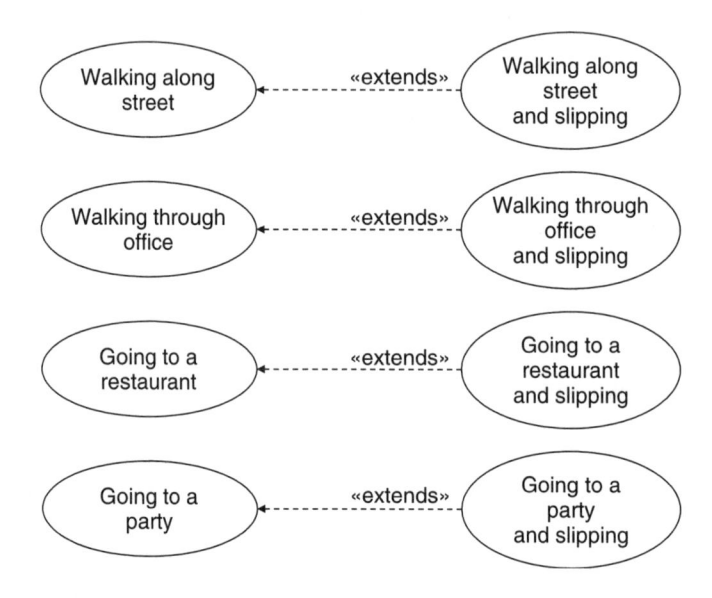

Figure 7-1 Using «extends».

7.3 Describing Boundary Conversations or Use Cases

As we saw in Section 5.4, conversations can be modelled beneficially as *bona fide* objects and the models structured using the standard object connectives of UML: specialization (inheritance), composition, association and message passing. When we looked at this earlier I rather skipped over the issue of message passing, so I try to remedy that now.

The composition (diamond) link is entirely equivalent to the «includes» stereotype, with the dotted arrows pointing from the composite to the components. They are completely interchangeable as notations. There is thus no ambiguity about the semantics of «includes»; either can be used without harm. The only restriction is that some CASE tools disallow the diamond notation in use case diagrams, so that «includes» must be used. A similar remark applies to the notation for message passing used in Figure 5-4, which may only be permitted on collaboration diagrams by some tools. In that case we need to invent a new stereotype called «send to», «handle» or some such. Figure 7-2 redraws Figure 5-4 in this way. Notice how, comparing with Figure 7-1, every exception adds only one use case – five use cases instead of eight in this example.

Message passing links give us a much better way of handling exceptions than is available with standard «extends» use cases, which suffer from the poor semantics referred to above and the proliferation of 'exceptional paths' in their documentation.

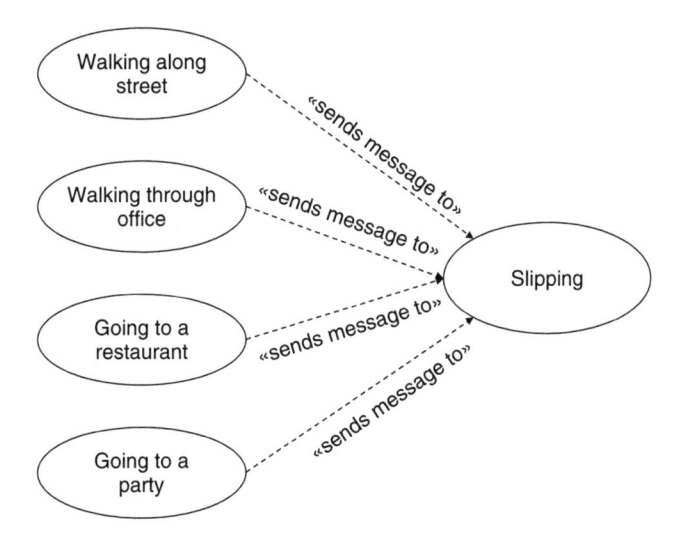

Figure 7-2 Using message passing in a CASE tool.

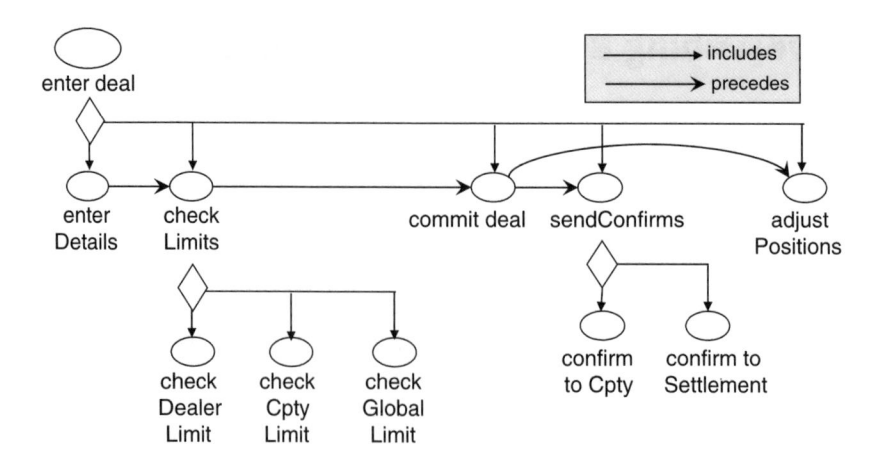

Figure 7-3 Decomposed collaboration.

Boundary conversations describe the features that the user of the system will be able to use. In other words, they describe the *services* that the system offers its direct users. These services are completely specified by their pre- and post-conditions. However, they cannot, as I have argued throughout this book, be understood without reference to the entire business process and the real user. The procedure must thus be this.

Model the process using either a network model (such as BPMN) or Catalysis conversations. Combine the process nodes or the conversations into collaborations and decompose to atomic level. Ask how such collaborations need to be supported by boundary conversations. Define these as services with clearly stated pre- and post-conditions. When we have done this we will be able to proceed further (iteratively) by extracting the object types that the services will rely on.

Let us return to the simple order processing example. Figure 7-3 repeats Figure 5-11 and shows the decomposed collaboration. How does this map onto the boundary conversation?

EnterDetails presupposes a conversation with the customer but from the point of view of system specification all we need is a service that offers to record such details; so there will be, most likely, a screen that displays a number of blank fields and behind which there is some validation. If the basic data are sufficiently complete and valid then we can move on to the credit (or limit) checks (the pre-condition on CheckLimits). Again, this is best seen as a reusable service. The commit service must perhaps be disabled should the credit checks not pass; this too will be expressed as a pre-condition.

Now, CheckLimits can involve up to three checks. Each of these may be seen as separate internal services, called or messaged by CheckLimits,

Name/number	**EnterDeal** #4.01
Conversation/Collaboration	Conversation
Collaborators (underline the initiator)	<u>Clerk</u>, System
Pre-condition	The clerk has or can access the following data: customer id, product id, quantity, etc.
Post-condition	Either a) A valid order is stored in the system, stock has been updated and confirmations sent, or b) the quote is rejected and the transaction rolled back.
Other business rules	A price may not be given after the customer has announced buy or sell.
Fatal errors	Machine crash: Roll back on restart.
Non-fatal errors	Credit checks fail: Do **RejectQuote** Customer conversation interrupted: Do **ArchiveQuote**
Includes	**EnterDetails, CheckLimits, CommitDeal, SendConfs, AdjustStock**
Performance post-condition	0.01 second trivial response

Figure 7-4 A service description (use case) template.

although it is probably best if only the aggregate service is published to users.

With Commit, we have two options: either there is a SendConfirms service that deals with sending whatever paperwork is required (DANs, invoices, affirmations, etc.) or the commit service will know how to invoke the relevant subservices (as in Figure 5-12). In either case the commit service invokes the adjustPositions (i.e. stock) services. One would presume that normally there is a separate stock management system that offers this as just one of its services. And so we are roundly back to the consideration of architecture.

In each case, the method advocated here is to describe the services by their pre- and post-conditions. In addition, we must document how fatal or rare errors are to be handled. Common non-fatal errors are best documented as separate use cases. Figure 7-4 provides a suggested template for such documentation, partially completed for purposes of illustration. Note its minimalism compared to the ones in wide use. Use case names are in bold.

Having documented the boundary conversations that describe all visible services and their crucial components (such as CheckLimits) – in this example these will probably be EnterDeal, DealerLogin, CapturePriceData, AuditDeals, MaintainStaticData and ReportP&L – the analyst must do two things: (a) document any internal collaborations implied by the model and (b) discover the object types that will need to be designed to implement the services: we must discover the type model.

7.4 Establishing the Type Model

Adopting a Catalysis approach makes this remarkably simple; everything we need is in the use case pre- and post-conditions. We can employ the simple textual analysis technique of Chapter 3 if need be, or just use our common sense in reading them.

In our running example, we obviously need types corresponding to Order, Product, Deal, Customer and Confirmation. And there must be attributes for quantity, positions and so on.

Figure 7-5 shows a first attempt at a type model that will work for order processing.

A good method here is to go through the boundary conversations in the manner of a walkthrough in a requirements workshop (cf. Graham, 2009). Here we do the same thing as a *Gedankenexperiment*. Let's do the simplest use case first: DealerLogin. It seems simplest to make the Dealer object responsible for storing and validating Username, password and any other required security or status data. In other words we must specify a Dealer component, with these attributes that will implement the DealerLogin service. In practice there will be a number of similarly simple System Admin services that control permissions and static data updates (CRUD use cases), but I will not explore that one here. The most interesting conversation is entering and validating a deal.

To complete this task we must first ensure that the correct data are collected. This tells us that there must be attributes for components representing customers and products. These, like Dealer, are Party/Place/Thing (green) components or core components. Recall that every green object has

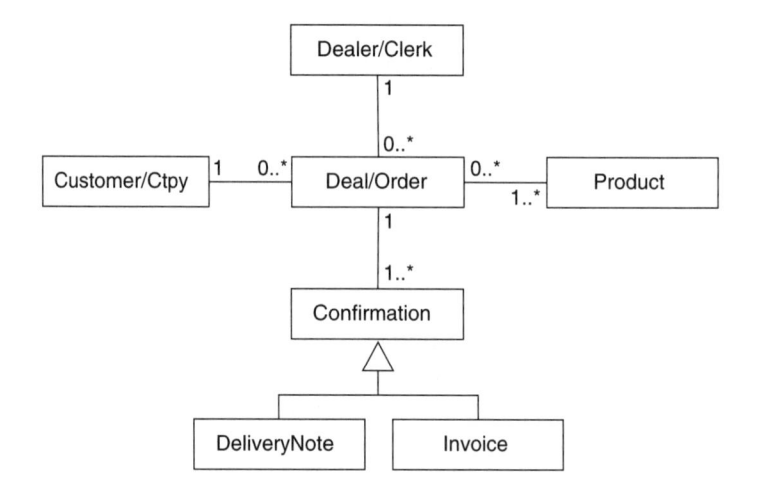

Figure 7-5 A type model.

a blue description. Next we need to apply the credit checks. This may already be a service represented by an existing system. As a component it is a pink Episode representing a business process. If the commit process results in a positive decision then we will need to create objects representing the various items of paperwork: Invoice and DAN, say. Of course, the stock level is an attribute of Product. This process leaves us with about seven components: Dealer, Customer, Product, CreditService, Invoice, DAN and possibly PrintServer. However, we know from the process model that there is some sequencing to be enforced. And we cannot rely on the clerk because of the danger of error. Which component should be responsible for this? There are two options: either we can cartoon the clerk by creating a (possibly mobile) intelligent agent with responsibility for this part of the control strategy[2] or we can delegate it to the Deal component. Most conventional systems developers adopt the latter strategy. Deal is then a process episode (pink) component which offers an EnterDeal service at the system boundary; it is precisely the top level collaboration that we investigated earlier but is now represented as a boundary conversation in which the machine has been given control knowledge that will control properly the clerk's parallel synchronization with the customer. We have used our understanding of the business process to INTERNALIZE THE PARALLELISM OF COLLABORATIONS; this is a very useful analysis pattern.

Notice that collapsing or internalization involves the equivalent of the database notion of a two-phase commit. If you want another example of this, think of a system to support arranging meeting between several participants and the business process that it will be embedded in.

It is important to note all the Episode components because it is these that often lead directly to the discovery of the services that must be designed and implemented but which our top level analysis has missed. To see how, we must now investigate components as finite state machines.

7.4.1 State Models

For components with significant complex state it is useful to use UML state charts or state transition diagrams (STDs). These diagrams are used to capture the dynamics of individual objects and are related to the object model as effective specification of operations and their assertions. Statecharts represent possible sequences of state change from a particular point of view. Each transition is a realization of a use case. This provides a handy completeness check on use case models.

As a motivating example, consider the states that a human being may take on as life progresses. Figure 7-6 shows states that a person's marital-status variable can take on. Rounded rectangles are the permissible states

---

[2]The idea of cartooning is discussed later in this chapter.

and the arrows represent legal changes of state. The small filled circle represents the creation of an instance conception (perhaps) and the small target symbol is the corresponding destruction of the individual (burnt, buried, eaten as carrion, etc.) Thus, one is always born into the single state – unless we introduce an engaged state and consider societies that arrange marriages, in which case you might be born engaged.

Notice the slightly subjective character of the states chosen: there is no engaged state and the inclusion of divorced as a state reflects the understanding of an earlier generation; the modern sensibility is that one becomes single after a divorce, thus simplifying the model – and indeed the world.

Of course, marital-status is not the only state variable of a person; one may be employed, unemployed or retired; one might be awake or asleep. In fact, there are very many dimensions of a person's state, each one corresponding to a separate state chart; consider just a few other states: gaoled, free, on-probation; busy, idle, skiving, in-a-meeting.

From a methodological point of view a key observation to make about state charts is that the transitions are precisely use cases: things that happen that change the state of the world, as described by their post-condition. This provides a check on the completeness of our use case and business process models. Catalysis promotes this as an iterative modelling strategy, as shown in Figure 7-6. Starting either with a process or a data model or both, we discover use cases, use their post-conditions to discover types and their attributes, then we construct state models for the interesting types and check to see if we have a transition that doesn't correspond to a use case. If we have them we conclude that we have missed a possibly important use case.

An object's significant states are determined by key arrangements of its attribute values. These and the valid transitions between them are captured by a state transition diagram. Figure 7-7 illustrates the basic notation. States, which can be regarded as Boolean attributes of the type or values of a particular 'state attribute', are represented by rounded rectangles labelled with their names. Transitions are labelled arrows connecting states.

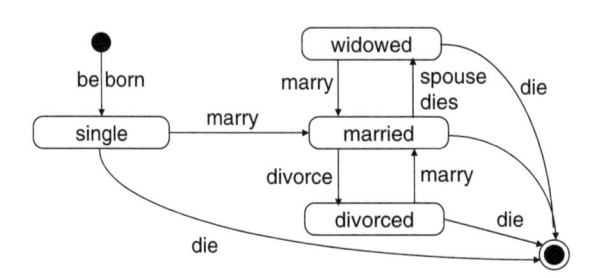

Figure 7-6 Some states of a person.

Figure 7-7 States and transitions.

Events that cause transitions to occur are written next to the arrows. Events may have attributes. For example, thinking of a calculator object, the event of pressing a key may have the attribute keyNumber. This avoids the need to have a separate event for each key. Events may have guards or pre-conditions. A guard determines a logical condition that must be true before the transition can take place. An action is a function that is executed – effectively instantaneously – after the transition occurs. States may have activities. These are functions that begin execution as soon as the state is entered and continue executing until completion or until the state is left, whichever is the earlier. A guard may mandate that the state may not be left until an activity is completed.

Henderson-Sellers (private communication) points out that novices often misuse and overuse activities. They effectively use their STDs as DFDs in this way. The use of activities is therefore not encouraged.

Figure 7-8 gives a simple example showing part of the life history of a pop-up menu. Initial and final states are shown as filled circles and ringed filled circles respectively as shown in this example. Start and End (Selected here) are not states but represent the creation and destruction of instances, so that the attributes become undefined.

States may be nested and partitioned into concurrent states to make the structure neater. Figure 7-9 summarizes most of the rest of the notation.

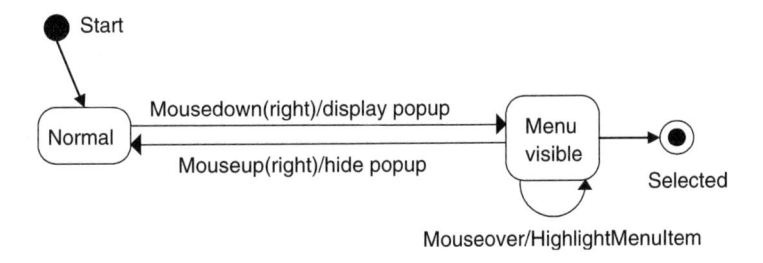

Figure 7-8 An example.

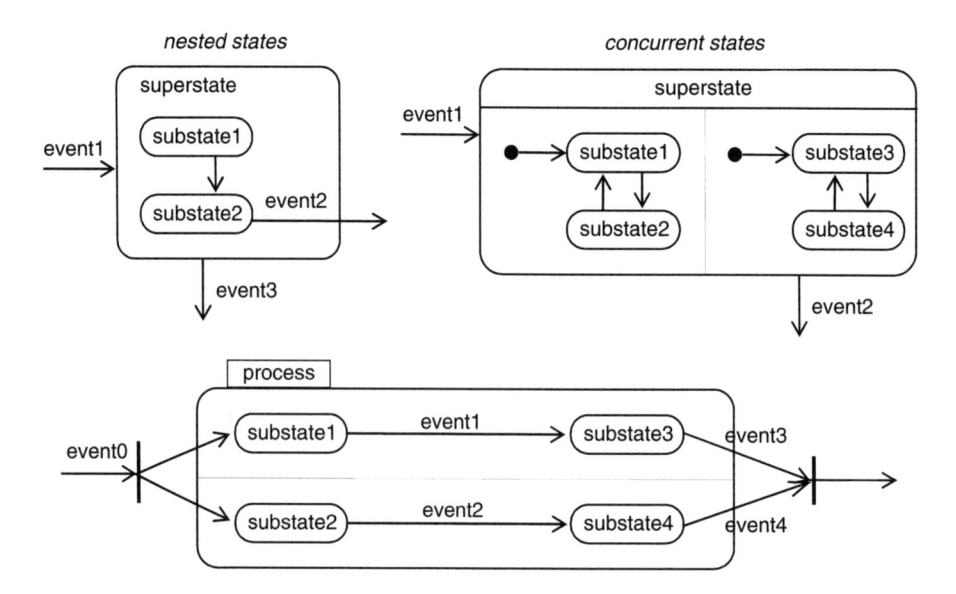

Figure 7-9 Statechart notation.

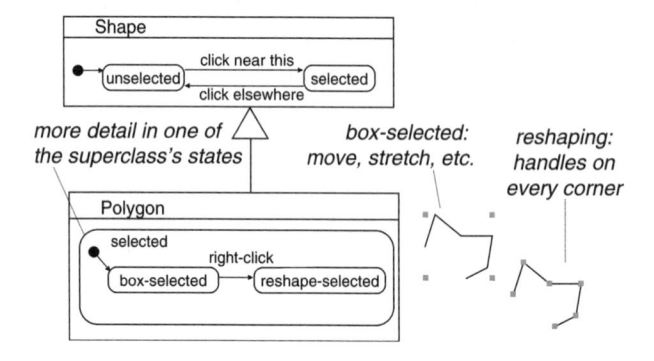

Figure 7-10 States and subtypes.

We have omitted some details such as start and end states to avoid clutter that would add little in the way of understanding the basic ideas.

Subtypes inherit the state models of their supertypes as illustrated in Figure 7-10, where the context is a simple graphical editor.

Sometimes it is useful to represent the states of a type as *bona fide* types; so that rather than considering people as employed or unemployed we could create types for employees and so on. These can be considered as rôles or as **stative types**. The latter view is useful when the attributes and behaviour are very different.

One problem with STDs is that they can sometimes become very complex very quickly. However, for objects with complex life histories the technique is invaluable for capturing information about both the business and the system. A good example of an object where the technique is suitable is a loan application. However, the very act of representing this business process as an object is sometimes questionable. It is often better to capture this kind of information in the business process model or as use cases, which then refer to classes such as Loans. The individual circumstances will dictate the best approach.

State charts, along with sequence diagrams, are useful for exploring and making explicit the way a particular business service is implemented.

STDs describe the local dynamics of each object in the system. We still need some techniques to describe global behaviour. However, the use of rulesets helps to encapsulate locally some aspects of global behaviour, as we have seen. Statecharts provide an additional way to visualize the problem and usually expose use cases that one has missed on the first pass. They also make it clear which process sequences are permissible.

In UML, states must be Boolean: you're either married or not married; you can't be a Don Juan and be 'a little bit married'. In principle, of course, we could build fuzzy state models; it's just that UML forbids it, which is a shame. Typical fuzzy states for a person might include tall, short, average for the height variable or obese, fat, average, skinny and super-model for body type. Hubert Matthews points out that fuzzy state machines may be usefully related to the concept of transactions[3]. Transactions have ACID properties, most of which are about ensuring that transitions are crisp. Perhaps one rôle for fuzzy state machines would be to give meaning to systems that have non-ACID operations. The ACID properties of a database transaction are as follows.

- Atomicity: Database updates must obey an 'all or nothing' rule; each transaction is said to be 'atomic' if, when one part of the transaction fails, the entire transaction fails. It is assumed that the system will maintain the atomicity of transactions in spite of any DBMS, operating system or hardware failure.
- Consistency: Only valid data will be written to the database. If, for some reason, a transaction is executed that violates the consistency rules, the entire transaction will be rolled back and the database will be restored to a state consistent with those rules. If a transaction executes successfully, it will take the database from one consistent state to another consistent state.
- Isolation: Multiple transactions that happen at the same time should not affect each other's execution. For example, if Hubert invokes a transaction against the database at the same time that Ian issues a different one; both transactions should operate on the database in an isolated manner. The database should either commit Ian's entire

---

[3]Private communication.

transaction before executing Hubert's or vice-versa. This prevents Ian's transaction from reading Hubert's intermediate data that will not eventually be committed and are only produced as a side effect.

- Durability: Transactions committed to the database will not be lost. This is ensured by using database backups and transaction logs that facilitate the restoration of committed transactions regardless of any subsequent software or hardware failures.

An example of a non-ACID database might be the normal file system on a computer, where updates can be partially applied without any kind of overall commitment boundaries or rollback itself. Another, more business oriented example is customer classification with, say, CRM systems, where having crisp boundaries for good, bad or average seems unnecessarily restrictive. The fuzzy truth values (Zadeh, 1965) for this would be based on average spend, credit limits, aged debt, payment record, number and value of orders, etc. It is almost as if current CRM systems are trying to be fuzzy without acknowledging it! But let us stick to crisp state models from here on.

7.5 Finding Services from State Models

In our running example, we discovered two potential process components: Deal and CreditSystem. It is the pink components which will implement these processes that are the ones most likely to have significant state models. We must now create and check the state models to see if all our use cases correspond to states and vice versa. Every state must correspond to a use case. As with process algebra-based models, state can be internal to the component as well as visible at the boundary.

As it turns out, the state model for an order can be immensely complex, especially for financial transactions in banks. In that case an order is Quoted, Agreed, Confirmed (by the bank), Affirmed (by the counterparty), Matched (to see if the confirmation and affirmation agree), Settled and so on. The matching process itself has a complex state model with substates like Matched_OK and Mismatched which lead to different courses of action, a mismatched deal usually involving manual invention which finds out what has gone wrong and even negotiation or legal or regulatory (compliance) action. Luckily most of this complexity will be handled outside the typical deal entry system that we are considering here.

The pattern we use is simple enough: CROSS-REFERENCE STATES TO USE CASES.

In implementation terms, in a Java environment, the pink components correspond to entity beans, but when implemented as an SOA or ESB co-ordinator they are session beans.

As I have said, there is another way to model the control strategy which makes Deal a much less complex (green) component. This approach corresponds to the philosophy of so-called intelligent multi-agent systems (Wooldridge, 2002). But, in an SOA context, we can also think of it as preceding implementation using a co-ordinator. I call this approach cartooning.

7.5.1 Cartooning Using Agents or Co-ordinators

In the normal style of development, agents – such as customers and clerks – are usually represented by rather unintelligent objects with few or no operations but typically several attributes. It is important not to confuse these internal representations, which cannot do anything except store static data, with their real-world counterparts that do exhibit, often complex, behaviour. Such internal representations of agents external to the system are nearly always persistent (green) components. The most usual approach, and the one described in the foregoing, models our intelligent customers and clerks as mere dumb data structures and the orders or deals – which are dumb pieces of paper in the real world – as intelligent objects responsible for several operations, such as the validation of customer credit limits or checking stock levels. There is a powerful alternative to this, which is to internalize part of the intelligence of the entities in the world as intelligent agents in the system. In an SOA these agents control how data-rich messages flow between services and be themselves be viewed as offering services.

In our example, we evidently have a clerk, a customer, a product and, of course, an order. Is the credit limit an attribute of the customer or is it the responsibility of a credit manager agent? In banking systems it is often the latter because credit lines are handled by specialized systems; usually legacy systems. But now we come to the really fascinating question from the agent-oriented perspective: How intelligent is the order itself? Do the credit validation rules belong to the Order component?

The knee-jerk reaction of the typical systems designer is to place the rule and a good deal of the behaviour in the Order component. But does this make sense to a typical user? I do not think it always does. In the world, customers and clerks are intelligent and exhibit behaviour. The order is a very dead, behaviour-free piece of paper. But our systems push all the behaviour into the order and strip it away from customers and clerks who are usually represented in database tables that store details like name, address and login codes. The most these objects do is to calculate things like current debt, usually by collaborating with other components such as Order. In one way this is sensible; real customers can place orders with us, but we certainly do not want the system representation of customer to be able to do this. Business would become just too easy – except that we probably either would not be paid or would be charged with fraud! However, in the case of the clerk it is less clear that this strategy is the right one.

The agent/co-ordinator perspective allows us instead to visualize an agent in the system called Clerk's Assistant. This agent can take responsibility for all the order validation and confirmation behaviour that is needed and let us strip it away from Order. This has three significant advantages:

1. If we are in a distributed system we can allow the assistant agent to be mobile with the attendant benefits of reducing network traffic and improving overall control structure.
2. Stripping the order of its behaviour may reduce the impedance mismatch between our new systems and legacy databases where orders are still stored, without behaviour usually.
3. The 'cognitive dissonance' between the system and the world is reduced. This means that discussions between users and developers are easier because they share a common model of the application. Smart clerks in the office are modelled as smart creatures in the computer (or partially so, because real intelligent computers don't and can't exist). Electronic orders are just as dumb as their paper counterparts.

Whether this approach is correct will depend entirely on the application and its circumstances. However, knowing that it is possible gives developers an extra tool of their trade. Next time you model a system, at least consider the choice.

It is a coincidence that, while the insertion of rulesets into objects (Graham, 1992, 2006) was not motivated by agent technology at all, this addition to object modelling seems to be pretty well all that is needed to model intelligent, possibly mobile agents. The original motivation was actually provided by a business process re-engineering project as long ago as 1989. Now it should be possible to see why precisely the same extension to object-oriented analysis needed to model business processes is needed to model system agents. The underlying metaphor is the same.

We can use internalized (or **cartooned**) agents to model the responsibilities of the sales clerk and his/her collaboration with customers. The agent stereotype can be thought of as internalizing within the system the real agents in the business world. With agents or co-ordinators representing more of the business logic, the order is modelled as a data structure that will probably correspond far more closely to the representation that may exist in the legacy order database. The agent is still accessed, like the order component, as a service that offers help in completing valid orders. However, the clerk agent may have other responsibilities – corresponding to those of the clerk in the real world.

7.6 Finding Business Rules

With business and software modelling, a large number of lessons can be learnt from AI systems built using semantic nets and from semantic data modelling. Specifications that exhibit encapsulation of attributes and operations are all very well but do not necessarily contain the meaning intended by the analyst or the user. To reuse the specification of a component we should be able to read from it what it knows (attributes), what it does (operations), why it does it and how it is related to other component or service interfaces. It is my position that this semantic content is contained not only in the static structures of association, classification, composition and messaging but by the assertions, invariants and rulesets which describe a component's behaviour.

The fact is that all semantics limit reuse, although they make it safer. For example, inheritance does so; and so does anything that makes the *meaning* of an object more specific. In system specification, both aspects are equally important and the trade-off must be well understood and managed with care, depending on the goals of the analysts and their clients.

One must also be aware of the need to decide whether rules belong to individual operations or to the service as a whole. There is no principled reason why operations cannot be expressed in a rule-based language. However, the distinction to be made here is not between the form of expression but the content of the rules. Rules that relate several operations do not belong within those operations, and rules which define dependencies between attributes also refer to the component as a whole. Conversely, rules that concern the encapsulated state of the component belong within one of its operations.

Thus we enhance our component models by adding a set of rulesets to each object. Thus, while an object is normally thought to consist of an identifier, attributes and operations, for us an object consists of identifier, attributes, operations and rulesets. **Rulesets** are composed of an unordered set of assertions and rules of either 'if/then' or 'when/then' form. This modelling extension has a number of interesting consequences, the most notable of which is that components with rulesets can be regarded as intelligent agents for BRMS developments.

It is widely agreed that it is quite insufficient to specify only the attributes and operations (the signature) of an object. To specify the object completely we must say how these are allowed to interact with each other and what rules and constraints must be obeyed by the object as a whole to maintain its integrity as such. Some languages, such as Eiffel, achieved a partial solution by using assertions. Assertions in such systems are of two kinds: assertions about the operations and assertions about the whole object. The former are typically pre- and post-conditions while the latter are called class invariants. Catalysis added what I have called invariance conditions to the operational assertions and we can generalize class invariants to rulesets – which can be chained together to infer new information. There are also assertion facets representing attribute constraints. Here are the definitions:

Attribute assertions
- **Range constraints** give limits on permissible values.
- **Enumeration constraints** list permissible values.
- **Type constraints** specify the class that values must belong to. Type constraints are always present and generalize the former two cases.

Operational assertions
- A **pre-condition** is a single logical statement that must be true before its operation may execute.
- A **post-condition** is a single logical statement that must be true after its operation has finished execution.
- An **invariance condition** is a single logical statement that must hold at all times when its operation is executing. This is only of importance for parallel processing systems (including business process models and SOA-based systems). Invariance conditions were first introduced as part of SOMA (Graham, 1991). Catalysis (D'Souza and Wills, 1999) distinguished two kinds of invariance conditions: guarantee and rely clauses.
- A **rely** clause states a pre-condition that must remain true throughout the execution of the operation it refers to. Should it be violated, the specification does not state what clients can expect as a result. The server is not responsible for maintaining the condition.
- A **guarantee** is a statement that the server must maintain as true throughout the execution of the operation.

The facets of an operation may include more than one assertion of any of these types. Assertions may be represented by state-transition diagrams as we shall see.

Object assertions and rulesets
- A **class invariant** is a single (possibly quantified) logical statement about any subset of the features of an object that must be true at all times (in Eiffel, which had direct support for invariants, this only applied to the times when a method is not executing). Cardinality constraints on attributes are invariants. Invariants can also be called **rules**.
- A **ruleset** is an unordered set of class invariants (or **rules**) and assertions about attributes together with a defined inference régime

that allows the rules to be chained together. **External rulesets** express second order information such as control strategy. **Internal rulesets** are (first order) sets of invariants. They may be written either in natural language, OCL (cf. Warner and Kleppe, 1999) or in an executable rule language.
- An **effect** is a post-condition that is conjoined with all other operation post-conditions of a type. An effect is usually of the form: (any change $f(x, x@pre) \Rightarrow$ condition). Effects can be expressed as rules. They are useful for the designer of a supertype who wants to impose restrictions on the operations that may be invented by subtype specifiers.

The normal assumption behind the above definitions is that the logic to be used is standard first order predicate calculus (FOPC). We make no such assumption although FOPC is the usual default logic[4]. Other logics that can be used include temporal, fuzzy, deontic, epistemic and non-monotonic logic. Each ruleset in a class determines its own logic locally, although it would be unusual to mix logics in the same class.

We have already seen the distinction between a type and a class: a type has no implementation. We can now distinguish between types and interfaces. An **interface** is a list of the messages that can be sent to an object with their parameters and return types. Depending on the interpretation, this may include the get and set operations on attributes. This concept is sometimes referred to as the **signature** of a type. A type on the other hand is a full specification including all the assertions that may be made about the type and its instances and all rulesets.

There are several techniques for discovering rules. They, and other useful guidelines, can be conveniently expressed as the following patterns.

- USE CASE POST-CONDITIONS ARE RULES (which we have already explored).
- WRITE THE CONSTRAINTS AS RULES. (This is a matter of style.)
- ASSOCIATION LOOPS CONCEAL RULES.
- ASK THE BUSINESS.
- ASSIGN RULES TO COMPONENTS.
- BASE ERROR MESSAGES ON RULES.
- POLICY BLACKBOARD.
- STORE RULES IN A REPOSITORY.
- ENCAPSULATE A REFERENCE.

---

[4]In Catalysis the default is Logic of Partial Functions (Cheng and Jones, 1990) which has clear treatment of undefined values. It is recommended reading for anyone who has applied logic to program specifications in earnest.

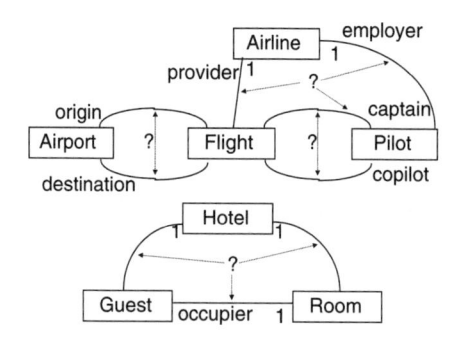

Figure 7-11 Cyclic associations suggest invariants.

I will start by looking at ASSOCIATION LOOPS CONCEAL RULES.

An invariant, or constraint, is a single rule that is always obeyed by the object whose scope it lies in. It is expressed using the domain ontology: the vocabulary provided by the type model. Example invariants or business rules for an airline management system might include: 'Every pilot must be the captain or co-pilot of up to one flight per day', 'The captain and co-pilot cannot be the same person' or 'Every flight must be flown by a captain who is qualified for this plane type'. Clearly, an invariant of a type can refer to the public interfaces of other types. Invariants can be expressed informally, as above, or using the high precision of OCL or other formal logic systems.

One possible source of rules or invariants is the existence of cycles in type diagrams. In fact, as we shall see later, any bi-directional association usually requires a pair of invariants – precisely because the pair of rôlenames is a loop. In Figure 7-11 we can see that all the indicated loops may possibly imply the need for one or more business rules to be stated. In the upper diagram, there are two associations between Flight and Airport that are equivalent to two attributes of Flight: the origin airport and the destination airport. Since there is a loop, the ASSOCIATION LOOPS CONCEAL RULES pattern tells us that we must ask if there is a rule hiding away here. The obvious one is that the origin and the destination should not be the same airport. However, what about joyrides? Indeed I remember when one could take Concorde from Bradford Airport, fly out over the Atlantic to make a loud bang (sonic boom) and return reliably to – yes, you guessed – Bradford. Thus, the potential rules found in this way may or may not hold true. The only sensible thing for the analyst to do in such cases is to ASK THE BUSINESS, i.e. go and consult a domain expert or business leader.

For another example, also in the upper diagram the pilot of a flight must work for the airline that provides the flight. The reader is encouraged to formulate rules for the other cycles in Figure 7-11.

Rulesets generalize class invariants and permit objects to do several things:

- Infer attribute values that are not stored explicitly.
- Represent database triggers.
- Represent operations in a non-procedural fashion.
- Represent control régimes.

Rules specify second order information, such as dependencies between attributes; for example, a dependency between the age of an employee and her holiday entitlement. Global pre- and post-conditions that apply to all operations may be specified as rules. A typical business rule in a human resources application might include 'change holiday entitlement to six weeks when service exceeds five years' as a rule in the `Employee` type. With rulesets the notation can cope with analysis problems where an active database is envisaged as the target environment.

Rules and invariants are used to make an object's semantics explicit and visible. This helps with the description of information that would normally reside in a repository, such as business rules for the enterprise. It can also help with inter-operability at quite a low level. For example, if I have an object that computes cube roots, as a client of that object it is not enough to know its operations alone; I need to know that what is returned is a cube root and not a square root. In this simple case the solution is obvious because we can characterize the cube root uniquely with one simple rule: the response times itself twice is equal to the parameter sent. If this rule is part of the interface then all other systems and system components can see the meaning of the object from its interface alone, removing thus some of the complexities of repository technology by shifting it into the object model.

The rules which appear in the rule window may be classified into several, not necessarily exclusive, types, as follows.

- Business rules local to a component.
- Policy rules, i.e. global business rules.
- Triggers.
- Exception handling rules.
- Control rules.

Local business rules typically relate two or more attributes and triggers relate attributes to operations. For example:

Business rule
```
If Employee.service_length > 5 then Employee.holiday= 25
```

Forward Trigger

```
When Employee.salary + SalaryIncrease
   > Employee.manager.salary
Set Employee.manager.salary = Employee.salary
   + SalaryIncrease*1.05
```

Notice that the first of these two simple rules could be implemented in two completely different ways. We could place a pre-condition on getHoliday that always checks Service_length before returning the value. Alternatively, we could place a post-condition on putService_length that detects whether Holiday should be changed on every anniversary. Clearly, the former corresponds to lazy and the latter to eager evaluation. The important point here is that we should *not* be making design decisions of this nature during specification or analysis. Using a rule-based approach defers these decisions to a more appropriate point.

Control rules represent the most esoteric type of rule in this classification. For example, in a system that uses dangerous multiple inheritance from classes, we should include provision for annotating the handling of conflicts arising when the same attribute or operation is inherited differently from two parent objects. Of course, types compose monotonically so this problem doesn't arise. This kind of discrimination can only be done with a class. One way to deal with it is to use rulesets to disambiguate multiple inheritance. One can then also define priority rules for defaults and demons. (A demon is a method that wakes up when needed, i.e. when a value changes, or is added or deleted.) Such rules can determine how to resolve the conflict that arises when an attribute inherits two different values or perhaps specify whether the default value should be applied before or after inheritance takes place or before or after a demon fires. They may also specify the relative priorities of inheritance and demons. As with attributes and operations, the interface of the object only displays the name of a ruleset. In the case of a backward chaining ruleset this might well include the name of the value being sought: its goal, e.g. If Route: needed SEEK Route:

Control rules are encapsulated within objects, instead of being declared globally. They may also be inherited and overridden (although the rules for this may be slightly complicated in some cases – see Wills (1991)). The benefit of this is that local variations in control strategy are possible. Furthermore, the analyst may inspect the impact of the control structure on every object – using a browser perhaps – and does not have to annotate convoluted diagrams to describe the local effects of global control. Genuinely global rules might be contained in a top level object, called something like 'object', and will be inherited by all objects that do not override them. Alternatively, we can set up global rules in a special POLICY BLACKBOARD object. Relevant classes register interest in the blackboard, which broadcasts rule and status changes to registrants as necessary. This uses, of course, a publish and subscribe pattern. Just as state transition diagrams may be used to describe the procedural semantics of operations, so decision trees may be found useful in describing complex sets of rules.

Control rules *concern* the operations and attributes of the object they belong to. They do not concern themselves. Thus, they cannot help with the determination of how to resolve a multiple inheritance conflict between rulesets or other control strategy problem related to rulesets. This would require a set of metarules to be encapsulated and these too would require a meta-language. This quickly leads to an infinite regress. Therefore multiple inheritance of rules does not permit conflict resolution. A dot notation is used to duplicate any rulesets with the same name. Thus, if an object inherits rulesets called POLICYA from two superclasses, X and Y, they are inherited separately as X.POLICYA and Y.POLICYA. The case of fuzzy rules is slightly different since fuzzy rules cannot contradict each other as explained in Appendix A. Therefore multiply inherited fuzzy rulesets with the same name may be merged. In both the crisp and fuzzy cases, however, the careful user of the method should decide every case on its merits, since the equivalent naming of the inherited rulesets could have been erroneous.

It is sometimes possible, in simple cases, to specify rules that must be obeyed by all control strategies for multiple inheritance. In the case where objects are identified with only abstract data types, i.e. constructed types representing relations, say, are not permitted – we have a clear set of three rules for inheritance:

1. There must be no cycles of the form: x is AKO[5] y is AKO z is AKO x. This rule eliminates redundant objects.
2. The bottom of an AKO link must be a subtype, and the top must be a subtype or an abstract type (i.e. not a printable object; not an attribute).
3. It must be possible to name a subtype of two supertypes. This rule prevents absurd objects, such as the class of all people who are also toys.

These rules are commended as model checks.

7.7 Ontology, Type Models and Business Rules

The process of specification is best approached iteratively. Figure 7-12 suggests an approach. We can either start with a process description using BPMN or conversation analysis, or we may begin – especially when migrating from important legacy systems – with the types evident in the

---

[5] A Kind Of, indicating a specialization.

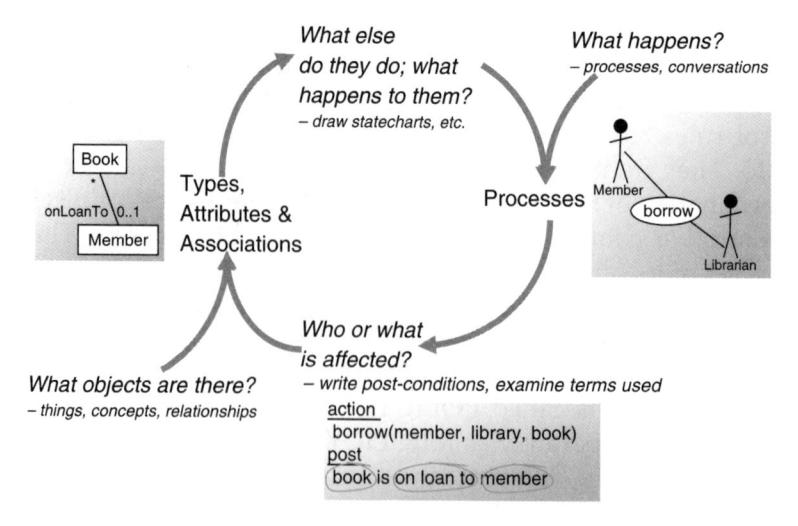

Figure 7-12 The specification process.

data model. Let us look at the process-led case, because there is no difference in procedure, wherever one starts. The procedure is this.

- Identify the processes or conversations at the system boundary.
- Write pre- and post-conditions and business rules for each of these.
- Extract types using textual analysis and other techniques.
- Refine the model and find new processes and actions using, perhaps, state models.
- Write pre- and post-conditions and rules for any new processes.
- Iterate until the model is stable (or time runs out!).

Of course, we could start the iteration by eliciting the rules but implicitly the rules are always *about* either a process or a type, so the diagram is right conceptually.

Rules only make sense in the presence of the type model, which provides their vocabulary or ontology.

7.7.1 Rules and Rule Chaining

Graham (2006), based largely on an analysis of other people's earlier work, defines a business rule as a compact, atomic, well-formed, declarative statement about an aspect of a business that can be expressed in terms that can be directly related to the business and its collaborators, using simple unambiguous language that is accessible to all interested parties: business owner, business analyst, technical architect, customer and so on. This simple language may include domain-specific jargon. Business rules are always interpreted against a defined domain ontology, i.e. a vocabulary expressed as a component model.

Business rules management systems separate the rules from data and control logic and maintain them in a repository. Rule-based systems are non-procedural. That is, the ordering of a set of rules does not affect their interpretation. Rules are grouped into rulesets and inference over and within rulesets is both possible and transparent.

Suppose we are asked to specify a life assurance advisory service. Here are the rules for such a simplified system as they might be expressed in a business policy or requirements statement.

> *The system needs to recommend a best policy for each client.*
>
> *An annuity is best for clients that are retired and risk averse. An endowment policy is best for clients that are young and not averse to risk. An equity-linked policy is recommended if the client is a mature adult and is risk prone or at least neutral about risk. A bond-linked policy is recommended for a client that is averse to risk unless the client is retired. In any case, we assume that a client is averse to risk if the client has one or more children.*

Rephrasing this as a ruleset encapsulated in an AssuranceAdviser component might give something like this.

```
Goal = Client.bestProduct
Regime = 'Backward'
If Client.status is 'retired'
  and Client.preference is 'riskAverse'
  then Client.bestProduct is 'Annuity'
If Client.status is 'young'
  and Client.preference is not 'riskAverse'
  then Client.bestProduct is 'Endowment'
if Client.status is 'matureAdult'
     and Client.preference = 'riskProne' or
client.preference = 'riskNeutral'
     then Client.bestProduct is 'EquityLinked'
If Client.preference is 'riskAverse'
  then Client.bestProduct is 'BondLinked'
If Client.children: > 0
  then Client.preference is 'riskAverse'
```

Note that backward chaining is being required to resolve this ruleset. In a procedural language we would have to put the rule about children first, in order to avoid asking for the client's preference unnecessarily. What happens under backward chaining is that the inference engine first seeks a value for Client.bestProduct and, failing to find one, searches for the first rule that has this on the right-hand side. Then it tries to 'prove' the

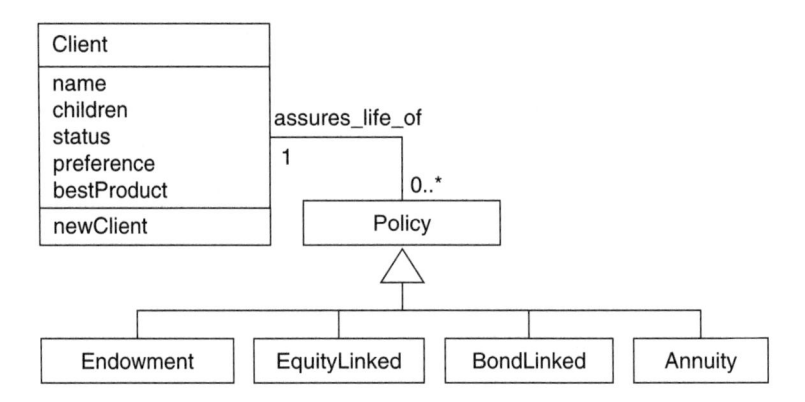

Figure 7-13 Ontology type model for the life assurance adviser ruleset.

left-hand side. In each case, it will need a value for Client.preference but, being a well-behaved inference engine, it does not just ask the user – we are assuming an interactive session – but looks for a rule with this attribute on the right–hand side. Failing to find further rules or data, it finally starts the dialogue by asking for the number of children. Only if the answer is zero will it ask for the risk preference. In a typical business rules system the programmer has to do absolutely *nothing* to achieve this behaviour.

Note the completely non-procedural character of this ruleset. The rule that fires first is written last. That is, the ordering of a set of rules does not affect their interpretation.

Implicit in these rules is the ontology given by the UML type diagram in Figure 7-13. Note that the association is irrelevant to the ruleset but that it implies a business process wherein, after advice is given, an actual policy may be purchased.

As another example application of rules, UML's qualifiers may be expressed as rules. For example, consider the many-to-many association between DOS files and directories. The Filename qualifier reduces this to a many-to-one association as illustrated in Figure 7-14. In general, qualification only partitions the sets. This is because qualification is relative; there is a degree of qualification. To avoid confusion we use rules such as 'Every file in the ListOfFiles attribute must have a unique name', a rule encapsulated in Directory. If FileNames is an attribute this can be avoided by writing FileNames[set of names] as opposed to [bag of ...] or [list of ...]. In UML we can write rulesets in an (optional) fourth

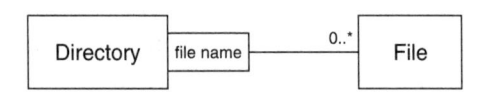

Figure 7-14 A qualified association in UML.

named compartment underneath the operations compartment of a type or class icon.

As with the description of business process semantics, rule-based extensions to object-oriented analysis help enrich the semantics of system models. This makes these models more readable and more reversible; more of the analysts' intentions are evident in the model.

As soon as we consider the inclusion of a substantial number of externalized business rules in our specification we might well consider the rôle of a business rules management system of some sort. The best such systems STORE RULES IN A REPOSITORY so that the rules may be better managed; if a rule changes then it only needs to be modified in one place. Furthermore, the repository usually offers version control and change management services. The advantages should be obvious. But there is a problem.

If services and the components that implement them are to be reusable then they should encapsulate all that they need to work properly so that they can be shared or ported to other systems. Thus, they need attributes, operations, QoS statements and business rules associated with them rather than separated out and bunged in the repository. Therefore we must ASSIGN RULES TO COMPONENTS or to the services they implement. This appears to be a paradox: we must store the rules centrally and we must encapsulate them locally.

The solution is to ENCAPSULATE A REFERENCE to centrally stored rules rather than to encapsulate the rules or rulesets themselves. If we port, we have to then duplicate the relevant parts of the repository but this is easy because the components know which rules are relevant. The circle is squared!

Of course, some rules apply to more than one service or component. We certainly would not want to encapsulate tens of references to such rules. Here again there is a useful and well-established pattern; we use a POLICY BLACKBOARD. Global rules that many services need to conform to are encapsulated in the policy blackboard service/component and other services register interest in it on a publish and subscribe basis so they can be updated if the rules on the blackboard change. Of course, the blackboard itself will not store the rules but ENCAPSULATE A REFERENCE to them.

Finally, making rules explicit in the specification allows us to exploit the rule-based style and BASE ERROR MESSAGES ON RULES. This strays into the territory of user interface design but helps service consumers to relate errors to stored code in a traceable and more understandable manner. If a rule engine is in use it can produce audit trails automatically based on actual rule executions, so that these too will follow rule wording.

See Appendix A for sketches of these and the other patterns mentioned.

7.8 Documenting the Specification

A specification is a description of a desired machine. In the context of SOA it is the description of a desired set of service interfaces and the specification of the components that will implement them. It says what the users may expect and what they must do to obtain correctly functioning services. It should also make reference to any business process models that provide the context for the specification, or which the services may be choreographed to implement.

Huge wordy specifications are to be avoided; the general principle is: only write documentation that will be used. For example, if you will be the designer as well as the analyst, you can defer some of the specification until you document the design. Also avoid comprehensive wall-sized diagrams of the type model. It is far better to fragment the diagrams and organize them around process or service descriptions.

Narrative descriptions of processes process and services are most useful, in our experience. They should be illustrated with relevant fragment of the type model and supported by a glossary of types. Relevant business rules should be included.

The documentation should also include deliverables inherited from the business process analysis: business objectives with measures and priorities, cross reference tables for conversations/processes and objectives and the process models themselves.

Above all, keep it simple and keep it as concise and as short as possible – but no shorter! Think about who could benefit from reading it and what they will really need to know in the future.

7.9 Associations, Rules and Encapsulation

I have already stated that cyclic associations in the ontology type model imply the presence of latent business rules.

In my formalism, as we have seen, objects encapsulate rulesets along with the usual attributes and methods. In this section we examine the notion of associations and their 'inverses' in some depth and point out some inconsistencies in current terminology within the database community that go back as far as Abrial's work. With the new foundation I then construct, I show how referential integrity rules can be embedded in types rather than attached to external associations, as is the current normal practice. I prove that, to maintain the principle of encapsulation and to represent the integrity of relationships, components *must* have rulesets; they are not an optional extra. The material is a little technical compared to the remainder of the chapter and the reader may skip it at a first reading.

I think that associations should point in one direction only because to do otherwise violates the principle of encapsulation. Several object-oriented methodologists have argued against my position, saying that you can always add link attributes to an association and create from it an association object type. However, this new object type must retain links to its progenitors. Therefore, if we accept this as a solution, these new relationships must in turn give rise to new association object types. At some point we must stop this process and will still have to represent the residual associations connecting our, now more numerous, set of classes. This is not to deny the utility of association object types. Some associations are so important that they are themselves concepts, i.e. object types.

Of course, in any particular case, one can find a natural place to stop this process. It is usual to create types out of associations only when the association has interesting properties in its own right. This still leaves us with associations between the newly constructed types and the types that were previously linked by the original associations. Thus, in *all* practical cases, we will have failed to convert *all* associations to types although we will typically have removed most of the many-to-many associations through this process. It is worth noting that while relational databases forbid the use of many-to-many relationships, they are not precluded by object-oriented databases. Thus the habit of always removing them, common among traditionally educated database designers, is not necessarily a good one.

I will now show how the problems alluded to above can be overcome by abolishing bi-directional associations in favour of uni-directional associations or **mappings**, which can be thought of as pointers embedded in object types, coupled with rulesets to preserve referential and semantic integrity. This last point is crucial. Without encapsulating class invariants in components there can be no way of storing referential integrity rules apart from as a part of some external and generally bi-directional association, and thus violating encapsulation.

A component may encapsulate public rulesets that concern the other public features of that component. They provide second order information about the class. For example, a single rule within a ruleset could represent a database trigger that causes a method to execute when an attribute changes value or it could represent necessary sequencing among methods. More unusually rules can represent the control régimes under which the class operates. For example, the rules could state whether default values should take precedence over multiple inheritance conflict resolution or vice versa. Rulesets for resolving multiple inheritance conflicts on numerical attributes can include mathematical formulae. For example, we could use such a formula to average the values of two conflicting, inherited attributes. Rulesets are unordered sets of production rules and are always subject to a defined inference régime. This means that classes can infer facts that are not stated explicitly.

Odell (Martin and Odell, 1995) also suggests that associations are really pairs of 'mappings' corresponding to the *rôles* of an association (Bachman, 1977). A mapping is a one-way connexion. It is part of the component (the client) and therefore does not break encapsulation. An association *à la* vanilla UML is external and does break encapsulation. We will examine Odell's argument and present a slightly firmer foundation in much the same spirit.

The obvious problem with replacing bi-directional associations with mappings is that there is now no obvious container in which to store referential integrity constraints. I must therefore now show how this is accomplished using mappings. Fortunately, rulesets provide a neat solution.

In order to regard 'associations' as pairs of rôles or mappings we must be prepared to store the relationships, if there are any, between these pairs of mappings. An example where this is important arises when there are integrity rules.

Basing himself on the terminology prevalent in work on databases and, especially, functional databases (Gray, 1984), Odell suggests that pairs of related mappings pointing in opposite directions are 'inverses' (in the sense of set theory). This is actually incorrect but close enough to the truth to make it worthwhile reiterating his set-theoretic foundations more rigorously.

In mathematics, a relation is a set of ordered n-tuples and a mapping is a single-valued relation. Consider two object types A and B. Forget that they are types and regard them simply as sets. Strictly speaking, a mapping takes elements of A to elements of B. However, such an interpretation does not capture the notion of association that we require, because it cannot represent one-to-many relationships such as the 'has children' association where A and B are both the set of all people. Odell, following a suggestion of Abrial and in conformity with the literature of functional data models, asserts that mappings are from the set to the power set and that an association consists of two 'inverse' mappings (Martin and Odell, 1995). This definition does not stand up to close scrutiny. To see this, consider the bi-directional publications association of Figure 7-15.

This can be broken into two mappings:

$$f': \text{Papers} \longrightarrow \mathcal{P}(\text{People}) \quad (f' = \text{writtenBy});$$

$$g': \text{People} \longrightarrow \mathcal{P}(\text{Papers}) \quad (g' = \text{wrote}).$$

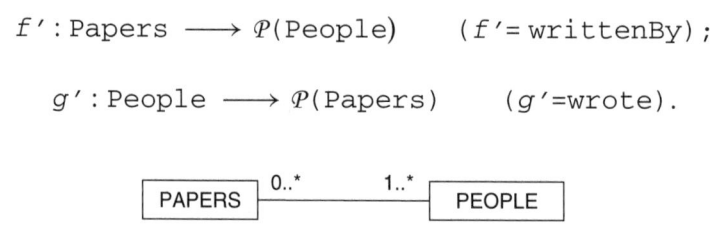

Figure 7-15 A bi-directional association.

where $\mathcal{P}(A)$ represents the power set of A: the set of all subsets of A. Actually, we could work with power types but only the set theory is relevant to the present argument. These functions cannot even be composed, much less satisfy the definition of being inverse to each other:

$$f'.g' = 1 \quad (g' \text{ is a right inverse of } f')$$

$$g'.f' = 1 \quad (g' \text{ is a left inverse of } f')$$

The correct formulation is to say that the mappings should go between the power sets, so that:

$$f: \mathcal{P}(\text{Papers}) \longrightarrow \mathcal{P}(\text{People})$$

$$g: \mathcal{P}(\text{People}) \longrightarrow \mathcal{P}(\text{Papers})$$

These mappings are completely determined by their values at singleton subsets since, for all subset S and T, $f(S \cup T) = f(S) \cup f(T)$. In this sense, these mappings may always be reconstructed from mappings whose domain is the set rather than the power set by setting, for example, $f(\{p\}) = f'(p) \, \forall \, p$.

Observe that, for any A, $\mathcal{P}(A)$ is a complete lattice with the preorder relation defined by set inclusion: $\supseteq$ (read 'contains'). In fact, the power lattice is a category with these inclusions as arrows. This is the basis of my claim that the two mappings are adjoints rather than inverses.

Taking any two arbitrary mappings in opposite senses between a pair of power types is not sufficient for a true association. Intuitively there must be some relationship between the pair. This definition enables one to represent many-to-many relationships properly and to compose the two mappings as originally claimed. However, in general, we still do not have to have an inverse pair as claimed by Odell. What we must at least have is that these mappings should be left and right **semi-inverses** (where the = in the definition of inverse is replaced by $\supseteq$):

$$\text{Rule 1: } f.g(\{p\}) \supseteq \{p\}$$

($f.g(\{p\})$ is the set of all the people that wrote (or co-wrote) papers written by p; this contains $\{p\}$.)

$$\text{Rule 2: } g.f(\{q\}) \supseteq \{q\}$$

($g.f(\{q\})$ is the set of all papers written by people who wrote q; this contains $\{q\}$.)

Intuitively, these two rules represent the minimal referential integrity constraint on a pair of mappings for them to constitute an association. In fact, we *define* an **association** as a pair of opposed mappings on the power types such that rules 1 and 2 above are satisfied. An association need not be strong enough to enforce referential integrity and I will show in Section A.2.3 how these conditions must be strengthened to achieve this.

7.9.1 Integrity Rules, Rulesets and Encapsulation

The above two conditions can be expressed by rulesets (or, more specifically, class invariants) encapsulated in the classes as follows.

Each object type corresponds to a set of classes that implement it. We choose one class as a representative. The mapping f is an instance attribute of the class Papers which can be written as writtenBy(People,1,n). This pointer to the People class indicates that a paper may be written by one to many people (authors). Then, in this example, g is an instance attribute of People, which would normally be written as wrote (Papers,0,n).

Since the associations are attributes that form part of the interface, an instance q of the class Papers can determine the set of instances of People that wrote the paper. Call that set of identifiers AuthorsOf(q). For each member of AuthorsOf(q), People can check its Wrote attribute and return the set of papers written by this author. Call this set WrittenBy (AuthorsOf(q)). Rule 2, above, just states that q is a member of this set, for all q in Papers. The rule is encapsulated by Papers. Dually, Rule 1 is encapsulated by People. The reader should work through the dual processing steps.

Inserting the obvious cardinalities we could write the attributes and Rule 2 in a more familiar style:

- For all papers there must be someone, possibly many people, who wrote the paper.
- For all papers q, q is a member of the set of papers written by people who wrote q.

For those readers more familiar with Smalltalk-like programming languages than with databases, the above can be thought of as being implemented by message sends rather than mappings.

It should also be noted that, since f and g are in the public interfaces of their respective classes, there is no violation of encapsulation when the rules are encapsulated. The existence of a mapping implies that the class stores the identity of the associated class and this, of course, gives access to its interface. Encapsulation would be violated if a class referred to an instance of another class, because this would be an assumption about the instantiation of the other class. Therefore, it is assumed that reference to instances happens via the class extension (which is part of the public interface of the class).

The suggestion above does not allow us to search for the association member that caused the integrity violation (as the rule is applied *a postiori*), although this is a necessity for any DBMS. To be able to provide a solution for this, the assumption that the other class can process its g function in the reverse direction (starting from the result) is not a violation of encapsulation. Starting from this, the first step would be to retrieve the set of authors of aPaper, wrote(aPaper), by sending a message to the People class. To ensure integrity it is then sufficient to compare the image of the returned set wrote(aPaper) under writtenBy with the Papers class's instance aPaper. This argument is made clearer in the next section.

Another way of looking at Rule 1 is to say that q is contained in the *union* of the individual sets of papers written by each author who wrote q (who are represented in the writtenBy association of the Papersclass). These sets are found in the People class by checking the wrote association for each author who wrote paper q. This, in itself, is insufficient to ensure referential integrity.

For example, imagine the case when a paper q establishes that it is in writtenBy({Hugh}). Author Hugh would then have to establish that paper q is in the image of its wrote association. In case author Hugh could not establish this association for any reason, Rule 1 in the Papers class would compare the union of the sets of papers written by the Authors who wrote q as provided by the People class. If paper q had also been co-written by other authors, the resulting set would contain q, even though author Hugh's wrote association does not contain paper q and integrity would be violated. Thus, the rule given does not allow us to search for the association member that caused the integrity violation, although this is a necessity for any DBMS.

The solution is to build the *intersection* (rather than the union) of all the applications of the mapping. If the intersection (of the sets of papers written by each author) does not contain paper q, you know that an integrity violation has occurred. Thus, People and Papers must contain rules that state:

$$\text{Rule 3:} \quad \{p\} \subseteq \bigcap_{qa \in g(\{p\})} f(\{qa\})$$
$$\text{Rule 4:} \quad \{q\} \subseteq \bigcap_{pa \in f(\{q\})} g(\{pa\})$$

An association with these rules encapsulated in its classes ensures referential integrity and gives a precise meaning to the intuitive notion of 'inverse' mappings, although:

PROPOSITION 1: Rules 3 and 4 are weaker conditions than saying that f and g are true inverses.

Proof: Assume that g is left inverse to f so that: $gf(Q) = Q$. Choose any q and let $pa \in f(\{q\})$. Then $g(\{pa\}) \subseteq gf(\{q\}) = \{q\}$. Therefore either $g(\{pa\})$ is empty or equal to $\{q\}$. Being empty would violate our assumptions. Therefore Rule 4 holds (actually with the inclusion replaced by a stronger equality).

That the converse is not true may be seen by considering a group of three authors, Hugh, Ivan and Jane, who all co-authored the two papers

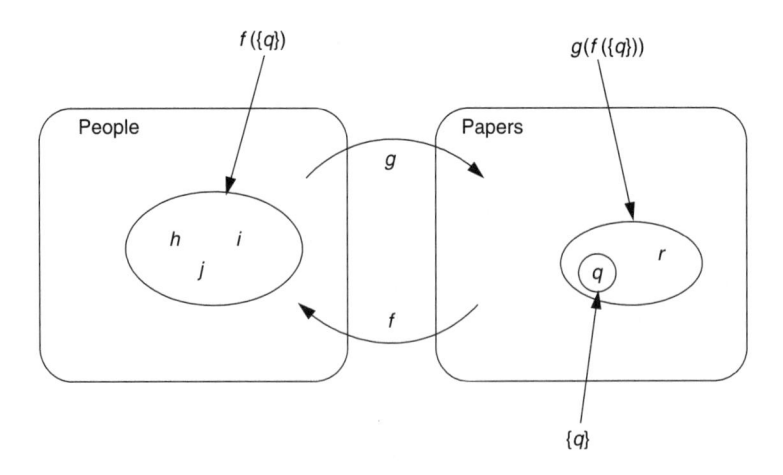

Figure 7-16 The counterexample of Proposition 1.

q and r. Here $\{q\}$ is a proper subset of $\{q,r\} = g(f(\{q\})) \cap g(f(\{r\}))$. Figure 7-16 illustrates this counter-example.

QED

To get true inverses we must assert equality in the two rules but this seems counter intuitive. Define a **strong association** to be a pair of mappings satisfying Rules 3 and 4. Also define such a pair as **strong semi-inverses**.

7.10 Summary

Understanding and modelling requirements requires a richer language than that needed to specify a computer system.

The requirements model should contain all of the following items.

- Prioritized measurable business objectives.
- Before and after versions of business process descriptions. These may include network models (e.g. models written in BPMN), mission grids or rich pictures based on conversations – or both. They may also include collaborations that show how conversations interact.
- Cross reference tables linking the objectives to the processes and conversations.
- Descriptions of the boundary conversations that are the starting point for specification.

There are problems with the conventional approach to use cases including the following.

- Overemphasis on functional decomposition.
- Lack of a clear definition and agreed interpretation.
- The inappropriate use of controller objects.
- Confusion over the relationship of use cases with scenarios.
- Lack of a notion of genericity.
- Lack of a notion of atomicity.
- Too much detail and too many use cases as a result of poor abstraction.
- Poor exception handling.

We can use the standard UML class diagram concepts to model conversations and use cases; the «extends» dependency violates object-oriented principles and should never be used.

Boundary conversations describe the features that the user of the system will be able to use. In other words, they describe the *services* that the system offers its direct users. Describe such services by their pre- and post-conditions. In addition, document how fatal or rare errors are to be handled. Common non-fatal errors are best documented as separate use cases.

Having documented the boundary conversations that describe visible services and their crucial components the analyst must do two things: (a) document any internal collaborations implied by the model and (b) discover the object types that will need to be designed to implement the services. Adopting a Catalysis approach makes the latter step remarkably simple; everything we need is in the use case pre- and post-conditions. We can employ the simple textual analysis technique of Chapter 3 if need be, or just use our common sense in reading them. Make use of Coad's colour patterns. Don't forget to INTERNALIZE THE PARALLELISM OF COLLABORATIONS (7). Use statecharts to increase understanding of the types and to find services. Then CROSS-REFERENCE STATES TO USE CASES (8). Consider cartooning users as agents.

Look for rules and policies. Remember that ASSOCIATION LOOPS CONCEAL RULES and use these other patterns where appropriate.

- USE CASE POST-CONDITIONS ARE RULES (9) (which we have already explored).
- WRITE THE CONSTRAINTS AS RULES (11). (This is a matter of style.)
- ASK THE BUSINESS (12).
- ASSIGN RULES TO COMPONENTS (13).
- POLICY BLACKBOARD (14).
- BASE ERROR MESSAGES ON RULES (15).
- STORE RULES IN A REPOSITORY (16).
- ENCAPSULATE A REFERENCE (17).

Our analysis process proceeds as follows.

- Identify the processes or conversations at the system boundary.
- Write pre- and post-conditions and business rules for each of these.
- Extract types using textual analysis and other techniques.
- Refine the model and find new processes and actions using, perhaps, state models.
- Write pre- and post-conditions and rules for any new processes.
- Iterate until the model is stable (or time runs out!)

7.11 Bibliographical Notes

Use cases were introduced by Ivar Jacobson and first presented in book form by Jacobson *et al.* (1992). RUP is largely based on Jacobson's Unified Process (1999). Kruchten (1999) is another treatment of RUP that concentrates more on the process than the notations.

CHAPTER 8

Standards

Standards are always out of date.
That is what makes them standards.
Alan Bennett *(Forty Years On, 1969)*

This short chapter summarizes various important standards that the modern business analyst should be aware of. Since SOA is essentially a standards-based technology, this is important. However, since standards are subject to rapid evolution, especially in this dynamic area of computing, I do not go into detail or repeat what has been said and some of the standards in earlier chapters. Instead, I have chosen to provide references from which the reader may obtain the latest information. Mostly, of course, these are references to web sites.

We divide the standards up into standards for business process modelling, standards for web services and other standards that are relevant in some way or other.

8.1 BPM Standards

The Unified Modelling Language (UML) contains at least three notations that are useful for business process modelling. The most widely used is the activity diagram described in Chapter 4. In Chapter 5 we saw how to model processes using UML use case notation. Finally, in some circumstances it is very helpful to use statecharts (see Chapter 7) although we have not really explored this in this book since it would normally be done as part of design as opposed to specification. UML is specified at:

- http://www.uml.org/

BPMN (Business Process Modelling Notation), which we met in Chapter 4, is a rich graphical notation that can be used to model transactional business processes and to generate BPEL executables from its diagrams. In future it will also be able to generate an open interchange format based on BPDM. BPMN is specified at:

- http://www.bpmn.org/

BPDM (Business Process Definition Metamodel) is the process metamodel under development by the OMG. It aims to standardize the BPMN to BPEL mapping and provide an open interchange standard for model exchange. BPDM is compliant with MDA (see Section 8.3). BPDM provides the capability to represent and model business processes independent of notation or method. This is done using a metamodel of how to describe business processes. The metamodel uses the OMG's MOF (Meta Object Facility) standard to capture business processes and to provide the XML syntax for storing and transferring process models between tools. BPDM is specified at:

- http://www.omg.org/technology/documents/br_pm_spec_catalog.htm

BPRI (Business Process Runtime Interface) is another MDA initiative under development that is aimed at administration and at user and system interfaces. A standard for the runtime artifacts of executing processes and the display of aggregated data in management dashboards and so on – those data used to measure process performance. The proposed standard will allow process information to be shared across vendor offerings and become accessible to third party tools. BPRI is described at:

- http://66.102.9.104/search?q=cache:Q3ID7PlYhRQJ:www.omg.org/news/meetings/workshops/soa-bpm-mda-2006/04-1_Baker.pdf+bpri+omg&hl=en&ct=clnk&cd=1&gl=uk

Another standards consortium, OASIS, maintains the WS-BPEL specification. BPEL is a programming language. It represents a process using XML with bindings to web services expressed in WSDL (see Section 8.2).

- http://www.oasis-open.org/committees/tc_home.php?wg_abbrev=wsbpel

The world wide web consortium's (W3C) Choreography Description Language (WS-CDL) is an XML-based language that defines how different web services and participants can interact. E-Business applications require the ability to perform long-lived, peer-to-peer transactions between participating services, within or across organizational boundaries Thus WS-CDL describes these by defining, from a global viewpoint, their observable common and complementary behaviour; where ordered message exchanges result in the achievement of some common business goal. It can do this between any type of participant regardless of the supporting platform or programming model used. Significantly, it can be used as a precursor to a BPEL implementation. W3C also maintains the following other choreography standards, though they have not had much impact on the mainstream of commercial computing: WSCI (Web Services Choreography Interface) and WSCL (Web Services Conversation Language).

WS-CDL is specified at:

- http://www.w3.org/TR/ws-cdl-10/

WSCI and WSCL are specified, respectively, at:

- http://www.w3.org/TR/wsci/
- http://www.w3.org/TR/wscl10/

BPQL (Business Process Query Language) is meant to be a management interface to a business process management infrastructure that includes a process server that provides an execution facility and a repository that provides a process deployment facility. The OMG has taken over development of the specification from the BPMI. It has yet to be published.

Finally there are three significant XML-based process execution languages, including BPML and BPEL. BPML (Business Process Modelling Language) was developed by the BPMI with similar aims to BPEL but, these days, of more theoretical than commercial significance. It is now under the auspices of the OMG. And the specification may be found on the OMG site. The Workflow Management Coalition (WfMC) developed another called XPDL, which is quite similar to WS-BPEL. The specification may be found at:

- http://www.wfmc.org/standards/xpdl.htm

OASIS looks after BPEL which I outlined in Chapter 4. It has been taken up vigorously by all the leading middleware and infrastructure vendors. The specification may be found at:

- http://www.oasis-open.org/committees/tc_home.php?wg_abbrev=wsbpel

8.2 Web Services Standards

Web Services specifications offer a communication bridge between the heterogeneous computational environments used to develop and host applications. We met them in Chapter 1.

XML is, of course, the root standard for the entire SOA enterprise. All web services standards and several business process modelling standards build on it in some ways. XML is documented in various good textbooks; Harold and Means (2004) is a popular one. The other chief standards are WSDL, SOAP and UDDI. In addition there is a whole family of WSDL-based standards for things such as security, reliable messaging and so on, usually referred to as WS-*. Specifications for these can be found on the W3C site (www.w3.org).

Here are the other relevant sites.

WSDL: http://www.w3.org/TR/wsdl

SOAP: http://www.w3.org/TR/soap/

UDDI: http://www.oasis-open.org/committees/uddi-spec/doc/tcspecs.htm

8.3 Other Miscellaneous Standards

UML, of course contains more than the activity diagram and SOA analysts will need to know about at least class, use case and state diagrams. When moving to the design of messaging within a SOA implementation, the UML sequence diagram is also a very natural and helpful tool. The UML specification is maintained by the Object Management Group (OMG).

Another important OMG specification is MDA (Model Driven Architecture) which is a software development approach the OMG announced as long ago as 2001: it has been influential though has limited take up in many industry sectors. MDA supports a form of code generation and provides a set of guidelines for structuring specifications expressed as models as described in Chapter 2 (Section 2.4). MDA principles can also be applied to other areas such as business process modelling where the PIM is translated to either automated or manual processes so that MDA is a good starting point for modelling a BPEL implementation. I think that the CIM is a better place to start with more general business process modelling – which is partly what Chapter 5 was all about. You can find the specification and other information at:

- http://www.omg.org/mda/

At the end of Chapter 4 and in Chapter 5, I introduced the notion of collaborative business processes. The nearest thing to this idea to be found among the myriad standards on offer is BPSS (Business Process Specification Schema) (an OASIS specification). The BPSS notion of collaboration is more restrictive than ours and it is, in some ways, closer to a choreography language – although a BPSS collaboration is a collection of legally significant message exchanges forming a transaction whereas choreography is concerned with higher level control flow of a set of transactions. Specifically, it is part of the ebXML system aimed at facilitating business-to-business electronic transactions. A transaction may be between multiple parties.

Specifications for ebXML, including BPSS, may be found at:

- http://www.ebxml.org/

Havey (2005) provides a good introductory summary of BPSS.

If you are considering using a business rules management system, there are some significant standards that you should know about.

SBVR (Semantics of Business Vocabulary and Business Rules) is an OMG standard defining the syntax and structure of fact and rule expressions. It is broadly a generalization of and evolved from RuleSpeak (Ross, 2003). One of its great benefits is that it helps companies fix on a standard way of recording their business knowledge, externalizing it from computer code. To see this consider the following rule taken from a project we did at a large life assurance office.

```
Rule 1

A plan may be issued to a planholder (rule outcome)
if all of the following conditions are true (if clause)
```
- `the product age validation tests are passed (ANDed statements)`
- `the payment method is valid`
- `the fees have been calculated`

  `unless the planholder has a history of fraud ('and not' clause)`

The first line is the **rule outcome** and is followed by the **if clause**. Of course we do not include the bracketed text in our actual rules. Note that the rule is easily extensible because of the use of the word 'all' (underlined for emphasis only) rather than 'both'; a new condition can be added with changing the rule text. This is far better than the usual if-then style. To define terms for the rule we also need **facts**, such as the following.

```
Fact 1: A plan must offer at least one benefit
Fact 2: The maximum age for a Whole Life assured is 72
```

The 'product age validation tests' have yet to be defined. We do this as follows.

```
Rule 2

The product age validation tests are passed (rule out-
come)
   if all of the following conditions are true (if clause)
• the ANB of the life is greater than the minimum age
    for the product
• the ANB of the life is less than or equal to the
    maximum age for the product
```

ANB is short for age next birthday. Note the implicit chaining together of the rules; Rule 1 doesn't make sense without the facts and Rule 2 (and possibly others)

We also need disjunctive (OR) rules, such as:

```
Rule 3

A premium may be loaded (rule outcome)
if at least one of the following conditions is true
(if clause)
• the medical questionnaire is unsatisfactory
    (ORed statements)
• the life has declared dangerous hobbies
```

To convince our client further of the value of this kind of standardization, we mined their existing specification and found the following phrase: 'A correspondent can be a Payer, Nominee, Cessionary, Life Insured and/or Correspondent'. And/or! Hardly rigorous, is it? But it is so easy for a busy analyst to do, and the same specification was positively littered with similar *faux pas*. Adopting the standard layout makes it almost impossible to commit such elementary ambiguities to paper. Here is the version we suggested (although it needed further refinement based on business knowledge).

```
Rule 4

A person can receive correspondence
    if at least one of the following is true
• The person is the Owner
• The person is a Payer
• The person is a Nominee
• The person is a Cessionary
• The person is a Life Insured
• The person is a Correspondent
```

The SBVR metamodel specification is designed to support interchange of business vocabularies and rules amongst organizations. SBVR is designed for use by business people and for business purposes independent of information systems designs although the actual specification is dauntingly large and complex. It is also intended to provide the business vocabulary and business rules underpinned by first order predicate calculus (FOPC) with a small extension into what it calls alethic or 'modal' (actually deontic) logic for transformations by IT staff into MDA PIM system designs. In most cases, such transformations will not be fully automated. Ross's RuleSpeak is an example of a rule notation that complies with SBVR. Rule authoring products such as RuleArts' RuleXpress support the SBVR directly. The emphasis on FOPC tends to make SBVR rather database-centric, although there is nothing in it which prevents a broader interpretation. On this broader interpretation, SBVR is intended to offer a business vocabulary for defining business vocabularies and business rules in completely technology-independent fashion.

Another OMG standard concentrates on the type models that must underpin any business rules or process models. The Ontology Definition Metamodel (ODM) aims to provide a common metamodel for a variety of knowledge representation techniques, with a key objective of supporting the semantic web. It includes MOF metamodels for RDFS, OWL, Topic Maps, Entity-Relation Diagrams, generic Description Logics in several formats and Simple Common Logic. The SBVR group has been co-ordinating with the ODM group for some time and SBVR supports a superset of the logic supported by ODM, and there are plans eventually for interchange between ODM/OWL and SBVR based on an MDA mapping. OWL (Web Ontology Language) is a web-standard language, written in XML, for processing information on the web designed to be interpreted by computers rather than people. The term 'ontology' refers here to a machine-processable representation of knowledge, designed for automated inferencing. In most cases it is structurally indistinguishable from a type model as discussed in Chapter 7. The chief audience for the ODM is the developers of rule engines or other tools that capture and prepare ontologies for inference engines from other declarative forms, such as UML models and structural business rules. In ODM ontologies, knowledge is assumed to be monotonic, i.e. over time knowledge can be added but not removed or contradicted.

The ODM is being developed concurrently with SBVR. The draft proposed ODM includes metamodels of several popular knowledge representation languages, with mappings between them.

SBVR covers vocabularies (ontology) and business rules. It makes a strong distinction between a concept and its expression. It does not standardize expression but does illustrate business rule expression in three ways: SBVR-SE (a structured English form that the standard itself uses),

BRS RuleSpeak and ORM (Object Rôle Models). Other languages and notations are encouraged.

These standards provide quite different viewpoints. ODM is to OWL as SBVR is to things like RuleSpeak. SBVR deals with business rules, which ODM does not cover. ODM is for ontologists (business thing analysts) and SBVR is for business users or business rule analysts. OWL is a semantic web standard, whereas SBVR is a business modelling standard.

Specifications for these standards can be found at the following sites.

- SBVR: http://www.omg.org/technology/documents/bms_spec_catalog.htm
- OWL: http://www.w3.org/TR/owl-ref/
- RDFS: http://www.w3.org/TR/rdf-schema/

Finally, there is a growing number of vertical industry ontologies, without which B2B process interactions are very problematical. Ontological standards, along with their obvious advantages for communication through documentation, support such things as straight-through processing, expand market opportunities, help develop more flexible relationships and meet global needs. In the Insurance and Life industries the emerging standard is ACORD (www.acord.org). The Oil and Gas sector ontology, one of the first to emerge, has been standardized as ISO29001. There are similar emerging standards for Banking and other industry sectors. Make sure you are aware of those relevant to the industries you work in.

Various business rules management system vendors offer 'knowledge packs': packaged ontologies that work with the vendor's rule engine and are meant to save users a great deal of modelling effort in the early months of development. Some of these are based on industry standards such as ACORD.

8.4 Bibliographical Notes

The UML standard is discussed in detail by Fowler (2003) and Graham (2001).

Havey (2005) describes several of the standards mentioned in this chapter and a few more besides, although the latter are probably less important in today's environment. Ehn (2004, 2005) provides detailed discussion of the various web services standards.

Graham (2006) discusses standards in the context of business rules management systems.

APPENDIX A

Requirements Engineering and Specification Patterns

> *God forbid that we should give out a dream of our own imagination for a pattern of the world.*
> **Francis Bacon (*The Great Instauration*, 1620)**

This appendix presents some thumbnail sketches of patterns that have been referred to in the text. They form part, but not all, of an emerging pattern language that also includes patterns for BRMS development (cf. Graham, 2006) and process and project management patterns (cf. Graham, 2009), not to mention usability patterns (Graham, 2003). Therefore, hooks to other patterns are sometimes incomplete as this is only part of the language.

Figure A-1 presents the patterns graphically and provides primary navigation. The pattern's numbers have no significance whatsoever, except to provide the reader with a quick reference when browsing this chapter.

Some patterns are terminal within this part of the language. A pattern being terminal does not mean that design thinking stops with it – merely that the language considers the further design issues as beyond the language's scope or ambitions. The other cases where the language terminates abruptly usually concern areas of some complexity that, in my opinion, are deserving of a pattern language in their own right. Where such pattern languages already exist, I have referenced them at the end of this appendix.

The simplest way to use the patterns is to consider pattern number one (ESTABLISH THE BUSINESS OBJECTIVES) first and then follow the links to the other patterns. It is best to have a concrete problem in mind when doing this. Eventually you will reach patterns that are terminal (represented in black on the diagrams). You should also try to construct sequences (or sublanguages) to deal with specific design problems or specific kinds of development.

Rules are made to be broken. The patterns in this chapter may be regarded as rules for successful analysis but it is better to think of them as

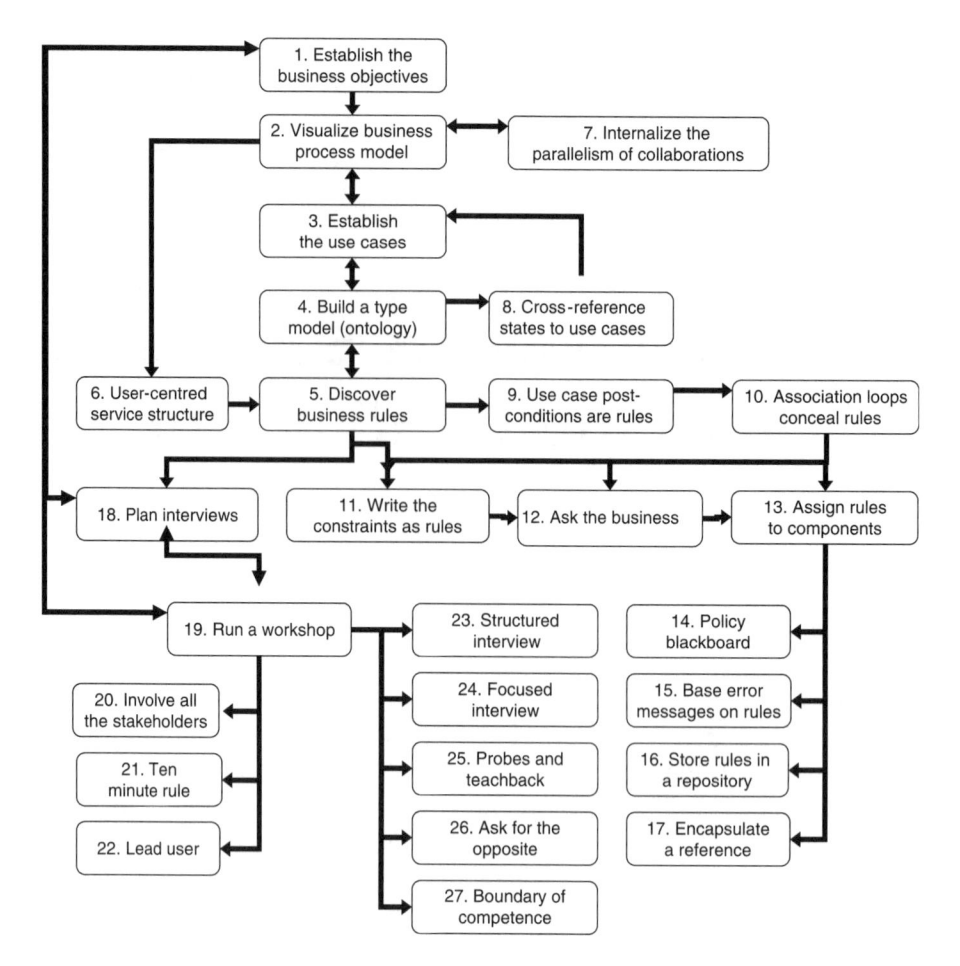

Figure A-1 Requirements patterns map.

providing suggestions, guidance and checklists of things not to forget to think about. If you do find yourself treating the patterns as rules then pause. Always consider the likely effects of breaking the rules and ensure that you understand the rules that you are going to break and the justification for doing so.

Each pattern is presented using the same layout, semantic structure and typographical conventions. These are very closely based on the structure pioneered by Alexander *et al.* (1977). The pattern number and name are presented first followed, optionally, by a list of alternative names – all in a black header. The alternatives, if present, are labelled aka (also known as) in the same header. Next comes what many people call a **sensitizing image**: a picture or diagram concerning, supporting or illustrating the pattern. In many cases this has been omitted for brevity.

After the sensitizing image we present the **Context** in which one would normally encounter the pattern. This section usually gives the names of patterns that one has already used or considered. This is separated from the body of the pattern by three tildes, thus:

~~~

Next, the Problem is stated in **bold text**. For the discussion of the **forces** that are at work and the way the pattern deals with them we return to plain text, i.e. text of the sort you are reading in this paragraph. This section may include quite diverse types of commentary and explanations. Where appropriate we highlight known uses of the patterns. Where this is omitted it is because the known uses are so obvious as to not need stating or because they have been intrinsic to the description of the forces and related discussion.

At the end of the discussion, where applicable, there is a reference to the chapter in this book wherein the pattern has been expanded upon.

Once the discussion is complete, I state or summarize the recommended solution in **bold text**. This section is highlighted in the margin with the word Therefore. This completes the body of the pattern; so we again delimit it with three tildes.

The next section describes the Resultant context and, unless the pattern is terminal, will include the names of the patterns that one may consider applying next. This information is partly represented in Figure A-1 by the arrows. Interpret these arrows as meaning 'supplies a potential context for'.

Following Alexander again, I have classified the patterns according to my degree of confidence in them. The pattern's 'star rating', shown next to its name, indicates this. Three stars means that I am totally convinced of the pattern's efficacy, having used it or seen it used successfully on many projects. Three stars may also indicate that there is some solid theoretical justification of the pattern in the literature and folklore of the subject. If there are no stars it means that I think this is a good idea but would like people to try and see. One and two stars are interpreted on the scale between these extremes in the obvious manner.

The lengths of the patterns vary. Partly, this reflects knowledge and experience of the patterns and therefore confidence in them. However, sometimes a short pattern merely reflects the fact that it is easy to describe and understand. In some cases the pattern is short because either a longer version of the pattern has already been published or an expanded version might be considered useful.

In Figure A-1 rounded rectangles represent patterns and an arrow from pattern P_1 to pattern P_2 is to be interpreted as meaning 'P_1 possibly generates a context for applying P_2 and indicates that the designer should consider applying P_2 whenever he/she has applied P_1'. Double headed arrows further suggest that a group of patterns will normally be considered iteratively and in parallel.

Pattern 1 — ESTABLISH THE BUSINESS OBJECTIVES ***

Context You are embarking on a business solution and system development project.

Problem **How can you be sure that the system will be fit for purpose and that project management can be both successful and agile in response to evolving requirements?**

Forces Many development methods encourage developers to start analysis with use case modelling or, at best, give little concrete advice on how to tie development to business goals. This can lead to dysfunctional results, unused systems or loss of focus during development. Furthermore, as requirements evolve during the project, there can be disputes over which use cases have priority for implementation before the next timeboxed delivery date.

When you decide to use timeboxes to control iterative, agile development you can only negotiate sensibly on evolving requirements if you have consensus on the things that will *not* change during the project.

Prioritizing objectives according to some scheme such as 'Must have, Should have, Could have', often presents difficulties because stakeholders insist that their favourite objective is a 'must' until discrimination is lost completely and the priorities are worthless. An objective numerical ranking can be achieved by pairwise comparison of the objectives but this can be very time-consuming. It is quicker and just as practically effective to let workshop participants vote, preferably from two points of view.

Example For example, give each person red and blue stickers to the tune of two-thirds of the number of objectives and let them place the stickers next to the objectives on a flipchart. Red might represent the view of the organization, while blue represent individual (or departmental) preferences. Next one may add the results (blue and red) together and open a discussion to ensure that there is a consensus on the priorities so computed.

A longer version of this pattern can be found in Graham (2003). It should also be noted that there

Refer to   Chapter 3.

Therefore   **Run a stakeholder workshop to establish the business objectives. There will typically be between 7 and 30 such objectives. Ensure each objective can be measured numerically and objectively; otherwise reject or reword it. Now assign numerical priorities to the objectives. The quickest way to do this is by voting and consensus-building discussion. Fix the objectives and priorities for the duration of the project.**

Involve as many stakeholders as possible. Make sure that potential users are represented. Find a good facilitator. Agree a mission statement to give context to the objectives.

~~~

Resultant context   Once the objectives and priorities are fixed you can safely move on to VISUALIZE THE BUSINESS PROCESS MODEL (2). To help you do this, PLAN INTERVIEWS (18) and/or RUN A WORKSHOP (19).

Pattern 2   VISUALIZE BUSINESS PROCESS MODEL **

Context   You have ESTABLISHED THE BUSINESS OBJECTIVES (1) and fixed their priorities. You are also committed to a service-oriented approach.

~~~

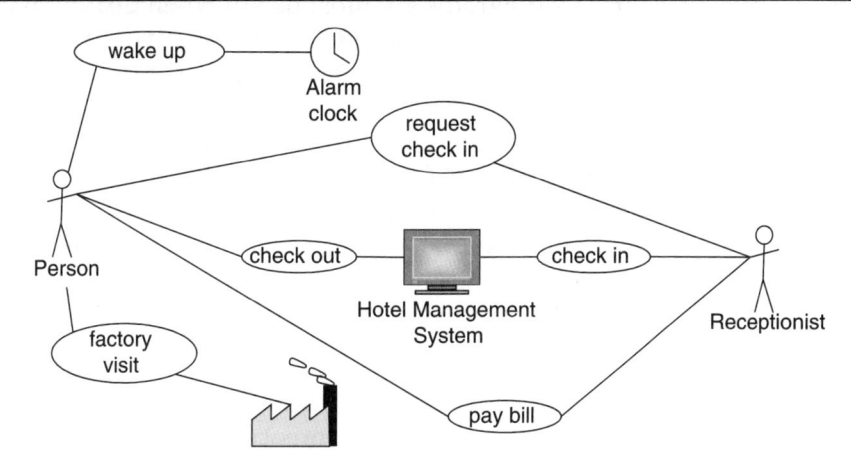

Problem	**How can you ensure that the development will take account of current or re-engineered business practices and procedures? The needs of stakeholders that are not direct users of the system must be understood – as well as those of the 'actors' in a conventional use case model. Do you understand the process fully? Is process automation a possibility? Do the processes, as they mostly will, involve any explicit or latent business rules?**
Forces	The philosophy of service-oriented architecture emphasizes that our focus must be on the real user as well as the user who actually interacts with the system; a conventional use case model tends to focus on the latter.

There are a few notational styles commonly used to represent business processes. In UML terms, we have activity diagrams or use case diagrams available. We also have BPMN. Activity diagrams are often useful but they can grow unmanageably large very quickly, often because they attempt to incorporate business rules (as conditionals, etc.) or because they model system activities. Also, they do not show 'who does what' very clearly; in that sense they are 'disembodied'.

BPMN diagrams are most useful when dealing with transactional, as opposed to collaborative, processes, especially when process automation in BPEL is being considered.

Use case diagrams tend to remain manageably concise and are ideal for emphasizing the contract-driven nature of business. Stating contracts for each conversation that occurs in a process can lead directly to statements of business rules. At a minimum, the pre- and post-conditions of the conversations (represented as use cases) always have a rule-like nature.

Known uses	The image above is meant to suggest that actors in use case diagrams should be stereotyped to look like what they represent; if it is a factory, make it look like one. This helps communication in workshop situations and beyond.

This technique has been used successfully on hundreds of projects known to me around the world over fifteen years or so. A longer variant of this pattern can be found in Graham (2003).

Refer to Chapters 4 to 6 describe the techniques that apply to this pattern.

Therefore **Understand first the network of agents and commitments that make up the business. Specify the conversations that take place at an appropriate level of abstraction, so that they are stereotypes for actual stories. Get people to tell these stories. Eliminate conversations that do not correspond to business objectives (or discover the missed objective). Ensure that every objective is supported by a conversation.**

Emphasizing the contracts that subsist in the business processes will assist in identifying business rules both now and later in the project.

Draw a rich picture of the whole of each business process. Use cases can be used in this picture to represent goal-oriented conversations between actors (including users, non-users, events and artifacts). Ensure that you discuss possible changes to the process, leading to a 'before' and 'after' process model. Use stereotypes in the rich pictures that are meaningful to the business stakeholders present.

Classify your processes as transactional or collaborative. Draw BPMN diagrams of the transactional processes to ensure you understand them and to help think about process automation opportunities.

~~~

Resultant context Now ESTABLISH THE USE CASES (3) in the context of the proposed system and the business processes defined. Understanding who the real users are will provide the correct context for building a USER-CENTRED SERVICE STRUCTURE (6).

INTERNALIZE THE PARALLELISM OF COLLABORATIONS (7) to make sure that there will be no absurdities in the process when the system is implemented.

This pattern is normally applied iteratively, in parallel with all the patterns in the group numbered 2–5.

Pattern 3   ESTABLISH THE USE CASES ★★★

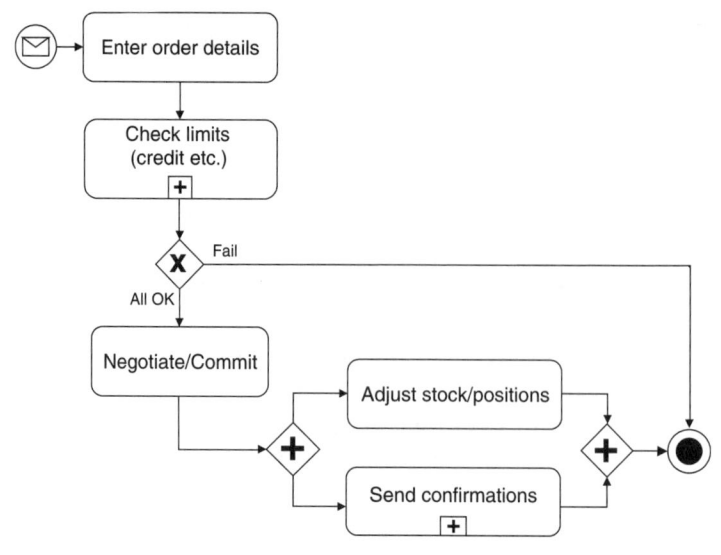

[Diagram: BPMN process flow — Enter order details → Check limits (credit etc.) → gateway (Fail / All OK) → Negotiate/Commit → parallel split to Adjust stock/positions and Send confirmations → join → end event]

Context
: You have constructed and visualized a 'before' and 'after' BUSINESS PROCESS MODEL (2) and, where applicable, INTERNALIZED THE PARALLELISM OF COLLABORATIONS (7).

∼∼∼

Problem
: **How can you specify the behaviour of a system and the services it must provide?**

Forces
: Use case modelling is a very well-known technique. However, current practice tends to produce over-complex use cases with far too much detail. Jacobsen, Fowler and Cockburn all give 'templates' for use cases, which exacerbate this tendency to 'over-document' although, to be fair, I think Cockburn did not intend to encourage their (mis)use.

  Theoretically, use cases are completely determined by their pre- and post-conditions. There is really no need to specify them further, apart from the need to state what should happen when the use case encounters an unrecoverable (i.e. fatal) exception. Recoverable exceptions are new, reusable use cases. No steps! No alternative paths!

  The second problem with current practice is the use of the semantically ambiguous «extends» association, which tends to over-complicate and enlarge models.

It is better to dispense with it and define exception handling by separate use cases, to which error handling messages are delegated.

Use cases correspond to what I have called boundary conversations.

Use cases can also be found by examining BPMN models; they correspond then to the activities of the model, but beware in case the latter conceal collaborations rather than conversations. In case they do you must INTERNALIZE THE PARALLELISM OF COLLABORATIONS (7).

Basically, use case modelling focuses on the functionality of systems as opposed to their data structure. Business process management based methods start with business activities and it is often easy to extract use cases from these, but beware the warning in the previous paragraph. Rule-based methods (e.g. Date, 2002; Halle, 2002) tend to start with the data model. The danger in that approach is that the service structure becomes data-centred rather than user-centred. Much experience says that a method that starts with functionality is both sounder and easier to understand.

Known uses
Use case modelling is a well-established technique for systems development and is part of most mainstream methods for object-oriented and component based development. A longer version of this pattern can be found in Graham (2003).

Refer to
Chapters 5 and 7.

Therefore
Extract the use cases from the conversations in the BUSINESS PROCESS MODEL (2). Write post-conditions for each use case. Compare the vocabulary of the post-conditions to the type model. Write use cases in stimulus–response form. Do not constrain unnecessarily the user's ability to perform steps in any particular sequence.

Use cases are ideal for high level specification but they must be formulated at the right level of abstraction. Very detailed use cases are an impediment to clear understanding. To avoid superfluous detail, define use cases by ONLY their pre- and post-conditions and, if necessary, remarks on what will

happen if there is a non-recoverable error during execution of the task. Write separate use cases to describe how to recover from other types of error.

Write explicit rules based on the pre- and post-conditions (the use case goals).

Ensure the use cases remain cross-referenced to the business objectives and that they inherit the priorities of the latter.

∼∼∼

`Resultant context`

Now BUILD A TYPE MODEL (4) by explicating the vocabulary needed to express the pre- and post-conditions. Use the use cases to DISCOVER BUSINESS RULES (5); ensure that they are executable and based on the type model.

Note the use cases that will be exported as services with your SOA.

Group the use cases into sets that can be implemented together; base your project timeboxes on these prioritized sets. Use the use case model to define tests and automate testing.

This pattern is normally applied iteratively, in parallel with all the patterns in the group numbered 2–5.

Pattern 4   BUILD A TYPE MODEL (ONTOLOGY) ***

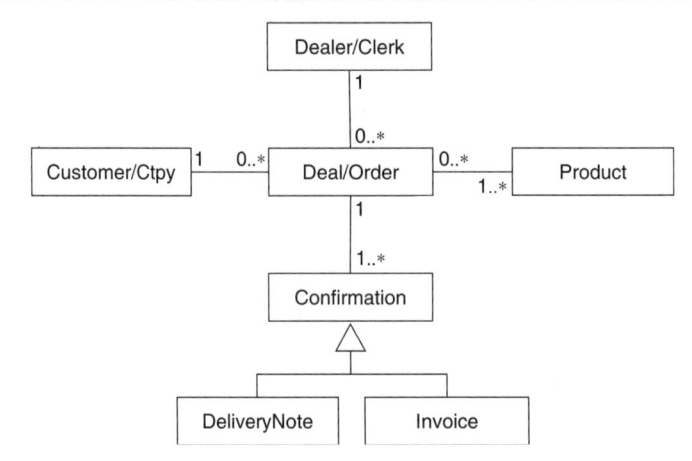

`Context`

You have ESTABLISHED THE USE CASES (3) and written their post-conditions. These statements or rules make no sense without a vocabulary: an ontology that gives the statements meaning.

∼∼∼

Problem	**How can you get a computer to interpret use cases and the business rules associated with them?**
Forces	Getting a machine to understand natural language statements is either impossible or quite beyond any known science. Therefore, we must help the machine by providing an ontology that gives precise meaning to the statements we use in rules or use cases. A UML type model is an ideal way to do this, although semantic networks may also prove valuable.
Known uses	Type modelling is a standard technique for software development although there are variations in its practice. It is assumed here that a theoretically sound method such as Catalysis (D'Souza and Wills, 1999; Andrews, 2009) or UML components (Cheesman and Daniels, 2000) is the basis for type modelling. It would be inappropriate to reproduce all the details of how to do type modelling here. A few remarks will suffice.

In the context of SOA and CBD it is a good idea to distinguish core (kernel), role and process (association) components – Date (2000), Cheesman and Daniels (2000) and Andrews (2009) all agree on this point. Core objects will be stored in lower architectural layers whereas role and process objects tend to be about specific applications. Also Coad and co-workers' (1999) colour patterns are often very useful in making similar architectural decisions. We discussed them fleetingly in Chapter 2.

Catalysis includes several subpatterns such as MAP TO EXISTING DATABASE (which concerns retrievals from legacy systems). These are worth getting to know.

Most BRMS products provide some level of automated support for this process. Haley Authority walks the user through the construction of the minimal type model needed to interpret the rules. JRules allows developers to import existing Java object models or UML models. At a minimum, all these products will fail to compile rules in the absence of an adequate type model. |
| Refer to | Chapter 7. |
| Therefore | **Read all the rules that you have discovered so far and especially the pre- and post-conditions of all the use cases. Define types that represent the vocabulary of** |

these statements. Some terms may be attributes of the types. Record how types are associated and note any cardinality constraints. Classify and interrelate your types using Coad and co-workers' colour patterns.

~~~

Resultant context

The type model will contain many business rules, some explicit, some hidden. We need to DISCOVER BUSINESS RULES (6). These two patterns may be applied in any order and their use will be iterative in most cases. That is, you can write the rules before type modelling or vice versa.

This pattern is normally applied iteratively, in parallel with all the patterns in the group numbered 2–5.

Pattern 5 — DISCOVER BUSINESS RULES

Context

You are building a business rules management system. You have ESTABLISHED THE USE CASES (3). You may have already BUILT A TYPE MODEL (4).

~~~

Problem

How can you discover business rules based on the type model? How can you find rules in other ways?

Forces

The forces at work here depend on how you have arrived at this juncture. Since you have a use case model, the obvious starting point is to rewrite the use case post-conditions as rules. For example, the post-condition of a simple business process such as a sale is 'The vendor has the money and the buyer has the goods'. The corresponding rules might be written as follows.

A sale may be recorded if both of the following are true:

- The Vendor's stock of money has increased by the price of the Goods.
- The Buyer has the Goods.

You can also find rules by examining the type model. Otherwise, you must consider interviews, data mining, workshops and various knowledge elicitation techniques.

Therefore

Rewrite the use case post-conditions as rules.

If there is no type model at the outset, you must use various knowledge elicitation techniques to discover rules. These are covered by the following patterns:

PLAN INTERVIEWS (18)
RUN A WORKSHOP (19)
STRUCTURED INTERVIEW (23)
FOCUSED INTERVIEW (24)
PROBES AND TEACHBACK (25)
ASK FOR THE OPPOSITE (26)
BOUNDARY OF COMPETENCE (27)

and by FILLED-IN FORMS (Graham, 2006). If there is a type model then we may also proceed as follows. First realize that ASSOCIATION LOOPS CONCEAL RULES(10). Then rewrite any cardinality constraints as rules (WRITE THE CONSTRAINTS AS RULES (11)).

Now BUILD A TYPE MODEL (4) or modify the existing one based on the terms used in the new rules discovered.

∼∼∼

Resultant context

This is a link pattern that leads to the patterns listed above, in the Solution.

This pattern is normally applied iteratively, in parallel with all the patterns in the group numbered 2–5.

Pattern 6 — USER-CENTRED SERVICE STRUCTURE

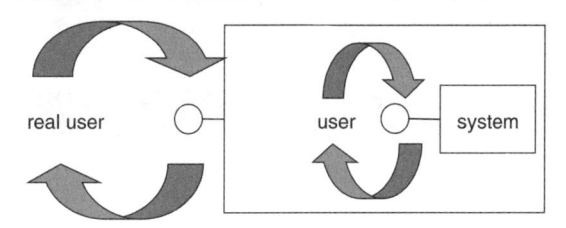

Context

You are building an application within a service-oriented architecture. You have defined and VISUALIZED A BUSINESS PROCESS MODEL (2).

∼∼∼

Problem

How can you ensure that the services and components that are provided are pitched at the right level of abstraction?

Forces	All too often, developers focus their attention on implementation concerns and thus arrive at a design mindset at far too low a level of abstraction compared to the needs of business users. They focus on technical collaborations rather than business processes; the latter often do not – indeed cannot – involve computers. For example, a parcel tracking system needs to understand that a real person has to collect a parcel; the IT systems really can't do that. The user that actually operates the computer is often not the 'real' user, in the sense of the person who gains the business benefit. Designing the system around use cases (in the conventional sense of actions at the system boundary) will lead to a system that does not serve the real users and whose services are not bundled appropriately for use.
Refer to	Chapter 1.
Therefore	**Focus on the 'real' user and upon use cases that represent business process that may occur away from the system boundary. Focus on *what* users want to do, rather than *how* they want to do it. Where possible, capture this essence in the form of business rules.** **Use the Coad and co-workers' colour patterns in your type model; the pink types are most likely to correspond to services.**
	~~
Resultant context	Since you have a clear idea about who the various kinds of users are, both real and hands-on, you can now better DISCOVER BUSINESS RULES (6).

Pattern 7 — INTERNALIZE THE PARALLELISM OF COLLABORATIONS

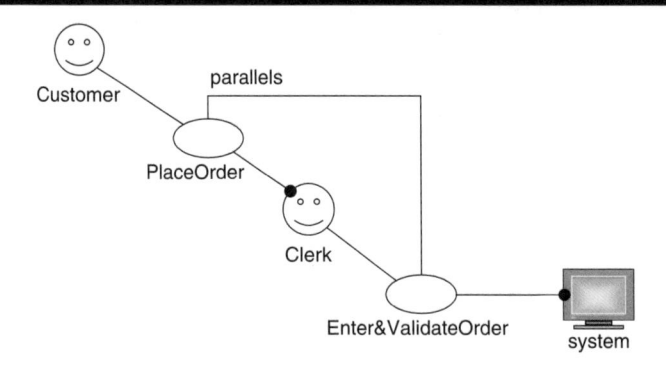

Context	You are building an application within a service-oriented architecture. You have VISUALIZED A BUSINESS PROCESS MODEL (2). You may have started to ESTABLISH THE USE CASES (3).
	∼∼∼
Problem	**How can you move from an understanding of processes that occur away from the system boundary to a model of how the system will interact with its direct users without introducing obstacles to the actual business processes or absurdities from the customer's point of view?**
Forces	Sometimes the business process involves two or more separate activities or conversations that interact or happen concurrently. This is readily understandable by users but will not fit well into a program specification where, often, the machine is given control over the process and this will affect the nature of the interactions among real users as well as computer users.
Refer to	Chapter 7.
Therefore	**Understand and visualize the business process as a real world activity. Decide at which points machine support would be useful and design a boundary conversation (use case) to the direct user that takes account of the fact that other people may be consulted during the conversation. Internalize only the essential control points of the process within this specification.**
	∼∼∼
Resultant context	Now go on to refine the BUSINESS PROCESS MODEL (2) further and ESTABLISH THE USE CASES (3).

Pattern 8   CROSS-REFERENCE STATES TO USE CASES **

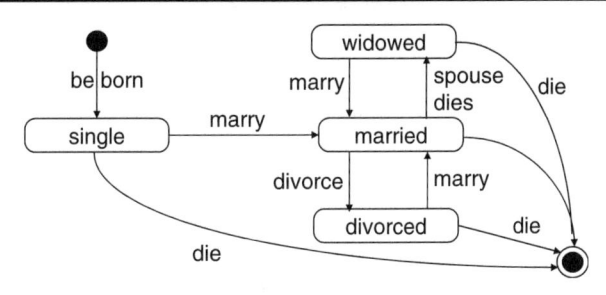

Context	You have VISUALIZED A BUSINESS PROCESS MODEL (2) and BUILT A TYPE MODEL (4).

~~~

Problem	**How can you ensure that there are no contradictions between the business process model and the type model?**
Forces	When you use several modelling notations it is easy for the diagrams to contradict each other. Cross-checking diagrams for consistency is a good idea but could be costly in time. However, some checks are very quick and simple. Do these first. State charts can give insights into business processes that are different and complimentary to, for example, BPMN diagrams.
Refer to	Chapter 7.
Therefore	**Check the type model for types that have a significant complex state and draw a state-transition diagram for these. Ensure that every transition corresponds to a use case in the use case model. See if you can gain further insights into a process by examining the statecharts.**

~~~

Resultant context	Now go back to ESTABLISH THE USE CASES (3) and refine them further with the benefit of this new knowledge.

Pattern 9 — USE CASE POST-CONDITIONS ARE RULES **

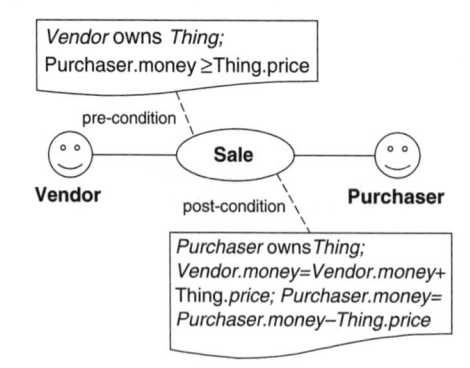

Vendor owns *Thing*;
Purchaser.money ≥ Thing.price

pre-condition

Vendor —— Sale —— Purchaser

post-condition

Purchaser owns *Thing*;
Vendor.money = Vendor.money + Thing.price; Purchaser.money = Purchaser.money − Thing.price

Context	You are trying to DISCOVER BUSINESS RULES (6).

~~~

Problem	**Are there any easy ways to discover business rules?**

Forces	The use cases appear functional in character if written using the 'template' style. However, if written as we have recommended here it is easy to see that their pre- and post-conditions are rules in disguise.
Refer to	Chapters 5 and 7.
Therefore	**Rewrite the use case pre- and post-conditions as rules.**

~~~

Resultant context	Now go on to the ASSOCIATION LOOPS CONCEAL RULES (10) pattern and ASSIGN YOUR RULES TO COMPONENTS (13). If possible STORE THE RULES IN A REPOSITORY (16).

Pattern 10   ASSOCIATION LOOPS CONCEAL RULES **

Context	You are trying to DISCOVER BUSINESS RULES (5) and have completed part of BUILDING A TYPE MODEL (4). You know that you must WRITE THE cardinality CONSTRAINTS AS RULES (11).

~~~

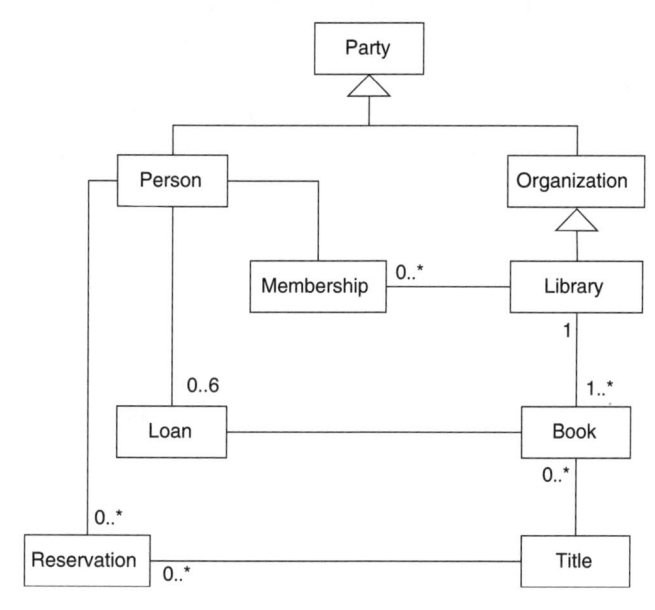

Problem	**How can you be sure that you have not missed any rules implicit in the type model?**
Example	In the image above, start with a person. Do they have a loan? If yes, choose one. Every loan is for a unique

book that has a unique title. Does the title have an outstanding reservation against it? If yes, go back to the person you started with. Does that person have a reservation? If so, is it for the same title? Perhaps the rule is: 'A member may not reserve a title which they have already borrowed a copy of'.

Therefore

Look for cycles (loops) in the type diagrams. Start at each type in the loop, choosing a generic instance of that type and follow the associations to another type. Ask if every route brings you to the same instance. Write down the rule that says it does.

~~~

Resultant context

The rules you have written down may not be true, so now ASK THE BUSINESS (12) and then ASSIGN THE RULES TO COMPONENTS (13).

Pattern 11 — **WRITE THE CONSTRAINTS AS RULES *aka WRITE THE CARDINALITY CONSTRAINTS AS RULES**

Context

You have started to BUILD A TYPE MODEL (4) and noticed that ASSOCIATION LOOPS CONCEAL RULES (10). You may even have ASKED THE BUSINESS (12) and found that some of these rules are correct. However . . .

~~~

Problem

Some rules are written as constraints in a style that does not fit with any obvious externalized form and they may just disappear into the documentation of the type model or, worse, the code. It is unclear at this stage whether there is any interaction (inferencing) among the constraints. How can you clarify the situation?

Forces

Writing rules in the style of constraints is useful if you want to rewrite them in OCL, as post-conditions in a language like Eiffel, using throw and catch in a language like Java or as database update constraints. On the other hand it may mean that there is a conflict of rule style with other rules elicited by other means. Furthermore, it may be hard to see if there are inferential connexions between constraints.

Example

Suppose we have the constraint 'The pilot must be qualified to fly the type of plane assigned to the flight'.

Clear enough, but not written as a rule. Why not try this?

```
A pilot may be assigned to a flight if all
of the following are all true:
  A plane has been assigned to the flight;
  The pilot is qualified to fly the plane
  type (of the assigned plane).
```

In this form it is much easier to see that inferences may be possible. Supposing we have other constraints that say, when written as rules:

```
A plane may be assigned to a transatlantic
flight only if it is a Boeing 777.
A pilot may be hired only if he/she is
qualified to fly Boeing 777s.
```

If we also know the fact 'The flight is a transatlantic flight' (which may, in turn, be inferred from its origin and destination), then the original constraint may be *inferred* to be true, eliminating the need to check it directly in the database or prompt the user for information.

```
Refer to
```
Chapter 7.

```
Therefore
```
Rewrite the cardinality and other constraints as rules using a standard style or rule template. Look out for possible inference patterns.

~~~

```
Resultant
context
```
Now ASK THE BUSINESS (13) to ensure the rules are (still) correct and whether your discoveries about possible inferences are valid. If you haven't done so already, DEFINE A RULE WRITING STYLE (Graham, 2006) and ensure that you have enforced it when using this pattern. Next, try to ASSIGN RULES TO COMPONENTS (13).

Pattern 12	ASK THE BUSINESS ** aka EXPERT REVIEWER

```
Context
```
You have discovered some rules, perhaps by exploiting the fact that ASSOCIATION LOOPS CONCEAL RULES (10) or by WRITING THE CONSTRAINTS AS RULES (11).

~~~

Problem	**How can you be sure that the candidate rules are indeed veritable rules?**
Forces	Having written a rule after much arduous analysis work, it is tempting to assume that it is true. This need not be the case. The temptation to make assumptions is very strong. For example, if air journeys have an origin and destination then one may jump to the conclusion that these have to be different. Indeed, mostly this is the case. But I remember the days when one could board Concorde at Bradford airport, fly out over the Atlantic for a rewarding sonic boom and then return to – yes, you guessed it – Bradford.
Therefore	**A competent user or domain expert must verify every rule. Check also that any inference chains among rules are valid.**

∼∼∼

Resultant context	Now that you are confident that the rules are valid, ASSIGN RULES TO COMPONENTS (13).

Pattern 13 — ASSIGN RULES TO COMPONENTS *

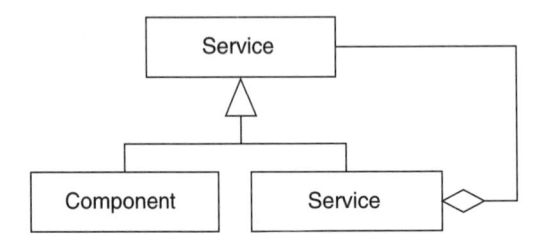

Context	You are developing a rule base. You have DISCOVERED BUSINESS RULES (5), possibly from ASSOCIATION LOOPS (10). You have asked the business (12) to validate the rules. Now you need to store and manage them. Component or service reuse is an important objective.

∼∼∼

Problem	**How can you maximize the reuse potential of processes, components and services and the rules that apply to them?**
Forces	Note first that services are built from components and that components, not services, are the units of

encapsulation and reuse; components are reused, services are shared. Service sharing is the basis of funding for reuse but is not the technical means of achieving it. In turn, services may be composed (recursively) of other services. This is an instance of Buschmann *et al*'s (1996) COMPOSITE pattern, as suggested by the above image.

Some rules obviously belong to component objects, or even to attributes of objects. Attribute constraints might include valid ranges (domains) or there could be rules about attribute default values. Object rules might include simple triggers (relating attributes to methods) or complex rulesets that search for the values of sets of attributes or even the applicable methods dependent on the data presented to the object. If such objects are to be reusable then we need to be able to take them out of one system and drop them in another.

This implies that the objects should contain or encapsulate everything they need to work properly if relocated to a new application. This encapsulating components must include, as well as their own attributes and methods, all references to components and services upon which they depend (i.e. have associations with or send messages to) and *all the rules* that describe how they behave. In other words, if you want reuse, components must encapsulate the rules that apply to them. That way, when you share a service or reuse a component you will get a package of everything needed for that thing to work properly.

On the other hand, the business rules approach recommends that rules should be stored in a central repository for ease of management and update. Also some rules may apply to several objects and be hard to assign to just one. We will need some extra patterns to reconcile these forces. But first...

`Therefore` **Where possible, assign rules and rulesets to the components that they are concerned with or constrain the structure or behaviour of.**

~~~

`Resultant context` Now consider if a POLICY BLACKBOARD (14) is needed, STORE RULES IN A REPOSITORY (16) and ENCAPSULATE A REFERENCE (17).

Pattern 14 — POLICY BLACKBOARD *

Context
You are trying to ASSIGN RULES TO COMPONENTS (14). In some cases this is easy but in others you face a quandary.

~~~

Problem
If a rule applies to more than one service or component, in which component should it be encapsulated?

Forces
Let's say that there are two candidate components, A and B, and that the rule talks about both of them. If you assign the rule to A then B ceases to be fully reusable because if you reuse it, its rules may be left behind. Assigning the rule to B causes the same problem for A. How about assigning the rule to both A and B? This would mean you have two points of maintenance for this rule. If you ENCAPSULATE A REFERENCE (16) and STORE RULES IN A REPOSITORY (17) then the maintenance problem goes away; A and B only *refer* to a centrally maintained rule in their interfaces. However, there may still be a conceptual problem.

Some rules may apply to several components and, as well as this, are naturally thought of as 'policy': policy that can change as the business evolves or at the whim of regulators or lawgivers. In such a case, there is an additional complexity in that the new rules may not correspond one-to-one to the old ones. In SBVR terminology, business rules are 'interpretations' of policy to make them 'actionable' or 'practicable'.

A policy blackboard is a central component designed to encapsulate such a policy statement. Rules only encapsulate a reference to these rules *in the blackboard*, which in turn should ENCAPSULATE A REFERENCE (16) and STORE its RULES IN A REPOSITORY (17). In addition to this, each component sets up an OBSERVER to the policy blackboard. There are two variants of this. Either the publisher (the blackboard) broadcasts all changes to rules in which interest has been registered to the subscribed components, allowing them to update their interfaces or stored rules accordingly (if this can be done) or it merely broadcasts an 'I have changed' message, leaving it to the subscribers to decide whether to ask for more information and, indeed, what action to take. To distinguish these alternative architectures we may think of them as subpatterns: PUSH POLICY BLACKBOARD and PULL POLICY BLACKBOARD.

It is sometimes useful, when the rules are grouped into rulesets in a complex way for example, to segment the policy blackboard into pigeonholes that contain different kinds of knowledge. Subscribing components can register interest in whichever pigeonholes they need to know about.

Such an approach not only makes maintenance changes easier to understand at the business level and implement at the technical level, but it also supports a model of complex, co-operative decision making. For example, services implemented as intelligent agents can collaborate in applying the rules to a problem they face, sharing knowledge through the policy blackboard. In that case, the blackboard component may also need methods for handling a problem-solving agenda – which, in turn, may be rule-based.

The alternative to pigeonholes is to divide the rules among several policy blackboards according to the provenance of the rules, e.g. accounting rules, stock control rules, rules of engagement, etc. This approach makes the blackboards themselves more reusable (shareable) but may introduce too much complexity or overhead in agent-based applications.

Example

'Each pilot scheduled for a flight must be qualified to fly the type of plane assigned to the flight' is a structural constraint. It is almost inconceivable that any policy change would reverse it. It is not, therefore, an obvious candidate for the policy blackboard, although it could just about conceivably be part of a 'safety rules' blackboard.

'We may not fly more than twenty flights a week out of Bangkok'. 'Our share of transatlantic flights must not exceed 20% of total transatlantic flights'. These rules look more like policy.

This pattern is a specialization of Buschmann, *et al*'s (1996) BLACKBOARD, which is, in turn, an architectural generalization of PUBLISHER–SUBSCRIBER (the GoF OBSERVER pattern).

Therefore

When rules refer to more than one object, consider encapsulating them (or references to them) in one

or more policy blackboard component. This is especially indicated when there is a stated distinction between rules that are 'policy' and those which merely describe the structural relationships between objects.

Remember, too, that it's generally not a good idea to have developers guessing which rules might change and which might not; life is full of surprises.

Resultant context

This pattern is terminal within this part of the language.

Pattern 15 — BASE ERROR MESSAGES ON RULES *

Context

You have elicited all or some of the rules and probably have ASSIGNED THE RULES TO COMPONENTS (10). Usability testing leads you to think about how friendly the error messages ought to be.

Problem

How can you ensure that users understand the messages that the system will issue without the need for extensive training or help facilities?

Forces

Rules must be executed by machines but understood by humans, sometimes including business analysts and users. When an error message is generated, this is done on the basis of the statements that the machine understands. The tendency, therefore, is to present error numbers (good to remove ambiguity in debugging) and language that users find hard to interpret. Rewriting the messages involves extra development work. But we have already stored the rules in a form at least close to natural language. Why not exploit that resource?

Therefore

Base as many error and other system generated messages as possible on the natural language versions of corresponding business rules.

Use explanation facilities (that usually work by unwinding the current rule execution stack) to answer as many How? or Why? questions as possible. Again, before presenting the explanations, convert the unwound rules into their natural language equivalents – as stored in the repository. If this is not possible consider handcrafting the natural language versions of explanations or presenting them through purpose-written non-natural-language interfaces.

~~~

Resultant context: This pattern is terminal within this part of the language.

Pattern 16 — STORE RULES IN A REPOSITORY ***

Context: You have developed externalized some rules. You have ASSIGNED RULES TO COMPONENTS (13), where possible.

~~~

Problem: **How can you make a complex system containing many thousands of business rules manageable?**

Forces: The trouble with encapsulating rules is that it can make them hard to locate. The situation is certainly better than it would be were the rules to be embedded in procedural code and there are cases where a rule so obviously 'belongs' to a component that it is easy to find it – by finding the component. However, in general, scattered rules will be hard to locate for maintenance. Furthermore there are other data that we may wish to store with the rules: author, date created, date retired, containers that realize the rule, etc. Thus, it is natural to consider storing all the rules and rulesets, together with related data and metadata, in a rule database or **repository**. Such a repository will ideally support full version control too.

The repository must include rules that are not implemented in a BRMS as well as those that are.

Just as we ENCAPSULATE A REFERENCE (17) when rules are related to a component, we may even realize the same rules in that component. When this happens the repository must store a reference to the realization.

Morgan (2002) gives a useful list of the sort of things that one might want to store in a repository. Halle (2002) gives step-by-step guidance on how to go about defining a repository, giving examples using the Usoft and Versata products.

Therefore   **Store *all* business rules and rulesets in a version-control-enabled repository. Include all data and metadata related to the rules.**

~~~

Resultant context   This pattern is terminal within this part of the language.

Pattern 17   ENCAPSULATE A REFERENCE *

Context   You want to make your services and components as shareable and reusable as possible but you also need to maintain and manage their rules centrally. You have ASSIGNed RULES TO COMPONENTS (13). Rules that apply to more than one component have been assigned to the POLICY BLACKBOARD (14).

~~~

Problem   **How can you enforce rule encapsulation and not end up with a fragmented, unmaintainable rulebase?**

Forces   Reuse implies encapsulation, although it may be hard to decide where to put the rules. Opposed to this, rule independence implies a separate rule layer. If you encapsulate you lose rule independence; if you centralize you lose the potential benefits of component reuse and service sharing. It seems to be a lose–lose situation. But there is a way out. Decide where the rules *should* go, but instead of storing the rules with the components to which they have been assigned, one can store a reference to these rules in the interfaces of objects that should encapsulate them.

Therefore   **Store the actual rules in the rule repository. When you create or specify any component, ensure that any rules associated with it are both stored in the repository and referenced in the specification and implementation of that component. Perhaps implement these references as methods that invoke the rules on the server. Do this also for the POLICY BLACKBOARD (14).**

~~~

Resultant context   This pattern is terminal within this part of the language.

Pattern 18	**PLAN INTERVIEWS** **

Context
: You are trying to VISUALIZE THE BUSINESS PROCESS MODEL (2), ESTABLISH THE USE CASES (3), BUILD A TYPE MODEL (4) and DISCOVER BUSINESS RULES (5).

Problem
: **How can you elicit the required knowledge from human beings?**

Forces
: People know stuff, lots of stuff. But sometimes they don't know – or can't articulate – what they know. If they do know what they know then all you have to do is ask (assuming no dishonesty or hidden agendas). If there is latent knowledge then you will have to consider more subtle strategies as exemplified by patterns 23 to 27 of this language.

    So why not just interview everyone? The trouble is that that is an expensive, time-consuming procedure. Furthermore, it is common to find that different people, when interviewed, give different versions of the truth, so you end up having to go round and round the stakeholders, confirming and clarifying points. This suggests that running a workshop is a far better approach. On the other hand, sometimes it is impossible to get people to give up the time to travel to a workshop. In such a case there is no choice but to interview the stakeholders.

    Interviews run better if they are planned.

    The interview plan can be used to give structure to a workshop, so any effort exerted in creating it is seldom wasted.

Refer to
: Chapter 3.

Therefore
: **Start by outlining plans for stakeholder interviews. The plan should include clear objectives for the outcome of the interview. Select interviewers who have some knowledge of the vocabulary of the domain and who can show humanity and adaptability. It sometimes helps if they have a little knowledge of business rules technology too. Be prepared to abandon the plan during actual interviews or workshops.**

Resultant context
: Before conducting expensive and time consuming interviews with all the stakeholders, consider RUNNING

A WORKSHOP (19). It is usual to conduct STRUCTURED INTERVIEWS (23) before FOCUSED INTERVIEWS (24).

Pattern 19   RUN A WORKSHOP ***

Context
: You are trying to VISUALIZE THE BUSINESS PROCESS MODEL (2), ESTABLISH THE USE CASES (3), BUILD A TYPE MODEL (4), DISCOVER BUSINESS RULES (5) and may have conducted or PLANNED INTERVIEWS (18).

Problem
: **How can you discover requirements efficiently, taking into account all the overlapping and possibly conflicting views of the stakeholders?**

Forces
: Interviews are time consuming and can lead to self-contradictory or incomplete information. Workshops, on the other hand, ensure that all participants have heard at first hand the contributions of others, which facilitates compromises where these are necessary. They also generate a sense of shared ownership of the project between and among the developers and users.

  On-site workshops may be prone to interruption but an off-site location is usually more costly but much more focus and relaxation is possible for participants.

  The idea is to drive through the core of the requirements gathering process in a very short time and certainly no more than a week. This implies strong, unbiased facilitation and real-time, technically savvy reporting of the proceedings. The facilitator acts as both guide and interviewer as the event unfolds.

Refer to: Chapter 3.

Therefore: **Organize and run a facilitated workshop. Try to hold it off-site. Use a facilitator who has no stake in the project. Appoint a skilled and enthusiastic scribe to record models, rules, decision and so on.**

~~~

Resultant context: Before running the workshop, make sure you INVOLVE ALL THE STAKEHOLDERS (22). At the beginning of the session announce the TEN-MINUTE RULE (21). Early on in the session identify a LEAD USER (22). Apply patterns 1 to 7 of this language iteratively during the entire session.

During the session consider using all or some of the following knowledge elicitation patterns: STRUCTURED INTERVIEW (23), FOCUSED INTERVIEW (24), PROBES AND TEACHBACK (25), ASK FOR THE OPPOSITE (26), BOUNDARY OF COMPETENCE (27).

Pattern 20 — INVOLVE ALL THE STAKEHOLDERS **

Workshop participation grid	*Strategic management*	*Tactical management*	*Operational management and clerical staff*
Sales	Sales Director National Sales Manager	Account Managers Regional Managers	Sales Staff Clerical and Telesales Staff
Marketing	Marketing Director	Product Managers	Marketing Assistants
Production	Distribution Director	Production Engineers	Warehouse Supervisors Machinists

Context: You are going to RUN A WORKSHOP (19).

~~~

Problem: **How can you maximize the workshop's coverage of the business area and business rules?**

Forces	Business people are busy but they are the people who have the knowledge. Not everyone affected by a proposed new business rules system can always be present at requirements capture workshops. A good and oft-quoted example is dealers in financial trading rooms, who are reluctant to leave their investment positions unattended. Furthermore, events involving absolutely everybody could be too large and unwieldy to be managed comfortably. Therefore, some users may act as delegates for their immediate colleagues, managers and subordinates. In the example given, dealer management often stands in for actual dealers. The selection of the right delegates for the task is a key determinant of the success of the event and the participants must at least include representatives of both the users of the proposed system and the development team.

The presence of key users is both more important and potentially more difficult to organize than one might think. Surely the identity of the correct participants from the user side is obvious and unarguable. Not necessarily! There are several factors to weigh.

Seniority may matter. More senior people may have a better grasp of the wider business issues being addressed in the workshop (or maybe just think they do) but the devil is always in the details and operational level staff are more likely to be familiar with the detailed intricacies of operations, which will be the things that will break a proposed system if they are not taken into account. So we need people from different levels of seniority – but then we need to be aware that some people will not like to be seen to contradict their boss in public. This is where the facilitator's job of setting ground rules and ensuring fair play becomes important.

Every stakeholder present *must* have authority to commit to the findings of the workshop. Ensuring that this signatory authority is in place is a key job of the sponsor.

The number of people present is hard to get right. The complexity of the interactions will rise exponentially with the number of participants, so life is easier the smaller the number – and the workshop is cheaper to run. But everyone affected by the proposed system should be represented. In the limit, this could mean half the company. What must be avoided is the situation of somebody feeling later that they were improperly overlooked. When the delivered system has a flaw, you do not want to be told that that some stakeholder or user was never consulted in the first place.

Before setting up the workshop, the sponsor, project manager and facilitator should have a prior meeting, generally led by the facilitator, to establish the participant list. They should examine all the options in terms of inclusions and exclusions, probe the emerging list for weaknesses and seek to rectify them and document the reasons for the final invitation list. It can be useful to develop a matrix of candidates, enumerating all the people who could conceivably attend and then compare possible combinations of candidates from the grid in terms of the impact on the workshop's success. Start with the company's organization chart and collapse the relevant components into a matrix where the rows are the organizational units, the columns represent approximate seniority levels within the organization and the cells contain names of logical job descriptions and possible candidates. Note especially that this document is *not* a formal deliverable, because the logical rôles may be the subject of discussion and change during the workshop.

As an example, consider a system to support a new process for product presentation, sales, order taking and manufacturing. This would affect *inter alia* the Sales, Marketing and Production divisions. A possible workshop participation grid is shown in the above image. One should ensure that the grid reflects the actual organizational structure, then fill in the names of the candidates for participation. Considering the options, one representative for each group may make the workshop too large. Beware of the dangers of arguing that a manager can always speak for the troops as well – because he/she used to be one. This may be true, but it is difficult for people to represent their own needs sincerely as well as those of someone else. The inevitable exceptions that do occur, as with the dealers alluded to above, should be handled with extra care and sensitivity. Otherwise, if any rôle is not to be represented at the workshop, then there is an assumption this rôle will not be affected by the new system – and this should be documented. Some sensitive issues can arise if this is a business process re-engineering project: some rôles may disappear altogether, and asking possible victims of reorganization to contribute enthusiastically to planning the wake may be regarded as unproductive, or in bad taste at the very least. The aim is to produce a participant invitation list along with a supporting document justifying the rôles represented and not represented, and the reasoning behind the choices made.

Users should attend the entire workshop. This is often easier said than done. Freeing people from important work, even for a few days, can have a significant business impact and cost implications. It is also sometimes the case that people will not wish to appear in any way 'dispensable'. Having people attending for a couple of hours, disappearing for a while, then coming back can be very harmful to the progress and ultimate value of a workshop. The sponsor and project manager must work hard with departmental managers to ensure that a block of time is made available to run the event as a block and not as a set of piecemeal sessions with a floating population of participants.

Where at all possible, the complete development team should attend the workshop(s). The challenge is to avoid the development of an 'us and them' attitude: where the user group states its requirements, the developer group goes away and produces something with little contact with or reference to the users. Only later do the users have the opportunity to tell them where they went wrong, when it is often too late to avoid project deadline pressure freezing the mistakes into the end product. The reason for having the whole development team present at the workshops is to help gain *shared* ownership of the system requirements: to understand more fully the content of the formal documents they may be dealing with later in the project. Importantly, all developers should feel involved in all parts of the project. Of course, someone may be on the team because of specialist skills because it is known that this will be a key component of the delivered system; but that person should not have the feeling that their contribution is just at the level of their own narrow specialism – they should be regarded as significant contributors to the system as a whole.

Lastly, if the group is very large, it often helps to organize breakout sessions whereby smaller subgroups resolve knotty issues and report back to the main workshop.

Therefore **Involve all the stakeholders: users, IT people, customers, legal experts, workers, managers, regulators, different business areas, whomsoever is affected or knowledgeable. Use the workshop participation grid to check that coverage is complete.**

~~~

Resultant context

This pattern is terminal within this part of the language.

Pattern 21	TEN MINUTE RULE ***
	aka TWO MINUTE RULE

Context You are starting to RUN A WORKSHOP (19). You need to ensure that discussion is focused while not wanting to restrict it so much that information is lost.

~~~

Problem **How can you shut up vociferous (and possibly senior) bores while ensuring that people with valuable information to add are given free rein?**

Forces Junior or diffident individuals sometimes find it difficult to contribute and senior or aggressive ones can easily dominate the conversation even though they may have less to contribute. You really don't want long off-topic exegeses in a tightly run workshop. However, so-called 'war stories' sometimes conceal valuable gems of information and sometimes it needs quite a long presentation to delve into the business rules and processes deeply enough. So exactly how can you, as facilitator, tell the MD to shut the f*** up without causing offence?

Therefore **At the start of the workshop, announce the ground rules. These may vary, depending on circumstances.**

They might include a rule that forbids critical remarks (typical of brainstorming workshops). But *always* announce a ten minute rule: no one may speak on a topic for more than ten minutes. Then, as facilitator, listen to the debate and ignore this rule totally when you feel that useful information is being added by the speaker. Only invoke it when Mr Bigmouth wants to show how clever and interesting he is. Invoke the rule and offer to 'take his issues offline'.

~~~

Resultant context
This pattern is terminal within this part of the language.

Pattern 22 — LEAD USER **

Context
You are starting to RUN A WORKSHOP (19). You know that disputes and impasses will inevitably arise.

~~~

Problem
How can you resolve such disputes quickly in order to move on to the next topic without bureaucratically curtailing the discussion or upsetting anyone?

Forces
In workshops, when a difficult technical issue arises and there is a significant silence – as people think about it – one often sees eyes turning to one person in the room. This person may or may not be the most senior individual but is clearly the focus of respect in the group. He/she could be a domain expert or a user or a skilled artisan; there are no rules for this. But he/she is the person whose shoulder is cried upon when technical or practical issues need to be resolved. A good facilitator keeps a weather eye open for such people. We call them **lead users** or **lead experts.**

In a workshop, the facilitator may decide to make the identification of the lead expert explicit, saying something like 'Can we agree that Emily is going to resolve issues like this one when we can't agree or just get stuck – at least for this week?'. Or it may be more prudent to keep quiet and just make sure that the lead expert is assigned to the teams given open issues to resolve and consulted by the project team regularly throughout the project. This is the right strategy when there is a danger of jealousy arising.

A lead user or lead expert should be appointed as early as possible to resolve disputes. It will be too late to get consensus on who the lead expert is to be after the dispute has arisen. This person will be one respected by other users/experts/colleagues and need not always be the most heavily involved in the project in terms of time spent. The lead user corresponds somewhat to what DSDM calls an *ambassador* user (Stapleton, 1997). Many users will only be consulted on an *ad hoc* basis and these then correspond to the *adviser* users of DSDM.

The lead user can help resolve another force: that of confidentiality. The group should be assured that any tapes made will be confidential to the project team and that they will be destroyed after use or, if required, returned to the lead user for destruction.

Therefore **Identify a lead expert or lead user early in any workshop or in any project. Such a person will resolve disputes and open issues and may also act as the conscience and guardian of the group. It is a matter of discretion (usually the facilitator's) whether the lead user is publicly acknowledged as such. Consult the lead user regularly throughout the project.**

~~~

Resultant context This pattern is terminal within this part of the language.

Pattern 23 — STRUCTURED INTERVIEW *

Context You have PLANNED INTERVIEWS (18) or decided to RUN A WORKSHOP (19).

~~~

Problem **How can you gain a high level overview of a business area, process or problem domain?**

Forces Structured interviews are high level. They are intended to uncover an overview of a topic or business problem. A structured interview should reveal the key rules, objects and concepts of the domain. Their coverage is 'broad and shallow'. It will result in elicitation of the key objects and concepts of the domain but not go into detail. In a workshop this corresponds to running a scoping session, where the same techniques can be used.

The plan for a structured interview is always pretty much the same:

- Agree the agenda with interviewee.
- Ask questions, put out PROBES (33).
- Review progress against objectives.
- Move on to the next topic.
- Review and compare with plan: have the objectives been achieved?
- If not, arrange next interview.

Therefore **Plan to execute structured interviews at the early stages of the project. Use the same techniques in the early parts of a workshop.**

Resultant context This pattern is terminal within this part of the language but structured interviews are often followed by FOCUSED INTERVIEWS (24).

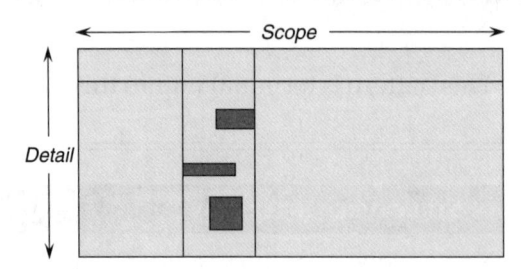

Pattern 24 — FOCUSED INTERVIEW *

Context You have PLANNED INTERVIEWS (18) or decided to RUN A WORKSHOP (19).

Problem **How can you uncover the details of business processes and rules within a business area, process or problem domain?**

Forces Focused interviews are meant to delve into the detail of one area of the problem space covered by structured interviews. Their coverage is 'narrow and deep'.

During the interview process it is essential to search for reusable elements – the grey rectangles in the above image. Analysts should select the area of the domain that gives either 80% of the benefit or 80% of the predicted complexity or reuse/sharing potential as the first area to explore – preferably both. This corresponds, ideally, to about 20% of the scope of the system.

The agenda for a focused interview depends largely on the domain. Focused interviews will be enhanced by applying various knowledge elicitation techniques or patterns such as VISUALIZE BUSINESS PROCESS MODEL (2), ESTABLISH THE USE CASES (3), PROBES AND TEACHBACK (25), ASK FOR THE OPPOSITE (26) and BOUNDARY OF COMPETENCE (27).

Therefore **Use a focused interview to uncover details. Use the same techniques in the later parts of a workshop.**

~~~

Resultant context: This pattern is terminal within this part of the language.

Pattern 25 PROBES AND TEACHBACK **

> I keep six honest serving men
> (They taught me all I knew);
> Their names are **What** and **Why** and **When**
> And **How** and **Where** and **Who.**
>
> R. Kipling, *Just So Stories*, 'The Elephant's Child'

Context   You have PLANNED INTERVIEWS (18) or decided to RUN A WORKSHOP (19).

~~~

Problem   **If you are interviewing or running a workshop and you suddenly can't think of the next question to ask, is there a formula to prompt you to think of a suitable question?**

Forces   It is essential in interviews of workshops that questions are open rather than closed. Open questions do not permit an answer such as 'Yes' or 'No' that closes further discussion or elaboration. Probes are merely particularly useful types of open question. Probes use all six question words emphasized in the above image.

There are five types of probe. A **definitional** probe asks 'What is a . . . ?'. A **directive** probe asks 'Why is that?' or uses the word 'how'. An **additive** probe is used when you say something like 'Go on'. A **mode change** probe could be a question like 'How would your colleagues view that?' or 'Can you give a more concrete/abstract example?'. Mode change probes are thus all about scope, viewpoints and generalization (inheritance). A **reflective** probe involves saying the equivalent of 'What you're saying is . . . '. In that case you are far better off when the expert replies 'No, I didn't mean that'. A 'Yes' doesn't give you the chance to ask 'Why?'.

Teachback generalizes the idea of reflective probes and involves interviewers, knowledge engineers or business analysts presenting their understanding to the users formally (perhaps with a slideshow) and receiving corrections thereby.

Therefore   **When the obvious question does not come to mind, ask yourself if one of the five probes will help. Consider using teachback when time permits.**

~~~

Resultant context   This pattern is terminal within this part of the language.

Pattern 26	**ASK FOR THE OPPOSITE ** ** aka KELLY GRIDS, LADDERING, CARD SORTS, CONCEPT MINING**

	———————OBJECTS———————					
CONCEPT	Rolls Royce	Porsche	Jaguar	Mini	Trabant	OPPOSITE CONCEPT
Economical	5	4	4	2	2	Costly
Comfortable	1	4	2	4	5	Basic
Sporty	5	1	3	5	5	Family
Cheap	5	4	4	2	1	Expensive
Fast	3	1	2	4	5	Slow

Context   You have PLANNED INTERVIEWS (18) or decided to RUN A WORKSHOP (19).

~~~

Problem   **Are there any other ways of digging out concepts that are not immediately present in the forefront of a user's or expert's consciousness?**

Forces   One useful knowledge engineering technique for eliciting objects or concepts and their structural relationships is that of Kelly (or repertoire) grids. These grids were introduced originally in the context of clinical psychiatry (Kelly, 1955). They are devices for helping analysts elicit 'personal constructs': concepts which people use in dealing with and constructing their world. Constructs are pairs of opposites, such as slow/fast, and usually correspond to either classes or attribute values in object-oriented analysis. The second dimension of a grid is its 'elements', which correspond to objects. Elements are rated on a scale from 1 to 5, say, according to which pole of the construct they correspond to most closely. These values can then be used to 'focus' the grid: a mathematical procedure which clarifies relationships among elements and constructs. In particular, focusing ranks the elements in order of the clarity with which they are perceived and the constructs in order of their importance as classifiers of elements.

To illustrate, first identify some 'elements' in the application. These might be components or concepts, but should be organized into coherent sets. For example, the set {Porsche, Jaguar, Rolls Royce, Mini, Driver} has an obvious odd man out: Driver.

The use of the technique in its full form is not recommended. However, questioning techniques based on Kelly grids are immensely powerful in eliciting new concepts, objects and attributes and extending and refining inheritance structures. There are three principal techniques:

- asking for the opposites of all elements and concepts;
- laddering to extract generalizations;
- elicitation by triads to extract specializations.

Considering the image above, we see that Sporty is a key concept for the user concerned. Asking for the opposite has produced not 'Unsporty' but the concept of 'Family' cars: not the logical opposite but a totally new concept. Thus, asking for the opposite of a concept can reveal a totally new one.

In laddering, users are asked to give names for higher level concepts. 'Can you think of a word that describes all these things: speed, luxury and economy?'. This might produce a concept of 'value for money'. It produces more generalizations of concepts.

Elicitation by triads is not a reference to a Chinese method of torture but to a technique whereby, given a coherent set of elements, the user is asked to take any three and specify a concept that applies to two of them but not to the third. For example, with {Porsche, Jaguar, Mini}, top speed might emerge as an important concept. Similarly, the triad {Mini, Jaguar, Trabant} might reveal an attribute such as `CountryOfManufacture` or the concepts of British and German cars. As a variant of this technique, users may be asked to divide elements into two or more groups and then name the groups. This is known as card sorting, since the elements or concepts are often written on small cards and laid on a table for sorting into groups.

All these techniques are first-rate ways of getting at the conceptual structure of the problem space, if used with care and sensitivity. Exhaustive listing of all triads, for example, can be extremely tedious and easily alienate users.

`Therefore` **For every concept presented, ask for its opposite and record the new concept if it is not a logical opposite. For every pair of concepts or objects, ask if there is a word that encompasses both; if there is, record the generalization as a new concept. For every triplet of concepts or objects, ask 'Can you think of a feature, attribute, operation or rule that is shared by two of these but not the third?'. Alternatively, write the names of all the concepts or objects on cards and ask users or experts to sort them into groups and names the groups. Record the group names as new concepts.**

~~~

Resultant context	This pattern is terminal within this part of the language.

Pattern 27 BOUNDARY OF COMPETENCE

Context	You have PLANNED INTERVIEWS (18) or decided to RUN A WORKSHOP (19).

∼∼∼

Problem	**How can you be sure that any business rules, as stated, always apply?**
Forces	Sometimes rules seem to be true because we have limited our perception to the familiar. But there may be unusual circumstances in which the rules cease to be valid. The most common example of this is where a rule is true only between defined applicable dates. A good BRMS will have facilities for handling such time-constrained rules. In general, one must beware of including rules that may fail when circumstances change. Rules that work fine for a British company may fail when it merges with a German one. These 'boundary conditions' must be made explicit in the way rules are stated and processes described.
Example	Suppose the domain is gardening and that we have discovered that 'regular mowing produces good lawns'. The analyst should not be satisfied with this because it does not show the boundaries of the intended system's competence – we do not want a system that gives confident advice in areas where it is incompetent. We need to go deeper. Thus, the next question asked of the expert might be of the form: 'why?'. The answer might be 'Because regular mowing reduces coarse grasses and encourages springy turf'. What we have obtained here are two attributes of the class Turf. 'Why does regular mowing lead to springy turf?'. 'Well, it helps to promote leaf branching'. Now we are beginning to elicit methods as we approach causal knowledge. To help define the boundaries, ask 'What else?' and 'What about...' questions. In the example we have given, the analyst should ask 'What about drought conditions?' or 'What else

	gives good lawns?'. These questioning techniques are immensely useful.
Therefore	**Always ask domain experts for the boundaries of rule applicability. Consider time, geography, culture, frequency, previous events and so on: anything that may vary. Make the boundary or applicability conditions explicit in process descriptions and rule statements.**
	~~
Resultant context	This pattern is terminal within this part of the language.

Related External Patterns

Related patterns that are important for the SOA analyst, process modeller, designer and project manager to know include the following. They follow on nicely from the patterns presented in this appendix.

- Colour patterns for designing type models (Coad, *et al.*, 1999). See also Andrews (2009).
- Basic business process modelling patterns (Aalst *et al.*, 2003).
- Enterprise integration patterns (Hohpe and Woolf, 2004) – these patterns are highly relevant to ESB and SOA message design (cf. Chappell, 2004; Andrews, 2009).
- Organizational patterns (Coplien and Harrison, 2005).

APPENDIX B

The Fundamental Concepts of Service Oriented Architecture

> *The mystification which dialectic suffers in Hegel's hands, by no means prevents him from being the first to present its general form of working in a comprehensive and conscious manner. With him it is standing on its head. It must be turned right side up again, if you would discover the rational kernel within the mystical shell.*
>
> **K. Marx, Afterword to Volume I of *Das Kapital* (1873)**

This appendix is a philosophical digression which the uninterested reader may wish to skip completely. Doing so will not affect your ability to understand the rest of the book but may help you organize your understanding better.

To analyse the fundamental concepts of SOA the method we bring to bear is a particular kind of dialectics developed in the 19th century by idealist phiosphers such as Georg Frederich Hegel and the materialist Karl Marx. The Wikipaedia gives the following definition:

> *Dialectics ($\delta\iota\alpha\lambda\varepsilon\kappa\tau\iota\kappa\eta$) is an exchange of propositions (theses) and counterpropositions (antitheses) resulting in a synthesis of the opposing assertions, or at least a qualitative transformation in the direction of the dialogue.*

As is often the case, Wikipaedia repeats the conventional wisdom about the Hegelian dialectic. I am not aware that Hegel ever presented it as Thesis–Antithesis–Synthesis in this way. This was a crude misconception that arose in the early to mid-20th Century and was much touted by Stanlinist 'theoreticians' and various of their academic hangers-on. In Greek, dialectic just means discourse or argument and so Plato's method is just as much a dialectical one as Hegel's is.

My variation on the dialectical method of Hegel and, indeed, Marx is extremely good for analysing all kinds of problems and I always use it when preparing any kind of talk or text. This applies even to fiction and it is significant that George Eliot translated and read Hegel immediately prior to penning Middlemarch – arguably her greatest work and even the greatest English novel of all time.

The essence of dialectics is the apprehension of objects in terms of categories. Aristotle was the first philosopher to formalize this and Kant built a whole intellectual edifice out of it (Smith, 1929). However, unlike Kant's fixed categories, Hegel's are dynamic; categories evolve as history unfolds. At its core is the assumption that the world is esentially binary. It has this in common with all Chinese philosophical systems and the systems of many presocratics, from Heraklietos of Elia onwards (Marx, 1841). There are no trinities in dialectics – including the holy trinity of Thesis–Antithesis–Synthesis.

The method proceeds as follows:

- Define the categories that apply to the subject matter.
- For each category find exactly two **aspects**: subcategories and the forces that make them oppose each other. (Note the methodological similarity to the approach of pattern writers.)
- Define (optionally) which force represents the 'leading aspect' (Mao, 1937).
- Now identify the **mediations**: the processes by which the forces transform the aspects. There are exactly two mediations per aspect pair. The mediations are said to **sublate** or **posit** each aspect within its opposite. You can think of this sublation as a lind of internalization.
- Next reify the mediations into aspects.
- Iterate.

Note that aspects are generally nouns and mediations are generally verbs.

Thus, to analyse a problem such as political economy, you might discover that the principal opposition is that between Labour and Capital. Labour uses Capital to produce values. Capital uses Labour to grow. In his *Grundrisse*, Marx (1861) argues that the mediations are named Production and Consumption. The mediations between reified Production and Consumption are called Distribution and Exchange. Money can be seen then as a reification of Exchange. And so on.

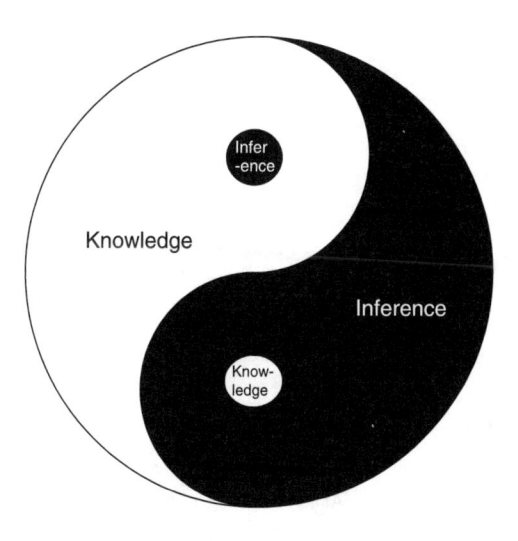

Figure B-1 The dialectics of business rules management.

In Graham and Jones (1988) I applied this method to BRMS using the schematic shown in Figure B-1. I also wrote there:

> *Quantum physics shows that we can no longer regard observers as independent from what they observe. Marcuse (1941) develops the alternative point of view especially clearly. Experience takes place in a world of which we humans are an internal part but from which we are able to differentiate ourselves. We do this by internalizing a representation of nature and checking the validity of the representation through continuous practice. But the very internalization process is a practice, and practice is guided by the representation so far achieved. This analysis leads to a ladder-like structure of concepts as shown in Figure B-2.*

More pertinently to a discussion of SOA in particular and technology in general, I later wrote (Graham, 1995):

> *There is a range of new software tools and a range of new developments in computing and software engineering. The effects of these technological opportunities on businesses are very difficult to predict. What we don't want is solutions looking for problems. We want our businesses to drive our use of technology. It could be argued that there is a contradiction between adaptability and complexity or, indeed, between a flexible organization and an organization that uses a lot of technology. The more complex the technology the more it inhibits change; the faster the requirements change the harder it is to build tools to support them. The resolution of this contradiction is to be found in the mediation of users and developers illustrated in Figure B-3.*

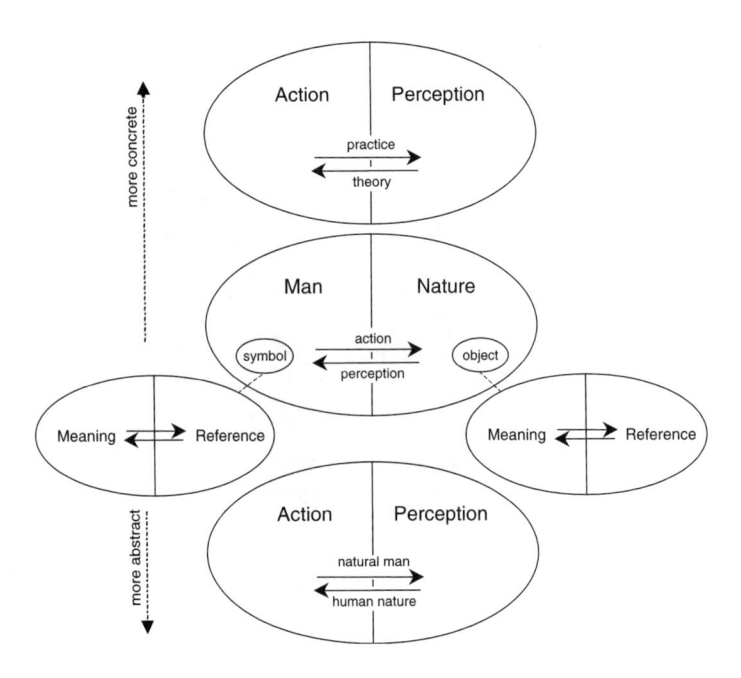

Figure B-2 Dialectical analysis of concepts.

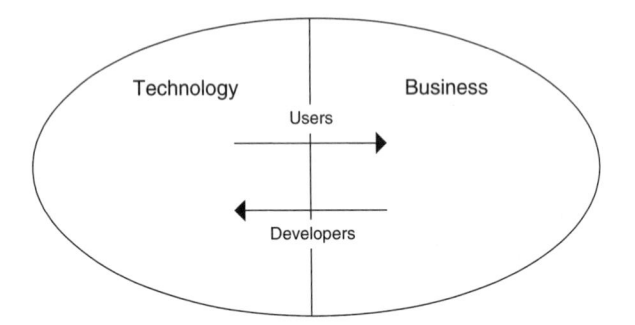

Figure B-3 Users and developers mediate the contradiction between the evolution of business and the freezing of solutions in technology.

Users apply technology to transform their businesses. Developers bring the business reality to the models built. Users reflect the business with technical models that developers turn into technically supported business processes. There is a further contradiction between developers and users in that they have different views of both the business and the model. The reflexion[1] of the business in the technology is the system model and

---

[1] The word *reflexion*, with the same root as *reflexive*, is to be distinguished from *reflection*. I use the former in the same way as Lektorsky (1984) to emphasize the rôle of the active subject in cognition, as opposed to the passive *reflection* of real-world entities in consciousness. Here it is used to signify the internalization of an aspect of a contradiction within the opposite aspect.

the reflexion of the technology in the business is the working, supported business process.

And later (*op cit.*):

We divided enterprises between business and technology (labour and capital) and then briefly examined the principal mediators of the contradiction; the developer and the user (production and consumption). We now turn to the technology itself ... regarded as the syntheses of the business, the developer and the user, internally reflected in either the business or the technology; a dual trinity. ... Users and developers may be viewed as opposites, united by the organization but divided by the technology. The unity arises from their common organizational purpose but technology intervenes, often preventing the user from carrying out certain tasks or at least separating the skills of users from those of developers. This latter separation corresponds to a useful division of labour, so that the schism represented by technology is not always a bad thing; leading to increased productivity. If we have adaptable systems, satisfied users and productive developers, we can achieve most of the goals of IT within a business context.

I also applied the method (*op cit.*) to understanding the fundamental concepts behind component technology, as follows:

Henderson-Sellers and Edwards (1994) suggest a triad or triangle of concepts consisting of:

1. *Polymorphism/Inheritance.*
2. *Abstraction.*
3. *Encapsulation/Information hiding.*

Berard (1993) points outs that the last three are closely related; abstraction being the process of identifying what information is important and visible, encapsulation the technique used to package these decisions and information hiding being the general principle that design decisions should be hidden. Further, I shrink from triads of this sort, which I do not believe occur in Nature or Thought and can obfuscate understanding. My approach is to look for the principal contradictions in terminology as in things. Thus, we could approach this question of finding the key concepts by starting with Polymorphism (having many forms) and opposing it to Monomorphism (having a single form or identity). These opposites interpenetrate each other. Every system is both polymorphic and monomorphic. However, it is a capital mistake to consider form in isolation from content. At this level, abstraction can be seen as the process that gives (ideal) form to (material or concrete) content. The opposite of abstraction is realization, which can be thought of as the instantiation of form: classes, concepts or structures.

These processes mediate the contradiction between form and content but are at yet too high a level to be useful. Let us examine one side of the dichotomy in more detail, the category of Form. Form can be singular (monomorphic) or manifold (polymorphic) as illustrated in Figure B-4. When we classify objects, we posit the oneness of their multiplicity. When we encapsulate, we collect variation and give it a single, but polymorphic, identity. Encapsulation collects individual operations and groups them into a multi-faceted unity. Thus encapsulation and classification (inheritance) become the key concepts mediating the contradiction between the oneness and multiplicity of system components. Now, this analysis has glossed over the fact that classification is merely a special case of relationship, i.e. that relationship corresponding to the verb to be or the copula is. Strictly, the arrow in the figure should be labelled 'relationship' or 'structuring', but classification is a very special, distinguished kind of relationship. Other distinguished relationships are composition (or aggregation) and usage. The arrows representing Encapsulation and Structuring can also be viewed as the internalization of Abstraction and Instantiation within the category of Form. All structures imply some sort of inter-object visibility. Where such structures interact we also have replicable 'patterns' (Coad, 1992; Madsen et al., 1993; Pree, 1995; Gamma et al., 1995; Gabriel, 1996). The general term we will use for the formation of patterns from objects is therefore 'structuring' but for simplicity we will sometimes talk of classification as a representative of this process. This is justified because this particular form of structuring characterizes object-oriented programming languages, which often do not have direct support for composition structures or patterns.

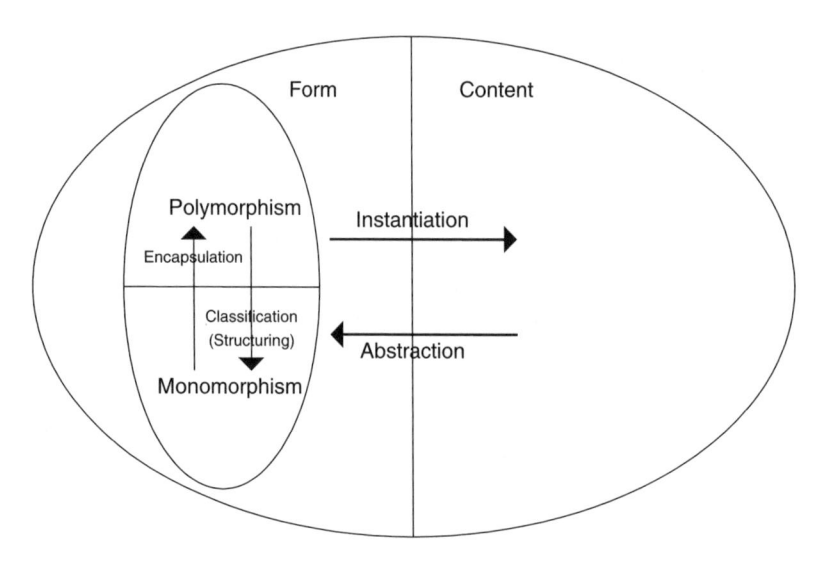

Figure B-4 Analysis of fundamental terms (form).

Figure B-4 can be read as follows. Consider a thing. Abstract from it to discover its form. That form has identity and may be looked at from many points of view. Now realize this form as a concrete instance. You have returned to the original thing but now it is an abstract model rather than the original. Conversely, if we start from an idea, a form such as a class, we can instantiate it and then ask what abstract properties the instance has. This is illustrated in Figure B-5 which expands the Content aspect of the contradiction.

Figure B-5 also shows how the concepts of object identity and message passing (visibility) arise as a result of the conflict between encapsulation and classification. Visibility is the internal reflection in the category of Content of the polymorphic within the monomorphic, which means that when you encapsulate a concept you do so within a context that needs to refer to it. Identity internalizes the singleness of the object within its manifoldness by classifying it as such.

In these, rather abstract terms, we can see that the most fundamental concepts of all are content and form; in particular polymorphism. In practical terms, however, the fundamental concepts are those that let us deal with the content and form of systems and their mediating processes of abstraction and realization. These are encapsulation and classification (or more generally structuring). We should avoid taking polymorphism as the fundamental concept since, like structuring in general, it is not definitional for object-oriented languages. There are polymorphic languages, such as ML, that are not object-oriented. This leaves us with encapsulation and classification as the fundamental, definitional concepts. This

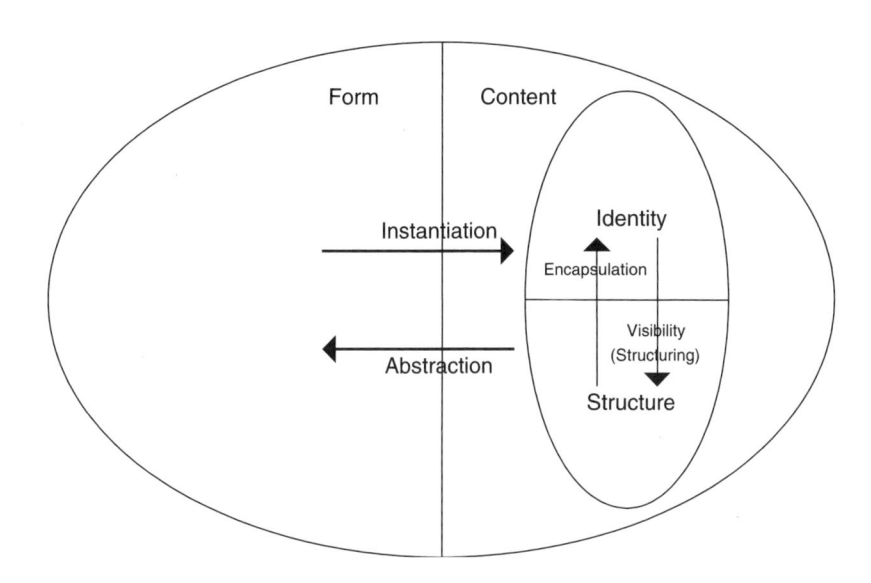

Figure B-5 Analysis of fundamental terms (content).

argument has also shown that polymorphism, abstraction, structuring, usage (message passing) and identity are also key concepts and how they are related. The ladder of concepts need not end or begin here and a deeper exploration is required to discover the nature of the relation between structuring and classification. However, we have made this diversion merely to emphasize the central concepts of object technology as encapsulation and structure, with classification being singled out as a particularly important kind of structure just as inheritance is a particular kind of polymorphism.

The question now is to apply the same analysis to SOA's fundamental concepts: abstraction, polymorphism, message passing and so on. At first it seems that the fundamental concepts are exactly the same as those for object-orientation or CBD, as presented in Figures B-4 and B-5.

- Services must have identity – in order to be discoverable (visible).
- Services can only be loosely coupled if they encapsulate their implementation.
- Services can be associated and composed (structuring).
- Services can, obviously, be classified (polymorphism).

However, there are two features that we must think slightly harder about: the self-routing and self-describing nature of messages and their statelessness.

Statelessness, as I have argued above, is properly only *transactional* statelessness. In other words, when a message is processed the processing is transparent until a transaction is deemed complete. Clearly this is a refinement of the notion of encapsulation.

Note that 'Embed route' means embed format translation in the message. Clearly there is more that could be said, but this analysis will suffice for our present purposes. It leads to the following statement of the fundamental, or characteristic, concepts of service oriented architecture.

Static concepts

- *Encapsulation*. This gives services unique identity and the property of being abstract.
- *Polymorphism*. This provides discoverability (visibility) and composability (structuring).

Dynamic concepts

- Message routing (based on rules).
- Message transformation (based on contracts).

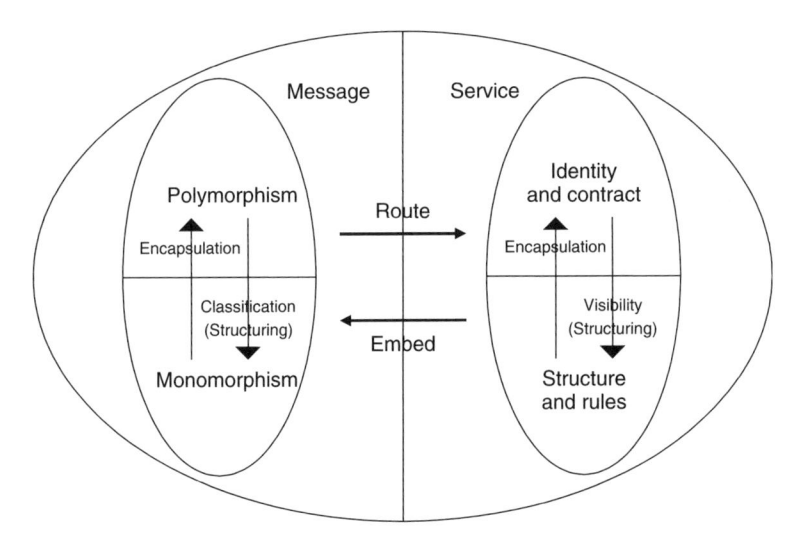

Figure B-6 Analysis of fundamental terms (messaging).

In a nutshell, the fundamental static concepts of SOA are encapsulation (abstraction/identity) and polymorphism (inheritance/classification/discoverability/visibility/composability). The fundamental dynamic concepts are message passing and rule embedding, which lead to rule-based routing and contract-based transformation as subsidiary (but no less important) fundamental concepts (see Figure B-6).

References and Bibliography

Aalst, W.M.P. van der, Hofstede, A.H.M. ter, Kiepuszewski, B. and Barios, A.P. (2003) Workflow Patterns, *Distributed and Parallel Databases* **14**(1), 5–51

Abbott, R.J. (1983) Program Design by Informal English Descriptions, *Communications of the ACM* **26**(11), 882–894

Alexander, C., Ishikawa, S. and Silverstein, M. (1977) *A Pattern Language*, Oxford: Oxford University Press

Allen, P. and Frost, S. (1998) *Component-Based Development for Enterprise Systems: Applying the SELECT Perspective*, Cambridge: Cambridge University Press/SIGS

Andrews, D. (2009) *Service Oriented Architecture: The Catalysis II Approach*, in preparation.

Austin, J.L. (1962) *How to Do Things with Words*, Cambridge MA: Harvard University Press

Bachman, C. (1977) The rôle concept in data models. In *Proceedings of the 3rd International Conference on Very Large Databases*, New York NY: IEEE, 464–476

Barfield, L. (1993) *The User Interface: Concepts & Design*, Wokingham, UK: Addison-Wesley

Basden, A. (1990a) Towards a Methodology for Building Expert Systems I, *Codex* **2**(1) 15–19, Uxbridge, UK: Creative Logic Ltd

Basden, A. (1990b) Towards a Methodology for Building Expert Systems II, *Codex* **2**(2) 19–23, Uxbridge, UK: Creative Logic Ltd

Bass, L., Clements, P. and Kazman, R. (1998) *Software Architecture in Practice*, Reading MA: Addison-Wesley

Berard, E.V. (1993) *Essays on Object-Oriented Software Engineering* – Volume 1, Englewood Cliffs NJ: Prentice Hall

Beyer, H. and Holtzblatt, K. (1997) *Contextual Design: Defining Customer-Centred Systems*, New York NY: Morgan Kaufmann

Blaauw, G.A. (1970) Hardware Requirements for the Fourth Generation. In F. Greunberger (Ed.) *Fourth Generation Computers*, Englewood Cliffs NJ: Prentice Hall

Blaha, M. and Premerlani, W. (1998) *Object-Oriented Modelling and Design for Database Applications*, Upper Saddle River NJ: Prentice Hall

Blum, B.I. (1996) *Beyond Programming: To a New Era of Design*, New York NY: Oxford University Press

Blum, B.I. (1998) *Software Engineering: A Holistic Approach*, New York NY: Oxford University Press

Borenstein, N.S. (1991) *Programming as if People Mattered: Friendly Programs, Software Engineering and Other Noble Delusions*, Princeton NJ: Princeton University Press

Bosch, J. (2000) *Design and Use of Software Architectures*, Harlow, UK: Addison-Wesley

Braune, R. and Foshay, W.R. (1983) Towards a practical model of cognitive information processing, task analysis and schema acquisition for complex problem solving situations, *Instructional Science* **12**, 121–145

Brooks, F. (1975) *The Mythical Man Month*, Reading MA: Addison-Wesley

Brooks, F. (1986) No Silver Bullet: Essence and Accidents of Software Engineering. In H.-J. Kluger (Ed.) *Information Processing '86*, Amsterdam: Elsevier

Buschmann, F., Meunier, R., Rohnert, H., Sommerlad, P. and Stal, M. (1996) *Pattern-Oriented Software Architecture: A System of Patterns*, Chichester, UK: John Wiley & Sons, Ltd

Carter, S. (2007) *The New Language of Business, SOA & Web 2.0*, Upper Saddle River NJ: IBM Press

Chappell, D.A. (2004) *Enterprise Service Bus*, Beijing: O'Reilly

Checkland, P. (1981) *Systems Thinking, Systems Practice*, Chichester, UK: John Wiley & Sons, Ltd

Checkland, P. and Scholes, J. (1991) *Soft Systems Methodology in Action*, Chichester, UK: John Wiley & Sons, Ltd

Cheesman, J. and Daniels, J. (2000) *UML Components*, Harlow, UK: Addison-Wesley

Chen, P. (1976) The Entity-Relationship Model: Toward a Unified View of Data, *ACM Transactions on Database Systems* **1**(1), 9–36

Cheng, J. and Jones, C. (1990) On the usability of logics which handle partial functions. In C. Morgan and J. Woodcock (Eds) *Proceedings of the 3rd Refinement Workshop*, Berlin: Springer-Verlag

Coad, P. (1992) Object-Oriented Patterns, *Communications of the ACM* **35**(9), 152–158

Coad, P., LeFebvre, E. and DeLuca, J. (1999) *Java Modeling in Color with UML*, Upper Saddle River NJ: Prentice Hall

Cockburn, A. (1997) Using goal-based use cases, *J. Object-Oriented Programming* **10**(5), 267 pp

Cockburn, A. (2000) *Writing Effective Use Cases*, Reading MA: Addison-Wesley

Connell, J.L and Shafer, L.B. (1989) *Structured Rapid Prototyping: An Evolutionary Approach*, Englewood Cliffs NJ: Yourdon Press

Constantine, L.L. (1995) Essential modeling: use cases for user interfaces, *Interactions (ACM)*, **2**(2), 355 pp

Constantine, L.L. and Lockwood, L. (1999) *Software for Use: Models and Methods of Usage-Centred Design*, Reading MA: Addison-Wesley

Coplien, J.O. and Harrison, N.B. (2005) *Organizational Patterns of Agile Software Development*, Upper Saddle River NJ: Prentice Hall

D'Souza, D.F. and Wills, A.C. (1999) *Objects, Components and Frameworks with UML: The Catalysis Approach*, Reading MA: Addison-Wesley

Daniels, J. (2000) Component contracts, Keynote Lecture at TOOLS Europe

Date, C.J. (2000) *What Not How: The Business Rules Approach to Application Development*, Reading MA: Addison-Wesley

Davenport, T.H. and Short, J.E. (1990) The New Industrial Engineering: Information Technology and Business Process Redesign, *Sloan Management Review*, Summer, 11–27

Davis, A.M. (1993) *Software Requirements: Objects, Functions and States, Revision*, Englewood Cliffs NJ: Prentice Hall

Dikel, D., Kane, D. and Wilson, J. (2001) *Software Architecture*, Upper Saddle River NJ: Prentice Hall

Dorfman, M. and Thayer, R.H. (1990) *Standards, Guidelines and Examples on System and Software Requirements Engineering*, Los Alamitos CA: IEEE Computer Society Press

Eason, K.D. (1989) Tools for participation: How managers and users can influence design. In Knight, K. (Ed.) *Participation in Systems Development*, London: Kogan Page

Ehn, P., Mollervd, B. and Sjogren, D. (1990) Playing in reality: a paradigm case, *Scandinavian Journal of Information Systems* **2**, 101–120

Ehn, P. and Kyng, M. (1991) Cardboard computers: mocking up hands-on-the future. In J. Greenbaum and M. Kyng (Eds) *Design at Work: Co-operative Design of Computer Systems*, Hillsdale NJ: Lawrence Erlbaum

Erl. T. (2004) *Service Oriented Architecture: A Field Guide to Integrating XML and Web Services*, Upper Saddle River NJ: Prentice Hall

Erl. T. (2005) *Service Oriented Architecture: Concepts, Technology and Design*, Upper Saddle River NJ: Prentice Hall

Flores, F. (1997) The leaders of the future. In P.J. Denning and R.M. Metcalfe (Eds) *Beyond Calculation: The Next 50 Years of Computing*, New York NY: Copernicus

Fowler, M. (1999) *Refactoring*, Harlow, UK: Addison-Wesley

Fowler, M. (2003) *UML Distilled*, 3rd Edition, Harlow, UK: Addison-Wesley

Gabriel, R.P (1996) *Patterns of Software*, Oxford: Oxford University Press

Gamma, E., Helm, R. Johnson, R. and Vlissedes, J. (1995) *Design Patterns: Elements of Reusable Object-Oriented Software*, Reading MA: Addison-Wesley

Gaur, H. and Zirn, M. (Eds) (2006) *BPEL Cookbook*, Bombay: Packt Publishing

Gause, D. and Weinberg, G. (1989) *Exploring Requirements*, New York NY: Dorset House

Graham, I. (1991) *Object-Oriented Methods*, 1st Edition, Wokingham, UK: Addison-Wesley

Graham, I. (1992) A Method for Integrating Object Technology with Rules, *Proceedings of Advanced Information Systems 92*, Oxford, Learned Information.

Graham, I. (1994) Beyond the Use Case: Combining task analysis and scripts in object-oriented requirements capture and business process re-engineering. In B. Magnusson, B. Meyer, J.-M. Nerson and J.-F. Perrot (Eds) *Tools 13*, Hemel Hempstead, UK: Prentice Hall

Graham, I. (1995) *Migrating to Object Technology*, Wokingham, UK: Addison-Wesley

Graham, I. (1996) Task scripts, use cases and scenarios in object-oriented analysis, *Object-Oriented Systems* **3**(3), 123–142

Graham, I. (1998) *Requirements Engineering and Rapid Development: An Object-Oriented Approach*, Harlow, UK: Addison-Wesley

Graham, I. (2001) *Object-Oriented Methods*, 3rd Edition, Wokingham, UK: Addison-Wesley

Graham, I. (2003) *A Pattern Language for Web Usability*, Harlow, UK: Addison-Wesley

Graham, I. (2006) *Business Rules Management and Service Oriented Architecture: A Pattern Language*, Chichester, UK: John Wiley & Sons, Ltd

Graham, I. (2009) *Managing Service Oriented Architecture Projects with Agile Processes*, Chichester, UK: John Wiley & Sons, Ltd

Graham, I. and Jones, P.L.K. (1988) *Expert Systems: Knowledge, Uncertainty and Decision*, London: Chapman & Hall

Graham, I., Bischof, J. and Henderson-Sellers, B. (1997) Associations considered a bad thing, *J. Object-Oriented Programming*, **9**(9), 41–47

Gray, P.M.D. (1984) *Logic, Algebra and Databases*, Chichester, UK: Ellis Horwood

Guttag, J., Horning, J.J. and Wing, J.M. (1985) *Larch in Five Easy Pieces*, Palo Alto CA: Digital Systems Research Centre

Halle, B. von (2002) *Business Rules Applied*, New York NY: John Wiley & Sons, Inc.

Hammer, M. (1990) Reengineering Work: Don't Automate, Obliterate, *Harvard Business Review*, July–August, 104–112

Harold E. and Means, W. (2004) *XML in a Nutshell*, Beijing: O'Reilly

Harrison-Broninski, K. (2005) Human Interactions: No Cheese is Made of Chalk. In S. Towers and M. McGregor (Eds) *In Search of BPM Excellence*, Tampa FL: Meghan-Kiffer Press

Havey, M. (2005) *Essential Business Process Modelling*, Beijing: O'Reilly

Hayes, P.J. (1979) The Logic of Frames. In D. Metzing (Ed.) *Frames, Conceptions and Text Understanding*, Berlin: Walter de Gruyter & Company

Henderson-Sellers, B. and Edwards, J. (1994) *BOOK TWO of Object-Oriented Knowledge: The Working Object*, Sydney, Australia: Prentice Hall

Hillstone, J. (1993) *PEPA: Performance Enhanced Process Algebra*, Report CSR-24-93, Edinburgh, UK: University of Edinburgh Press

Hoare, C.A.R. (1985) *Communicating Sequential Processes*, Englewood Cliffs NJ: Prentice Hall

Hohpe, G. and Woolf, R. (2004) *Enterprise Integration Patterns*, Boston MA: Addison-Wesley

Jackson, M.A. (1983) *System Development*, Chichester, UK: Prentice Hall

Jackson, M.A. (1995) *Software Requirements and Specifications*, Harlow, UK: Addison-Wesley

Jackson, M.A. (1998) A Discipline of Description, *Requirements Engineering* **3**(2), 73–78

Jackson, M.A. (2001) *Problem Frames and Methods*, Harlow, UK: Addison-Wesley

Jacobson, I., Christerson, M., Jonsson, P. and Overgaard, G. (1992) *Object-Oriented Software Engineering: A Use Case Driven Approach*, Wokingham, UK: Addison-Wesley

Jacobson, I., Ericsson, M. and Jacobson, A. (1995) *The Object Advantage: Business Process Re-engineering with Object Technology*, Wokingham, UK: Addison-Wesley

Jones, C. (1986) *Systematic Software Development using VDM*, Englewood Cliffs NJ: Prentice Hall

Kelly, G.A. (1955) *The Psychology of Personal Constructs*, New York NY: W.W. Norton

Kleppe, A., Warmer, J. and Bast, W. (2003) *MDA Explained. The Model Driven Architecture: Practice and Promise*, Harlow, UK: Addison-Wesley

Krutchen, P. (1995) The 4+1 View of Software Architecture, *IEEE Software*, November, 42–50.

Kruchten, P. (1999) *The Rational Unified Process*, Reading MA: Addison-Wesley

Lektorsky, V.A. (1984) *Subject Object Cognition*, Moscow: Progress Publishers

Lientz, B.P. and Swanson, E.B. (1979) Software Maintenance: A User/Management Tug of War, *Data Management*, April, 26–30

Macaulay, L.A. (1996) *Requirements Engineering*, London: Springer-Verlag

MacLean, R., Stepney, S., Smith, S., Tordoff, N., Gradwell, D. and Hoverd, T. (1994) *Analysing Systems: Determining Requirements for Object-Oriented Development*, Hemel Hempstead, UK: Prentice Hall

Madsen, O.L., Moller-Pedersen, B. and Nygaard, K. (1993) *Object-Oriented Programming in the BETA Programming Language*, Wokingham, UK: Addison-Wesley

Maiden, N.A.M., Cisse, M., Perez, H. and Manuel, D. (1998) *CREWS Validation Frames: Patterns for Validating Systems Requirements*, London: Centre for Human Computer Interface Design, City University

Mao, Z-D (1937) On Contradiction, in *Selected Works*, Beijing: Foreign Languages Press

Marcuse, H. (1941) *Reason and Revolution: Hegel and the Rise of Social Theory*, London: Oxford University Press; Second Edition 1955, London: Routledge & Kegan Paul

Martin, J. and Odell, J.J. (1995) *Object-Oriented Methods: A Foundation*, Englewood Cliffs NJ: Prentice Hall

Martin, J. and Odell, J.J. (1998) *Object-Oriented Methods: A Foundation (UML Edition)*, Englewood Cliffs NJ: Prentice Hall

Marx, K. (1841) *Differenz der demokratischen und epikureischen Naturphilosophie*, Doctoral dissertation, University of Jena; English translation: Moscow: Progress Publishers, 1976

Marx, K. (1861) *Grundrisse der Kritik der Politischen Öknomie*, unpublished manuscript; First published 1953, Moscow: Foreign Languages Publishing House; English translation by M. Nicolaus 1973, Harmondsworth, UK: Penguin

Marx, K. (1961) *Capital*, Volume I, Afterword to the Second German Edition, translated by S. Moore and E. Aveling, Moscow: Foreign Languages Publishing House

Milner, R. (1989) *Communication and Concurrency*, Englewood Cliffs NJ: Prentice Hall

Milner, R. (1993) The Polyadic Pi-Calculus: A Tutorial. In F.L. Brauer, W. Brauer and H. Schwichtenberg (Eds) *Logic And Algebra of Specification*, Berlin: Springer-Verlag

Morgan, A. (2002) *Business Rules and Information Systems: Aligning IT with Business Goals*, Boston MA: Addison-Wesley

Mumford, E. (1986) *Designing Systems for Business Success: The ETHICS Method*, Manchester: Business School

Naur, P. and Randell, B. (Eds) (1969) *Software Engineering: Report on a Conference Sponsored by the NATO Science Committee 7–11 October 1968*, Garmisch, Germany: NATO Science Committee

Ould, M. (2005) Five Fables and their Lessons. In Towers, S. and McGregor, M. (Eds) *In Search of BPM Excellence*, Tampa FL: Meghan-Kiffer Press

Pawson, R. and Matthews, R. (2002) *Naked Objects*, Harlow, UK: Addison-Wesley

Perry, D.E and Wolf, A.L. (1992) Foundations for the Study of Software Architecture, *Software Engineering Notes* **17**(4), 40–52

Peterson, J.L. (1981) *Petri Net Theory and the Modelling of Systems*, Englewood Cliffs NJ: Prentice Hall

Petri, C.A. (1962) *Kommunikation mit Automaten*, Ph.D. Dissertation, Bonn: University of Bonn

Pohl, K. (1993) The three dimensions of requirements engineering. In C. Rolland, F. Bodart and C. Cauvet (Eds) *Proceedings of CAISE'93*, Paris: Springer-Verlag, 175–292

Pree, W. (1995) *Design Patterns for Object-Oriented Software Development*, Reading MA: Addison-Wesley

Ross. R.G. (2003) *Principles of the Business Rules Approach*, Boston MA: Addison-Wesley

Ross, R. (2005) Business Rules and Business Processes: Win-Win for the Business. In S. Towers and M. McGregor (Eds) *In Search of BPM Excellence*, Tampa FL: Meghan-Kiffer Press

Rumbaugh, J., Booch, G. and Jacobson, I. (1999) *The Unified Modelling Language Reference Manual*, Reading MA: Addison-Wesley

Schank, R.C. and Abelson, R.P. (1977) *Scripts, Plans, Goals and Understanding*, Boston MA: Lawrence Erlbaum Associates

Searle, J.R. (1969) *Speech Acts*, Cambridge: Cambridge University Press

Senge, P.M. (1990) *The Fifth Discipline: The Art And Practice Of The Learning Organization*, New York NY: Doubleday; London: Random House

Sharble, R.S. and Cohen, S. (1993) The object-oriented brewery: a comparison of two object-oriented development methods, *ACM Sigsoft* **18**(2), 60–73

Shaw, M. (1990) Prospects for an Engineering Discipline of Software, *IEEE Software* **7**(6), 15–24

Shaw, M. and Garlan, D. (1996) *Software Architecture: Perspectives on an Emerging Discipline*, Englewood Cliffs NJ: Prentice Hall.

Short, J.E. and Venkatramen, N. (1992) Beyond business process redesign: Redefining Baxter's Business Network, *Sloan Management Review*, Fall, 7–17

Simons, A. (2000) On the Compositional Properties of UML Statechart Diagrams, *Proceedings of the 3rd Conference on Rigorous Object-Oriented Methods*.

Smith, N.K. (translator) (1929) *Immanuel Kant's Critique of Pure Reason*, London: Macmillan

Stapleton, J. (1997) *Dynamic Systems Development Method: The Method in Practice*, Harlow, UK: Addison-Wesley

Stern, R. (1990) *Hegel, Kant and the Structure of the Object*, London: Routledge

Suchman, L.A. (1987) *Plans and Situated Actions: The problem of human–machine communication*, Cambridge: Cambridge University Press

Szyperski, C. (1998) *Component Software: Beyond Object-Oriented Programming*, Harlow, UK: Addison-Wesley

Towers, S. and McGregor, M. (Eds) (2005) *In Search of BPM Excellence*, Tampa FL: Meghan-Kiffer Press

Wand, Y. (1989) A Proposal for a Formal Model of Objects. In W. Kim and F.H. Lochovsky (Eds) *Object-oriented Concepts, Databases and Applications*, Reading MA: Addison-Wesley

Warmer, J. and Kleppe, A. (1999) *The Object Constraint Language*, Reading MA: Addison-Wesley

Webster, J. (1996) *Shaping Women's Work: Gender, Employment and Information Technology*, London: Longman Sociology

Wieringa, R.J. (1996) *Requirements Engineering*, Chichester, UK: John Wiley & Sons, Ltd

Wills, A.C. (1991) Specification in Fresco. In S. Stepney, R. Barden and D. Cooper (Eds) *Object-Orientation in Z*, Berlin: Springer-Verlag

Winograd, T. and Flores, F. (1986) *Understanding Computers and Cognition*, Reading MA: Addison-Wesley

Witt, B.I., Baker, F.T. and Merritt, E.W. (1994) *Software Architecture and Design – Principles, Models and Methods*, New York NY: Van Nostrand Rheinhold

Wooldridge, M. (2002) *An Introduction to Multi-agent Systems*, Chichester, UK: John Wiley & Sons, Ltd

Young, J.Z. (1986) *Philosophy and the Brain*, Oxford: Oxford University Press

Yourdon, E. and Constantine, L.L. (1979) *Structured Design: Fundamentals of a Discipline of Computer Program and Systems Design*, Englewood Cliffs NJ: Prentice Hall

Zadeh, L.A. (1965) Fuzzy Sets, *Information and Control* **8**, 338–353

Zadeh, L.A. (1971) Similarity relations and fuzzy orderings, *Information Sciences* **3**, 177–200

Index

Page numbers in *italics* refer to figures, those in **bold** to tables; n signifies a reference to a footnote, App. to an appendix.

abstractions 102, 105
   essential 105
   in use cases 186–7
accidents 104–5
ACID (Atomicity, Consistency, Isolation, Durability) properties 197–8
ACORD 23, 228
Action Semantics Language (ASL) 59
actions 131, 155
Active Endpoints 128
activities 195
actors 12, 16, 141, 161
   defined 81
agents 131, 140–1, 161–2
   cartooning using 199–200
   external 141
   internal 141, 200
   as objects 142
   rule-based 184
agile development 114
AI script theory 146
AKO (A Kind Of) links 207
Andrews, Derek 181
applets 51
Application Programmer Interfaces (APIs) 22, 38, 59, 66
applications 4

archetypes 38–9, 103–4
architectural description languages (ADLs) 32–4
   key requirements for 33
architectural vision 68
architecture *see* software architecture
Aristotle 104
assertions 202
   and rulesets 202–3
association loops conceal rules 57, 89, 204, 219, 245–6 App.
associations 212–18
   bi-directional 214–15, *214*
   definition of 215
   strong 218
   of types 213
   uni-directional 213
AT&T 166
atomicity 197
   and use cases 186
attributes 195
   Boolean 194
   and rules 205

B2B 20, 228
Basden, A. 95
Bass, Larry 32–3, 40
Baxter Healthcare 159, *160*

BEA 21–2, 127–8
Blaauw, G.A. 32, 36
black boxes 14, 57
Blaze Advisor 22
Blum, Bruce 34–6
Boehm, Barry 37
Booch notation 38
Borenstein, N.S. 34
Bosch, J. 38–40
boundaries of competence 269–70 App.
boundary conversations 158
   description of 189–91
BPEL programming language 23, 114, 118, 120, 127–9, 222
   and BPDM 222
   and BPMN 128–9, 222
BPEL4People 128
BPEL4WS 127
BPELJ 128–9
BPMI 223
BPMN2BPEL 128
Brentano, Franz 104
British Petroleum 166
Brooks, Fred 31, 35–7, 104–5
business
   aligning IT with 3–8
   asking the 204, 247–8 App.
   definition of 140
business component model (BCM) 177
business objectives 232–3 App.
   establishing and prioritising of 89–93
business objects 101
business ontology 101
business policy statement 209
business process 161
   definition of 139–41
   handling exceptions in 147–9
   internalising parallelism of collaborations in 193
Business Process Definition Metamodel (BPDM) 222
business process innovation 113
business process management 112–13
   failures of 114
business process modelling (BPM) 52–3, 111–37
   basic patterns 270 App.
   the human side of 135–6
   of large enterprises 165–79
   need for 111–14
   networked 115
   origins of 111–14
   and SOA in the large 165–73
   standards 221–3
   summarised 114–16
   visualisation 233–5 App.
Business Process Modelling Language (BPML) 223
Business Process Modelling Notation (BPMN) 23, 116, 118–27, 140
   activities 120
   and BPEL 128–9
   events 119–20, *119*
   flows 118, *119*
   fundamental patterns 121–3, *121–2*
      communication 123
      process 122–3, *125*
      workflow 123
   gateways 120, *120*
   model of moving home *133*
   standards 222
Business Process Query Language (BPQL) 223
business process re-engineering (BPR) 76, 112–13, 159
   and the mission grid 170
Business Process Runtime Interface (BPRI) 222
Business Process Specification Schema (BPSS) 130, 225
business processes
   incompatible 55–6, *56*
   rely and guarantee conditions of 158
business requirements
   statement of 209
   to specification from 181–2
business requirements model, items in 182
business rules 55, 109, 207–12
   as contracts 174
   definition of 208
   discovery of 240–1 App.
   and domain ontology 89, 109–10, 209
   finding of 201–7

inter-process 174
in the mission grid 173–6
and requirements 88–9, 109
business rules management systems
(BRMSs) 22, 201, 211
rule repositories in 211
typical products 22
business service implementation, and
state charts 197
Butler Cox Group 42

C# 50, 129
C++ 2, 42, 50
Calculus of Communicating Systems
(CCS) 131
Cape Clear 22
card sorts 97, 266–9 App.
Carnegie Mellon University
(CMU) 33–4
cartooning 193
using agents or
co-ordinators 199–200
CASE 98
message passing in tools 189, *189*
case studies
air-transport industry 19
aircraft design 74–5
aircraft fuel loading 17–18
Baxter Healthcare 159, *160*
call centres 18, 124–5, *125*
conversation on house buying 144–5
design of web radio station 12–13
hotel check in 81–2, *82*
hotel support system 53–5, *54*
investment bank trading 125–7,
157–8, *157*
lending library users 17, 174–5
life assurance using SVBR 225–6
order processing and auto-pricing
system 4–5
patient monitoring 85–6, *85–6*
stationery ordering service 124–5,
125, 155–7, *156–7*
Catalysis 57, 129, 155, 181–2, 192, 194
default logic 203n
Catalysis II 181
catalysis conversation analysis 139–63

categories 104
CATWOE (Customers, Actors,
Transformation processes,
Weltanschauung, Owners and
Environment) 78
change management 26–7
Checkland, Peter 77–8, 82
choreography 129–30
standards 222–3
Choreography Description Language
(WS-CDL) 222–3
class invariant 202
classic requirements, and use
cases 78–85
classification, zoological 47–8, *48–9*
co-ordinators, cartooning
using 199–200
Coad, P. 103, 158, 162
COBOL 2, 72
code, mathematical proofs of
correctness 75
collaboration scripts 185
collaborations 155–60, 162
atomic 185
checking model consistency 160–1
decomposed 190, *190*
effects of 51
essential 185
internalising parallelism of 193, 219,
242–3 App.
in order processing *157*, 190
rely and guarantee conditions of 158
and scenarios 186
collaborative work support 113
colour patterns 103, 158, 162, 192–3,
198–9, 219
for designing type models 270 App.
commanded behaviour 87, *87*
commitments, goal-oriented 140
Common Object Request Broker
Architecture (CORBA) 20, 50
Communicating Sequential Processes
(CSP) 131
communication 131
by agents 140–1
ports 13–14
with UML 79

competence, boundary of 269–70 App.
component based development (CBD) 42–3, 45, 50–3
components 33, 45, 49–57, 69
   conversations as 149–50
   designing and coding 62
   for flexibility 53–4
   relating services to 56–7
   and rules 211, 248–9 App.
   with rulesets 201
   and services 174
computer independent model (CIM) 59, 224
Computer Science 34–5
computer supported co-operative work (CSCW) 113
concept mining 266–9 App.
conditions 202
connectors 33
   large-scale 54–6
connexion 87
consistency 197
Constantine, Larry 42, 185
constraints 84, 108–9, 202, 204
   and rules 246–7 App.
constructs, in grids 96
context 230 App.
context diagrams 81, 107
contextual enquiry 77
contracts 140–1
   as business rules 174
   of conversations 151–5
control rules 206–7
controller objects 184
conversations 141–5, *142–3*, 155–63
   associations between 149
   atomic 185
   boundary 158, 182, 189–91
   checking model consistency 160–1
   as components 149–50
   contracts of 151–5
   decomposition of 153, 162
   essential 185
   goals of 151–5
   handling exceptions in 147–9
   order processing 155–7, *156–7*

   pre- and post-conditions of 151–3, *152*
   rely and guarantee conditions of 158
   request canonical form notion of 144
   sale 151, *151*
   scripts 145–9, 162
      atomic 150, 162
      relationships among 149–50, *150*
      written in SVDPI form 150, 162
   side-scripts in 148, *148*
   six-fold structure of 143
   and stereotypes 145–9, 162
   structure in SOMA *144*
   subscripts in 149
   symbol for 162
   as transactions 143
Cook, Steve 45
cookies, storage of 65
copper mines 171
corporate data models 166
COTS packages 36
counterparties 126, 155
CRUD matrix 45, 154
CRUD use cases 187, 192
Customer Relations Management (CRM) 135, 170, 198
customer value propositions (CVPs) 166
customers 166
   reasons for exasperation with IT 3
   services for 13

data dictionaries 72
data flow 142
data flow diagrams (DFDs) 72, 195
Database Management System (DBMS) 216–17
databases 214
   ACID properties of 197–8
datastores 184
DCOM 50
decision trees 72
delivery logistics *160*
demons 206
Descartes, René 104
design
   by contract 51
   task-centred 76

usage-centred 77
user-centred 76
diagrams, as process definitions 115
documentation, for specification
    modelling 212
domain model 58
domain ontology 88
    and business rules 89, 109–10, 209
DOORS 73
dot notation 207
DSDM 91
durability 198

ebXML 225
Effective Technical and Human
    Implementation of Computer-based
    Systems (ETHICS) 75–6
effects 203
Ehn, P. 76
Eiffel 201–2
    classes 50
8 Omega 177
Electronic Data Interchange (EDI) 20
elements, in grids 96
elicitation by triads 97
Empiricism 102, 105
encapsulation 42–3, 45–7, 49, 184,
    212–18
    of references 254 App.
    of rules 211
    and SOA 64
    violation of 51
endpoints 13, 28
Enterprise Application Integration
    (EAI) 20, 22, 29
enterprise integration patterns 270 App.
Enterprise Service Buses (ESBs) 21–2,
    21, 24, 29, 38, 40–1
    as message brokers 46, 61
    and message design 270 App.
    and PIMs 59
    spaghetti in *21, 25, 25*
    tools 63
    typical vendors of 22
Entity Relationship (ER) modelling 72
Epistemology 102
ergonomics 74

Ericsson 78, 182
error messages, and rules 211, 252–3
    App.
essence 104–5
ethnography 76
ethnomethodology 74, 76–7
event schemata (Martin/Odell) 116
events 195
exceptions 147–9
    fatal and non-fatal 147, 162
expert reviewers 204, 247–8 App.
exposure 126
eXtreme Programming (XP) 54
Exxon 43

file transfer protocol (FTP) 63
first order predicate calculus
    (FOPC) 203, 227
flexibility, components for 53–4
Flores, F. 140, 143–4
flow relations 132
Ford 112
4+1 View Model 37, 40
functional requirements 83–4
fuzzy rules 207
fuzzy state models 197

Garlan, David 32–4
Gedankenexperiment 192
generification 185–6
global behaviour 197
global rules 206
goals
    of conversations 142, 151–5
    external 166–7
    internal 167
    shared 166
    subsidiary 166
    and tasks 98, 142
groupware 113
guarantee 202
    conditions 158
guards 195

HaleyRules 22
Harrison-Broninski, K. 135
Hegel, Georg W.F. 104–5
Heidegger, Martin 104

Henderson-Sellers, B. 195
Hoare, Tony 131
Honest John's Prices Inc. 14
house of quality 77
human computer interaction (HCI) 17, 76
human factors theories 74
Husserl, Edmund G.A. 104
Hyperdesk 50
Hypertext Transfer Protocol (HTTP) 22, 61, 65

IBM 21–2, 127–8, 166
   grid-based technique 177
   Rational Unified Process 37
IDEF0 116
IEEE standards 72–3
implementation, constraints on 84
implementation model 58
information display 87
information providers, on-line 14–15
information technology (IT)
   aligning business with 3–8
   and customer exasperation 3
inheritance 47, 51–2
   implementation 52
   interface 52
   rules for 207
integrity rules 216–18
interfaces 69, 153
   changes to 47
   outbound 50–1
   and types 203
internet 61
interviewing techniques 93–6
   heuristics 95
interviews
   focused 264–5 App.
   planning of 255–6 App.
   structured 263–4 App.
intranet 61
invariants 204
   and rulesets 205
   and semantics 205
   see also rules
isolation 197
issues, non-functional 108

J2EE 15, 59, 129
Jackson, Michael 4–6, 35, 72, 85–8
Jackson Problem Frames 73
Jackson System Development (JSD) 72, 74
Jacobson, Ivar 73, 78, 80–1, 184, 187–8
Java 42, 50, 72, 128–9, 198
JMS 22, 61
Johns Hopkins University 34
JRules 22
judgments, analysis of 105–6, **105**
Just Do It (JFDI) 73

Kant, Immanuel 104–5
Kelly grids 96–7, *97*, 266–9 App.
Kipling, Rudyard 94
knowledge elicitation 74
Kruchten, Phillipe 37–8, 40

laddering 96–7, 266–9 App.
language
   common 3–8
   natural 90
   protocol 129
Larch 72
legacy systems 199
   wrapping of 66
Linnaeus, Carolus 47
logical rôle s 168–9
loose coupling *see* services, loosely coupled
Lotus Notes 76

maintenance
   high costs of 45
   localization of 46–7
   sources of costs in 43, *43*
mappings 213–16
   semi-inverses 215, 218
Markov models 131
Marx, Karl 104
Matthews, Hubert 197–8
Mazda 112
message buses 61
message passing 49, 189, *189*
message-oriented middleware (MOM) 20–1, 29, 61
   typical products 21

messages
    elimination of duplication by 46, *46*
    preventing information loss 65
    and state maintenance 65, 69
    and statelessness 64
    SWIFT funds transfer 146
Microsoft 51, 127
    interfaces 53
    MQ 21
migration 58
    strategies 26–7
Milner, Rob 131
mission grid analysis 166–73, *167*, *170*
    business rules in 173–6
    C-F/D grid 170–1, *170*
    hypercubes 172
    normal steps in 172, 178
    as roadmap for SOA 176
mission statements 171
Model Driven Architecture (MDA) 52, 58–60, 107, 222, 227
    specification 224
    transformations 60, *60*
modelling 22, 29

    of business processes 52–3, 111–37
    key steps in 62
    of objects 79
models 6–8, *7*
    checking consistency of 160–1
    of large enterprises 165–79
    state 193–8
    types of 78–9
modules 9, 32
MoSCoW ranking 91–2
MQSeries 21
Mutual Benefit Life 112

.NET 15, 41, 59
network process models 111
non-functional requirements (NFRs) 39

OASIS 127, 222–3, 225
Object Constraint Language (OCL) 59, 80, 107, 204
object discovery techniques 101–6
Object Management Group (OMG) 58, 78, 116, 222–5, 227

Meta Object Facility (MOF) 222, 227
    web site 80, 224
object modelling 79
object request brokers (ORBs) 20–1
Object rôle Models (ORM) 228
Object Technology 96, 184
object types 213
object-orientation (OO) 42–3, 45–6, 48
Object-Oriented Requirements Capture and Analysis (ORCA) 77
Object-Z 72
objectives 161
    measures for 90
    prioritisation of 90–3, *92*, **92**
Objectory method 78
objects 45, 49–57
    accidental 105
    business 101
    controller 184
    essential 105–6
    identification of 105
    nature of 102, 104–5
    and rulesets 200, 205
    use cases as 187
Odell, J.J. 214–15
OMT 183
ontology 102, 105, 207–12, 227, 238–40 App.
    business 101
    definition of 88
    domain 97, 109–10
    model for ruleset 210, *210*
    types in 153–4, *153*
Ontology Definition Metamodel (ODM) 227
OOPSLA 1994, 184
OpenDoc 50
OpenStep 50
Oracle 59, 128
orchestration 129–30
order processing
    activity diagram for *117*
    decomposition of collaboration *157*
    service implementation of 159, *159*
    type model for *192*
organisational patterns 270 App.
outsourcing 18–19, 169

Parasoft 24
Pareto 80/20 principle 93–4
participatory design 76
patterns 41
  and pattern languages 41
Pawson, Richard 115
payback 62
PD4J 128
PegaRules 22
Performance Enhanced Process Algebra (PEPA) 131
Perry, Dewayne 37
Petri nets 72, 118, 130–4
  contents of 132
  model of moving home 134
  simulation 132, 133
Phenomenology 104–5
pi-calculus 131
PL/1 2, 72
places 132
platform independent model (PIM) 59, 224, 227
platform specific model (PSM) 59
Pohl, K. 73–4
policy blackboard 206, 211, 250–2 App.
polymorphism 42, 46–9, 51
ports 14, 28, 131
  entry 13–14, 28
  exit 13–14, 28
  rejected message 13–14, 28
positions 126
power lattice 215
probes 94, 265–6 App.
  types of 95
problem analysis techniques 72
problem context diagram 85
problem diagram 86
problem frames 85–8, 109
  library of 87
procedure flow charts 118
process algebra 130–4
process categories 169
process definitions, as diagrams 115
process documentation, main items in 178
process engineer 114
process improvement 113

process interactions, types of 175–6
processes
  assigned to logical rôle s 168–9
  business 17
  comprised of tasks 115
  customer facing 169
  differentiating 169
  modelling high priority 172
  for order processing 4–5, 5
  prioritising of 171–2
  stative 64
profiles 39
programs
  in the computer 35
  in the world 35
projects, failure of 1–3
prototyping 72
Ptech method 116

quality function deployment 77
quality of service (QoS) 14–15, 24, 28, 39
  constraints 51
quick wins 26

Rational Unified Process (RUP) 184
RDFS 227
references, encapsulation of 254 App.
rely clause 202
rely conditions 158
repertory grids 96–7, 97
repositories, for rules in BRMSs 211, 253–4 App.
requirements 4, 109
  and business rules 88–9, 109
  definition of 73–4
  formulation of 83–5
  functional 83–4
  non-functional 84
  in problem diagrams 86
  references 86, 109
  soft techniques for elicitation 93–106, 110
  statements of 108
requirements analysis 74, 107
requirements document 4
requirements elicitation 74, 107
requirements engineering
  approaches to 71–110

    based on human factors 73–8
    conventional 71–8
        CREWS 77
    definition of 73
    and formal methods 73
    modelling problem of 3–4
    and specification patterns 229–70 App.
    and use cases 73
requirements model, items in 182, 218
requirements pattern map *230* App.
Requisite Pro 73
reuse 105–6
Reuters 14
rich pictures 82–3, *82*, 166
RPCs 50, 66
    mechanism across network 61
rule embedding 49
RuleArts 227
rules 212–18
    and attributes 205
    central storage of 211
    classification of 205
    and components 211, 248–9 App.
    concealed by association loops 57, 89, 204
    and constraints 246–7 App.
    control 206–7
    error messages based on 211, 252–3 App.
    fuzzy 207
    global 206
    integrity 216–18
    local encapsulation of 211
    repository for 253–4 App.
    and rule chaining 208–12
    and second order information 205
    and semantics 205
    techniques for discovering 203
    and use cases 244–5 App.
rulesets 201–2, 209, 216–18
    and assertions 202–3
    and backward chaining 209
    external and internal 203
    and inference 213
    and multiple inheritance 206–7
    and objects 200, 205

    ontology type model for 210, *210*
RuleSpeak 225, 227
RuleXpress 227

SADT 72
SAP 61, 128
scenarios 37, 39
    and collaborations 186
    and use cases 81, 184–6
script theory 77, 146
scripts
    collaboration 185
    of conversations 145–9, 162
SeeBeyond (Sun) 22
Seibel 61
semantics 201
    and invariants 205
    and rules 205
Semantics of Business Vocabulary and Business Rules (SBVR) 23, 225–7
    metamodel 227
    structured English form (SBVR-SE) 227
semiotic acts 141–2
semiotics 77, 140
    definition of 141n
sensitising image 230 App.
sequence diagrams 118
service consumer 9
service contract 9–10
service description template *191*
service design 58
service level agreements (SLAs) 14
service modelling 7–8
service oriented architecture (SOA)
    application development with 63
    benefits of 23–6, 29
    and BPM in the large 165–73
    business drivers for 19–20, 28–9
    critical success factors of 27, 30
    definition of 8–19
    fundamental concepts of 271–9 App.
    message design 270 App.
    metamodel for *56*
    mission grid as roadmap for 176
    pitfalls of 24–5, 29
    principles of 1–30

service oriented architecture (SOA)
    (*continued*)
    for developing, maintaining and exploiting 66–8
    and software architecture 57–63
    technical difficulties of introduction 67
service provider 9
service supplier, and information 19
services 9, 28, 45, 155–60
    abstract 10–12
    atomic 57
    autonomous 10–11
    as a black box 14, 28
    and the business 11
    and components 174
    composition of 10–11
    description template *191*
    design of 63
    discovery of 10–11
    extendable 14
    external 14–15, *15*
    finding from state models 198–200
    implementation of 68
        order processing 159, *159*
    loosely coupled 10–11, *10*, 13–14, 42
        and SOA 64
    perfect 14
    pre- and post-conditions of 190–1
    process for understanding 190
    properties of 9–11, *11*
    real users of 12
    reusable 11
    state management 66
    stateless 10–11, 63–6
    stative 63, 66
    transactionally stateless 64
    user interface of 12
    user-centred structure 241–2 App.
session beans 198
Shaw, Mary 32–4
simple information systems 87
Simple Object Access Protocol (SOAP) 9, 22, 61, 66, 68, 224
simple workpieces 87
simulation modelling 79
Smalltalk 216

objects 50
Smith, Adam 111
SOAPSonar 24
soft systems method (SSM) 74, 77–8, 107
    key concepts of 78
soft systems research 77–8
software, real-world-based 52
software agents 9
software architecture 31–70
    archetypes in 38–9
    component-based *45*, 49
    of conventional computer system 44
    definitions of 31–42, 57
    as design rational or vision 37–41
    development view of 37
    emergency fixes 44
    4+1 View Model of 37, 40
    as high level structure 32–7
    and implementation 36
    layers of 60, *60*
    logical view of 37
    maintenance costs 43, *43*
    physical view of 37
    process view of 37
    product-line approach 38–40
    profiles 39
    and reuse 41–2
    scenarios-based view of 37, 39
    and service oriented architecture (SOA) 57–63
    service-oriented *45*, 49
    structured methods 42–3
    system instantiation 39
    through the ages 42–9
    transformations 40
software crisis 31–2
software engineering 31–2
    human-oriented 34
Software Engineering Institute (SEI) 33–6, 57
SOMA 51, 99
    structure of a conversation in *144*
Sonic (Progress) 22
SonicMQ 21
specification modelling 58, 181–220
    documentation of 212
    from business requirements 181–2

procedure for 207–8
specification patterns
   1: establish business objectives 232–3 App.
   2: visualise business process model 233–5 App.
   3: establish use cases 236–8 App.
   4: build type model (ontology) 238–40 App.
   5: discover business rules 240–1 App.
   6: user-centred service structure 241–2 App.
   7: internalise parallelisms of collaborations 242–3 App.
   8: cross-reference states to use cases 243–4 App.
   9: use case post-conditions are rules 244–5 App.
   10: association loops conceal rules 245–6 App.
   11: write constraints as rules 246–7 App.
   12: ask the business 247–8 App.
   13: assign rules to components 248–9 App.
   14: policy blackboard 250–2 App.
   15: base error messages on rules 252–3 App.
   16: store rules in a repository 253–4 App.
   17: encapsulate a reference 254 App.
   18: plan interviews 255–6 App.
   19: run a workshop 256–7 App.
   20: involve all stakeholders 257–61 App.
   21: ten minute rule 261–2 App.
   22: lead user 262–3 App.
   23: structured interview 263–4 App.
   24: focused interview 264–5 App.
   25: probes and teachback 265–6 App.
   26: ask for the opposite 266–9 App.
   27: boundary competence 269–70 App.
   and requirements engineering 229–70 App.
specifications 4
speech acts 141–2, 144
five types of 141
spell-checking 64
spreadsheets 161, 167, 173
SQL/Server 59
SSADM 72
stakeholders 66, 166
   involvement of 257–61 App.
standards 221–8
   BPM 221–4
   miscellaneous 224–8
   web services 224
Standish Group 1–2
state
   maintenance of 65, 69
   management services 66
   notion of 64
   tracking of 65
state charts 72, 117, 193, 221
   and business service implementation 197
   notation of 195–6, *196*
   and use cases 194, 219
state models 193–8
   finding services from 198–200
   of a person 193–4, *194*
   subtypes 196, *196*
state transition diagrams (STDs) 132, 193, 195–7
states
   Boolean 197
   and transitions 194–5, *195*
   and use cases 198, 243–4 App.
stative services 63
stative types 196
stereotypes 142
   of conversations 145–9, 162
SWIFT funds transfer messages 146
swimlanes 116–17, *117*
   in BPMN 120
system design 58
   conceptual integrity of 35–7
systems analysis 74
task analysis
   fundamental activities of 99
   hierarchical 97–101, 146
   and human IP theory 101

task analysis (*continued*)
  objectives of 100
  user 77
task description 100
tasks 115
  atomic 99–100, 185
  centrality 99
  definition of 98
  expression of 99
  external 98
  and goals 98, 142
  internal 98
  representativeness 99
  typicality 99
TCP/IP 22
teachback 95, 265–6 App.
techniques
  behaviour-orientated 72
  data-centred 72
  function-centred 72
technology drivers 20–3
terms 88
textual analysis 102–3, **103**
Thompson (Datastream) 15
TIBCO 21
tokens 132
Toyota 166
transactions
  ACID properties of 197–8
  conversations as 143
  and fuzzy state machines 197
  stateless 64
transformations 61, 87
  architectural 40
transitions 132
  firing of 132
  and states 194–5, *195*
triggers 205–6
Trireme International Ltd 181
Tuxedo 21
type models *192*, 207–12
  building 238–40 App.
  establishment of 192–8
types
  associations of 213
  and interfaces 203
  signature of 203
  stative 196

UBS 166
Udell, John 49
Unified Modelling Language (UML) 16, 23, 38, 78, 107
  activity diagrams 116–18, *117*, 140, 219
  basics 78–80
  benefits of 79
  and BPM 221
  and business objects 101
  case notation 139, 183, 221
  case symbols 142
  classes 50
  diagram types of 79
  modelling limits of 89–90
  origins and influences *80*
  qualified association in 210, *210*
  specification 224
  state charts and diagrams 193
  and use case diagrams 187
United States of America (USA), defence projects 1–2, *2*
Universal Description, Discovery and Integration (UDDI) 22–3, 224
University of Karlskrona-Ronneby, Research in Software Engineering group (RiSE) 38, 40
Usage-Centred Design method 185
use case analysis 73
use cases 4–5, 12, 16–17, 39, 69, 77
  big 17
  business 81
  and classic requirements 78–85, 107
  CRUD 187, 192
  description of 189–91
  establishment of 236–8 App.
  generification of 185–6
  inappropriate use of controller objects 184
  lack of atomicity 186
  lack of clear definition 183–4
  lack of essentiality 185–6
  lack of genericity 185–6
  latent 84–5, *85*

as linked tasks 186
models 80–3
  nested *16*
  with system boundary 81–2, *82*
as objects 187
overemphasis on functional decomposition 183
poor exception handling in 187–8
poor level of abstraction 186–7
problems with 182–8, 218–19
and rules 244–5 App.
and scenarios 81, 184–6
and state charts 194
and states 198, 219, 243–4 App.
symbol for 162
template *191*
using «extends» in 187–8, *188*, 219
user involvement 2
user task analysis 77
users
  leading 262–3 App.
  real 12–13, 16–19

value chains 140
VB 50
VBX 50
VDM 72, 74
Versata 22
Viacom 43
vocabulary 88
Von Neumann architecture 44, 69

web 65
Web Ontology Language (OWL) 23, 227
web services 9, 21, 29, 61
  standards 22–3, 224
Web Services Choreography Description Language (WS-CDL) 130
Web Services Choreography Interface (WSCI) 130, 223
Web Services Conversation Language (WSCL) 223
Web Services Description Language (WSDL) 9, 22–3, 127, 222, 224
WebLogic 22, 59
Websphere 22, 59
Winograd, T. 140, 143
Wolf, Alexander 37
Wolf Research 34
workflow, process focus of 113
workflow analysis 76–7
workflow automation 113
Workflow Management Coalition (WfMC) 223
workflow systems 140
workshops 256–7 App.
  ten minute rule during 261–2 App.
World Wide Institute of Software Architects 36
world wide web consortium (W3C) 222–4
WS-* 22, 224
WS-BPEL *see* BPEL
WS-HumanTask 128
WSFL 127

XLANG 127
XML 20, 22–3, 68, 127–8, 130
  and message transport 46, 66
  standards 224
  syntax 222
XPDL 223

Young, J.Z. 102
Yourdon 72

Z 74